European Intellectual History Since 1789

third edition

ROLAND N. STROMBERG
University of Wisconsin–Milwaukee

Prentice-Hall, Inc.
Englewood Cliffs, New Jersey 07632

Library of Congress Cataloging in Publication Data

STROMBERG, ROLAND N (date)
European intellectual history since 1789.

Originally published under title: An intellectual
history of modern Europe.
Bibliography: p.
Includes index.
1. Philosophy—Europe—History. 2.–Europe—
Intellectual life. I.–Title.
B791.S84–1981   190   80-19941
ISBN 0-13-291955-9

Editorial production/supervision *Edith Riker*
Cover design by *Miriam Recio*
Manufacturing buyer *Edmund W. Leone*

Poetry on page 279 is from C. Day Lewis,
Selected Poems (New York: Harper & Row, Pub.,
1967).

Printed in the United States of America

10   9   8   7   6   5   4   3   2   1

Prentice-Hall International, Inc., *London*
Prentice-Hall of Australia Pty. Limited, *Sydney*
Prentice-Hall of Canada, Ltd., *Toronto*
Prentice-Hall of India Private Limited, *New Delhi*
Prentice-Hall of Japan, Inc., *Tokyo*
Prentice-Hall of Southeast Asia Pte. Ltd., *Singapore*
Whitehall Books Limited, *Wellington, New Zealand*

To Mary

One cannot live without ideas; every step one takes is directed, if not by a conscious, at least by an unconscious or sub-conscious idea.

ARNOLD HOTTINGER

All human history is fundamentally a history of ideas.

H. G. WELLS

The narrowest life is the one into which there enter the fewest ideas.

VERNON LEE

There is but one thing more interesting than the intellectual history of a man, and that is the intellectual history of a nation.

MOSES COIT TYLER

The drama of Europe is a spiritual drama, a drama of the mind.

GEORGE BERNANOS

Contents

7

8

Preface

The reception accorded both the first edition of this book (1966) and the second (1975) was pleasant indeed. The publisher and I received many favorable comments from those teaching and writing in this field at colleges and universities small and large (and a few secondary schools too). I would like to thank all those who encouraged me by these comments, and would do so by name here, were it not that the list is a very long one. Many—students as well as teachers—offered helpful criticisms and corrections, and for these I am grateful.

The book evidently has served usefully in a large number of courses in modern history. On the basis of this reception one might feel justified in making few changes. Yet I have felt a need to do more than that, chiefly because the subject is one in which rapid development has taken place during recent years. Some alterations of fact or stress have been dictated by additions to knowledge coming from recent books, or by an improvement in my own education derived from closer study of certain areas, or perhaps by an alteration in our own *Zeitgeist* impelling a change in our outlook on the past. One chapter I found myself almost entirely rewriting was that on Marx; what a revolution has taken place in Marx studies since the discovery of a mass of new material which coincided with a freeing of Marxism from the Stalinist grip and the efforts of a host of students who looked with fresh eyes on this old subject! In general, though, I have not so much changed as added. This is especially true of the more recent period, where so much has happened in the realm of thought. The bibliography, of course, has been updated.

The preface to the first edition spoke of the need for a basic textbook in modern European intellectual history, combining adequate coverage with relative brevity, a nucleus around which one might build a course by adding source readings and other supplementary reading. Such a book "should be fairly concise, well-informed, attractively written, well-organized . . . full enough to raise the issues and introduce the topics that need to be introduced, above all able to stimulate the student to more exact investigations, and supply him with the references he needs to carry on these; yet not so long as to become tedious, and to drown the beginning student in detail." This goal has not been basically altered.

The earlier preface made the obvious point that this book rests on the labors of many other scholars working in the history of ideas who must supply the building blocks for any such synthesis. This battery of inquirers now has greatly increased. "The average citizen wants to know about his heritage of civilization, which is contained in a fabric of thought so old and complex that guides are urgently needed," the first preface observed. The citizens want to know about the world in which they live, we might add, a confused and churning world concerning which one observation at least would not be challenged: Ideas are in ferment. And some of them, alive and vital today, are very old ideas. Radical youth, for all its "nowism," seems to thrive on the thoughts of those early Victorian thinkers, Marx and Kierkegaard, while neoconservatives resurrect Burke and Tocqueville. Debates about the role of science in cultural life are as fresh in the era of Snow and Leavis as they were in the time of Huxley and Arnold, or Newton and Swift. In brief, ideas which were born one or two or even three centuries ago are highly relevant to our present situation.

Whether or not it is true, as H. G. Wells urged, that all history at bottom is a history of ideas, certainly there are those to whom intellectual history is the most exciting kind of history, combining as it does, or should do, the special excitement of Man Thinking with an attempt to show this thinking in its connections with the realm of fact and action and as part of a larger cultural unity. Comments on the nature and status of intellectual history are best expressed elsewhere. A preface is a place to acknowledge debts; these, in addition to those mentioned, include (in this as in the first edition) the author's students, who over the years have given him knowledge and inspiration as well as satisfaction.

Roland N. Stromberg

Introduction

To "trace the history of the human mind," said Hume, is the task of the historian, as distinct from the chronicler. Voltaire added that "it is better to know how men thought in former times than how they acted." A great deal of intellectual history has crept, willy-nilly, into history, it being impossible to keep out the men and women of ideas. A current collection of readings offered to students of the beginning college course in Western civilization includes selections from Plato, Aristotle, the Bible, Cicero, Augustine, Aquinas, Machiavelli, Rabelais, Luther, Calvin, Bodin, Descartes, Locke, Bossuet, Rousseau, Burke, Tocqueville, Marx, Nietzsche, Sartre, and Camus. Obviously it would be difficult to justify their exclusion from such a course. One wonders, though, to what extent most freshmen are equipped to grapple with these formidable adversaries.

We no longer restrict history to politics or public events, if for no other reason than that these cannot be "understood" without reference to the climate of opinion in which they took place. The deeds of Charlemagne cannot be understood apart from the peculiar mixture of ideas and values that made up the mind of his age, a mind quite different from ours. Nor, to come closer to home in both space and time, can the deeds of Thomas Jefferson be understood except in the context of the Enlightenment—a "lost world," as one Jefferson student has cogently argued. Some men and women of ideas "made history" directly— Luther, for example. Others, who did not, contributed so much to those who did that we cannot leave them out: Robespierre had his Rousseau, Lenin his Marx. "If ideas in politics more than elsewhere are the children of practical needs," J. N. Figgis has written, "none the less is it true, that the actual world is the result of men's thought. The existing arrangement of political forces is dependent at least as much upon ideas, as it is upon men's perceptions of their interests." "Not ideas, but material and ideal interests directly govern man's conduct," Max Weber held, but he added, "Yet very frequently the world images which have been created by ideas have, like switchmen, determined the tracks along which action has been pushed by the dynamics of interest." Nothing is false than the view, often associated with a kind of vulgar Marxism (Marx never held it), that ideas are merely the mechanical reflection of some supposedly nonintellectual material interest. There is nothing mechanical about an idea. Created in the mysterious ways of individual genius, it will then be acted upon in the realm of social reality and can partly decide the nature of that reality. Or, as Lord Acton observed, if people are stimulated by the hope of material gain, they can also be stimulated to action "by political or religious motives with no hope of material profit, and a certainty of material loss." Nothing is greater than the power of an idea; if greatest "when its time has come" (that is, when it agrees with the direction of social evolution), the idea yet remains an indispensable part of the recipe for meaningful action; even if it runs against the main flow of social evolution, an idea can be important.

Here is not the place to go into the troublesome question of just how *ideas* and *interests* act together in history. It is enough to observe that they do interact, that they are the "two faces of reality," in Jean Lhomme's expression, which one sees in all the great issues of mankind. Ideas are quite commonly found first in the mind of some unworldly person, a recluse like Bentham, an obscure pauper like Marx, a poor vagabond like Rousseau; then they are taken up by men and women of affairs, who, as John Maynard Keynes observed, snatch them from the air, perhaps without knowing that they came from some scribbler of yester-day.

The interaction of historically important ideas with the social milieu from which they emerge and which they in turn influence—this is, broadly, the domain of intellectual history. The separate disciplines, such as philosophy, the sciences, or political theory, insofar as they study their past ideas tend to do so unhistorically, treating them substantively and as if they arose in a vacuum. It must remain for the intellectual historian to show how these ideas interacted with social reality, with past ideas, and with each other. At any particular time and place there is a specific set of influences on the human mind, which includes (1) the legacy of past ideas available to people at that time, (2) a social context, consisting of all sorts of phenomena prominent in the environment of the times, political, economic, and so forth, and (3) other contemporary strains of thought and expression. If, for example, we wish to grasp the thought of Nietzsche, we have to know the older thinkers who influenced him (a great many reaching back to the Greeks), some more than others, such as his immediate predecessor Schopenhauer; also his social atmosphere, of nineteenth-century bourgeois culture, together with such events as the Franco-Prussian War and the Bismarckian supremacy; and finally other significant intellectual movements of his time, among them French estheticism, Darwinism, socialism, and so forth. A recent European scholar has remarked, "There is room for a disciple whose aim is to assess the factors which influence the human mind in one period or in one region," this being his definition of the realm of intellectual history.

What validates or testifies to the importance of intellectual systems? Few of them, if any, can stand the test of absolute logic: The great philosophies have all turned out to be postulates at bottom, mere assertions, fiats, resting on something assumed to be true without proof. This is quite as true of allegedly "scientific" structures such as Marxism, Newtonian physics, or logical positivism as it is of more patently "metaphysical" ones. The reason they appear and are adopted, become popular and influential, is related to factors other than the merely immanent laws of thought. These factors, it may be suggested, are historical and social; historical, in that ideas evolve in time as one generation hands down its thoughts to others who take them up and use them as a point of departure—the endless dialectic of intellectual history; social, in that the selection of some ideas rather than others for emphasis and discussion has to do with the structure of social reality at a given time—the issues, atmosphere, and great events of the day. Even genius must create with reference to the external social world it finds at hand; it cannot just create in a vacuum.

Intellectual history as an academic discipline is fairly new and probably has yet to complete the task of clarifying its scope, methods, and content. Clearly the subject matter is intensely interesting, for those with a flair for ideas. Some do not have this taste and should probably avoid the subject. Indeed, other historians, fact-minded, often lack it, which is perhaps a reason why they suspect intellectual history. Defined as the study of the role of *ideas* in historical events and processes, intellectual history is admittedly a difficult art. In this connection one scholar observes that historical writing of the usual sort "often fails to apprehend the slow subterranean movements which minds inclined to be too matter-of-fact find intangible"[1]—those movements of the mind, of ideas and ideologies and tides of taste, which never appear overtly in history until one day, perchance, they explode in a French Revolution. While the details of politics and administrations and wars are studied in the most minute detail, because they are neatly documented in archives and can be grasped by the matter-of-fact mind, the role of ideas may be dismissed in a vague phrase or two. The need for careful and precise studies in intellectual history is now recognized and is being met.[2] But much work remains to be done.

Writing some years ago, that philosopher so celebrated in the "history of ideas," Arthur O. Lovejoy, noted the unnatural fragmentation of the study of ideas, apportioned out among at least twelve "disciplines."[3] While students of literature, of the arts, of science, theology, education, social thought, and so forth, each cart away a portion of the body of Western thought, to dissect it minutely in the privacy of their chambers in isolation from each other, the whole organism perishes of this process, and there is no one to restore it to life unless a discipline called "history of ideas" can do so. The specialist work done by the various departments of learning is extensive and valuable, but badly needs to be collated. And a service may be rendered to these various departments themselves, for Milton's poetry cannot be understood apart from the poet's store of general ideas, nor can Darwin's science be fully grasped without this context. That sometimes disparaged entity, the *Zeitgeist*, the "spirit of the age," assuredly does exist. Coleridge, perhaps, put it best: "Such as is the existing spirit of speculation, during any given period, such will be the spirit and tone of the religion and morals, nay even of the fine arts, the manners, and the fashions." (Nor is this the less true, he added, "because the great majority of men live like bats, but in twilight, and know and feel the philosophy of their age only by its reflections and

---

[1]Henri Peyre, "The Influence of Eighteenth-Century Ideas on the French Revolution," *Journal of the History of Ideas,* January, 1949.

[2]See some apposite remarks in the introduction to Walter M. Simon, *European Positivism in the Nineteenth Century,* 1963.

[3]"The Historiography of Ideas," in *Essays in the History of Ideas,* 1948.

refractions.") Later culture historians have attached much importance to the *generation* as a key to the discovery of that mysterious but omnipresently real set of the mind which permeates all aspects of the thought and expression of an era.

As an introductory textbook, in a difficult domain of study still far from mature, this volume need offer no apology for its defects. Introductory textbooks are intended for the important function of introducing the as yet fairly unsophisticated student to fields which it is hoped he will further explore, with the aid of the suggestions for additional reading supplied. This book should of course also be supplemented by outside readings in the sources of intellectual history. Asked what to read, Walter Pater advised students to "read the great authors whole; read Plato whole; read Kant whole; read Mill whole." Excellent advice, but a little impractical for many students. This textbook is not meant to substitute for the reading of the great thinkers, but rather to prepare for or supplement that task. It is, indeed, not meant to be more than a serviceable text for college courses. It has arisen from a number of years of experience in teaching such a course in modern European intellectual history. Intellectual history, as it seems to us, should provide an introduction to the most important—from a general cultural viewpoint[4]— "ideas" (intellectual systems, movements of the mind) in the cultural heritage; it should relate these ideas to the social and political background so far as possible; it should show the continuity and lineage of thought; it should indicate the relevance of the ideas to general culture.

Most especially, perhaps, as a *history* of ideas, a presentation of this sort should provide a sense of history. That means a sense of the living context of reality, and it means a sense of the flow and movement of things. Too often the great thinkers and the great ideas are drained of life by being presented as disembodied abstractions. The historian wants to see Kepler in his classroom at the moment when he stumbled upon what seemed to him a great truth, and which really was not, but which launched him on a lifelong quest destined to alter the mind of the West. He wants Kepler's unhappy childhood and restless adolescence. (Arthur Koestler, that great contemporary writer, has done this in *The Sleep-*

---

[4]Philosophy students, attuned to the analytical mood, often do not find the intellectual history course satisfying because it is not much interested in the truth or falsity, consistency or inconsistency, of intellectual systems or philosophies and is therefore prone to linger over some not interesting from this point of view, while ignoring others that are. Rousseau and Marx are not great philosophers and the essentially analytical mind soon grows impatient with their cloudy terms and vague ideas; they are historically and existentially of the highest importance, that is, they posed questions relevant to their age and of deepest significance for the human situation of modern times. It has been noted that specialists in whatever field, from economics to theology, will choose figures different from those selected by historians for their general cultural interest.

walkers.) He wants Voltaire's misspent youth and Rousseau's neuroticism and Marx's proud poverty; Locke's bourgeois prudence and Nietzsche's madness—all the human story of the great thinkers.

Nor should they, intellectual historians feel, deal only with the great thinkers, for Croce was right in observing that the spirit of an age is sometimes better found in the second-rate thinkers, and the spirit of the age must always be close to what historians of ideas seek. It is the general direction of the movement of thought that concerns them. From earliest times to the present, the great army of thought has marched—some individuals ahead, some in the rear, a large straggling army—steadily past one milestone after another, leaving behind some ideas, fashioning new ones, transforming old ones. We do not know the ultimate destination of the long trek, if it has any. But where we have been and what we have learned is worth knowing, for each of us is a part of the army, anxiously searching for signposts and wondering where, in the endless chaos of things, we are. History orients us.

It also equips us to live. To understand the past is to be able to live fully in the present. To be acquainted with the intellectual heritage of our long and rich Western civilization is to be a civilized person and to be prepared for constructive thinking. The object of this book is to present the most important general ideas in modern European history, not in isolation but as part of the stream of history. As Dr. Johnson said, "There is no part of history so generally useful as that which relates to the progress [?] of the human mind, the successive advances of science, the vicissitudes of learning and ignorance, the extension and resuscitation of arts and the revolution of the intellectual world."[5]

THE MODERN EPOCH

Few deny that the French Revolution ushered in the specifically modern epoch of history. The Revolution in some measure looked to the eighteenth century "philosophers," to Rousseau and Voltaire and Montesquieu and Diderot, for its inspiration and ideas; but it soon swept beyond their prescriptions (which were hardly in agreement with each other) to explore political frontiers previously unheard of. Examinations

[5]Some additional references on the definition and methodology of intellectual history: Franklin L. Baumer, "Intellectual History and Its Problems," *Journal of Modern History,* September, 1949; John C. Greene, "Objectives and Methods in Intellectual History," *Mississippi Valley Historical Review,* June, 1957; Peter Burke, "Ideas Have a History," *The Listener,* February 9 and 16, 1967; Sir Isaiah Berlin, Introduction to Marc Raeff, *Russian Intellectual History: An Anthology* (New York: Harcourt Brace Jovanovich, 1966); Hayden White, "The Tasks of Intellectual History," *Monist,* Vol. 53, 1969, pp. 600–30; Leonard Krieger, "The Autonomy of Intellectual History," *Journal of Historical Ideas,* October–December, 1973; Roland N. Stromberg, "Some Models Used by Intellectual Historians," *American Historical Review,* June, 1975.

of the role of Rousseau's and Voltaire's ideas in the Revolution impressively document both the extensive nature of this role and its amazingly chameleon-like character: The revolutionaries constantly quoted the Enlightenment giants but just as constantly made these words mean entirely different things. Apart from its specific content of novel political ideas, including equality, individualism, democracy, nationalism, and socialism, the Revolution was so massive that people could not help thinking of it as ushering in a new epoch in every department of life. Then the reaction to its violent excesses entailed opposition to all those ideas that had presumably inspired it, and a kind of intellectual counterrevolution against the Enlightenment, associated with Edmund Burke, took place. The titanic struggles of the twenty-five years after 1789 left the entire civilization forever altered, socially, politically, and intellectually. This era of revolutions dominates the early part of the nineteenth century.

The nineteenth century falls rather naturally into three parts, from the viewpoint of *Zeitgeist* and history of ideas. The morning is the Romantic and Revolutionary age, lasting from about 1789 to 1832 or perhaps 1848. It is marked by convulsions both political and moral, an intellectual revolution, and a great deal of creativity emerging from its storm and stress. Its heroes of thought are Kant and Fichte and Hegel; Burke, Chateaubriand, Saint-Simon, Fourier; the Romantic poets; the renovators of political philosophy; the creators of new social doctrines. It is an age in which people felt old moorings give way and wondered where the storm would blow them.

Then, during the noonday of the century, calm returns and there is time to take soundings. Doubts and tensions remain, but this Victorian period is marked by relative stability and by the undertaking of extraordinary efforts at synthesis. This is the time of Comte, Marx, Darwin, and Mill. Realism replaces romanticism in literature and the arts; science, the ultimate realism, mounts the pedestal as the modern god; visions of utopia in politics and society suffer a severe blow with the failure of the revolutions of 1848. There is disenchantment, but there is also success, on solid if pedestrian foundations, the kind of success and solidity the adjective "mid-Victorian" conveys.

The evening brings its gloom and uncertainties; unquestionably a darker mood strikes Europe late in the century, from about 1885 down to the stunning collapse of 1914. If the average man remained complacent and hopeful, post-Darwinian and post-Marxist Europe produced a crop of amazingly insightful thinkers who were exploring domains never heretofore much known, zones of fearful nonsymmetry. The unconscious irrational, or the prerational, interested those who dominate this epoch—Nietzsche, Freud, Bergson, Sorel, Max Weber. In part, this mirrored the experiences of an epoch which brought vast movements of population from farm to city, vast increases in population with the accompanying problem of "mass," almost terrifying technological "advances." In this period artists and intellectuals became increasingly estranged or alienated from society, yet were creative as seldom before. The "modernist" mood and movement began.

Of all watersheds, 1914 is rivaled only by 1789 in the modern world; nothing after the terrible World War—to the coming of which intellectuals had actually contributed strongly—could be the same. Shattered visions of infinite progress littered the postwar landscape, and Western civilization suddenly found it had no other values to fall back upon. It tried to invent new ones, tried even to restore old ones, but watched the world descend into even lower depths of war and degradation. The response of thought to the challenge of "decline and fall" was at times nothing less than heroic. If this was the age of Hitler and Stalin, it was also the age of Toynbee and Sartre, as well as of Le Corbusier and Picasso, Lawrence and Joyce. From the awful devastation and slaughter of World War II, Western civilization made a remarkable recovery. And its thought has been dazzlingly prolific—too much so, perhaps, an embarrassment of riches, an excess of self-consciousness which explodes and fragments into an urban society losing all intellectual as well as social unity. Surmounting one crisis of depression and war, the civilization met new ones of order and legitimation.

Throughout this period of the nineteenth century and beyond, powerful forces were at work transforming the social structure in which ideas operate—vast processes of population growth, urbanization, technological progress, and new social stratification. "The concentration of population in cities," a British student of urbanization, A. F. Weber, noted near the end of the nineteenth century, had been "the most remarkable social phenomenon" of that century. Yet by present standards it had hardly begun. These teeming urban masses were uprooted from their traditional folk cultures to become consumers of ideas and values supplied by urban intellectuals. "What bonds link the two million inhabitants who crowd into Paris?" asked Baron Haussmann, the redesigner of Pairs, in 1864. "For them Paris is a great consumers' market, a vast workshop, an arena for ambitions." A place of marvelous stimulation where keenness of mind fed on rapid communications and the competition for prizes, the metropolis, growing toward megalopolis, was also a place of restless discontent. And it was a place where an essentially new class, the intellectuals, specialists in ideas, sellers of ideological wares, arose as never before. (The term *intellectuels* was first popularized in France at the time of the Dreyfus Affair, 1894 to 1900.)

This volume, then, tries to take the Europeans from the French Revolution through the tumultuously changing nineteenth century and into the tragic, turbulent, creative twentieth. It begins with them emerging from an aristocratic into a democratic society, from an agrarian and commercial era into an industrial and technological one. It observes their thinking as they are carried on a tide of modernization that leaves them confused and buffeted creatures, victims in part of too much knowledge, too many ideas that escape their control. Alienated, they need to rethink and put to constructive use this remarkably rich inheritance of thought and expression.

1

Romanticism and Revolution: 1789–1815

*What is the good of curbing sensuality, shaping the intellect,
securing the supremacy of reason? Imagination lies in wait as
the most powerful enemy.*

GOETHE

I have seen the beginning and the end of a world.

CHATEAUBRIAND

*He would not yield dominion of his mind
To spirits against whom his own rebelled.*

BYRON

At least three revolutions, the French, the romantic, and the Kantian, occurred in the 1780s, with their direct impact carrying on through the next several decades to leave a deep mark on the entire modern world. To these, general history must perhaps add the Industrial Revolution. Contemporaries were prone to regard them as but different aspects of a single revolution. Thus the conservative Francis Jeffrey in 1816, discussing "the revolution in our literature," attributed it to "the agitations of the French Revolution . . . the hopes and terrors to which it gave occasion." Some recent scholarly students of romanticism have been inclined to endorse this verdict. And the German poet Heine, speaking of Immanuel Kant, remarked that "with this book (*The Critique of Pure Reason*) an intellectual revolution began in Germany which offers the strangest analogies with the material revolution in France . . ." and, he added, to the reflective mind is of equal importance. This judgment was endorsed by Karl Marx, who observed that the Kantian revolution in philosophy was the intellectual counterpart of the French Revolution in politics. It only remains to connect Kant with romanticism, and of course, that is a common juxtaposition—not that the two things were quite the same, but that Kant's successors and disciples, Fichte and Schelling, provided philosophical grounding for the romantic poets.

Clearly these three important developments, in politics, literature, and pure philosophy respectively, did interact and sometimes blend. It is not clear that they were of similar origin. Kant was working on problems bequeathed to philosophy by Locke, Berkeley, Leibniz, and especially Hume; he wrote his chief books before the Revolution, and his basic position does not seem to have been affected by that event, though it stirred him deeply, even in his ivory tower at Königsberg. (But Jean-Jacques Rousseau demonstrably influenced both Kant and the French Revolution.) The Revolution, needless to say, owed nothing directly to the German philosopher on the shores of the Baltic, whose abstruse speculations were unknown in 1789 to all but a few. As for romanticism, which also can be traced back to Rousseau, it most clearly announced its arrival in Germany around 1781, with the writings of Schiller and the young Goethe, in a context that seems neither politically revolutionary nor at all interested in technical philosophy. The young Goethe was mostly interested in mystical religion. Schiller's *William Tell* was to inspire many a revolutionary, but it was not written until 1804.

Causation in history is a tricky problem, never simple. Monistic dogmas that assert the invariable priority of one factor, such as technological change or the rise of a social class, do not stand the test of careful criticism. Material, social, and intellectual factors continually interact on each other. It is not clear that they do so within the matrix of a single system, so that one can speak of the unity of an historical epoch. Any historical period contains within itself many processes and themes, not necessarily all knit together in a seamless web; there are always loose ends.

One can say with assurance that there was restlessness and malaise in the 178Us. The American Revolution, an event of the profoundest significance for Europe, not least France, concluded successfully. The French monarchy was in deep trouble before 1789, reeling toward bankruptcy, apparently unable, since the failure of the Turgot reform effort in 1776, to install necessary reforms. In Great Britain, a political organism weakened by the American defeat faced impending great changes, as reformers demanded a more democratic and representative

Parliament. In the realm of literature and thought, there were some equally disturbing signs. The German drama of *Sturm und Drang* (storm and stress) was a strong reaction against Enlightenment classicism, while the turn toward mysticism and religion expressed itself in France in such figures as the popular *Philosophe inconnu,* Saint-Martin. Hamann, Swedenborg, and Blake are other examples in diverse quarters of Europe.[1] The 1780s was a glorious decade that gave us Mozart and the American constitution as well as Kant, in many ways the climax of the Enlightenment. But the leaders of the great *philosophe* era were falling away. Voltaire died in 1778, Rousseau in the same year, Hume in 1776, Diderot in 1784, d'Alembert in 1783, Condillac in 1780, Frederick the Great in 1786. Buffon and Franklin were octogenarians. These illustrious passings signaled the demise of an age. Many sensed change in the air—even before the French Revolution arrived to confirm it.

Though Enlightenment strains continued on, to be seen in such prominent schools as British utilitarianism and Political Economy, the Revolution ended by discrediting much of it. It was accused, by the important conservative manifesto of Edmund Burke, of having led France to disaster through its simplistic and abstract conception of people, its utopian quest for a perfect social order. It was now said to have been metaphysical, a charge it had once itself leveled at the past. It had invented fantasies and called them Reason. It had thrown out the really important things in life, such as religion and tradition and concrete human ties, in favor of slogans about human rights which, in practice, only invited the godless to slaughter each other. Europe, the conservative foes of revolutionary France believed, would have to purge itself of this disease which, erupting in the Terror, had its roots in the sick cynicism of Voltaire, the wild dreams of Rousseau. In Burke and his numerous followers strains of romanticism interacted with the reaction against the Revolution that affected most of Europe's major intellectual figures by 1798, continuing on through the Napoleonic wars and into the post-Napoleonic Restoration.

THE FRENCH REVOLUTION

Some historians of the French Revolution tell us that we should not speak of a *French* Revolution. Jacques Godechot states, "In fact, the French Revolution was only one aspect of a Western, or more exactly an Atlantic revolution, which began in the English colonies in America

---

[1]Robert Darnton, *Mesmerism and the End of the Enlightenment in France* (1968) interestingly recounts another reaction against rationalism that appeared in the 1780s, becoming almost a mania for a time. Darnton points out that mesmerism had a distinct radical component, being adopted as a kind of anti-Establishment gesture by a number of the future leaders of the Revolution.

shortly after 1763, extended through revolutions in Switzerland, the Low Countries, and Ireland, before reaching France between 1787 and 1789." From France it bounced over to Germany, Switzerland, Italy, and other parts of Europe. One might object that it is foolish to compare the rumblings in Holland or Ireland with the French Revolution for significance and scope and that the later revolutions came about precisely because France's had done so. But it is certainly true that the French Revolution from the beginning exerted a worldwide influence, and, if this was because of French prestige and influence throughout Europe, it was also because the Revolution produced ideas for which the whole Western world was ready.

What were the great ideas of the Revolution? Some of them seem self-evident and therefore pedestrian today, but they were not so familiar then, and they were given vibrant new meaning by the marvelous events of 1789: popular sovereignty, self-determination of peoples, equality of rights. And nationalism. The French joyously toasted *la patrie* of which they were all, equally, the children now: no more Bretons, Angevins, or Dauphinards, any more than nobles and commoners. The whole conception of the political society changed. The king could no longer be King of France; he must (if he stayed) be King of the French, for he owed his power to the people. The special privileges and rights of the nobility, renounced by the nobles themselves in an orgy of ideological altruism, were no more; all citizens were equal before the law, with equal access to office, equal liability to taxation. Much of the Revolution's mystique went into that word *citoyen*. The Nation, then, was born—a community of citizens sharing equally in rights and duties, not a class hierarchy. If people did not like the government they had, they should have a right to change it. And they had a right to speak up freely, according to the Declaration of the Rights of Man and Citizen, that great manifesto of the Revolution.

Those who alleged a certain vagueness and utopian character in the ideology of the Revolution would, of course, be right. It was an apocalyptic moment, and all kinds of millennial ideals came forth. Universal peace was one of them, ironically enough in view of what the Revolution, in fact, soon brought to Europe. Numerous orators repudiated the very right to make war, and the Assembly solemnly adopted a resolution of this sort in 1790. Two years later, France was at war with the monarchies of Europe, and only that incurable ideologist, Maximilien Robespierre, was still (for the time being) a pacifist. It had been expected that all mankind would be brothers. In fact, "popular sovereignty" or "self-determination" entailed war, because Europe's political order did not correspond to this principle. Nor would it have been possible to decide what this slogan meant exactly, in practice, in many parts of Europe.

Faced with the need to transform the largely negative character of the initial revolution (the first Constitution resounds with *il n'y a plus*— "there no longer exists"), eighteenth-century ideas were called upon. Rousseau especially was to be quoted incessantly by leaders of the Revolution. Enlightenment political theory tended to be vague and utopian. Nor was it all of a piece. Montesquieu disagreed with Voltaire, Voltaire with Rousseau, and Rousseau, if not with himself, at least with some of his followers. It is easy to identify at least three major strains in the Revolution, perhaps more. The first period of the Revolution was in the hands of the moderates, who did not wish drastic change; the intellectual idol of this phase was Montesquieu, the goal a limited, constitutional monarchy on the English model. Then, in terms of the chief Revolutionary factions, came the Girondin, Jacobin or *Montagnard,* and *sans culotte* or perhaps Babeuvist forces—in broader ideological terms, roughly liberal, democratic, and socialist.

The Girondins admired Voltaire, his disciple Condorcet being one of their brain trust. Not lacking in revolutionary zeal, the party of Brissot, Condorect, and Mme. Roland was anticlerical, antiaristocratic, and inclined to a doctrinaire liberalism based on Montesquieu and Locke along with Voltaire (though Mme. Roland also admired Rousseau, an ambivalent figure). These were the upper bourgeoisie, insofar as a class label might be roughly pinned on them. They believed in natural rights of the individual and were suspicious of excessive state power. Constitutional government with "checks and balances" but not too much democracy appealed to this group, who perhaps betrayed their bourgeois outlook as much in their deistic anticlericalism as in the law against workers' associations passed in 1791. Anglophile admirers of the British constitutional system, they bequeathed much to nineteenth-century French liberalism, always weaker than in Britain but not without its influence. They lost out in the struggle that developed, were destroyed, and sent to the guillotine by their enemies on the Left. It is significant that under the impact of events they moved toward democracy. Initially hostile to universal suffrage, some of them came around to it. Condorcet's constitution of 1793, which never went into effect, included universal suffrage and a single legislative assembly, ideas approved by the American friend of this group, Benjamin Franklin. But executive and judicial checks on the will of this assembly were to exist. If the Gironde moved close to a type of democracy under the pressure of events during the Revolution, its position should be distinguished from Jacobin democracy.

The left-wing Jacobins developed an unusual conception of democracy based on Rousseau's social contract and general will, or their construal of these concepts. Their goal was equality, and the idea of the general will together with the mass or mob action on which their power often depended caused them to glorify the people *en masse*. Robespierre

and Saint-Just accepted a dictatorship of Reason, with themselves representing the "people." This strain of thought had relatively little regard
for individual rights or parliamentary institutions, which seemed to it
selfish and corrupt. The Jacobin constitution of 1793 provided for no
separation of powers, no limit on the power of the state, no guarantees
of individual liberties. It sanctioned a plebescitary or democratic dictatorship, based on the popular will but with power delegated to a small
number of people. Jacobin democracy with its frank worship of the mob
spirit is difficult for Anglo-Saxons to grasp, but it has been a potent
tradition in France. Democratic in a deep sense, with a feeling for the
common man *en masse*, a desire to bring the people directly into government (Robespierre wished to build a stadium holding twelve
thousand people to allow the crowd to watch the legislators), and a
passion for equality, its disregard of legal processes and individual rights
may have been reflected in the Reign of Terror, though that abnormal
episode ought not to be charged to ideology alone. (Later Jacobins
showed a keen concern for individual justice: Consider the glorious fight
of Georges Clemenceau, a century later, on behalf of Captain Dreyfus.)

Robespierre was the great ideologist of the Revolution and leading
personality during the hectic bloody days of the Republic of Virtue. It is
significant for his love of Jean-Jacques that he believed in the worship of
a Supreme Being; atheism, he declared, is aristocratic. He was a believer,
but his true God was a kind of abstract embodiment of the People.
Effective mass orator, he was coldly unhappy in most of his relationships
with concrete, real people. With a sensitivity that caused him to tremble
at the sight of blood, he could order the death of thousands in the name
of humanity. All that Edmund Burke meant when he accused the Revolution of abstract theorizing and a want of practical judgment is embodied in Robespierre, the man of austere principle who hated the in-
trigues of practical politics and became a bloody dictator because he
would not compromise.

Robespierre was not the most radical product of the French Revolution. Jacobinism was not socialistic though it accepted the supremacy
of community over individual in the spirit of Rousseau's social contract.
Danton, Robespierre, and Saint-Just assumed a right to regulate property in any way necessary, but the social order they believed to be best
was one in which every citizen held a little property, as Rousseau had
suggested. This might well be designated as a petty-bourgeois or
artisan-workman utopia.

Socialism did appear in the French Revolution though it did not
get far. Babeuf and Buonarrotti, revolutionary socialists, attempted an
insurrection in 1795 (the Conspiracy of the Equals) but failed badly.
Nevertheless they began a powerful tradition. Somewhat inarticulately
they hated property, commerce, luxury, while extolling the virtues of

poverty, equality, honest labor. They, too, took their inspiration chiefly from aspects of the writings of Jean-Jacques, which partially articulated their natural class feelings. Morelly, an obscure writer, had developed Rousseau's thought in a more socialistic direction just before the Revolution. Mably and Holbach also wrote in a similar vein and reached large audiences. These were mostly poor men and their words are significant as among the first sounds from the lower depths. Like the Levellers and Diggers of the English Revolution, the left-wing Jacobins and the Equals spoke briefly for classes hardly yet represented at all in literate thought; the revolution had stirred the pot sufficiently to bring them momentarily to the top, then they subsided. But this time their voices were not forgotten. Buonarrotti survived to become a link with the socialism of the 1840s, and Parisian revolutionary radicalism lived on in other firebrands such as Blanqui. This *sans culotte* socialism spread over Europe quickly, making an appeal to doctrinaire representatives of the poorer classes. It was, after all, close to elemental Christianity. Russo, the Italian Babeuvist, echoed Savonarola's medieval call to the rich to throw away their jewels.

These extremes tended to discredit the Revolution. The initial joy with which it was greeted all over Europe turned to disillusionment as the 1790s wore on, and the Revolution led to civil war, persecution, terror, international war. At first all the intellectuals of Europe were enchanted by it, including dozens who later became its bitter foes. "Bliss was it in that dawn to be alive." Not only Wordsworth but Maistre, Chateaubriand, Kant, Fichte, Novalis, Goethe, Coleridge, Southey, and many others felt this. Rousseau had passionate admirers in England, like the father of Thomas Malthus, who asked only to be known as "the friend of Rousseau." Gilbert Wakefield, a Rousseau disciple, was imprisoned in 1799 for allegedly expressing a wish that the French would invade and conquer Britain. Everyone at this time, too, was reading Gibbon, whose *Decline and Fall of the Roman Empire*, which he had finished in 1787 after more than twenty years of labor, radiated a republican spirit—or did it only seem so in the atmosphere of 1789? The Roman state had begun its collapse with the very first emperor, and Christianity had finished it off, the great historian seemed to be saying.

But the Revolution seemed to lose its way and turn to violence, rapine, and injustice. It ended with the Reign of Terror and the awesome spectacle of the revolution devouring its own children. The result was a reexamination of the premises of the Age of Reason and a rejection of them that aided the turn toward romanticism.

The Revolutionaries had seemed to cling to eighteenth-century rationalism. It was not the romantic Rousseau they worshiped, but the utopian rationalist of *The Social Contract*. Before his suicide in a revolutionary prison, Condorcet, the disciple of Voltaire, wrote his hymn to unlimited human progress under reason. The Republic of Virtue and of Terror paraded the Goddess of Reason through the streets. Volney (*The Ruins, 1791*) theorized that empires fall from an insufficiency of natural religion and too many priests. Robespierre, in his meteoric path upward to grand inquisitor and then downward to victim of the Terror he had instituted, carried Rousseau's words with him everywhere. Little wonder that some who watched turned away in disgust from eighteenth-century thought, holding it responsible for the failure of the Revolution.

Critics of the Revolution

Edmund Burke's great indictment of the Revolution stood out above all others. It was eloquently answered by Tom Paine and others; the conservative reaction did not entirely sweep the field. But it tended to dominate. Historians still debate the element of validity in Burke's charges against the Revolution, but it would probably be generally agreed that he was right in holding that *philosophe* thought on politics was both too vague and too doctrinaire, in an area where these qualities are peculiarly dangerous. A scholar has observed concerning the thought of Helvétius and Holbach that they "must answer for the fact that they ultimately offered nothing beyond pious wishes" for an enlightened despot, ignoring "institutional structure" altogether.[2] One can readily find fantasies in which it was simply assumed that revolution would somehow install good government and do away with all evils— crime, hatred, deceit, envy, lawsuits, prisons, poverty—presumably by a sweep of the pen. No more monumentally innocent thought can be imagined. It would still be found in the Revolution of 1848.

The famous Declaration of the Rights of Man and of Citizen, manifesto of the Revolution, is a case in point. Attempting to reduce the formula for political justice to a few axioms, it revealed considerable confusion and subsequently was completely ignored. It might mean everything or nothing. "Men are born and remain free and equal in rights." "The purpose of the state is to secure the citizen in enjoyment of his rights." What exactly were these rights, and how could the state maintain them? They were said to include "the unrestrained communication of thought and opinions," as well as "a sacred and inviolable right to property"; but in both cases there might be exceptions, "in cases of evident public necessity." Similarly equivocal were statements that "the law ought to prohibit only actions hurtful to society" and "ought to impose no other penalties but such as are absolutely and evidently necessary." Would anyone disagree about the principle, but could any two

[2]Everett C. Ladd, Jr., "Helvétius and D'Holbach," *Journal of the History of Ideas*, April–June, 1962.

people agree on the all-important matter of just what these actions and penalties were?

Critics of the "natural rights of man" school such as Jeremy Bentham have claimed that such rights are either equivocations or tautologies—meaningless slogans. But clearly they have an emotional value. At that time their concrete referents were real enough. For example, Robespierre in his younger days attacked the law that "inflicted civil infamy upon the innocent family of a convicted criminal" (John Morley) as well as another that denied civil rights to children born out of wedlock. Such remnants of irrational barbarity fell before this wave of political reform. The reforms of the Revolutionary era were real enough, though stated in an abstract way. And had they not been so stated, they might never have been secured. In their attempt to bring about the final perfect state of humanity, the Revolutionary ideologists overstated their case and spoiled it, but en route to its ultimate failure as an apocalyptic movement, the Revolution achieved all sorts of useful changes in the lot of humanity. The old order of inequality, with its relics of the seigneurial system in the countryside, its unequal taxation and denial of equal economic opportunity, its unjust and arbitrary laws, disappeared forever. This is what the Revolution meant and why it has always been celebrated joyously in France.

But it meant something else in England—something suggested by that cartoon in which an ugly assassin armed with faggot and dagger is offering to give "liberty" to Britain. Secure (as most English thought) in their own liberties, the work of history and experience and not slogans and theories, Britain looked with horror on the bloody and turbulent French scene and found itself at war with revolutionary imperialism. From this position it produced the leading works of the counterrevolution, most notably that of Burke.

Edmund Burke's renowned book of 1790, *The Reflections on the Revolution in France*, has been, and probably always will be, the subject of violent disagreement. But its distinction is usually admitted even by those whose ideology forces them to be its foe on principle. Burke claimed that the Revolution went wrong because its leaders tried to scrap an entire political system and put a new one in its place overnight; he related this mistake to the outlook of the *philosophes*, the political rationalists whose method lacked realism in an area where abstractness is fatal and the nondoctrinaire approach is vitally necessary. On neither of these points has he lacked adversaries, then and later. But he made a strong case on both scores, though it may be hard to see how the mistakes could have been avoided. It is true that the wholesale abolition of an entire order in France in 1789 created immense confusion during the transformation period. "Feudalism" was declared at an end, which meant the dissolution of such institutions as the army, local government, the judicial system, the clergy. As for the *philosophe* political ideology, it did indeed consist in good part of general maxims without careful attention to detail and so was more helpful in tearing down than in building back up.

Whether Burke's analysis of the Revolution was right or wrong, the events in France stimulated him to formulate his political philosophy. A soaring eloquence and dazzling sense of the subtle texture of actual politics lent to Burke's book a memorable quality; as a piece of literature, it is one of the pioneer works of the new school of romanticism. The leading idea emerging from this eloquence and this subtlety was that society is a vast and complicated historical product that may not be tinkered with at will like a machine; it is a repository of collective human wisdom to be regarded with reverence, and if reformed at all it must be with due respect for the continuity of its traditions. There were other related ideas: that a political community is something made by history, an unanalyzable bond between people which makes free government possible; that the social organism has its "natural aristocracy," which the commoner sort of people must and do, in a healthy society, respect; that general rules and abstract principles are no help in politics.

With a disdain for the "abstract rights" proclaimed by the French, he tried to make clear the real rights of man: Burke certainly believed in rights, but he stressed the degree to which those entering civil society must give up some of their liberties in order to gain the advantages of government. He distrusted the restless innovators who had no patience to search out the wisdom of their ancestors but must draw amateur blueprints for the total reconstruction of society, as if they were the first to think. The science of government is not for these, whose visionary schemes "in proportion as they are metaphysically true, are morally and politically false." These "smugglers of adulterated metaphysics" knew not man—or God. Burke felt that Western political society was sound only on Christian foundations. To Burke two human needs were evident above all: history and religion. The human being is a religious animal who, without Christianity, would turn perforce to some other, and probably less satisfactory, faith—not a bad prediction of what has actually happened in recent times. A social animal, the human being would be no more than a beast if cut off from the sustaining fabric of ancient custom and tradition. Reverence toward God and toward the social order are therefore the two great duties, and they are linked, for history is the revelation of God's purpose.

There is irony, and perhaps confusion, in the fact that Burke accused the *philosophes* of being "metaphysicians," they whose banner always bore the motto "Down with metaphysics." He turns their own weapon against themselves. It seems that Burke is right, if we think of some of the cruder post-Rousseau political pamphleteers. But Burke's

own empiricism has roots in the better sort of Enlightenment political thought, Hume and Montesquieu especially.

The Irish politician deeply influenced all subsequent conservative political thought. Edition followed edition of the *Reflections,* all over Europe. Louis XVI personally translated it into French. For this popularity, its timeliness and what seemed an uncanny prophetic quality (Burke announced the failure of the Revolution before it had failed, it seemed) were partly responsible, along with the richness and color of the style. Stripped of its rhetoric, Burke's thought may not appear extraordinary, but its phrases would echo long afterward.

Perhaps it was not necessarily "conservative" in the most obvious sense of this word. In suggesting an empirical approach to the enormous complexity of human affairs, in place of the vague sloganizing of the *philosophes,* Burke may well be viewed as the founder of a real science of social reform, rather than as a hidebound conservative. He was certainly not opposed to change, if properly carried out, and his own career, that of a person of humble birth, consisted of one passionate crusade after another, on behalf of American independence, Ireland, India (the Warren Hastings affair), and against the French Revolution. "The most urgent need of his nature was always some great cause to serve—some monstrous injustice to repair." This tempestuous Irishman was temperamentally as little a conservative as well can be.

But there was, of course, the conservative Burke—or, since he almost created the school, the Burke traits that came to be thought of as conservative. The feeling of piety for the social order, the mistrust of hare-brained reformers with a one-shot plan, the organic conception of social growth, these were the foundations of the conservative faith. A great deal of Burke has been accepted as essential political wisdom for anyone who wants to participate in politics as it always is and must be, rather than merely shout slogans from a distance. A modern socialist, Harold Laski, declared that "the statesman ignorant of Burke is lost upon a stormy sea without a compass."

Burke's thought was a sort of idealized and conceptualized version of the traditional rural order of society, with roots reaching far back into recorded time. Nineteenth-century liberals and socialists applauded the decline of that society, which they saw as brutalized, narrow-minded, backward, and inequalitarian. "From the village street into the railway station is a leap across five centuries from the brutalizing torpor of nature's tyranny over man into the order and alertness of man's organized dominion over nature," George Bernard Shaw wrote. Writing a few years into the twentieth century, Bertrand Russell rejoiced that "this whole order of ideas has vanished from the civilized world"—ideas of hierarchy and authority, intolerance and subordination, religious dogma and social constraint. Russell, the liberal (despite occasional flirtations

with socialism), rejoiced in the freeing of the individual to fulfillment as a creative person emancipated from the tyranny of society. Shaw, the socialist, looked forward to a new and rational organization of society based on science and not superstition. And yet, throughout the nineteenth and twentieth centuries (it was never stronger than in quite recent years) a nostalgia for the country accompanied a horror of the city, of industry and technology and the dissolving of human ties. Burke's image of the primeval "natural" order of humanity, before corrupted by commerce and cities, never died.

The *Reflections on the Revolution in France* was a work of genius, written at white heat, blazing with indignation and charged with eloquence—an eloquence that is a bit too much for some modern readers ("Burke never takes the trumpet from his lips"), yet makes a gorgeous effect. It deeply influenced his generation and contributed not only to the anti-Revolutionary cause but to the romantic taste. In his youth, in the 1750s, a struggling young lawyer turned literary man, Burke had written a treatise called *The Sublime and the Beautiful*, which has often been seen as a landmark in the evolution of taste from neoclassical to romantic. He argued that while the realm of the "beautiful" is indeed subject to the familiar classical rules about harmony, proportion, elegance, and so forth, there is another realm, the "sublime," which inspires fear, awe, which does not civilize and socialize us as the classical does but makes us feel alone, exalts and exhilarates us. Burke was always a little romantic, his career was exceedingly so, and his last great work is, perhaps paradoxically, as romantic in style as it is conservative in content. So in a way the great spokesman of the counterrevolution was a revolutionary, too.

The Bonapartist Era

Insofar as he was trying to defend tradition and "prescription" as the "guardians of authority," Burke was swimming against the tide of the times. Despite its excesses and horrors, the French Revolution happened and, as Lord Acton later remarked, "it taught the people to regard their wishes and wants as the supreme criterion of right"; it accustomed men to change and swept away the old order beyond hope of recovery. Even Burke did not imagine, realist that he was, that it would be possible to restore the *status quo ante* in France. Soon the troops of France spread the Revolution all over Europe. The dictatorship of Napoleon (1800 to 1814) turned most of thinking Europe, even thinking France, against the Revolution, but the Bonapartist victories continued to overturn the old arrangements of Europe.

Against the rule of Napoleon, a good many of France's leading men and women of letters protested and went into exile, though some

(like Bonald) came back when the anarchy was over and order restored by a vigorous ruler. Benjamin Constant, Mme. de Staël, and Chateaubriand headed the brilliant crowd of refugees, to whom Bonapartism was purely and simply tyranny. There were others, like Goethe, who never lost faith in Napoleon, seeing in him the man of destiny whose mission it was to unite Europe under a single progressive law. In France, beginning in the period just before Napoleon (the Directory), the so-called Ideologues reacted against political failure and disillusion by becoming severely objective, seeking to study the human mind as strict scientists. (They were the ancestors of those antiseptic moderns, the "behavioral scientists.") This was the time of Laplace, Lamarck, Cuvier, and other great French scientists, indicating that the more detached subjects could flourish under Bonaparte. Laplace crowned the "classical mechanics," perfecting Newton, and was the author of a famous *Système du monde,* which undertook to explain the operations and evolution of the universe without recourse to Newton's *deus ex machina.* ("Sire, I have no need of that hypothesis," he responded when Napoleon asked him about God.) Cuvier and Lamarck began the controversy over evolution. The Italians, Galvani and Volta, were installing the age of electricity. Napoleon did admire the sciences and thought it important to encourage them in every way possible.

Within France, however, political controversy could hardly exist, and freedom of speculation was limited. Not that Bonaparte was, personally, anything other than the most emancipated of thinkers. Enormously cynical, he delighted in shocking people with his atheism in private conversation; but, believing that "only religion gives the state firm and lasting support," he would not tolerate any public irreligion. "You must form believers, not reasoners," he told the teachers of a state school for girls. Since "the stability of marriages serves the interest of social morality," the Code Napoleon was severe on adultery, but privately Napoleon called it "a mere peccadillo, an incident at a masked ball . . . a most common occurrence." Women he regarded as "mere machines to make children," and intellectuals and artists he affected to despise; therefore Mme. de Staël, an intellectual and artistic woman, was his *bête noire.* But many of Napoleon's outrageous opinions were, as they so often are, a kind of defense mechanism of an ego unsure of itself in this domain and cannot quite be taken seriously. He claimed, for example, to be "insensitive to what is called style," but he obviously was not. An omnivorous reader, he missed little that went on in the world of art, science, and philosophy and often commented on it shrewdly. Nevertheless, we feel he was sincere when he wrote that "the statistics of my army are, as far as I am concerned, the most enjoyable literary works in my library and those which I read with the most pleasure in my moments of relaxation!" But one should not be unjust to this remarkable man; in some ways his insatiable curiosity, especially about scientific matters, was hardly less than epochal. On his expedition to Egypt in 1798 he took along two hundred scholars to investigate that fascinating but still largely unknown land of antiquity. He shared and advanced the historical and orientalist interests of the times. He did not, however, admire the new literary fashion of romanticism that belonged to his foes, Mme. de Staël and Chateaubriand. Speculative thought and letters did not flourish in France in the years of Napoleon.

Abroad, the leading theme was a rallying of forces against Bonapartism. The *mystique* of the French Revolution gradually lost what force it had had in England. In 1794, Tom Paine's reply to Burke (the *Reflections* did not lack answers), *The Rights of Man,* sold like hot cakes, and the London Correspondence Society caused a fear of the French Revolution happening in Great Britain. William Godwin's *Enquiry concerning Social Justice* was very much in the French spirit, a rationalist utopia based on the ideal perfection of individuals. Though repeating Rousseau's indictment of existing property relations as theft, Godwin's utopia differed significantly from most of the French in being antistatist. In Britain, the idea of a natural order of society took the *laissez-faire* form: Society will run itself if left free from interference. The Physiocrats also believed this, but the idea took deeper root in the Whiggish environment of England. Tom Paine claimed that "the common consent of society, without government" can perform all the necessary functions heretofore discharged by government. The rest ought to be dispensed with, and would be as men approached perfection: "Government, like dress, is a badge of lost innocence." Laws regulating property and morality are, as Godwin observed, useless if men are not virtuous, and unnecessary if they are.

The combination of Adam Smith, Rousseau, and the spacious fields of America's sturdy, self-reliant citizens brewed this heady dogma in the mind of Paine. That it was not exclusively American was indicated by Godwin, father-in-law of the poet Shelley and husband of the women's rights author, Mary Wollstonecraft—a group around which much of the political Left in Great Britain revolved. Godwin was so suspicious of the state and indeed of all forms of institutional organization that he attacked public education, among other things. "Did we leave individuals to the progress of their own minds," Godwin believed, "without endeavoring to regulate them by any species of public foundation, mankind would in no very long period convert to the obedience of truth." This was the ultimate *laissez-faire.* Godwin believed, as H. N. Brailsford once remarked, that all men are as rational and virtuous as Swift's Houyhnhnms.

England was to be the land of liberalism, and Godwin no doubt is significant for the British bent of mind. But after some initial popularity, he was regarded as a crank and was the only man ever known to have caused Coleridge to lose his temper. British opinion turned away from the French Revolution and all radical thoughts during the long wars with France. Coleridge was among those who, earlier enthusiastic for the Revolution, "threw away his squeaking baby-trumpet of sedition" and combated the revolutionary heresy with all his strength. Coleridge ranks with Burke, to whom he owed much, as a founding father of English conservatism. But the sometime radical journalist, William Cobbett, joined the anti-Jacobin cause too, indicating that this mood was well-nigh universal in Britain. The Evangelical movement within the Church of England, led by William Wilberforce, was a reaction against the deistic laxities of the eighteenth-century church, thus a reproach to the infidel French.

Popularly, there was much millennial excitement in the air. Estimates of the number who followed the alleged prophetess Joanna Southcott in London from 1803 to 1814 ranged as high as fifty to one hundred thousand. Although not the first by any means to announce the second coming of Christ to be at hand, this unlettered Devonshire countrywoman became a sensation; her message fitted the unsettled times, when fears of a French invasion combined with much economic distress from rising prices and unemployment. Such strange religious outcroppings among the urban poor trying to adjust to urban life were to become familiar in many places thereafter. Thomas Macaulay was amazed: "We have seen an old woman, with no talents beyond the cunning of a fortune teller, and with the education of a scullion, exalted into a prophetess and surrounded by tens of thousands of devoted followers; and all this in the nineteenth century; and all this in London." It was the beginning of a career of popular culture in the cities that would often amaze the intellectuals; at this time there was a kind of popular romanticism reflected in religious emotionalism.

Controversy about Napoleon remained to the end. William Hazlitt, the famous literary critic and essayist, was described by a friend as "prostrated in mind and body" when he learned of Bonaparte's final defeat; "he walked about unwashed, unshaven, hardly sober by day, and always intoxicated by night" for weeks, until one day he awoke as if from a stupor and never touched alcohol again. His friend Haydon, author of the above description, believed that Napoleon had criminally betrayed the true cause; and yet on the great man's death in 1821 he reflected in his diary that "posterity can never estimate the sensations of those living at the time" about Napoleon—how his rise, his glory, and his fall affected men. Shelley found himself warming again to Bonaparte when he saw what followed:

I hated thee, fallen tyrant! I did groan
To think that a most unambitious slave
Like thou, should dance and revel on the grave
of Liberty. . . .

                                    I know
Too late, since thou and France are in the dust,
That Virtue owns a more eternal foe
Than Force or Fraud. . . .

These were exciting times. It is not surprising that romanticism arose in those twenty-five hectic years from the first dawn of revolution in 1789 to the final defeat of Napoleon in 1815.

NATIONALISM

Germany gave birth to nationalism in reaction against humiliation by the French. Herder and Fichte, giants of German thought, preached it along with humbler writers and organizers of youth (Arndt, Jahn, Kleist). The Enlightenment had been cosmospolitan. Fichte became convinced that this was another one of the errors made by that now politically discredited era. If France gave the world the Enlightenment and the Revolution, did not Germany have something to give? Every nation has its day, and the German day might be the greater for being so long postponed. Defeated in war by Napoleon, the Germans were assuming the cultural and intellectual leadership of the world in this time of Goethe, Schiller, Kant, Beethoven. A cultural people should have a great state. Germany must wake up politically, as she had done artistically and culturally. (*Addresses to the German Nation, 1807.*)

J. G. Herder's contribution to nationalism stands out in the intellectual career of a many-sided genius. Romanticism blended with nationalism in his thought. It was a humane and liberal nationalism, by comparison with some manifestations of that spirit; it meant, to Herder, the self-fulfillment of peoples who thereby make their contribution to humanity. He glorified the people, the *Volk*, exaggerating a strain already met with in Burke (there is wisdom in the collective consciousness of the people, that is, in traditions). Herder went seeking the songs of the people "on the streets, in alleys and fish markets, in the simple roundelays of the peasant folk." He has been compared to the American poet Walt Whitman in this respect, and indeed he deeply influenced Whitman. Mystical adulation of the national genius could lead in dangerous directions, perhaps, but at least Herder did not suggest them. He simply believed that nations exist, that peoples have their national cultures, and that these should be developed as the source of a valuable literature and art. The democratic element in this romantic nationalism is apparent.

Napoleon I met his downfall during 1814 and 1815, and conservative Europe gathered at Vienna to try, as far as possible, to restore order based on principles of tradition, prescription, monarchy. But forces had been set in motion which could not be halted, though they might be slowed or deflected. Between 1815 and 1830, Restoration France and conservative Europe produced some notable attempts to develop the conservative ideology, but it also saw the elaboration of the liberal, democratic, and socialist political philosophies. These political "isms" will be dealt with in the next chapter. Meanwhile we may note that of all these, the most potent "ism" in the nineteenth century was to be nationalism, affecting even the smaller and lesser peoples of Europe. The English and the French had long suspected they were nations, the Germans were finding it out, the Italians soon would discover it; but we also catch a glimpse of the Danes, who previously had had no inkling of their separate nationhood, seeking to restore the ancient Danish tongue and old Danish customs, while Gothicism in Sweden represents a similar impulse. The Belgians will find that they cannot live under a Dutch king, no matter how beneficent his rule and how logical and beneficial the larger political unit is, for they are different.

Nietzsche, in a characteristically impatient moment, burst out that Napoleon had tried to unite Europe, but reactionary nationalism had interfered to botch his plans. It may later have seemed reactionary; but for at least the first half of the nineteenth century, nationalism was regarded as liberal, progressive, and democratic. It meant the right of peoples to be free and self-determined, not merely because freedom in any of its guises is a good thing, but because the idea had been deeply implanted, by such as Herder, that each people has a sacred mission to make its unique contribution to the symphony of nations. And it meant, concretely speaking, the struggle of Germans to escape the dominion of France, later of Poland to throw off the tyranny of the tsar, or Italy to free herself from the Austrian yoke. It thus enlisted the support of idealists and activists, democrats and radicals, all who rejoiced in a struggle for justice against tyrants.

The shaping of a larger community, forged from local, regional loyalties, appealed to many in this historically minded era as a step forward on humanity's road to some future utopia. Nationalism blended readily with democracy, another of the age's shibboleths, because the nation was the crucible for a people of equal rights. Indeed, for a while nationalism was almost the common denominator of all ideologies and all social processes in the nineteenth century. For better or worse, Europe was to divide into numerous national cultures in the nineteenth century—a process accompanied by disruptions and upheavals. This vast and epochal process was in part a movement of the mind. More will be said about it later. Certainly that other of our three revolutions, the romantic, had much to do with it.

Immanuel Kant and the Revolution in Philosophy

Born in 1724, the man who became the greatest of modern philosophers did his most creative work in the 1780s, against the background of the crisis in Enlightenment thought. Rousseau made a deep impression on Immanuel Kant, as he did on so many of this generation. Indeed little that was discussed during the Enlightenment escaped the attention of the omniscient little professor of Königsberg. The young Kant, brought up in the reigning German philosophical school of Leibniz as systematized by Christian Wolff, showed strong scientific interests and entered into some of the typical *philosophe* controversies; thus we find him contributing his bit to the Lisbon Earthquake argument of the 1750s, begun by Voltaire, about the problem of evil. But it was particularly the work done by Berkeley and Hume to undermine the confident certainties of rationalism that engaged his attention. It was only in his middle age that Hume awakened him from his "dogmatical slumber." He found Hume's skepticism most unsatisfactory and, like the Scottish "commonsense" philosophers (but more effectively than those simpler souls, whom he ridiculed), determined to rescue men from it, restoring their confidence and vitality. Kant was an *Aufklärer,* a spokesman of the Enlightenment. But his powerful mind, in attempting to refute Hume, penetrated into ground beyond the frontiers of that movement. He made what he called a "Copernican revolution" in philosophy and was, in later years, compared to the French Revolution in his impact on thought. Heinrich Heine writes: "With this book (*The Critique of Pure Reason*) an intellectual revolution began in Germany which offers the strangest analogies with the material revolution in France, and, to a more reflective mind, appears to be of equal importance.... On both banks of the Rhine we see the same break with the past, all respect for tradition is revoked."

One of Kant's major objectives, then, was to rescue science from Humean skepticism. Hume took his departure from Locke's empiricism, which held that the only real knowledge comes from sense experience, and there is nothing in the mind except what comes to it from the senses. He demonstrated—and Kant accepted his demonstration as "irrefutable"—that through the senses alone the human mind cannot encounter reality at all, nor can it have a science founded on anything but "opinion." We have only an unrelated sequence of sense impressions. The principle of cause and effect cannot be derived from experience; we simply assume it arbitrarily; it may only be an accident of our mental processes.

Kant's reply was roughly as follows: The mind or intellect, far from being passive or negative, contains the organizing principles that *impose order on experience.* The mind contains forms and categories which are the basic concepts that give meaning to experience. These "fundamental conditions of thought itself" are *a priori,* that is, not derived from experience. Kant, in what he describes as the hardest metaphysical work ever done, specified these forms and categories: two forms of perception (space and time), twelve categories of the understanding (for example, cause and effect).[3] These correspond to the types of judgment of Aristotelian logic, that is, the types of quantity, quality, relation, modality. All minds contain these categories, thus mind is a fundamental unity—reason is "transcendent."

Thus our minds condition and, indeed, determine knowledge by being as they are. Agreeing with Leibniz, Kant denied that there is nothing in the mind except what the senses bring in; there is the mind itself, which sorts out, classifies, relates this raw material, making it intelligible. We will not here, of course, follow Kant in all his arguments and terminology. From his powerful analysis, it is enough to say, emerged a picture of mind as creative, not passive, and of reason as something *a priori,* thus rescued from the skepticism of an empiricist approach. Goethe interpreted Kant to mean that "had I not borne the world in myself by anticipation, I would have remained blind even with eyes that see." It is not our senses that enable us to experience reality, but a preformed structure within the mind that prepares us to receive and understand sensory impressions. It is not the "solid" data of sense that provide the basic cement of science; it is something given within the mind, something like those "innate ideas" Locke had sought to banish as too mysterious or occult.

Because of a debate that arose, it must be added that Kant was evidently not an "idealist" in the sense that some of his followers were. He does not say that reality is a *creation* of the mind. Things are out there, and in striking our senses, they provide the indispensable, primary data of knowledge. The point is that we could not "understand" them if we did not have minds equipped with a rational structure. Kant is pointing out that the world outside must appear to us in a certain way because of the kind of mind, as well as the kind of senses, that we have. If we put on red-tinted glasses, things look red, though they really are not all red; and we also have our built-in sensory apparatus, so that colors, odors, and so forth appear to us as they do because of the way that apparatus works. Kant adds the important point that things appear rational—classifiable and subject to order, such as cause and effect, identity, comparison—not

[3]Kant's categories are: quantity: unit, plurality, totality; quality: reality, negation, limitation; relation: substance and accident, cause and effect, community; modality: possibility, existence, necessity. It is usually held today that Kant's categories, too dependent on the logic of his day, do not hold up; but this is not to say that basic categories of the understanding do not exist.

because of the way *they* are but because of the way our minds are. The mind makes sense out of experience; it would be senseless without mind. But the external world exists; Kant is not denying that, nor that we must have its stimuli for the mind to work on in the knowing process. If precepts without concepts are blind, as someone said, concepts without precepts are empty.

This was only part of Kant's examination of the knowing process, and it must be added immediately that the sort of knowledge we have been talking about—scientific knowledge, taken from experience as worked on by the categorizing intellect—was not, to him, knowledge of ultimate reality. This domain of science is perfectly valid; Kant's goal was to rescue science from skepticism, and to represent him as a foe of science (the view is not uncommon) is a gross error. He himself made some contributions to the sciences, in which he was always interested. But it is a particular sort of knowledge, appropriate to the practical or useful realm only; it is knowledge of appearances, not of substance. In the famous Kantian language, it is the *phenomenal,* as opposed to the *noumenal,* world. It relates to the properties of things, not the "thing-in-itself." Kant's other great objective, the inspiration for which he perhaps derived from Rousseau, was to rescue the realm of *value* from the scientists. Thus he sets up two sharply different categories. The realm of science, which is useful knowledge, deals with the phenomenal world, the world of appearances. The realm of value, of religion, is intuitive and deals with the noumenal world, the world of substantive reality. Kant thinks that the two realms must not be confused. One of his achievements was to riddle the proofs of God's existence derived from the facts of physical nature—arguments extremely popular during the eighteenth century, especially the "argument from design." From ontological argument to argument from design, Kant devastated all these venerable "proofs" with such effectiveness that few dared revive them. The proofs appropriate to science have nothing to do with God, Kant believed, for they can never give us values.

There is nevertheless the noumenal realm. Kant was not quite sure whether we can know it at all. He seemed to think that in moments of moral or esthetic experience we can glimpse it fleetingly, and these hints were to be built upon by the romantics who followed him. The human soul, a thing-in-itself, by quite other roads than the analytical reason, may make contact with other things-in-themselves. Kant seems ambiguously poised between the Enlightenment and romanticism here. On the one hand he said that he "had to deny knowledge to make room for faith," which he clearly much wanted to do. His most widely quoted sentence is that in which he proclaims the equal wonders of the two realms, the starry heavens and the moral law. On the other hand Kant seldom departed from his Enlightenment hardheadedness, was certainly

[handwritten margin notes: "Why is there a Noumenal world? No proof. Just taken on Faith?"]

no mystic by temperament, and was not at all sure about our being able to make contact with the noumena at all. Perhaps we are condemned to live in the phenomenal world as far as intellectual activity is concerned, while being aware that there is another world, the real world, which we can never know—at least in this life. Each of Kant's realms is flawed for humanity. From the scientific, phenomenal one we can get clear and useful knowledge, but it is knowledge of appearances only. From the spiritual, noumenal realm we could get ultimate truth if we could reach it, but ordinarily we cannot do so.

Kant nevertheless at times put great stress on his rescuing of religion from the clammy grip of science so as to restore faith to its true estate. The existence of God, freedom of the will, the soul, these things cannot be proved by scientific argument. But when we move from "pure reason" to the "practical" or moral reason, we are in a realm which is in its own ways quite valid though different. Pascal's "the heart has its reasons" was close to Kant's meaning. Our moral consciousness exists and is entitled to great respect, though its knowledge is not the kind appropriate to science. Though we cannot prove them, we have to assume the existence of some noumena, for example God and human freedom, especially for moral purposes.

Kant's writings on ethics were among his most celebrated. Consistent with his general point of view, he argued that valid rules of conduct cannot be found in experience but must be sought in pure reason. Can we find the "categorical imperative" which reason must recognize as the basic principle of morals? It cannot be found in circumstances, Kant stated in a profound and subtle piece of argumentation, but in the moral agent, the person. That which is good in itself is the Will, when it is good; and a will is good when it is rational. The moral worth of an action is determined by the motive, not the result; it is Duty, the rational resistance to evil impulses, that is the highest moral faculty. In the end Kant reached his famous statement of the "categorical imperative": Act so that your action is one you would want to be a universal law, or, in his other version of it, always treat people as ends, not means. (If you act in a way you would *not* want everybody else to act, you are selfishly using them as means for your ends.)

Beyond Kant's formal arguments, which do not constitute proof that he found the key to ethics, is an assertion of faith in rationality and human dignity that is the main source of Kant's amazing appeal. Many who could not follow his formidable trains of reasoning were captivated by his general spirit. In the last analysis Kant's message is a tragic one. We are finite and imperfect creatures torn by contradiction and unable to plumb the ultimate secrets. We come against ultimate mysteries— "antinomies," such as nature and culture, freedom and authority, the individual and society in conflict—which our reason can never resolve.

As soon as we start to learn a little, Kant reflects, we grow old and die. In this respect Kant was not a typical romantic.

It is interesting to compare the dualism of Kant with the other great dualisms of Western thought—Plato's, Ockham's, Descartes's. To Plato, the realm of essences or ideas alone is real and knowable; to Kant, it is alone real, even more so, but it is scarcely knowable, certainly not knowable by the reasoning intellect as Plato thought. To Descartes, there are two realms, the physical and mental, one the domain of necessity and the other of freedom; there is something of this in Kant but, again, Descartes felt the physical world to be perfectly knowable in a way that Kant could not. Kant is closer to William of Ockham and to Pascal. Science is one thing, religion another; two wholly different kinds of cognition are appropriate to them; we cannot pass from one to the other.

Kant's successors tended to quarrel about what he meant, and it is plain that with but a slight twist his "critical philosophy" might be made the foundation of several different systems. Some Kantians forgot about the thing-in-itself and became either idealists, arguing that the world is completely a mental construct, or positivists (phenomenalists), urging that we do not and cannot know what ultimate reality is and had better remain content with the orderly arrangement of our observations. Others developed Kantian noumenalism in a romantic or mystical direction, stressing the role of the poetic or religious intuition in touching the deepest reality by nonscientific methods. Kant himself, as we have said, was hardly a romantic by temperament; but the romantic era was beginning as he wrote and his immediate followers in Germany tended to be either idealists or romantics, sometimes blending the two. There is no doubt a sense in which Kant is the uncle, if not the father, of romanticism.[4] But we ought not to forget that the bulk of his work was directed towards clarifying scientific philosophy and that his contribution here was enormous. It is part of the wonder of the Königsberg philosopher that he greatly advanced both of those different domains of the mind which he so sharply separated, the scientific and the esthetic-religious.

Kant's dualism nevertheless was unsatisfactory for many who had been accustomed by the Enlightenment to clear and final conclusions. Phenomena and noumena, pure reason and practical reason, seemed completely divorced, a situation not felt to be satisfactory. Fichte and Schelling, his immediate successors in German philosophy, sought for a unifying principle that would weld the divided self and divided world of thought together. Impressed by Kant's "transcendent" structure of rea-

---

[4] Wilhelm Busch, the jolly children's poet whose *Max and Morris* (1865) is the German equivalent of *Alice in Wonderland*, wrote in his autobiography that he was fascinated by Kant though he could not understand him, and found that *The Critique of Pure Reason* left him with a delighted interest in the secret places of the mind "where there are so many hiding places."

son, they wished to broaden it so as to bring pure and practical reason together under one roof. Kant stimulated future philosophy by the problems he left, as every great philosopher does.

But in both of Kant's two realms, the "Copernican revolution" is evident: The human mind is creative, not passive, whether it is working as scientist or as seer. It is an active agent, far from the wax of Condillac; it imposes order on nature, even in the scientific process. Kant reminded scientists that Galileo had understood the necessity of hypothesis, asking questions of nature; pure empiricism is poor scientific method. The creative mind is as much a necessity in science as in poetry. This is well understood today; Kant, probably more than any other modern thinker, established it firmly.

Kant made significant contributions to political and ethical thought too. For our purposes it will be sufficient to note the *liberal* implications of these. In making *duty* a linchpin of his system, Kant may have betrayed his Prussianism; but his political thought generally stressed individual freedom, the moral autonomy of the person, human beings as ends. There were even Kantian socialists in the nineteenth century who pointed out that the rule of treating people as ends and not as means, as persons not as things, invalidates the labor system of capitalism, which makes the workingman a commodity. Some attempted to blend Kant and Marx.

These liberal features, along with the attack on rational proofs of God's existence, caused Kant's writings to be banned for a time in his native country. But his political thought also stressed the reign of law, obedience to duly constituted authority; it sought to resolve the dilemma of liberty and authority (a dilemma of which Kant was very conscious) through just and general laws. History is the story of the education of humanity toward freedom under law. Thought should be free. Kant was one of those who "wished to be warmed by the fire of the French Revolution but not burnt up by it"; he was a moderate liberal with a horror of violent revolution. He believed a republic to be the best form of government (not a pure democracy which is irrational). If Kant stresses authority, he also believes in liberty. His political thought is perhaps a little trite; his well-known essay on universal peace does not take us much farther than the usual utopian exhortations. But Kant's deep respect for the individual was rooted in his great Critical Philosophy: One can readily see that he made the human mind and the inner self more important and sacred than did the Lockeans. They would have it determined, passive, dictated to by external conditions; to Kant it is hub and focus of all, it is self-determining and free insofar as noumenal, and even in its phenomenal aspects, it dictates to nature rather than being dictated to. The final purpose of all creation, Kant suggests, is our full realization as moral beings.

Kant came soon to be regarded as the greatest of modern philosophers (Hegel disputed the title with him in the nineteenth century, but clearly Kant made Hegel possible) as well as a notable contributor to moral, esthetic,[5] and political ideas. It seemed that he brought an end to the typical Enlightenment philosophy by rejecting both its empiricism and confused skepticism in favor of a new form of rationalism. The peculiar Enlightenment formula of commonsense empiricism was not tenable after his criticisms and reconstructions. He also gave hints to both the romanticists and the liberals, to whose influence the next generations largely belonged. The intellectual revolution of this era was bigger than Kant, but he was somehow an integral part of it.

POST-KANTIAN PHILOSOPHERS

The grand lineage of German philosophy in its golden age began with Kant and ended with Hegel a half century later. In between lay several others, most significantly Johann Gottlieb Fichte and Friedrich Wilhelm Joseph von Schelling. Here a very brief summary will suffice. Fichte, brought up on the writings of the French *philosophes,* praised the French Revolution and subsequently wrote much of significance on political, social, and economic subjects—especially his famous *Addresses to the German Nation* (1807), inspired by the Prussian defeat at the hands of Napoleon, which we have mentioned. He also had a good deal to say about religion and was, in fact, dismissed from the University of Jena in 1799 largely because of his excursions into this arena, bringing on him the charge of atheism. (A sort of pantheism would, of course, be closer.) He was not very romantic in temperament; philosophy, he thought, should be a science. But he adopted and preached a philosophy of idealism, believing that anything else leads to determinism and materialism, which destroy human dignity. According to the vision of reality that Fichte developed, the universe consists of an absolute Ego which is like our own consciousness, a unique, free activity which strives to realize itself in perfect self-awareness and is the foundation of all nature. Leaving aside the technical jargon, which probably mystified all but a few, this vision of reality dramatized the human will or consciousness as hub and center of the universe because an expression of the absolute spirit of which the universe consists. Spirit or idea makes up reality, and our spirits, represented by our basic consciousness, an indescribable but intuitively certain thing,[6] are the concrete manifestations of this world spirit. One might

---

[5] In *Critique of Judgment,* Kant sought to establish an objective, transcendental basis for artistic taste, while recognizing subjective elements also.

[6] Consciousness is the foundation of all thought and experience, yet we cannot find it in thought or experience because it cannot be objectified, cannot be made an object of thought or experience, Fichte pointed out. Sartre and the existentialists have made the same point.

say without too much distortion that, according to Fichte, each of us is God, or a part of God—if we equate the "absolute" or "world spirit" with God. So, if Fichte was technically not a "romantic," he introduced an intoxicating idea which in the broader sense was very romantic: that the world is spiritual, that we are a part of that spiritual world, and that in moral experience especially we can touch the uttermost sublimities of the universe.

Schelling, a disciple of Fichte and friend and collaborator of Hegel, whom he influenced, produced a stream of writings, especially between 1797 and 1802, which developed the idealist outlook into what he called Transcendental Idealism. He put greater stress than Fichte on physical nature as the objective form of the Absolute and pointed out the road Hegel was to follow in many respects. Perhaps the most striking feature of his thought was its representation of artistic creation, the act of esthetic intuition, as the supreme achievement. In it the unconscious and the conscious forces, representing the two forms of the Absolute, are fused in synthesis; it is in art that the infinite manifests itself in finite form.[7] Coleridge and all the romantic poets absorbed Schelling eagerly, for understandable reasons; he provided a metaphysical basis for the artist such as had never before been known. Romanticism's glorification of the poet as seer, as "unacknowledged legislator of the human race," as discoverer and purveyor of loftier truths than the merely logical, relates closely to Schelling's thought. Much later in his career Schelling opposed Hegel's excessively abstract rationalism by offering a kind of foreshadowing of existentialism; he influenced Kierkegaard, who listened to his lectures at Berlin in the 1840s. He came to reject all abstract, conceptual thinking as "negative philosophy," inferior to concrete, existent realities. He showed a keen interest in the history of religious mythologies, like Jung in our time. In this his earlier preference for art may perhaps be seen continuing.

Fichte and Schelling may seem to have travelled a long way from Kant, who so far as he lived to meet their ideas evidently repudiated them. But Kant had started them off. This extraordinary spate of German philosophizing concluded with the titanic figure of Hegel, consideration of whom we shall postpone for a moment. The whole of it cut a wide swath in intellectual Europe in the first half of the nineteenth century. It combined keen and searching thought with daring speculation and a good deal of moral sublimity. Later, especially in the non-German world, it seemed excessively "metaphysical" and might be dismissed as empty bombast. From another point of view it revealed about

---

[7]To further explain, the unconscious is the real, or objective, physical world, the conscious the realm of the ideal and subjective. Both are parts of the Absolute. Their destiny is to be merged in one, the objective becoming merged in the subjective and vice versa. This happens when the artist shapes nature, or cooperates with it, as Michelangelo carving a statue.

as radical a perspective as Europe had seen. For it may be noted that Fichte, Schelling, and subsequently Hegel offered a philosophical alternative to religion, substituting their Absolute for the Christian conception of God. A prominent feature of this metaphysical faith was man's place in it as almost the equivalent of God. The Absolute was not quite just the individual human Ego writ large, but it came close to being that, at least in the popular interpretation of these philosophies. The human consciousness reflects and participates in the divine. Man's art and moral experience are in effect cosmic forces working in and through him. German idealism united with romanticism to deify the mysterious forces working in the human soul and so to introduce that theme of "titanism" so marked in the nineteenth century and, according to some, so dangerous. "Glory to Man in the highest," sang the poet Swinburne.

At any rate the lofty and searching inquiries of the great German philosophers of the Kantian age captured humanity's imagination. Near the end of the century South African General Jan Smuts, having made his fortune and reputation by the age of thirty, decided to retire. "I prefer to sit still, to water my orange trees, and to study Kant's 'Critical Philosophy,'" he said. It could have been any thinking person's dream. Kant—together with his children—came close to meaning *philosophy* for the nineteenth century.

The Germans soon found their way to England, chiefly by way of Coleridge. They were less well known in France until around 1850; the Enlightenment carried on more strongly there, represented by Condillac's empirical psychology. But eventually the impact on French thought, and on Italian, was to be strong. Meanwhile France was not without idealist and romantic philosophic strains, as, for example, Maine de Biran and Victor Cousin.

THE ORIGINS OF ROMANTICISM

Romanticism is sometimes said to have begun with Rousseau, and particularly with that amazingly successful novel *La Nouvelle Hèloise,* which had all Europe weeping in 1762. Certain romantic affinities can be found in other eighteenth-century writers, notably the English poet James Thomson (d. 1748), while the poets Gray and Cowper are often classified as "preromantics" bridging the gap between Dryden and Pope on the one end and Wordsworth and Coleridge on the other. (And, indeed, it is possible for Geoffrey Clive to separate out a whole "romantic Enlightenment.") It may be questioned, though, whether "preromanticism" is a very useful concept. The criterion is passion or emotion, but this is not really the right one. The sentimentalism of the age of Julie and Pamela made itself at home in the Age of Reason and had little in common with what later came to be called romanticism. But at any rate

Rousseau strongly influenced practically all the romantics of the next generation or two; it is hardly too much to say that in France the figure of Jean-Jacques, shrouded in mists of legend, became deified. Before long the German writers Goethe and Schiller took up the romantic manner, the former's *Sorrows of Werther* rivaling *La Nouvelle Hèloise* in its ability to reduce all manner of people to tears, while the *Sturm und Drang* (storm and stress) plays of the early Schiller were to be show-pieces for many years. (*The Robbers* was written in 1781.) The chief disciples of Rousseau at first seem to have been the Germans; in France the influence of the rationalist Enlightenment continued, with Voltaire getting his tremendous triumph in Paris near the end of his life in 1778. But the restless decade of the 1780s, with its Saint-Martin mood, has been mentioned.

Then came the Revolution, which tended to halt literary and intellectual life, diverting all attention to the political melodrama being enacted at Paris. Some Frenchmen for a time suspected romanticism as too German to be patriotic. But in 1801 to 1805, French romanticism asserted itself with the powerful figure of Chateaubriand, the leading literary personality of his day. With *Atala* and *René* a new mode of literature had arrived, it was widely recognized. Chateaubriand was the father, as Rousseau was the grandfather, of all subsequent French romantic literature.

Meanwhile in England the young poets Coleridge and Wordsworth were experimenting with a new poetry they rightly felt to be nothing less than revolutionary. They, along with the poet-seer William Blake, began English romanticism in the years just before the turn of the century, but it remained obscure for some time. Blake printed his own books, *Songs of Innocence* (1789) and *Songs of Experience* (1794), but they were neither noticed nor understood for a number of years. He was known slightly as designer and engraver, but evidently not at all as poet, until well into the nineteenth century.

The Revolutionary and Napolionic wars were going on; Chateaubriand became an exile from Bonaparte's dictatorship and even Coleridge and Wordsworth took up political pamphleteering. In Germany romanticism continued to flourish uniquely: A group that included Frederick Schlegel and his brother August in Berlin, Novalis and Schelling at Dresden, and Jena called themselves romantic and threw out ideas important to the philosophy of the movement, to which it is necessary to add the theology of Schleiermacher (1799) and the music of Beethoven (1800). All this was in the years from 1798 to 1801—romanticism's moment of creative fruition. But its popular triumphs lay ahead.

Picking up momentum, romanticism reached its maximum of influence in the years from 1810 to 1830. Wordsworth and Coleridge began to achieve fame and were joined by Shelley, Byron, and Keats

A Romantic poet, Lord Byron in Albanian dress, 1813. (London, National Portrait Gallery. Portrait by T. Phillips.)

to make up the most renowned group of poets in England's history, all of whom are customarily labeled "romantic." In 1813 the Swiss-born Mme. de Staël, a glamorous figure who wrote, made love, and fought Napoleon with equal verve, popularized the Germans in France with her celebrated work *D'Allemagne.* France succumbed to romanticism between 1820, when Schiller's *Maria Stuart* (composed in 1801) took Paris by storm, and 1830, when Victor Hugo's *Hernani* caused the wildest tumult in the history of the French theater but emerged triumphant. Hugo and Lamartine, along with the novelist Alexander Dumas, the avowed leaders of the romantic movement, were the most popular and distinguished writers of their age. At the same time the painter Eugene Delacroix headed a school which called itself romantic.

    In the 1830s a "romantic" influence may be seen in many directions, and indeed for the rest of the century that influence never ceased to exist, being so absorbed into the texture of thought and expression that "nothing after it could be the same." But it became diffused. A partial reaction against it set in. We must not think of romanticism as ever quite sweeping away all opposition. In France, where a strong classical tradition existed, Hugo was denied admission to the Academy five times, the last time in 1836, and warfare between romantic and classic never ceased to enliven the theatrical season, at least. In 1829 the Academy denounced romanticism as that which "puts in disorder all our rules, insults our masterpieces, and perverts mass opinion." Eighteenth-century taste, classical and rococo, remained popular at the high tide of romanticism. In England, embittered literary reactionaries helped bring on Keats's early death, his friends believed. The greatest German literary figure in history, Goethe, who contributed to romanticism early in his career, eventually declared that classicism is healthy and romanticism diseased. Unconverted "classicists" always existed and, indeed, there was something of a classical revival contemporary with romanticism. If we grant that the romantics had carried away most of the prizes by 1830, they were under attack from the younger generation of the forties and fifties as too pompous and theatrical. Broadly speaking this next generation preferred to absorb its romanticism, if at all, in carefully filtered form.

Yet between 1760 and 1840—to take the widest time span (the creative zenith coming then in the middle of it)—Europe had been hit by something new, exciting, and controversial. We have yet to define what this was, having only named its landmarks. What was romanticism? The question has puzzled the more literal-minded for a century. A definition is elusive. Someone declared that this inability to define romanticism is the scandal of the century. The word took on many meanings. The romanticism of Chateaubriand was Catholic, and, reacting against the Revolution, became Royalist; but the romanticism of Victor Hugo was (eventually—Hugo began as a conservative) republican, liberal, even revolutionary. It was romantic to suffer, to pray, to fight (as Byron did for Greece), to venture on far voyages, to commune with nature, to have a sense of history. It was romantic to love passionately and transcend the conventional moral boundaries, but the eighteenth century, now old hat, had done this too, like all other centuries. It was romantic to read about the Middle Ages and to admire the pseudoprimitive bard Ossian,[8] but also to adore the days of classical antiquity—"fair Greece, sad relic." Fate was romantic; so was soul-baring. What was not, if done with the proper spirit? Romanticism was a mood and a style much more than a doctrine; moods and styles are hard to define.

The ambiguity of the term is carried over into everyday speech, in which today the word "romantic" is widely but quite variously used. It can mean charming or pretty ("What a romantic place!"); mysterious; old ("romantic old house"); sexy; quaint; young and exciting; impractical, visionary, dreamy; heroic and glorious. To be sure it cannot mean

---

[8]Between 1760 and 1763, the Scotsman James MacPherson published three volumes purporting to be literal translations from the legendary ancient Gallic poet Ossian, a sort of Celtic Homer of the third century A.D. Suspected by a few at the time and confirmed by later scholarship was the fact that little if any of this material really came from such a source, most of it being made up by MacPherson himself. But this "romantic" verse enjoyed wide popularity throughout Europe, much though Johnson inveighed against it ("Sir, a man might write such stuff for ever, if he would abandon his mind to it").

anything; one would never use it to mean dull, mediocre, staid, cautious, and this tells us something; yet its range of meanings is quite wide and even includes possible contradictions.

As part of the early nineteenth-century revolution in ideas, romanticism "has become a label for half a dozen things that have only an accidental connection" (Christopher Dawson). He instanced the following: expressing one's emotions, love of nature, intuition as a source of truth, the quest for new experience, the view of society as organism rather than machine. This is not an exhaustive list. In drama it meant departing from the classical "rules," to the great indignation of the traditionalists; in poetry it meant, to Wordsworth at least, using simple rather than "literary" language and writing about plain people rather than fancy ones.[9] In a clever essay Arthur O. Lovejoy once showed that these various meanings can be made to seem flatly contradictory and suggested that we must speak of romanticisms—not one thing, but a number, that happened to coincide in roughly a single period and have sometimes gotten badly confused. Romanticism, Lovejoy pointed out, has meant a belief in progress and a spirit of reaction; a return to Christianity and a naturalistic humanism; also various other philosophies arrantly at odds with each other. In concluding that "the word 'romantic' has come to mean so many things that, by itself, it means nothing," Lovejoy came near the truth; and yet of course we must not conclude that therefore it did not exist at all. The mood of an age may be nonetheless real for being illogical. Future historians will find it as difficult to say exactly what existentialism was as present ones do to define Renaissance, Enlightenment, or romanticism. Historical phenomena take on many accretions as they pass through society; they become involved with other phenomena and eventually lose themselves in the common stream. Any major movement of the mind inevitably accumulates a crowd of different associations and meanings as it spreads. It becomes rather like our political parties: too big to stand for any one creed on which all its followers might agree, except the vaguest sort of generalities. But we do not for this reason infer the nonexistence or meaninglessness of Democrats and Republicans. It is, in fact, possible to argue the reverse: that whenever we find a doctrine that everyone knows about but no one can quite define, we are in the presence of a major intellectual revolution. ("The indefinable word is the essential one," Chesterton noted, terms such as love, good, blue cannot be defined, but only illustrated, because irreducible.)

Without question, romanticism was such a revolution. We are in

---

[9]The word *romantic* derives from the medieval "romances," so named because written in the vernacular (French) rather than in classical Latin. Thus in returning to popular speech, and trying to find folk themes, romantics were loyal to the basic meaning of their movement.

danger of losing this truth if we seek too narrow or precise a definition. Behind the *forms* of romanticism, which were various, lay a deep spiritual change, often vague but nonetheless mighty. Critics of romanticism, then and later, charged that it was a fever which rejected all discipline and, by being out of proportion with nature, refusing to accept boundaries, became a dangerous malady, "an assault delivered on the modern soul by all the combined forces of disorganization" (René Doumic). To them it was nothing less than the destruction of the sense of balance on which European civilization had rested ever since the Greeks invented classicism with its message of nothing in excess, everything in proper proportion, each element in its due place. On the other side, friends of the new spirit believed that it had for the first time emancipated Europe from a timid orthodoxy and opened minds and hearts to poetry, to real religion, to true philosophy, to sincerity rather than artificiality. It was, said Sismondi, a "Protestantism in letters and the arts," a demand for liberty against authority in style; some have added that it was nothing less than an ultimate Protestantism (without dogma) in all ranges of life—a defiant Promethean rejection of all constraints on the free spirit of the individual man.

TYPES OF ROMANTICISM

Leaving such sweeping claims aside for the moment, we may try more precisely to state the range of romantic attitudes. First, romanticism began in *reaction against* the eighteenth century, that is, against rationalism, mechanistic materialism, classicism, all the dominant ingredients of the Enlightenment. Youth looked for new ideas and found them in Rousseau, subsequently in Kant, Fichte, Burke. A chief weakness in the Enlightenment was its neglect of the imagination, its externalism and absence of anything inward or deeply esthetic. It denied religious emotion; it ignored the mystery and terror of existence in its effort to make all things clear. All common sense and broad daylight, it became uninspiring and unthrilling. It lacked what the French call *frissons*, or thrills, and its literary style was, or came to seem, flat, conventional, unenterprising. Likewise its ethic of selfish hedonism, along with its mechanical and materialistic view of the universe, could appear as ignoble or dull.

Consequently the romantic era is filled with cries of rejection. "I, for my share, declare the world to be no machine!" exclaimed Thomas Carlyle, repeating the German idealists. The eighteenth century had said that it was. Burke speaks of reason being "but a part, and by no means the greatest part," of human nature, while Coleridge says that the "calculating faculty" is inferior to the "creative faculty." This rejection of the analytical reason in favor of an intuitive "eliciting of truth at a flash" was very close to the heart of romanticism and represented, in good part, another reaction against the Enlightenment. In literary form, romanticism rebelled against the "rules" imposed on drama or poetry by the classical formula, and against classicism's preference for the general rather than the concrete. "We are not to number the streaks of the tulip," classicism had pronounced. Romantics wanted to do just that. Romantics sought religion—a source of *frissons,* if nothing more—because rationalists scorned it. Chateaubriand declared that nothing is pleasing except the mysterious; the mysterious had been the great common enemy of all the *philosophes.* So, too, with "enthusiasm."

That which had been sensible moderation now seemed like torpor, or worse. The eighteenth century, "soul extinct but stomach well alive," in Carlyle's phrase, became a byword for crass materialism; Thackeray called it an age of gluttony. "The man of Locke" was to be scorned. "I mistrust Locke," Schelling announced; virtually all the romantics shared this contempt for that earthbound philosophy. (Some romantics made use of Locke, but if so they read him as meaning that the senses, that is, the feelings, and immediate experience, are to be trusted above the abstract reason.) "Unable to believe but terrified of skepticism," the peculiar "heavenly city" of the eighteenth-century philosophers with its "faith of reason" was now seen to be uninhabitable. Carlyle spoke for the romantic generations in repudiating its hedonistic ethic or pleasure-seeking spirit as unworthy of humanity: "the pig philosophy" he called it. (It was still vigorously alive in Carlyle's Britain in the guise of Jeremy Bentham's utilitarianism; the two schools could not abide each other.) This reaction against "the pursuit of happiness" as swinish sensualism pushed the romantics into some very lofty poses: Man was once again to be Promethean hero, world-conquering adventurer, sublime sage or saint—anything except that simpering courtier of the eighteenth century whose only goal in life was satisfaction of creature comforts. Keats, who certainly celebrated the sensual pleasures, regarded them as the doorway to transcendental realms of knowledge, not as ends in themselves.

The Age of Reason had been an Age of Prose; and so romanticism meant poetry, or a new kind of poetic prose such as Chateaubriand wrote. Romanticism was, after all, primarily a literary movement, though it spilled over into all branches of life. Eighteenth-century poetry had become on the whole unsatisfactory. "Crushed by rules, and weakened as refined," this polite literature usually failed to communicate sincere feeling, was overly formalized and abstract; it was Dr. Samuel Johnson, no romantic,[10] who noticed this much:

---

[10]From his famous Dictionary, definition of "Romantick":
1. Resembling the tales of romance; wild. . . .
2. Improbable; false.
3. Fanciful; full of wild scenery. . . .

From bard to bard the frigid caution crept
While declamation roar'd and passion slept.

Hazlitt, though not uncritical of the new poets, affirmed that

> Our poetical literature had, towards the close of the last century, degener-
> ated into the most trite, insipid, and mechanical of all things, in the hands
> of the followers of Pope and the old French school of poetry.

In revenge, the romantic poets gave full vent to what Locke had disparaged as "the conceits of a warmed or overweening brain." For a later
taste as well as an earlier, they often sought too many "grand effects,"
they bared their souls and gushed too much. Still, few would deny the
mighty debt to literature owed to the poets of the romantic generation.
They revitalized language, and, among other things, brought poetry to
the people. Too vast to be estimated is the force exerted on millions of
people, heretofore hardly reached by the printed word, by romantic
literature: Think of Musset and Hugo in France, Shelley and
Wordsworth in England, Goethe and Kleist in Germany, Emerson and
Longfellow in the United States, Bobbie Burns in Scotland. Or think of
Pushkin and Lermontov in Russia, reminding us of the universality of
this movement in the European cultural world—Pushkin, who clapped
his hands and shouted "O you Pushkin, you son of a bitch" after writing
a play in the new mode, which he felt, though he could not define. These
and their imitators molded the consciousness of the nineteenth century,
it is not too much to say. They made poetry something more than
rhymed reason; as image and symbol, haunting the imagination, it
shaped the feeling for life in its own unique way.

Mounting "an insurrection against the old traditions of classicism,"
the romanticists achieved a virtual revolution in the canons of art and
literature. One measure of that revolution may be found in attitudes
toward the art of the Middle Ages. Ever since the Renaissance, Gothic
architecture had been dismissed as crude and barbarous. Gibbon said
that the Piazzo San Marco in Venice contained "the worst architecture I
ever saw." Ruskin, only a few decades later, pronounced it the most
beautiful of human creations (*The Stones of Venice*). Each of us must make
up his own mind about this, but in general the romantics prevailed, most
people today grant the beauty of St. Mark's and of the Gothic cathedrals
in general. The French Revolution started to pull down those "piles of
monkish superstition"; the Gothic Revival of the 1830s tried to renovate
them and imitate them. Similarly, it may surprise us to learn that the poet
Dante had been held in considerable disdain. In the eighteenth century
Thomas Warton had spoken of the *Divine Comedy* as "disgusting," and a
follower of Voltaire pronounced it the worst poem in all the world.
Dante's reputation was made by the romantics, by Blake, Byron, Shelley,

and Coleridge, enthusiastically seconded by Carlyle, Tennyson, Browning, and Ruskin a bit later. A popular product of the romantic revolution, much fancied today by collectors of the unusual, was the Gothic novel, with its eerie atmosphere and supernatural events, its werewolves and ruined abbeys and diabolical happenings. Thus the taste for the medieval could go to extreme lengths. The mysterious, the exotic, the irregular, the sublime and even the grotesque now became appealing.

In a similar way the taste for wild nature, for mountains and deep forests, was largely a romantic reaction; pure neo-classical taste considered the Alps hideously unkempt and would have gone some distance out of the way to avoid them.[11] "Nature" was a word much on eighteenth-century lips, but it did not usually mean the woodlands wild. Rousseau's *Reveries of a Solitary Walker* passed down to Chateaubriand and to Lamartine's *Meditations;* and everyone knows how important nature was to Wordsworth and Thoreau. This attachment to the trees and flowers and hills had, or came to have, a metaphysical foundation which, forming a link to philosophical idealism, is one of the leading ideas of the age. Rousseau believed vaguely that nature soothes and calms us, returning us to fundamentals and reminding us of deeper truths than those of human society. Wordsworth, without much philosophy, felt keenly

> . . . a sense sublime
> Of something far more deeply interfused,
> Whose dwelling is the light of setting suns
> And the round ocean and the living air,
> And the blue sky, and in the mind of man;
> A motion and a spirit that impels
> All thinking things, all objects of all thought,
> And rolls through all things.

In Germany, where philosophy had been stimulated by Kant and where romanticism from the first interacted with it, this pantheistic sense of spirit in nature, "rolling through all things," received explicit formulation. How Kant's critical philosophy created a revolution in philosophy, and how this led on to the other great German philosophers (Fichte, Schelling, Hegel) has already been pointed out. There were philosophers who specifically called themselves "romantic"; and there were idealists, like Fichte, who contributed to the popular conception of romanticism in certain ways. Broadly speaking, the result was to present a vision of reality as basically spiritual, and to suggest in some sense a

---

[11]Despite neoclassical preference for neat symmetry, the eighteenth century had permitted a place for much that was not "beautiful" but nevertheless somehow impressive, under the title of "the sublime." Romantics—*cf.* the young Burke's notable essay—developed this concept. Especially was this true in England, never as orthodoxly neoclassical as France. "Mountain gloom and mountain glory" (Marjorie Nicolson) was celebrated by some eighteenth-century sublimists.

unity of this world spirit linking us to nature. The post-Kantians in various ways postulated a fundamental knowable unity, spiritual in nature—a mind-stuff underlying and giving form to the appearances, corresponding to the mind-stuff we have in us, and which we contact when we are using our minds creatively. Fichte called it the Ego, adopting an idealist position in which thought is the basic reality and stressing moral experience; Schelling spoke of the Absolute, of the union of object and subject in the human consciousness, and of the paramountcy of esthetic experience. All this might seem rather Teutonically mystifying to most people; on any showing it was difficult and academic, for these worthies of German philosophy were all university professors. But it got outside the classroom, as the poets Novalis and Hölderlin and Richter transformed its abstract words into concrete poetic symbols. And as esthetic doctrine it was tremendously influential.

Many people came to hold, more or less loosely, something like this idealist-romantic position, meaning that we can see God or a higher reality in Nature, actually commune with it, feel its basic kinship to our own souls. Nontechnical, semipopular romantic idealism may be found in Thomas Carlyle's first book, *Sartor Resartus,* wherein this vivid writer gave expression to the idea that "the external world known to our senses and explored by our sciences is mere Appearance. Reality is its divine, unseen counterpart, standing to Appearance as Soul stands to Body" (D. C. Somervell). "Transcendentalism" became a byword among the literary of both France and America from 1820 to 1840; the name of Ralph Waldo Emerson is enough to remind Americans of its potency. This heady doctrine might persuade people that all the appearances, social conventions, for example, are a fraud, and that all of us can be godlike if only we dare to search our own souls. It was close to mystical pantheism, a heresy long known to Christianity, whereby the god-intoxicated felt that they might communicate directly with deity. Often it had explicit roots in Neoplatonism; William Blake's mysticism has been traced to this source, and these writings were also prominent in the omnivorous reading of Coleridge, who claimed that he had found mysticism in many of the ancients before he read the Germans. There was also a discovery of the Indian religiophilosophical tradition at this time. "The pantheism of the Orient, transformed by Germany," E. Quinet wrote in 1841, was responsible for what he called a *"renaissance orientale."* (But the discovery and translation of the Hindu classics owed most to an Englishman, Sir William Jones, and a Frenchman, M. Anquetil-Duperron.)

The romantics added the thought that it is above all the artist, the poet, who feels the Infinite Spirit when creating. Working intuitively, the artist "elicits truth as at a flash" (Coleridge), truth deeper than the experimental or analytical. Poetic images are symbols of nature, keys to reality. The visionary-religious element in romanticism is perhaps to be found in its most remarkable state in the works of William Blake, the English artist-seer-poet. Taking quite seriously the identification of his own thoughts with the soul of the universe,[12] Blake believed it was the mission of the poet and artist to be a religious prophet, endowing the old religious truths with new meaning. A "symbolist" before the French school that was to bear this name later in the nineteenth century, a discoverer of the "archetypes of the unconscious" before Jung, Blake gave new names to the gods and spoke of building a "new Jerusalem" in England. His haunting, childlike songs touch closely on perennial religious and moral experience.

The church called the New Jerusalem was associated not with Blake but with the writings of the eighteenth-century Swedish seer Emanuel Swedenborg (d. 1772), whose visionary writings interpreting the Christian scriptures became popular, especially in England, in the early nineteenth century. There is still a Swedenborgian society in England; there was considerable American interest, too. The German romantic theologian Friedrich Schleiermacher (*Discourses on Religion,* 1799) sought to transpose Christianity from dogma to interior experience—a faith experimentally true, true to the meaning and purpose of life when its doctrines are transformed into concrete human terms. This idea grew familiar in the nineteenth century and merged with the "liberal" Christianity which dismissed Biblical literalism arguing that the "essential" truths of Christianity are deeper and broader. Romantic theology stressed inward emotional experience as a criterion of faith, and interacted with a revival of evangelical, pietistic Christianity. Already begun by the Wesleyans in the eighteenth century, this movement was quite popular from about 1780 to 1825. Various fervent if unorthodox sects arose. Alexander of Russia succumbed to one and tried to write it into the Holy Alliance of 1815; the socialist Saint-Simon preached a "new Christianity" to go with his Enlightenment social science. The Evangelical movement within the Church of England, beginning at the end of the eighteenth century, greatly influenced the whole Victorian era. More intellectual, the celebrated "Oxford Movement" produced John Newman and others in England in the 1830s; in rebellion against materialism and utilitarianism, these Anglicans shared with the romantics a poetic and spiritual emotionalism, a sense of history, a medievalism. Some Oxonians stayed within Anglicanism but revived the "high church" tradition; others followed Newman to Rome.

Popular manifestations of the return to religion included the American "great revival" of the earlier nineteenth century on the fron-

---

[12]Compare Gerard de Nerval, the French romantic poet: "The human imagination has invented nothing that is not true, either in this world or the next."

tier and the evangelical movement in Britain which reached the lowest classes. But many of the major writers shared it. Chateaubriands's *Genius of Christianity* was a leading work by one of the most celebrated of romantics; Wordsworth and Coleridge, if not Shelley and Byron, sought Christian piety. Eighteenth-century scoffing at the gods was no longer in vogue. Often unorthodox and verging on pantheist heresy, the feeling for religion was not the less strong for that.

Politically, romanticism was ambiguous. Coinciding with the French Revolution, it could not help but interact with it. At first the romantics hailed the Revolution with delight, joining figuratively with the young Wordsworth as he danced with the French people. Then they turned against it, listening to Burke's great indictment, which is charged with many feelings close to the heart of romanticism. The Revolution stood for eighteenth-century rationalism and failed for that reason; it was, in fact, reactionary. Most romantics distinguished between the French Revolution as a particular historic event and the broader movement of history it imperfectly embodied. They did not doubt that humanity was on the march, seldom wanted to go back to the eighteenth-century "old regime," but agreed that the French Revolution had degenerated in a cynical and vulgar imperialism, because of its false groundings in Enlightenment materialism. In his famed history of the Revolution, Thomas Carlyle regarded it as having failed because it did not (until Bonaparte) produce any "great man." But the advocate of hero worship condemned the old regime also for having failed to provide inspired leadership, a sure sign of decadence. Romantics might, like Wordsworth, retain a rather naive Godwinian faith in human perfectibility, believing however that this utopia would come when we realize our *inner* powers of consciousness, something not to be attained by changes in forms of government.

Coleridge's political odyssey may be taken as typical: Interested in politics and at first enthusiastic for the Revolution, he wrote an ode on the storming of the Bastille; his *Ode to France,* 1798, records his disillusion and despair. "In Mr. Burke's writings the germs of almost all political truths may be found," he thought, but he also thought Burke had gone too far in his hatred of the Revolution. There must be a moral basis of policy; Kant's categorical imperative, that persons are not to be treated as things, is the great foundation. Coleridge was a staunch foe of economic individualism and of the pseudoscience of political economy, which he regarded as "solemn humbug." The mystic bonds that tie people together shape the almost sacred entity of Society, which is a reflection of the divine, as much so as physical nature. This *organic* view of society, opposed to the eighteenth century's alleged atomistic individualism, was a marked romantic trait. Coleridge's political insights are deep, but he failed to communicate any very coherent platform; he had too much awareness of the complexity of things, and felt the great need was not for a program but for human understanding.

The others in the galaxy of great English Romantic poets illustrate the political ambiguity of romanticism. If Wordsworth and Coleridge ended as Tories, Byron, by far the most popular poet of his day, was an aristocratic revolutionary, who defended the Luddites, died fighting for Greek independence, and wrote much about rebels; though, in view of Byron's life, we cannot but feel that he more nearly spoke his mind when he asked for "wine and women, mirth and laughter." Shelley, that "beautiful and ineffectual angel," was also full of revolt at times:

> Men of England, wherefore plough
> For the lords who lay ye low?

but more full of poetry and the love of beautiful women. The greatest of these poets, John Keats, simply had no discernible politics; nightingales interested him far more. "Romanticism," the authors of a book about it assert, "fostered sympathy for the oppressed . . . and looked forward to a new social system, a Utopia" (W. V. Moody and R. M. Lovett). So it did, doubtless. But another writer (C. Grana) tells us, with equal accuracy, that "romanticism included a revival of political traditionalism, neo-feudal at times, decrying social fragmentation and exalting a sense of unspoiled community, born of spontaneous loyalty to ritualized customs." And we should have to take account of others who, like Keats or Alfred de Musset, were innocent of political convictions altogether.

But the great events of revolution and war wove themselves through the texture of feelings of all the writers. Stendhal, in his essay on "Racine and Shakespeare," remarked that those who had lived through such times, who had experienced the Terror and marched with bloody feet through Russian snows with Napoleon, could no longer be moved by the chaste tragedies of classicism. The blood stirred by these mighty happenings and warmed by revolutionary slogans, demanded stronger meat and drink. The political thought of romanticism was diverse, but whatever it was it demanded and created excitement. The young Hugo, worshipping Chateaubriand and abhorring the Revolution, was royalist, conservative, and even reactionary, but it was out of strong emotions and also a love of liberty. He simply thought that a false liberty and democracy had led to despotism, the enslavement of the people in the name of slogans about equality. Later he became a liberal, radical, or revolutionary (reversing the conventional picture of men growing more conservative with age). The fact is that Hugo was always passionate, always idealistic, always libertarian; the modes in which he expressed this spirit changed with the times, that was all.

Nevertheless the confusion in romanticism is amply evident in its political thought. We have only to observe that an organic view of society is widely regarded as most typical of it, but how are we to adjust this vision of collectivism with the spirit of revolt and individual self-expression, even alienation, which was also a romantic attitude? Between Coleridge opposing the English reform bill of 1832 and Hugo on the barricades, there seems a decided gulf. No doubt German philosophy could provide a shaky bridge between the ego and the cosmos, but there seems little to be gained by trying to cover positions so various with a single term.

THE MEANING OF ROMANTICISM

A century of scholarship and criticism has sought in vain for a single definition of romanticism. From this, some have drawn the conclusion that the term is useless, that no such thing existed, rather a number of different things that somehow got lumped together owing to sloppy thinking. In any case, was romanticism the same in Germany, France, Great Britain, Spain? Plainly, it took on regional variations. Should not one study the concrete—this Spanish poet, that German philosopher, Wordsworth, Keats, Coleridge—and forget about the elusive general? This has almost been the direction of literature studies in recent decades. Still, the term *romanticism* survives despite all efforts to kill it. It survives because it *is* a useful term to cover a number of striking if not identical cultural phenomena of the period from 1780 to 1830. The philosophy, literature, and general *Zeitgeist* of this period had enough in common over large areas to justify the use of some general word to describe it. Possibly we should use several terms; but we can, if we like, choose to subdivide the one term, qualify it, mark the exceptions—but retain it.

All kinds of definitions, divisions, and distinctions have been offered. Of these, it seems useful to distinguish the *negative* romanticism, which was a reaction against the Enlightenment, against neoclassicism, materialism, hedonism, and the like, from the positive romanticism, which was largely a gift of German philosophy—the philosophy of subjective and intuitive truth, spiritual nature, and the poet's role in bringing the two realms together in conscious creative experience. It may be useful, too, to sort out things which got interlocked with romanticism but were not essentially of it, such as the political explosions of the times, nationalism, democracy, the reaction against the French Revolution. It is also helpful to sort out things which, while characteristic of numerous romantics, were not at all new, such as Byron's sexual morals. And the careful student will take note of national differences. Thus the English romantics, despite Byron and Keats, were a more chaste and prudent lot than the Germans, reflecting the stability of English life and its strong bourgeois morality. French romanticism wore the badge of anti-Revolution with special prominence. Romanticism was weakest in Spain and Italy, especially in the latter, perhaps because of the pervasive influence of classicism on the Italian landscape. (The Gothic had been weakest there too.)

When all is said, the romantic revolution is linked to Kant and the French Revolution as a vital aspect of what was perhaps the most exciting and creative period of modern times. If one wishes to hazard a definition of the basic factor in this intellectual revolution, it would be *subjectivism* or the participation of mind in shaping reality. It has been said that no one previously had conceived the knowing process except in terms of the object known; now the subject came into the picture. The mind partly creates the external reality it grasps. Coleridge objected that "Newton was a mere materialist. Mind, in his system, is always passive—a lazy looker-on in an external world. . . . *Any system built on the passiveness of mind must be false.*" This was the central insight of the romantics: The mirror and the lamp, as an important critical study has put it—the mind creates truth rather than simply reflecting it. And in this sense romanticism, though many aspects of it went out of fashion after a time, has left its stamp on the contemporary Western world.

Subjectivism worked itself out in the unique romantic conception of the free individual, freed from the rules, from moral conventions, from all external restraints. In the concept of genius, romanticists found their central literary conception. Bound by no rules, they made their own. By no means is everyone a genius, but conceivably all *might* be. At any rate they do arise—a Homer, a Shakespeare, a Goethe—and they make the pattern for others to follow. In the last analysis we follow and should worship the actions of genius. Carlyle, in his famous *Sartor Resartus,* repeated the message of Goethe as an antidote to skepticism and lethargy; arise, WORK, do what thou canst do. Hero worship, and the gospel of work, affected people in all walks of life in the nineteenth century; they were romantics without knowing it. (The American Westward Movement has been seen as essentially romantic.)

It may be suggested then that romanticism was a literary and intellectual counterpart of the new principle of individualism in society—and this despite the fact that romantics often inveighed against individualism. The old regime had been corporative and organic, a society of estates and classes; after the French Revolution, one had a society of equal individuals. The literature of the eighteenth century, as we earlier noted, was a social literature which sought essentially not to express the personal soul but to communicate the common ideas. Romanticism was the former. Men had begun their modern fate of loneliness in the crowd, or their modern privilege of individual self-development, as one may choose to put it. The stable order of countryside would soon be challenged and overcome by the city's anonymity. A collection of individuals replaced "society," as Jeremy Bentham and the Utilitarians divined. One stood or fell by one's own unaided efforts. Romanticism was a literary retreat to the individual ego which, seen or not as part of a larger world soul, remained as the one solid basis of life.

Arthur O. Lovejoy, that great student of ideas, found the fundamental romantic trait to be diversity, as over against Enlightenment standardization and simplification—the search for unique particulars, rather than universals and generals. So stated, the change embraces a great deal of this age of revolution, counterrevolution, and romanticism. Romanticism's stress on diversity relates to some general features of nineteenth-century civilization. That civilization was in many ways more diverse and less unified than the older one. Aristocratic and cosmopolitan, the eighteenth century had *a* style, even though one might note exceptions to it. The nineteenth was to be eclectic in its architecture, pillaging the past for borrowed styles; it was to offer a "generous confusion" of modes in the arts and in ideas; it divided into separate national cultures. It was a much more pluralistic civilization. Man was parceled out in men, as the poet Rossetti put it—which he, looking backward nostalgically, took to be a sign of the decadence of Europe. Unconsciously perhaps, romanticism reflected the atomization of European society. Despite its nostalgia for unspoiled nature and simple countryfolk, romanticism was more at home in the city than the country—in Dickens's London or Balzac's Paris, where amid many horrors one found teeming, exuberant life.

Despite its occasional lapses into modish *Weltschmerz* or Byronic *Menschenhass,* romanticism on the whole shared the general optimism of the earlier nineteenth century. Romantic writers exhibited a lyric exuberance, a love for life. Nothing today, the great critic Lionel Trilling once remarked, can compare with the exhilarating effect of Keats's letters—destined, as he was, to die a young and tragic death from the great nineteenth-century killer, tuberculosis. Their minds soared, their spirits aspired to ecstatic heights, they escaped earthly bondage. A new inspiration visited poetry and swept into the other arts. "In 1813 music had newly become the most astonishing, the most fascinating, the most miraculous art in the world," Shaw wrote. The marvelous energy of Beethoven would carry into the great romantic composers, Chopin, Schumann, Berlioz, Brahms. Whatever its possible confusions of thought, the romantic generation of European expression saw an outburst of creative energy and inspiration not matched since the Renaissance and seldom equaled since; it fertilized the rest of the century and continues to this day, for all subsequent European literature and music is indebted to it. The visual arts, despite a Blake and Delacroix, seemed less affected, perhaps because painting and sculpture are essentially classical in spirit, depicting repose and equilibrium rather than—as in a Beethoven sonata or symphony—the ongoing rush of powerful feeling.

2

The Birth of Ideologies: 1815–1848

From the thunder of Napoleon battles, to the jabbering of Open-vestry in St. Mary Axe, all things announce democracy. Democracy is everywhere the inexorable demand of these ages, swift fulfilling itself.

THOMAS CARLYLE

I alone shall have confounded twenty generations of political imbecility and it is to me alone that present and future generations will owe the beginning of their boundless happiness.

CHARLES FOURIER

We preached everywhere and at all times. Exactly what it was we preached it is hard to say. . . .

ALEXANDER HERZEN

THE EUROPEAN SITUATION 1815–1848

The profusion of political and social "isms" in Europe after 1815 was a consequence of the situation people faced in that year. Especially acute in France, the crisis affected all Europe, for none of it had been untouched by the Revolution and Napoleon, and much of it had been as profoundly altered as France itself. Bonaparte had destroyed the old order in Italy and Germany and had brought sweeping innovations wherever his legions marched. Now the Revolution and its great leader were vanquished. But was it possible to go back to the old regime of 1789

as if nothing had happened? Even the most reactionary did not really
believe that. If one could not believe in either the old order or the new,
what lay ahead? All over Europe the need was felt to take soundings and
mark out some course. Europe seemed to be rushing into a yawning
void. Clearly the old Europe was dead—ten centuries of civilization
washed out. The new Europe had failed morally and now physically
from the Reign of Terror to the coup d'état of Bonaparte and so to his
military defeat after a terrible war. But Europe was going on, filled with
all kinds of half-understood dynamisms such as democracy and industrialization. Did they portend destruction or creation, rebirth or decadence?

In France the impulse to order showed itself strongly. Laissez-faire
liberty did not appeal to the rationalist French mind. Both conservatives
and socialists shared a desire to define and shape the reconstruction of a
positive social order. But this must be done in a new way, and there was
widespread realization that science and fact, not metaphysics and
dogma, had to form the foundation. In Great Britain liberal individualism was much more prominent. In both countries political and
social ideologies constituted the leading intellectual interest. Even in
Germany is that true; for while the great Hegel reigned as the last of the
classical lineage of German philosophy and produced a system some
found too metaphysical, his chief interest was in human history and its
political order; his disciples included critical historians such as David
Strauss and social ideologists such as Karl Marx.

The greatest need in Europe after 1815 was for political and social
reorganization following the destruction of the old order by the French
Revolution. The peace settlement at Vienna in 1815 tried to do this in
the arena of practical politics; it partly succeeded and partly failed.
Popular movements, such as nationalism in Germany and Italy or
working-class radicalism in Britain and France, reflected the deep dis-
turbances of a society undergoing rapid economic and social change
along with political uncertainty.

Socially, one marked the decline of the old aristocracy and the rise
of a new class, an upper bourgeoisie of commerce, finance, and industry.
The period of a few years from 1815 to 1830 witnessed a generally
conservative spirit, the product of the reactionary victors of the long war
against Bonapartism; in France it was the time of the attempted Bourbon restoration, in England the Tories continued their power, and in
Germany Prince Metternich's Austrian conservatism controlled affairs.
But the underlying social realities defeated the attempt to preserve aristocratic domination. The revolution of 1830 sweeps aside the restored
monarchy in France; the great Reform Bill of 1832 signals the demise of
old-fashioned Toryism in Britain.

The middle classes had begun their long reign. There was at this time considerable class consciousness among speakers for this group. Power must be transferred from the landed oligarchy to the "intelligent middle and industrious classes," said Richard Cobden, an oracle of British liberalism. These classes distinguished themselves from the "mob" below as carefully as from the aristocracy, or what was left of it, above—from both of which they differed in possessing the traits of industriousness, sobriety, and morality, they thought. (The upper classes and the lower, someone remarked, were united by the bond of a common immorality in sexual matters—the former having advanced beyond morality, the latter having not yet encountered it.) The new bourgeoisie were serious, frugal, upright, hardworking and, according to some critics, hardhearted. Certainly they were builders of wealth in this vigorous morning of the Industrial Revolution, very proud of their achievements, inclined to be scornful of those who contributed less, as they believed. Distinctions must be noted within the "bourgeoisie"; the term is too broad to be meaningful. In France, at least, the "grande bourgeoisie," who dominated the Orleanist Monarchy from 1830 to 1848, was a haughty coterie of rich bankers and industrialists who were "political liberals but social conservatives," having little regard for their social inferiors and absolutely no taste for democracy. In France, the 1830 revolution brought a "liberalization" of the suffrage to the degree that perhaps one in forty adult French males voted as compared to one in seventy-five before. In Great Britain, after the great Reform Bill of 1832, one in five had the vote. In the Continental revolutions of 1848 a lower bourgeoisie joined with workers in demanding universal suffrage. Britain escaped that revolution because to a much greater extent its lower as well as upper bourgeoisie were enfranchised.

The word *bourgeois* became an epithet in two circles: the socialists and the literary. It was alleged that the middle classes were indifferent to the arts as well as to the sufferings of the poor. The stereotype of the bourgeois (as depicted in a Daumier caricature, for example) had some basis in reality. It is true, for example, that the Benthamite *Westminster Review* regarded literature as inappropriate to civilization, while the liberal *Economist* along with Herbert Spencer coolly considered it better to starve the poor than to administer public charity. But one must remember the strength of this "industrious and intelligent" bourgeoisie. By and large they *were* in possession of a large share of those not altogether contemptible characteristics, industry and intelligence. They were creating wealth as it had never been created before. If their natural habitat was the bourse or the factory rather than university or parliament, they did produce powerful speakers in this age: not merely Samuel Smiles with his propaganda of self-help, but such as Cobden, Bright, Thiers, Guizot.

It is also necessary to keep in mind the point once made by Balzac, the astute French novelist and observer of the "human comedy": If the bourgeoisie destroyed the nobility, a combat would immediately ensue between the bourgeoisie and the people beneath them. The weapons with which the bourgeoisie had brought down the aristocracy—charges of special privilege and unearned income, demands for more democracy and equality—could obviously be turned on them by the others. Coleridge, opposing the extension of the suffrage in 1832, warned the middle class that they would be unable to stop by giving the vote just to themselves but would eventually have to give it to all. Carlyle warned them that by refusing to look after their workers, they would drive them to social revolution; the feudal landlords had at least given protection to their serfs, whereas the new factory owners gave them no human sympathy, only an inadequate wage. So the "social question" arose early and socialism became a factor, though unable to overturn the rule of the bourgeoisie. Few serious thinkers were ever quite happy with the new organization of society, or lack of it, under middle-class industrialism.

RESULTS OF THE FRENCH REVOLUTION

The most basic change wrought by the French Revolution (in principle, for most of Europe) was that which Henry Maine capsulized in the phrase "from status to contract." The Old Regime had been hierarchical, organic, inequalitarian, and corporative. Treating people neither as individuals nor as equals, it had yet contained a place for all within the society. Within fifty years of the French Revolution, Thomas Carlyle could develop a considerable nostalgia for it on the grounds that the serf at least had had a protector, humble though that role was. The Revolution proclaimed equality and freedom. People were free to make their own way; they were also free to starve. The medieval peasants had held land and duties by custom (status); the nineteenth-century workers had lost this security; they could rise, but if they fell there was, in principle, no one to rescue them.

From this enormous change issues a series of nineteenth-century ideological statements. The socialists were indignant that human labor had been turned into a commodity and claimed that "bourgeois freedom" was only a disguise for the greater exploitation of labor. More objectively, historians pointed out that the opposition of classes had been increased, not diminished, by the abolition of the old feudal ranks of society; now all were theoretically equal but marked off from one another by just the possession of wealth, a thing more likely to breed jealousy and bitterness. The gap between rich and poor became greater, not less, and the poor had less protection. In *Past and Present*, Carlyle asked his contemporaries to consider "Gurth, born thrall of Cedric the Saxon," who, though not exactly "an exemplar of human felicity . . . to me seems happy, in comparison with many a Lancashire and Buckinghamshire man, of these days, not born thrall of anybody!" "The Revolution ended one inequality and gave birth to another," as a later French writer summed it up. The new inequality was both more obvious and less tolerable. Plutocracy had replaced aristocracy. Legal, juridical equality meant a rat race in which the weaker or unluckier were ground into the dirt by the more energetic and less scrupulous.

The results of the French Revolution led by and large in the three main directions of nineteenth-century social thought: liberal, socialist, and conservative. Those who were content in the main with the abolition of the old regime and the installation (more or less by default) of legal equality and free competition were liberals; those who pined for a return of the ancient order of things, or what they imagined that order to have been, were conservatives; the socialists, for their part, pronounced the work of the Revolution incomplete—it had established a formal but not a real equality, a political but not an economic one. A new ruling class of the moneyed had replaced the old one and was even worse:

> They have given us into the hands of the new unhappy lords
> Lords without anger or honour, who dare not carry their swords,

as G. K. Chesterton subsequently wrote ("The Secret People"). The germ of socialism had appeared very soon after the Revolution in Babeuf's unsuccessful "conspiracy of the Equals" of 1795. All during the nineteenth century, victory in this three-horse race went to the bourgeois liberals, for while socialism remained a utopian dream of the future, those who dreamed of restoring the past were equally ineffective.

If the new "bourgeois" leaders could sometimes express feelings of disdain for the lower classes, they did not entirely neglect their welfare. Rejecting most plans of state assistance in accordance with their approval of the "night watchman" state that only "prevented crime and preserved contracts," bourgeois liberals could not deny that their maxim of "a fair field and no favors" required some social services. Education was perhaps the leading case of this sort. "The schoolmaster was abroad" in these years, in Europe as well as in the United States, where the name of Horace Mann became a household word. Guizot, who scorned the multitude, nevertheless put through the educational reform of 1833, called the charter of French primary education. It was far from installing free and universal elementary education, but by requiring every commune to maintain a public primary school, it began the movement that led in this direction. Probably the nineteenth-century bourgeoisie have been overly blamed for their alleged callousness toward the poor and the workers. Still, their creed did not allow for much social welfare legislation by modern standards. The political economists wrote their basic textbooks.

The great nineteenth-century economists were engaged in developing a highly specialized, formidably exacting branch of knowledge, with rare success; they were arbiters of public policy and beacons of light to the powerful industrial bourgeoisie.

Writing in 1831 on "The Spirit of the Age," young John Stuart Mill remarked that "a change has taken place in the human mind.... The conviction is already not far from being universal that the times are pregnant with change, and that the nineteenth century will be known to posterity as the era of one of the greatest revolutions of which history has preserved the remembrance, in the human mind, and in the whole con-stitution of human society." In 1830, France had a revolution, sweeping aside the restored Bourbons and establishing a constitutional monarchy; in 1832, Great Britain, too, entered into the liberal era with the passing of the great Reform Bill after a severe political struggle. But with the progress of the so-called industrial revolution, the rise of what Carlyle named the "social question," and a steady trend towards popular democ-racy, there was to be no stability on the basis of the settlements of 1830 to 1832, which provided for neither a democratic suffrage nor a welfare state. They were in fact political and social orders dominated by the upper classes and offered little to either the workers or the lower middle class, who were to join in making the revolutions of 1848, proving, however, incompatible allies. The 1830s witnessed a rise of interest in socialism and related ideas, brought violent insurrection to some districts (for example Lyons in 1831), and then gave way to the "hungry forties," at the end of which major revolutions swept Europe from one end to the other.

An unprecedented ferment of social and political thought pre-pared the way for the revolutions of the year 1848, a secondary tremor hardly less earth-shaking than the first quake of 1789. Various sorts of socialism, democracy, social democracy, and liberalism mingled in another apocalyptic moment, when many expected the deferred social millennium. Again came apparent failure and disillusion. But in fact 1848 marked the permanent arrival, if not the absolute victory, of both democracy and socialism. The ideas that grew up in the period from 1815 to 1848 are the political and social ideas or ideologies with which the Western world has been living ever since. They are, then, of the utmost importance.

CONSERVATISM

The rise of a conservative ideology began with Edmund Burke, and all subsequent members of this school were basically indebted to his *Reflections on the Revolution* (see Chapter 1). Coleridge, as we have noted, built on Burke's foundations in England, though his political thought was somewhat scattered. Writing under the impact of his own later (1798) disillusionment with the French cause, he did not go as far as Burke in rejecting all rationalism in politics; he joined him in the respect for tradition, the organic sense of society, and the feeling for a moral order in history. His influence flowed down through the nineteenth century as a strong philosophic source of British enlightened Toryism; John Stuart Mill declared that Coleridge and Jeremy Bentham, the utilitarian, were the two opposing seminal figures in nineteenth-century British thought. The contrast must be noted for American students: British and European conservatism has been an enemy of laissez-faire. Coleridge believed in government regulation of manufacturers, government aid to education, the duty of the state to enhance the moral and intellectual capabilities of its citizens in all sorts of positive ways. Conservatism abhorred and was set over against the individualism of the "liberals," who preached free competition and no state intervention in the economic order. Related to the rural squirearchy, it was certainly not equalitarian or leveling (Coleridge opposed the Reform Bill of 1832) but was deeply humanistic and more likely than liberalism to support governmental welfare measures for the poor. The leading hero of factory reform and other humanitarian measures in early industrial England was the Tory, Lord Shaftesbury. The Coleridge tradition passed to such writers as John Ruskin, who described himself as "a violent Tory of the old school" and violently denounced the materialistic and unprincipled society of industrial England. It also passed to Benjamin Disraeli, with his conception of a democratized Conservative party leading the way to social reform on behalf of the workers.

It was in France, though, that the conservative ideology developed most prominently. There were a few liberals in post-Napoleonic France (1815 to 1830), for example Benjamin Constant and Mme. de Staël, those old foes of Bonaparte, who stressed constitutionalism, civil liberties, a limited monarchy, parliamentarianism. In this camp, too, one might put Chateaubriand, whose career now turned to statesmanship as he struggled to make the system of parliamentary monarchy work. But even these French "liberals" do not seem to have had much of the spirit of Benthamite individualism, then becoming dominant in Britain. Nor were they the dominant voices, distinguished though the thought of Constant was. France in the 1820s produced two brilliant streams of thought from opposite directions: Right and Left. These were the conservatives and the socialists. The conservative camp included Joseph de Maistre and the Vicomte de Bonald as its chief ornaments.

Born in 1753 of aristocratic Savoyard family, the first of these was early a follower of Rousseau. In the 1780s he became interested in the occult Christianity pursued in the circle of the Marquess de Saint-Martin, "the unknown philosopher," as he signed himself, but dropped the attachment when the Church pronounced against it. A provincial senator, happily married, Maistre would never have made himself a famous figure in the history of thought had it not been for the French Revolution. Initially he was known as a liberal or even a Jacobin. But he fell afoul of the Revolution in 1793 and went into exile. At Lausanne in Switzerland he frequented the society of M. Necker and his celebrated daughter, Mme. de Staël, and met Gibbon, the historian. At that time he began to put together his thoughts on the origins of the Revolution, the reasons for its failure, and the means of reconstructing France. These were themes to which the thoughts of many turned in these dramatic years.

Bonald was in exile in Heidelberg at the same time, and Maistre wrote to him in 1796 that "your spirit and mine are in perfect accord." They had to wait out the Napoleonic years; Bonaparte, though he read and admired a book of Maistre's in 1797, could not secure the loyalty of the man who had made himself the spokesman of French royalism. Maistre worked as a diplomatist for the King of Sardinia, going to St. Petersburg as ambassador in 1803. The rugged integrity of this Savoyard (a people noted for this trait), who separated himself from his family whom he deeply loved, whose faith in France did not waver through the darkest days, added to the eloquence of his prose and the charm of his personality. He was a writer of genius and a scholar of great learning, as even his foes conceded. In St. Petersburg he wrote his chief works: *On the Pope, On the Gallican Church, Evenings in St. Petersburg.* After the fall of Napoleon and the restoration of Louis XVIII, Maistre returned to France to receive considerable acclaim, and his books, now published in France, earned him the reputation of chief theoretician of the Bourbon restoration; he died in 1821, just as he was gaining this long-deferred but well-earned recognition. Bonald, whose ideas were quite similar (he lacked Maistre's grace of style but was rather more systematic), lived on to reign as the high priest of the monarchists, joined, among others, by the youthful and fiery La Mennais, who would later take up a different crusade. But of these, Maistre's writings are the best known.

Negatively, Maistre's thought was marked by a cold fury against the whole *philosophe* school. He wished to "absolutely kill the spirit of the eighteenth century." In this sense these "ultraists," as they were known, were reactionaries. The lucid intellect of Maistre concluded that the *philosophes* had introduced the poison that had induced the sickness of the Revolution; the poison must be purged from France's body before it could be restored to health. Maistre would not even allow Voltaire and company the virtue of common honesty. They were great criminals; to like Voltaire is the sign of a corrupt soul; the very visage of the great satirist bespoke his service of the Devil. Locke, Hume, Voltaire, Rousseau were all evil or at the very least horribly misguided men. Here Maistre was simply a polemicist, a vigorous and eloquent one, turning Voltaire's weapons against himself and assailing the mockers as they had once assailed the church.

However, once the poison had been cast out, these "reactionaries" saw the additional task of reconstructing society and tried to show how it might be done. Here they proved immensely stimulating and influenced many who did not at all share their ideological preconceptions; they even, and most notably, influenced the socialists, Saint-Simon being the best example. They combined keen intelligence with penetrating insights into the weaknesses of the liberal or democratic order, while also contributing some fruitful ideas about methodology in the social sciences. They were aware that one could not go back to 1789, much though they may have regretted the Revolution, which Maistre could only explain as having been sent by God to punish France for its sins. Maistre was not the "prophet of the past," as a wit dubbed him. It was necessary to establish a new political philosophy; this was the age of ideology, with mere habit no longer sufficing; "the intellectual principle has taken priority over the moral principle in the direction of society," as Maistre put it. Living in a France which had seen the failure of the Republic and then (defeated in frightful war) the collapse of the dictatorship that succeeded it, and which now found itself trying the uncertain experiment of a restored Bourbon monarchy, Maistre and Bonald hoped to explain clearly why republics always failed and only monarchies could provide political security. The task stimulated them to a wide-ranging investigation of political and sociological phenomena.

Their argument made extensive use of the idea that the natural order of society is historical and traditional, while individualism and democracy are diseases resulting in social anarchy. Take away the discipline imposed by church, monarchy, nobility, each in its proper place in the orbit that is natural to France (nations have character; each has a form of government suitable to it; you must not tamper with this truth by an arid rationalistic universalism), take this away, and the result will be disorder, corruption, decay. Written constitutions are crude and artificial; the true constitution of a people is written in the hearts of its people and expressed in its ancestral customs. The school of Maistre, Savigny, and Haller[1] was historical; they held that wisdom in politics comes from experience only, that is, from a discriminating study of the past and from the understanding of national character as revealed in history. Abstract theory had caused much damage, they believed; igno-

---

[1]Savigny was spokesman for the historical school of jurisprudence in Germany, Burkean in its stress on the organic evolution of the law rooted in tradition. Haller, a German Swiss, held similar views. The latter's nostalgia for the Old Regime in its corporate, organic, and inequalitarian aspects was especially strong.

rance of and contempt for history was the prime source of political error.

Their arguments in favor of absolute monarchy may now make tedious reading, but the conservative school had a considerable influence on nineteenth-century thought. Bonald has been called the founder of sociology; he certainly influenced Comte, who is more frequently granted that title. Alexis de Tocqueville's famous *Democracy in America,* which might be called the pioneer work of sociological analysis, was much influenced by these writers. (See La Mennais's comments on democracy in his 1825 book, *De la religion considerée dans ses rapports avec l'ordre politique et civil,* volume I. It looks as if Tocqueville were testing the hypotheses of La Mennais: that democracy leads to despotism, enshrines mediocrity, causes people to be restless, rootless, and godless, and makes money the only idol.) Whereas their recommendations for the good society came to little, their critical analysis of the social changes overtaking France, their investigations of such matters as what effect the loss of religious faith or of social hierarchy will have on politics and society, were truly stimulating. Their appeal from the abstract theories of the rationalists to positive historical facts and careful sociological investigation bore fruit in many students after them, who admired their methods, while not necessarily sharing their political prejudices.

A deep awareness of the tragic aspects of the human situation marks Maistre's thought. In politics he was in a sense not illiberal; he wished to see the monarch checked by tradition and by local institutions in a "pluralistic" society, as in the Old Regime. His recent editor, Jack Lively, has pointed out how close he was after all to Rousseau, whom he thought he hated. Like Bossuet, Maistre distinguished an "absolute" monarchy from an unlimited or despotic one. In a notable argument set forth in *Du Pape,* he argued that the papacy might mediate between the sovereignty of the state and the liberty of the individual. The argument impressed few, least of all the pope, but it indicates Maistre's desire to mitigate the authority of the state (which he felt necessary) in some way, lest it become tyranny. He did not think democracy the answer, not at least for France (he conceded that England had it in its national character to live as a republic). It would only lead to a new Bonapartism. How accurate that prophecy was the events of 1848 to 1851 would reveal. Too much the polemicist and marred by corroding hatreds, Maistre remains a major figure because of his flashes of rare insight.

A recent writer (Benjamin N. Nelson) has observed that "a society founded on sheer egoism . . . will undergo atomization, anomic loss of a sense of belonging." It then leads to totalitarianism by reaction, modern totalitarianism being an effort to substitute for "subtle and satisfying forms of organic solidarity" by "imposing the yoke of mechanism." In other words, a natural community being absent, there is flight from the intolerable rootlessness and anonymity of modern urban life towards some kind of statism. The case for the conservatives of nineteenth-century France must rest on some such point as this, and it would seem to be one of enduring pertinence.

British Utilitarianism and Political Economy postulated free self-reliant individuals, the "mainspring of social progress" because their energies were released by the knowledge that what they gained would be their own, capable of enriching themselves and thereby also enriching the nation, capable also of enlightening and educating themselves. But an accompaniment of this far from unworthy idea was the loss of a social sense. The market was an impersonal force, though it regulated the relationships of society—impersonal and selfish. Society became only a collection of individuals, and thus something necessary to humanity was lost, for though we like to assert our individuality, we cannot do without membership in a community. The conservatives, whatever their sins in other respects, surely performed a valuable service to modern Europe in defending the community against atomization.

Moreover the conservatives typically disliked commercialism as well as mass democracy, and they had a deep sense of human dignity. Their values tended to be rooted in the stable society of the countryside where everybody knows everybody else and the impersonality of the city is abhorrent. In both England and France there were "Tory radicals" throughout the century who sided with the working class against the capitalists on matters of social reform. They produced a strong vein of social criticism. Coleridge, Carlyle, Disraeli, and perhaps Ruskin might be put into this category in England—a distinguished heritage of social thought, by no means reactionary, holding up the ideal of a society that was aristocratic, but not plutocratic, socially responsible rather than ir-responsible, opposing the social neglect of laissez-faire with a pater-nalism of the upper class.

Saint-Simon, the socialist, acknowledged his debt to Bonald, who taught him that society is "an organic machine whose every part contrib-utes to the movement of the whole," not a mere collection of separate and unconnected individuals. The conservatives and the socialists had something in common, and that, an important idea: the social principle. But the conservatives saw society as the will of God, favored obedience to political authority, believed religion to be a necessity, abhorred revolu-tion, and could scarcely accept either equality or democracy. Agreeing in the conviction that society must be ordered and organized, wherein they both differed from the nineteenth-century liberals, conservatives and socialists disagreed about the nature of that organization and its source. For the socialists held to an Enlightenment faith that human reason might contrive an ideal organization and establish it all at once. Conser-vatives, with a wisdom they thought they had learned from the melancholy experiment of the Revolution, held this to be impossible and disastrous. No opinion lay closer to the heart of conservative doctrine than a mistrust of what Burke called "the fallible and feeble contrivances of our reason." It mistrusted political theories and believed that we must fall back on existing rooted institutions which represent a kind of collective wisdom of the ages and which have at least worked. The liberals and radicals believed people could do better; the conservatives feared they might well do worse. They would rely on the allegedly natural social order, which seemed to mean just the *status quo*. Their defect was that the age was seething with change, and there was no stable order of things.

LIBERALISM

Though conservatives tried to put down an anchor against the currents of change, no task was less promising in this first half of the nineteenth century. It was, as a recent historian has observed, the most revolutionary half-century in history up to that time. Everyone felt whirled away by the pace of change; "We have been living the life of 300 years in 30," Matthew Arnold's father, the famous schoolmaster, remarked. "Can we never drop anchor for a single day, On the ocean of the ages?" Lamartine poetically wondered. By and large, it was a hopeful half-century, with all its perplexities and turbulence—much more hopeful than the latter half. There is an exuberance about its writing that reflects this basic optimism; one sees it in the titanic creative energies of a Dickens or a Balzac, as well as in the explosion of hopeful solutions for all the problems of humanity. "The period was full of evil things, but it was full of hope," Chesterton wrote in his book about Charles Dickens. Its typical giants, like Victor Hugo, dreamed vast dreams of progress and threw themselves furiously into their tasks. So it was not, on the whole, a good time for conservatives, and after a few years of success following the fall of Napoleon, they gave way to more hopeful people who presided over an era culminating in the great liberal-democratic-socialist revolutions of 1848.

Liberalism was a term rather like romanticism, broad and vague, and still is. By general agreement it was strongest in Great Britain, which had an ancestral sort of liberalism (though the word was not used in any systematic way until the 1830s) embracing civil liberty and parliamentary government. The English had not known absolute monarchy and had been living under the mildest of European governments since 1688. Fondly recalling such landmarks as the Magna Carta and the Bill of Rights, the English considered themselves freer than any other people and typically looked with amused contempt on the political broils of the French and other Continental lesser breeds. The storms of the French

Revolution caused some curtailments of this liberty between 1795 and 1820, producing toward the latter date, at the time of "Peterloo"[2] and the repressive Six Acts, what has been called the ugliest estrangement between English government and people since 1688. But this did not last, and under Whig auspices a series of parliamentary measures between 1825 and 1840 could be called "liberal" in that they extended the range of freedoms: commercial (removal of tariffs, monopolies, restrictions on trade), personal (freedom of press, religion), and political (more representative elections to parliament, extension of the suffrage in 1832).

There were other aspects to this "liberalism," for example opposition to factory legislation and to trade unions, which may seem illiberal by modern standards but were in accordance with maximum freedom of individual entrepreneurs from government regulation. Free speech was restored: In 1819 the Habeas Corpus Act had been suspended, journals and pamphlets taxed, publishers imprisoned for criticizing the king— but by 1832 these restrictions had been substantially removed. (On the Continent, Metternich more successfully repressed freedom of the press—a "modern scourge," the great conservative said, inconsistent with organized society—and seven German professors at Goettingen became martyrs to the censorship of ideas that was a part of the "Metternich system.") In 1829 the Catholic Emancipation Act and repeal of the Test Acts removed political disabilities from non-Anglican Christians, though the Established Church remained and Jews were not similarly relieved for thirty more years.

It cannot be said that the Whigs who supported these last actions were moved by flaming slogans about human rights; they were practical measures. The Reform Bill of 1832, bitterly opposed as it was, left four out of five Englishmen without the vote. At the same time, in the name of "liberal" principles, the most "liberal" of the English supported the harsh Poor Law of 1834 and fought the Ten Hour Bill. Even the most radical of them, like Francis Place, felt that granting any great amount of welfare relief to the laboring poor would "encourage idleness and extinguish enterprise." A courageous band fought to abolish slavery within the British Empire, but a considerable number of these were not "liberals" but Churchmen and Tories. All in all, early nineteenth-century liberalism was a somewhat curious thing as we view it today, and it requires some explanation.

It was associated with two notable intellectual systems of the period: the utilitarians and the political economists. Utilitarianism was

[2]A massacre at St. Peter's Fields in Manchester on August 16, 1819 was ironically called Peterloo, recalling the famous British victory over Napoleon at Waterloo. The Manchester Yeomanry, a police force, attacked or got into a battle with a crowd being addressed by Radical orators.

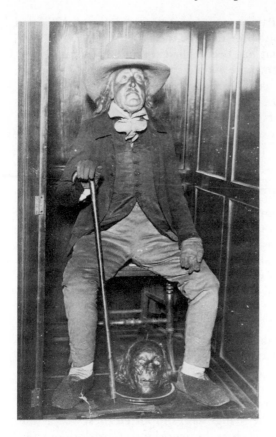

Jeremy Bentham's body, as he requested, still sits in the board room of University College, London. The real head is the one on the floor. (London, BBC Hulton Picture Library.)

the offspring of that strange genius, Jeremy Bentham. Bentham had been writing as early as the 1770s and was an old man in 1810 when his school began to become prominent; he belonged to the later Enlightenment and never departed from it in essential spirit. Decidedly no romantic, Bentham was a thoroughgoing rationalist, a scoffer at religion, a man without poetic instincts and almost, it seems, without emotions. John Stuart Mill, son of Bentham's leading disciple, described in his famous autobiography the inhuman regimen under which he was raised, and which finally caused him to have something like a breakdown. His relief came only when he found consolation in poetry and philosophy. After this dramatic and symbolic experience, Mill wrote a series of essays in which he presented Bentham and Coleridge as the two seminal influences of the century. The romantic-conservative and the utilitarian-liberal, rivals and opposites, sent forth two different strains of thought and feeling which even Mill's wise and catholic mind could not quite reconcile, though he strove to do so.

The lineage of utilitarianism can be traced back to various earlier sources. Helvétius, the French *philosophe,* had announced as a momentous .discovery the apparently trite idea that good government is that which secures the greatest happiness of the people. He also shared, if somewhat confusedly, the Physiocratic idea that about the best thing government could do to this end was to leave people alone—certainly, to leave trade alone. The recipe for maximum happiness was left somewhat vague in the pages of Helvétius's *Treatise on Man.* In Britain, Francis Hutcheson had used the phrase "greatest happiness of the greatest numbers," and David Hume had arrived at a form of "utilitarianism" when in his criticism of the social contract he had concluded that it was a fiction that might be dispensed with: "It is therefore on opinion only that government is founded." That is to say, there is no sort of sanction for government on rational analysis except the usefulness of that government in the eyes of its citizens. (Hume could scarcely have supported Bentham's view that an objective, rational standard of utility is possible, however.) William Paley, in his influential textbook *Principles of Moral and Political Philosophy* (1785), accepts this and defines utility as the sum of happiness. A law is good or bad accordingly as it increases or lessens this total of well-being.

Based on Enlightenment hedonism, utilitarianism was severely rationalistic, sweeping aside claims of sentiment or habit in government and requiring laws and institutions to justify themselves on the practical grounds of welfare achieved. Utilitarians were the direct opposites, and of course the violent adversaries, of Burkean conservatives in wishing total and immediate reform on theoretical or *a priori* principles. Sweep away the whole of a decrepit, illogical system, they urged, and replace it with a bright new model built on scientific foundations. They proposed breathtaking changes: Instead of two houses of parliament there should be just one, aristocracy along with monarchy should go, the common law should be replaced by a codified one; prisons should be reformed, schools should be reformed, everything should be reformed. Most radical of all was the suggestion of democratic, i.e., universal suffrage,[3] which the utilitarians reached in typical fashion by reasoning that we are the best judges of our own interest and "each should count as one." In behalf of these proposals, the followers of Bentham, including James Mill and many others, wrote pamphlets, edited magazines, tried to elect members of Parliament, and in general crusaded eagerly, inspired by their belief that they had at last found the exact science of government.

They were an interesting and powerful group, reaching their peak

---

[3]For a tribute to Bentham's feminism see Miriam Williford, "Bentham on the Rights of Women," *Journal of the History of Ideas,* Jan.–March, 1975. But Bentham changed his mind several times, and his final inclination was evidently to restrict suffrage not only to adult males but to literate ones, although "every individual of the human species" should be a part of the "public opinion tribunal."

in the 1820s as an organized movement but radiating influences down through the whole century. If they were in many ways exceedingly "radical" (a name they proudly adopted), they were in other ways not so much so, according to some standards. They stoutly defended private property, basing their case on the self-interest of free individuals. There was always some tension between the reforming and the individualistic tenets of utilitarianism. In the 1820s they worked closely with other "radicals," including working-class groups, and helped push through the Reform Bill of 1832. After that, they tended to lose their crusading zeal (perhaps the inevitable fate of a movement) and to become more conservative, or more pragmatic, working piecemeal for specific small changes and dropping their demands for total reconstruction of all society. They did not cease to do useful things; to take but one example, though an illustrious one, Edwin Chadwick undertook the sanitary reform of London in the 1840s as a utilitiarian disciple. From the total reconstruction of society to sewage systems was a considerable decline, though not necessarily a discreditable one. But later utilitarians tended even more strongly toward laissez-faire or the limited state, which respected individual property rights and did not regulate private business. In this respect they adopted the views of the political economists and parted company with socialists. The utilitarian position had always based itself squarely on the enlightened self-interest of individuals.

Bentham and his followers believed they had formulated an exact science of government. Hardheaded, they rejected the Natural Rights school, which was one form of liberalism reaching back to John Locke and the Whig revolution. Such alleged rights, apart from and above positive law, are either meaningless or false, they held. "Liberty" is not an absolute right; concrete liberties must be embodied in legislation to be meaningful, and the nature of such legislation should be determined by exact investigation into real circumstances. Bentham shared with Burke this one trait, at least, that he wished to get rid of metaphysical rubbish in politics and law and bring everything back to the touchstone of measurable human happiness. He believed that he could measure human happiness. The sum of individual happiness is the social goal, at which legislation should aim. Bentham thought that he could perform the herculean task of providing an objective measuring-stick for happiness on which all might agree. He invented a "felicific calculus."

The Benthamite principle of social welfare as the sum total of units of individual happiness, a total which could in principle be measured rather exactly, thus providing the basis for a science of welfare, lasted a long time; as late as 1920, A. C. Pigou, a British economics professor, claimed to have solved the problem of finding this exact science (*The Economics of Welfare*). The effort to make an exact science of welfare economics must nevertheless be regarded as a failure and illusion.

Bentham's notion of it certainly was inadequate and received many criticisms and subsequent restatements. But for all his extravagances, Bentham had a genius for practical reform. From his tireless pen flowed a series of projects for the practical reform of everything: schools, prisons, courts, laws. Some of them were fanciful, some ingenious. By sheer energy and perseverance, Bentham and his followers forced upon the public constant consideration of the questions, "What good is it? Can it be improved?"

Utilitarianism spread beyond its native shores to exert an influence in other countries as far afield as Russia, Spain, and Latin America. It offered a simple and rational rule for reform and had the merit of avoiding nebulous sloganizing as well as revolutionary radicalism; it was hardheaded and practical. But its individualistic foundations rendered it less acceptable in France. There the key social theorists of this period, whether conservatives like Maistre, socialists like Saint-Simon, or bourgeois thinkers like August Comte, stressed the social principle and were more statist.

It was this school of utility that Carlyle attacked as piggish and that sent the amiable Coleridge into a rage. Bentham and James Mill cared nothing for the arts, dismissing poetry as nonsense in the best or worst tradition of the Enlightenment; they cared nothing for "society," seeing in it nothing more than a group of individuals. Selfishness and hedonism seemed enshrined in their utterly unheroic ethics. The romantic-conservative, Coleridge-Carlyle temperament could not understand them. Nor, indeed, were they popular anywhere at first; they were radicals, as Lord Brougham remarked in 1827, "in their religion intolerable atheists, in their politics bloody-minded republicans...." Bentham's immense body of writing (the best known being *Principles of Morals and Legislation*, 1789) is marked by few if any graces of style. It is rather more prolix and formless than the works of his forerunners in the English tradition, Hobbes and Locke, but it does swarm with ideas for practical reform. Bentham's creed of self-interest has doubtless gone out of style in the twentieth century, but it appealed mightily to the nineteenth-century bourgeoisie and was conceivably a suitable polity for that day — witness the enormous growth of wealth in Great Britain. His method of attacking social reform piecemeal, assailing it with factual research, and avoiding large nebulous slogans, continued in the Fabian Socialists later with the goal being rather different but the method similar. It seemed to suit the English genius—individualistic, empirical, mistrustful of general ideas and metaphysics. And it can be interpreted as a creed for the English bourgeoisie in particular.

But the ethics of utility is not sheer egoism. One ought to do that which makes for the most good for the whole, that is, the sum of units of happiness; perhaps this might indicate one's extinction. In sharp opposition to Kant, utilitarian ethics judged an act by its consequences, not its inherent quality. Critics noted that, strictly followed, utilitarian rules of conduct might lead to euthanasia or genocide: killing an ill-tempered old man whose death would make his amiable sons and daughters very happy, or doing away with minorities. (If a law discriminating against blacks makes the white majority very happy, it should presumably be enacted, according to Bentham's principles.) Such odd inferences suggest that Bentham, whose embalmed body, in accordance with one of his eccentric wishes, still sits today in a room at University College, London, had scarcely fully reasoned out his alleged exact science of government. In the last analysis the Hermit of Queen Park Square takes his place in that gallery of ambitious utopists whose prescriptions fail to bridge the gap between theory and practice. But it may at least be said of him that his theories did less harm than others of that ilk.

POLITICAL ECONOMY

Closely related to and allied with utilitarians in the camp of British liberalism were the political economists. In the early nineteenth century the brilliant beginnings in economic thought made by the French Physiocrats and by Adam Smith reached maturity in the writings of such people as Thomas Malthus, David Ricardo, J. B. Say, and Nassau Senior. Say, along with Sismondi, kept up the French contribution, but in the main the British took over this subject. Perhaps this was because its determined individualism suited the British temperament, tradition, and experience. It is significant that Sismondi defected to socialism, while in Germany there were "romantic" economists such as List and Mueller who rejected the individualistic premises of the British "classical" economists. In Britain, too, the great Scottish writer Thomas Carlyle joined Coleridge and other poets and moralists who were dismissed as mere amateurs and sentimentalists by the economists,[4] in deploring the "dismal science." But it flourished and developed influence uniquely in the British Isles. The prestige of the political economists reached a high point with the 1817 publication of Ricardo's *Principles of Political Economy*, followed by Say's *Treatise* in 1821. Popularizations such as those of Mrs. Marcet (1816) and Harriet Martineau's stories in the later 1820s carried the message from on high to the common man in somewhat simplified form. It was the message of the hour, almost bedside reading for modish literates; it became "high fashion with the blue ladies to talk political economy." This ascendancy continued, on the whole, with the

---

[4]John Stuart Mill, in his discriminating and appreciative essay on Coleridge, said that "in political economy he writes like an arrant driveler, and it would have been well for his reputation had he never meddled with the subject." In turn Coleridge regarded political economy as "solemn humbug."

assumption being that an exact science had been perfected. In 1856 a distinguished member of Parliament remarked that "Political Economy is not exactly the law of the land but it is the ground of that law." Leaders of government sought the advice of the economists and parliamentary committees turned to them for guidance.

What was the message? The economists were in fact not a completely homogeneous group by any means. They had their heated debates. It is possible to identify a left wing and a right wing, led respectively by James Mill and J. R. McCulloch. Malthus and Ricardo engaged in a memorable debate about effective demand, to which John Maynard Keynes returned a century later in search of new truth and found Malthus righter than Ricardo, though for a century it had been thought otherwise. As for the greatest of them, David Ricardo, it is hard to know where to put him. Though often associated with the most brutally pessimistic of those who spoke of an "iron law" keeping wages down to the sustenance level ("the natural price of labour is that price which is necessary to enable the labourers, one with another, to subsist and perpetuate their race, without either increase or diminution"), he led to a kind of socialism and was best known for denouncing the landlord as virtually the enemy of society, thus precipitating class war in England. Ricardo evidently believed much less than Adam Smith that there is a natural order of harmony in economic affairs. He saw the landlord and the factory owner as natural foes. Rents raise the price of food, which raises wages, which causes profits in manufacturing to fall. And it was difficult to avoid the conclusion, on Ricardo's premises, that the wage worker is at war with the employer, since the latter must force wages down in order to keep profits up. The long struggle in British politics over repeal of the Corn Laws, or protective tariffs on grain, during which liberal manufacturers like John Bright attacked Tory landlords as parasites, sprang in good part from Ricardo's theory about rents; Owenite socialists took their inspiration from his Labour Theory of Value and Karl Marx built a system on it.

Yet of course the main message, especially in the popularized version of political economy, was that of individualism and laissez-faire. Smith and the Physiocrats had claimed that in accordance with a law of nature the "invisible hand" causes individual and social objectives to coincide, the rule of laissez-faire generally sufficing, via competition and the profit incentive, to secure the most efficient production and distribution of wealth. "The whole art of government," Smith had thought, "lies in the liberty of men and things." His successors may have moralized less, but they continued to assume that the free competitive system is the best and that state intervention seldom serves a useful purpose. Even if the major political economists never believed in eliminating all government—they assumed a secure infrastructure of authority, in fact—"mercantilism" was well on its way to becoming a synonym for the dark ages of economic thought. Merchants and statesmen began to accept free trade, which had by about 1820 (witness Baring's petition from the London merchants to Parliament in that year) become business orthodoxy. Say's law of the market posited automatic adjustment between production and consumption. The wage fund theory asserted the futility of any "artificial" attempts, such as by trade unions, to alter the sum available for wages. In one of Miss Martineau's little tales a strike takes place, and some wage increases are granted as a result, but the owner then informs the workers that it is necessary to fire some of them. If some workers get more than their share, others will get less.

In another of her stories it is explained how public expenditure on the poor raises tax rates, which discourages capital and thus intensifies the problem of unemployment. And the Reverend Thomas Malthus had by this time profoundly affected many with his famed tract on population, arguing that population always tends to increase up to the limit of sustenance, thus ensuring perpetual poverty unless something really heroic is done to break the gloomy cycle. The "hard line" Poor Law of 1834, based on an attempt to deter rather than relieve poverty by making welfare relief both hard to get and unpleasant, was actually far from a new medicine. In the eighteenth century Bernard Mandeville, Daniel Defoe, Arthur Young, and a host of others took it for granted that "the poor have nothing to stir them to labour but their wants, which it is wisdom to relieve but folly to cure," that in brief the poor must be kept poor or they will not work, and that too much charity encourages idleness. "It cannot fail to happen," Turgot had written before Adam Smith, "that the wages of the workman are limited to what is necessary to procure him his subsistence." But the prestigious teachings of political economy were thought to have lent credence to this venerable belief.

James Mill observed that capital tends to increase less rapidly than population, and the growth of capital cannot be forced; it must make its own pace. The classical economists would certainly have listened with bewilderment or perhaps amusement to the recent debate about just how to go about "creating economic growth" by the activities of various governmental agencies. Their world was strictly bounded by the limitations of nature; they saw the laws of diminishing returns and increasing population as probable barriers to any great improvement in the overall lot of the human race. They permitted themselves only an occasional hint of a brighter future.

Yet they became the respected arbiters of policy. This was a triumph not only for their obvious intelligence but also for the readiness of the middle classes to receive the message of hard work and austerity. Classical political economy appealed to the Puritan spirit of the industrious small manufacturers and business people who were climbing from poverty to riches in the favorable economic climate of England during and soon after the Napoleonic War. The slogan of the industrial middle class was self-help. The creed which Carlyle thought a monstrous, inhuman "gospel of mammon" seemed to them the law of life and of progress. As Great Britain assumed the leadership in industrialization, it was the presence and the power of this class, more perhaps than any other single factor, that was responsible for its success. They had energy, and the system of competitive capitalism provided them with incentive.

The British economists were both much admired and cordially disliked, and excited a vigorous countermovement. Socialism took its point of departure from the economic inequalitarianism as well as the economic individualism or selfishness of their teachings. Bentham, who had supported political and legal equality, accepted economic inequality. There must be, he wrote, equality in the sense that each of us is entitled to the just fruits of his own labor. But since people have unequal talents and energies, this will mean unequal rewards. Compelling people to share the fruits of their labors with others, the only practical way of securing economic equality, not only violates justice but will prove disastrous. Coleridge reached exactly the same conclusion—a rare example of agreement between the two leaders of rival schools. It is difficult to overstate the importance for the nineteenth century of this apparent truth that one must choose between civil and economic equality, one cannot have both; as students of ethics would put it, it is the problem of personal versus distributive justice.

The great utilitarian admitted that on other grounds equal distribution of wealth was desirable as contributing to the greatest happiness of the greatest number. (The principle of diminishing utility, he pointed out, means that the addition of a unit of wealth to one who already has a good deal of it brings less pleasure than it does to one with less of it.) Thus was posed the dilemma: In the name of social justice and economic efficiency, one sanctioned inequality and hence unhappiness.

Into the making of British middle-class liberalism, expressed in the famed "Manchester School" headed by John Bright and Richard Cobden, went some other ingredients than the intellectual doctrines of utility and political economy. Bright was a Quaker; Manchester was a provincial center. The rising capitalists of the Industrial Revolution were heavily nonconformist in religion outside the old aristocratic establishment; they were new men. As dissenters they had had to fight discrimination; Bright said he had to be a liberal because of the persecutions his people had endured. Scripture played as much part in the Manchester creed as political economy. The Bright-Cobden school went into their great crusade against the Corn Laws, symbol of a hated landlord aristocracy, with Bible phrases on their lips and the spirit of a moral crusade in their hearts. Tennyson ridiculed Bright as "This broad-brimmed hawker of holy things," a selfish moneybags hypocritically pretending to be religious. But the close student of Bright knows there was more to it than that. Self-interest was there and political economy contributed its share, but so did a kind of Puritan conscience, which was something more than a mask for self-interest, though it is easy to see why its enemies made this charge. A part of the liberal creed was passionate hatred of militarism and war that led Bright to stand out courageously against the Crimean War. If his Quaker faith dictated pacifism, so did the tenets of economic liberalism: Free trade would do away with war, which was an avocation of the idle aristocracy; nonintervention should be the rule for nations as for individuals. Thus did religion, economics, and interest blend together to make up the faith of liberal England.

Thus, clearly, there were several strains in early modern liberalism, not always in exact agreement with each other, yet they all tended to agree broadly on a negative conception of the state, on something approaching laissez-faire as an ideal. The Natural Rights school of Locke stressed resistance to arbitrary and tyrannical government while enshrining private property as one of the basic, inalienable human rights. The utilitarians built their system on the rational self-interest of free individuals. The political economists pointed toward the largely self-regulating economic order. To this must be added the religious nonconformists whose whole history disposed them to be suspicious of establishments and rules imposed by the state.

Of course, the achievements of the French Revolution in general, meaning the liquidation of the old class society (which came more slowly in England, but did come), left a kind of automatic liberalism in effect. The Old Regime having been destroyed, people became equal—equal under the law, that is, of equal rights, opportunities, status. That such an equality might mean, practically, a larger amount of real, economic equality did not occur to people until they saw what happened. Socialism, Harold Laski has written, was based on "the realization that the liberal ideal secured to the middle class its full share of privilege, while it left the proletariat in its chains." With allowance for rhetorical embellishment, the statement comes close to expressing the essence of the matter. Liberty—the liberty of all citizens to prosper or fail in accordance with their energies, abilities, and luck, the law maintaining a scrupulous impartiality and the state refusing to intervene to protect the weaker or less fortunate—meant inequality and even injustice. It meant that those who succeeded had both the protection of the law and the accolades of society, while those who failed, for whatever reason, might expect to hear only that most ancient of cries, *vae victis*.

SOCIALISM

About the same time as conservatism and liberalism were developing, socialism entered vigorously upon the scene. In 1822, Charles

Fourier, son of a Besançon merchant, published his *Traité de l'association*, a work not exactly greeted with wild acclaim when it appeared, one among multitudes of strange schemes for the total reconstruction of society, but destined in time to a greater fame than any of these. Between 1814 and 1822 the eccentric Count Saint-Simon, who modestly called himself a combination of Bacon, Newton, and Locke, sent forth a spate of books; the basis of his claim to be the first important socialist has usually been approved. Meanwhile in Britain, Robert Owen, the Scottish factory owner, was popularizing his plan, by example, for a more social organization of industry; thousands came to New Lanark to inspect it. Sismondi had broken with the laissez-faire economists, repelled by their selfish atomism and apparently callous disregard of human beings. The word *socialism* does not seem to have come into use until the 1830s, but the idea itself was forming in the 1820s. "Associationalism" was a term then in use.

Naturally, it had earlier roots. Leaving aside the strong tradition of communalism in both Platonism, the Church, and medieval feudalism, and in Christian millenarianism present from medieval times, we can find strands of socialism in the Enlightenment, along with the stronger element of laissez-faire individualism. By no means consistently a socialist (indeed, he sometimes called private property "sacred"), Rousseau, in one memorable passage that shocked Voltaire, regretted the origins of private property in an initial act of usurpation. Someone said, "This is mine!" and got away with it, ending the idyll of primitive communism and ushering in greed, civilization, and all their accompaniments. From Rousseau's concept of the General Will—the will of society as a whole, something more than the sum of individual wills—many of his disciples derived a strong statism. Rousseau's *Social Contract* taught that all rights are derived from society, without which they could not exist; the state, therefore, is justified in regulating property; there is no absolute right of property; if property exists it is at the sufferance of society. Rousseau believed that private property should be permitted to exist but should be approximately equal and represent only what one earned with one's labor. Moreover, he considered the pursuit of wealth an evil, a source of modern society's ills. Though to describe Rousseau as a socialist would be to commit an anachronism, some of his attitudes fed into the nineteenth-century stream of this school. His influence did not encourage the kind of socialism that stressed greater productivity and wealth, for he thought the good life was one of Spartan simplicity.

Morelly, called "the only consistent communist among the eighteenth-century thinkers," combined Rousseau's General Will with his attack on private property to arrive at a crude socialist theory. Equally crude, yet fervently sincere, was the thought of those who backed "Gracchus" Babeuf in his rather pathetic Conspiracy of the

Equals in the latter days of the French Revolution (1795). Robespierre, that "child of the ideas of Rousseau," had been willing to use the power of the state ruthlessly in accordance with the General Will concept but had basically been a Jacobin democrat who did not wish to abolish private property. Babeuf, however, advocated a "distributive socialism," a common pool of property to which everyone brings earnings that are then carved up equally. "Nature has given to every man an equal right to the enjoyment of all goods." The same nature that provided the basis for bourgeois property rights might be turned in another direction. A passion for equality and a belief that private property creates inequality moved these simple, poor people.

Like romanticism, socialism is a large word covering a multitude of rather different things. There have been various sorts of socialism, though one may link them all by certain common denominators. The first half of the century brought forth a profusion of schemes and plans, some of them seemingly weird and most impractical, yet supplying the basic ideas for all subsequent socialist thought. The eagerness with which people produced and imbibed socialist ideas in this period relates to the general feeling that some new plan of social reorganization was desperately needed, to a discontent with the liberalism of legal equality *cum* free competition, and to the continuing ferment of ideas stemming from the Enlightenment, romanticism, and the French Revolution.

The pioneer socialists were a colorful and interesting lot. Robert Owen, though born a poor boy (as one of thirteen children, he went to work at the age of nine), rose to become a wealthy and successful factory owner in a rags-to-riches story. A man of boundless energy, he went into business for himself at the age of eighteen in Manchester, getting in on the burgeoning cotton textile industry, and later bought the mills at New Lanark in Scotland, destined to become internationally celebrated. But he also found time to read and was clearly influenced by the "philosophic" ideas of Rousseau, Godwin, and other Enlightenment thinkers. At New Lanark he set to work reforming the ignorant, degraded mill hands (largely children) who worked long hours in unsanitary and dismal surroundings. He reduced working hours, improved housing, established schools, banned alcohol, set up communal stores where goods were sold at fair prices, organized pension and sick funds—and found that it paid, for the workers worked better. He was the benevolent dictator of a model community to which visitors began to come from all over the world. Owen's fame as an enlightened employer was such that when he visited the United States in 1825 he was invited to address a special joint session of Congress. He was at this time a respectable example of philanthropy and "benevolence," widely approved qualities, but he soon lost his respectability as he embarked on a variety of schemes for the total reformation of society. He attempted to found a highly unorthodox Rational Religion, a kind of secular-social morality which may be compared with Saint-Simon's New Christianity. But most of Owen's enormous energy went toward attempts to duplicate the New Lanark idea by planting other model socialist communities, sinking the whole of his substantial fortune into such schemes. Though the community at New Harmony, Indiana (which Owen bought from the Rappites[5]), is the best known, there were numerous others of varying sizes in the United States and the British Isles. They invariably failed but attracted thousands of eager experimenters, enchanted by the thought of helping to found what Owen called a New Moral World, to be marked by the spirit of community rather than selfishness.

The Owenite communities, like the later Fourierist ones, seemed, alas, to prove the validity of the liberal-utilitarian claim that people are moved only by their self-interest. The Owenites adopted a simple form of Ricardian socialism in which they attempted to devise a medium of exchange based on labor power to escape capitalistic exploitation of the worker. This proved unworkable. Owenite communities tried to abolish the family, seen as a bastion of private property and egoism, in favor of some form of communal living arrangements—a feature which, along with the religious unorthodoxy, shocked and alienated the neighboring populace. The communities were ill-managed, since Owen could not be everywhere and few of his disciples possessed his organizing genius. They attracted a gorgeous miscellany of unscreened free spirits, cranks, idealists, misfits, and parasites. Often in America the abler members caught the spirit of frontier individualism and went off to become proprietors for themselves. An endless number of such reasons might be given for the almost invariable collapse of these enterprises. Owen was not discouraged; later, in the 1830s, he threw himself into the Grand National Trade Union cause, which also collapsed after a spectacular beginning. Owen never tried to found a political party, regarding himself as missionary and educator. In its day the Owenite movement made a tremendous stir. "In the peak years 1839–1841," writes J. F. C. Harrison, author of the best book on Owenism, "two and a half-million tracts were distributed; 1450 lectures delivered in a year, Sunday lectures attended by up to 50,000 weekly." More than one hundred Owenite journals existed at various times. In the 1820s, when evangelical religion was popular, Owenism took on the qualities of a sectarian religion; later, there were Owenite Halls of Science.

After all this stir, the Owenite movement died away upon the death

---

[5]The early historian of socialism, J. H. Noyes, called the Shakers and Rappites "the real pioneers of modern socialism." These were religious communitarian sects, the former being an offshoot of Quakerism, while Father Rapp stemmed from the German Pietistic tradition (cf. the earlier Moravians and Mennonites). Essentially this was just a version of Christian monasticism.

of its remarkable founder in 1857, leaving little behind except a memory. (The cooperative movement, largely fathered by the Owenites, is an exception.) The same was true of other British socialist tentatives of this period, associated with the so-called Chartist movement among the working classes. They seemed to lack adequate intellectual foundations. Was it the incurable individualism of the English that caused the failure of socialism there?

THE FRENCH SOCIALISTS

France gave birth to more doctrines of *mouvement social* than any other country. Sismondi, in 1819, attacked laissez-faire economics, urging that the state intervene to regulate the use of property for the well-being of the community. Political economy based itself on an assumption of human selfishness and took human nature as it is. Adam Smith had posited the "economic man," seeking his own advantage, and made this self-seeking individual the key to his system; so did Ricardo, perhaps even more. That everyone wishes to obtain additional wealth, as efficiently as possible, Senior made his starting point. It should be noted that the supremacy of individual desires was a keystone of the whole structure of liberal economics. Suppose the state directs its citizens to produce something they are not producing. The view of the classical economists was that this must mean a diversion from what is desired to what is not, and this was a sufficient refutation in their eyes. Some romantic economists protested that the nation might wish to elevate itself by choosing a standard of production other than just what people want; it might wish, for example, to create more musical instruments and fewer evening clothes for the wealthy. This cannot be refuted by the classical economists, except that they would simply dismiss it as "uneconomic," that is, going beyond their system. They would add that a directed economy must burden itself with an expensive bureaucratic system, whereas the undirected one is largely self-running. But in large measure they identified efficiency with meeting the desires of individuals.

It was this individualist and egoist principle that critics of liberal economics, including Sismondi and, in Germany, Fichte, resented and assailed. Their moving impulse was an ethical desire to create something nobler than a selfish scramble, a "mere congeries of possessors and pursuers," as Lord Keynes once called it; or, again, a rational impulse to *plan* rather than leave matters to a chaos of contending individual wills. The difficulty was that this led to highly authoritarian structures in which an intellectual elite planned for and governed the entire community.

Whereas it was the simple passion of the poor to equalize themselves with the rich that inspired Babeuf, an intellectual passion to impose order, to *plan* the whole economy, was especially marked in the case of socialists such as Sismondi and, especially, the extremely important Frenchman, Saint-Simon. Claude Henri de Rouvroy, Comte de Saint-Simon (1760–1825), was a French aristocrat who traced his ancestry back to Charlemagne. He fought in the American Revolution and was wounded at Yorktown. During the French Revolution he made a fortune in financial speculations, narrowly escaped the guillotine, and then, like Owen, poured all his fortune into his schemes for a new moral and social world, dying in dire poverty. Between 1802 and 1825 he exuded a stream of writings and journals and left behind a cult.

Saint-Simon did not suggest equality, but rather a hierarchy. He looked upon society as one great workshop whose efficient organization was the main task of modern times. Science could surely answer this need, Saint-Simon thought, and he proposed an elite of social engineers planning and running society on scientific principles. He rejected democracy; the crowd cannot govern. He added, later, the need for a new public religion, a "new (rationalized) Christianity," also presided over by a priestly elite. One can see why this eccentric nobleman appeals to the present Communists of the Soviet Union, who grant him a place with Marx and Lenin among the makers of modern communism. On the other hand, Saint-Simon did not usually suggest class war or the dominance of the "proletariat." The new elite should be drawn from the industrialists and engineers. "Technocracy," a later scheme which enjoyed a brief vogue in the 1920s and 1930s, expressed more nearly what was in Saint-Simon's mind than did Marxism. Perhaps, indeed, this is the way the world is going, whether in the West or in the Communist world today.

Rather like Jeremy Bentham in England, Saint-Simon was an eccentric who succeeded in planting an idea that percolated down through the nineteenth century in his native France. The Emperor Louis Napoleon (1851 to 1870) was one of his influential disciples, even writing a book on *The Extinction of Poverty.* Certain aspects of his thought were carried on by August Comte (Chapter 3). Saint-Simonianism was not necessarily "radical," as noted; its "captains of industry" might be industrialists, and Saint-Simon was quite willing to accept even the Bourbon monarchy if this regime would back his plan. Like the Physiocrats of the preceding century, Saint-Simon preferred enlightened despotism to democracy. He announced a new epoch marked by industrialism and the power of scientific and technological knowledge, and he called for a new aristocracy to replace the defunct orders of church and nobility. He stressed increased productivity to satisfy material wants, agreeing with Bentham that the social goal is "happiness," which he defined largely as the satisfaction of physical wants. All this could be as attractive to a business person as to a proletarian, perhaps, though the element of state compulsion might be repellent. As a matter of fact, Saint-Simon inspired most notably a number of public-spirited administrators who wanted to impose a rational plan on the disorderly economy. One of the leading disciples, Pierre Enfantin, was later prominently associated with the building of the Suez Canal; a passion for huge enterprises of this sort marked the Saint-Simonians. The French down to the present have shown less enthusiasm for the free, unregulated economy and society than have the English. It is possible to see at work here the urge toward order and lucidity of the French mind, always influenced by classicism and rationalism. It might be added in regard to Saint-Simon that he was not a nationalist, but advocated and predicted a European society and economy.

Saint-Simon and Thomas Carlyle, who owed much to him, reiterated their message that Europe had entered the industrial age, the "mechanical age," a new epoch calling for wholly new methods of government and thought; they called attention to the fact that the "social question" (Carlyle) was the burning issue of modern times and would not be solved by laissez-faire negativism. They did not have any exact blueprint for this new order but were sure that the "captains of industry" would have to assert leadership rather than content themselves with profits; they were sure that society needed a plan ("That Chaos should sit empire in it, that is the Worst," Carlyle exclaimed). These ideas, vigorously expressed, exerted an incalculable influence in Europe. It is impossible to imagine Marx and the other later socialists without this background.

Charles Fourier, a sweet and saintly sort of person, thought in terms of social harmony, cooperation, "association." He may be regarded as the prototype of that variety of socialist to whom these things are values in themselves. In him it is easy, though, to detect the continued influence of the eighteenth century. Like the Physiocrats he presumes a preordained harmony and a perfect plan for society, only unlike them, he does not believe in the separateness of the individual atoms but thinks they must be placed in association according to an exact formula. Everybody has a precise niche in Fourier's carefully constructed plans. Science, speaking through Fourier, has determined the organization of the community down to the last detail. The ideal community must contain between sixteen hundred and eighteen hundred people, with a certain proportion of each occupation and age group and psychological types; they are to be housed in certain types of buildings; they rise at specified hours, and so forth. There are communal dining halls; no one is to be left, or let, alone. It is rather monastic (Fourier was religious) and rather depressing. It had the attraction of being a precise plan, where others had been vague. It suggested the perhaps enduringly important idea of a balanced society. And Fourier promised the elimination of all vice, crime, unhappiness. The state will become unnecessary. Fourier declared that his scheme was completely voluntary. He hoped, by setting up model communities, to demonstrate the superiority of his cooperative system to the competitive anarchy of the economists, against whom he launched violent diatribes. He wished to make labor enjoyable instead of unpleasant. Many experimental communities did indeed come into being, inspired by the pages of the *Treatise on Association;* most of them were not very successful, as we might guess.

In his attitude toward sexual morality and the family, Fourier was far bolder than any other early socialist, a fact responsible for much recent interest in him. A bachelor himself, Fourier identified the monogamous family as the root institution of bourgeois selfishness, and in his utopia there would be instant divorce, total promiscuity, complete sexual "emancipation" in which couplings would take place in all sorts of combinations; man was not meant for one woman alone, or even several, the "harmonian man" clearly believed. Some have seen an anticipation of Freud in his "passional attractions" or of Wilhelm Reich in his connection between sexual and economic oppression.

We can smile at Fourier, but we may be surprised at the number of people who took him seriously enough to try out his scheme. Harriet Martineau, the liberal Englishwoman who may be supposed to have had no special love for socialists (Coleridge regarded her as an incorrigible social atomist), wrote that the principle of cooperation "will now never rest till it has been made a matter of experiment." It was. Numbers of the sturdy individualists of New England founded Brook Farm on Fourierist lines, with predictable results. The fad for socialist communities, to which Robert Owen and his son had contributed, took on fresh life under Fourier's influence. Indeed, Fourierist ideas spread all over the world. The Russian scholar Zilberfarb, a leading Fourier expert, finds traces in eastern Europe, Scandinavia, Latin America, China, as well as other European countries; in Russia, between 1845 and 1849, Petreshevsky spread the ideas of "Sharlia Fure" by connecting them with the Russian peasant village, the *mir*. Perhaps, via eastern Europe, the present Israeli *kibbutz* owes something to Fourier. Though it was (and still is) common to laugh at Fourier's dreams, this retired merchant, who fed his cats and waited each day for the millionaire who would finance his schemes to save the world, was an interesting and important figure. More than Owen or Saint-Simon, Fourier was a keen psychologist who tried to base his social system on an examination of human nature. He did not, like the Owenites, wish to abolish private property, because he thought it too deep a human instinct to eradicate. The trick is to harness this force and make it serve the public interest. The proper collaboration of interests, as well as passions, leads to a happy community. A gentle and nonrevolutionary socialist, hating strife, seeking concord, bucolic and joyful, Fourier's utopia was perhaps not a thing of this world.

Etienne Cabet, author of the 1839 utopian romance *Voyage to Icaria*, was a "communist" in the sense of vesting total ownership and absolute power in the community—a veritable police state, suppressing all freedom of thought, in the name of an ideal society where economic efficiency was joined to perfect social harmony. The "Icarians" joined the Owenites and the Fourierists in establishing social communities in the New World (Illinois, Iowa, Texas), one of which survived until 1898 though, in general, the utopian ideal was not realized in practice.

Thus there were various kinds of socialism. Agreeing in their desire for some sort of social control over private property and individual rights, the socialists differed in the degree of control they would exercise, in its manner, and in its institutionalization. In the thought of Saint-Simon, Fourier, and Cabet, socialism is sometimes vague and often foolish, but it was an exciting beginning.

Modern socialism and communism have lain so heavily under the influence of Karl Marx that his predecessors in this field sometimes are forgotten. One book on Marxism does not even mention Saint-Simon, Fourier, and their numerous offshoots; it says that Marx is the "heir of Jan Hus, Thomas Moore (*sic*), Thomas Paine, and Jean-Jacques Rousseau." Doubtless he was, but in a much more meaningful sense he was the heir of the numerous socialists who had filled the press of Europe with their schemes and debates all through the years when Marx and Engels were growing up. Marx had more theoretical and philosophical talent than most of them; he syncretized a great many of their systems, marrying revolutionary Babeuvist communism to Saint-Simonian and Owenite conceptions in a Hegelian ceremony. But he really created few, if any, of the various ideas he strung together so ingeniously. To a large extent this creativity belonged to the half-mad Saint-Simon and the eccentric Fourier, along with their whole generation of (mostly French) messiahs of "social science."

More of them appeared than there is space for: The names of Jones and Harney in Great Britain, of Rodbertus and Weitling in Germany (before Marx), and of the numerous disciples and offspring of Saint-Simon and Fourier in France are among them. Victor Considerant carried on Fourier's work. A remarkable group of Saint-Simonian "apostles" formed a community in Paris where they attempted to live the famous formula of "to each according to his need, from each according to his ability" before dispersing to carry the message into the world. Here was a veritable chaos of socialistic ideas. Socialism before Marx reminds one of Protestantism before Calvin—in danger of perishing from its very profusion and popularity, in need of discipline and unity to save it. A rigorous logician of iron will would come in both cases to impose that discipline, at the cost of variety. Karl Marx would have recourse to the resources of German philosophy in this task, so that it is logical at this point to turn to the thought of the last and perhaps greatest of the German classical philosophers flourishing during these years.

HEGEL

French political and social thought, British economic theory, and German philosophy were the three outstanding areas of new ideas in the period from 1815 to 1830, it was frequently said. In 1831, G. W. F. Hegel died, Kant's successor as the leading German philosopher and much more a system-builder than the essentially critical Kant. Hegelianism so triumphed in academic circles that by the end of the century, even in Great Britain and the United States (where there was a certain resistance to this kind of thought), the leading philosophers were largely of this school, while in very unacademic circles it also spread widely, especially through the theories of Karl Marx and other socialists who owed much to Hegel.

Hegel's was a vast, labyrinthine, and, according to some, impenetrable system which despite its difficulties exercised this enormous influence. It may be well to ask what message, stripped of all the technicalities, ordinary cultivated men got from Hegel. One of them, the Russian socialist Belinsky who wrote that when he read Hegel he was overcome with emotion and the world took on a new meaning, got the message from Hegel's famous formula, "What is real is reasonable and what is reasonable real." This meant that all of history is the unfolding of reality itself, the idea or mind of the universe; what happens in history is in effect the writing of a book of which God is the ultimate author, but in which humans participate. For those who believed Hegel, history and human affairs no longer were chaotic, jumbled, or meaningless; every great event had its place in an unfolding plot which, when the book was finished, would be seen to have no loose ends, nothing put in without purpose. As Belinsky wrote, "For me there was no longer anything arbitrary or accidental in the course of history."

Undoubtedly Hegel's approach to human history *was* a revelation. He did not invent it; to go no farther back, an interest in history as rational process was taken up by Herder, a pupil of Kant. He wrote an essay on the "Idea for a Universal History from the Cosmopolitan Point of View" in 1784, on which Kant commented, following which Fichte, Schelling, and others made it a leading topic in German philosophical circles. The famous formula of thesis-antithesis-synthesis, the dialectic of history, which Marx took from Hegel, was evidently first suggested by Fichte, not Hegel. (Nor did Hegel consider it the only kind of process.) The original impulse to the new historicism probably came from Vico, writing in the earlier eighteenth century (*The New Science*, 1725, 1744); but that Neapolitan philosopher was not in step with his times. Voltaire was much more typical of the Enlightenment in seeing the past as without any continuity or regular path of development; a record largely of "crimes, follies, and misfortunes" illuminated by occasional and rather inexplicable epochs of reason, most of it without any interest to the philosophical mind. (What point is there in studying the superstitious Middle Ages or the ghastly wars of religion?) Yet at the end of the eighteenth century one of the great paths of discovery for the European mind was that of continuous secular progress, and others besides Hegel saw it. Saint-Simon incorporated into his socialism, before Hegel and Marx, the notion that history has a will of its own: "The supreme law of progress of the human spirit carries along and dominates everything; men are but its instruments...." He was at pains to correct those eighteenth-century philosophers who saw only darkness in the Medieval period; not only had it played its necessary part in its own day, but from its womb came the next age: "If historians had analyzed and examined the Middle Ages more deeply ... they would have recorded the gradual preparation of all the great events which developed later and would not have presented the explosions of the 16th and following centuries as sudden and unforeseen." From Rousseau had come what F. C. Lea has called "the romantic myth": progression from alienation to reunion, through civilization to a higher perfection at the end of historic time, when a perfect art, fully realized personality, and an ideal society would exist. Such popular elements of historicism lay about in every direction when Hegel applied his philosophical skills to the task of shaping from them a huge intellectual synthesis.

German philosophy had been searching for the underlying ideal unity of things. Hegel would show that this was a process working itself out in time. Behind the apparently fortuitous jumble of events, the philosopher-historian can discern a great process at work which is nothing else than thought, the Idea, working itself out in reality.

To identify the German philosopher only with his philosophy of history would be incorrect. The self-unfolding of the eternal Idea includes nature as well as humanity. A formidable polymath, Hegel knew a great deal about the sciences and lectured on them as well as on the law, the state, politics, religion. His famous *Phenomenology of the Spirit* is a kind of psychology, seeking to link inner consciousness with the outer pattern of historical evolution while showing how a motive force implicit in the interaction of internal and external leads onward and upward, in an endless dialectic of change. "All the great philosophical ideas had their origin in Hegel," a twentieth-century existentialist, Merleau-Ponty, enthusiastically exclaimed.

In reaction against Kant's critical philosophy, which had seemed to leave the world of thought in pieces, Hegel aspired to a magnificent, if often cloudy, totalism that saw the universe as one great whole. (Hegel claimed to have overcome Kant's "antinomies" or ultimate logical contradictions by his principle of development.) Yet the development of human affairs was by far the most important element in Hegel's thought. The self-realization of the Spirit, as it grows to full consciousness, takes place in and through human history; we are the instruments this divine Spirit has chosen with which to realize its cosmic purposes. Those purposes were to fully realize the potentialities of mind, to bring the Spirit to full self-consciousness, to perfect what Hegel called freedom.

Marxists, while recognizing Marx's great debt to Hegel, later charged Hegel with being too "idealistic" in locating the source of change not in material circumstances but in pure intellectual development. "History is mind clothing itself with the form of events." In 1845 and 1846 Marx ridiculed Hegel for preposterously endowing metaphysical categories with physical or human existence. Marx thought Hegel had found the right *method* but had the subject of the process wrong, seeing it as abstract idea or consciousness rather than as real flesh-and-blood people; he had "enveloped it in mysticism." Humans, Marx held, are active creatures realizing themselves in work rather than thought, engendering thought as they work; one must begin with this sentient creature, not with a ghostly spirit. But it is questionable whether this diatribe that occurred as Marx left his native land and denounced "the German Ideology" is an accurate interpretation of Hegel. For Hegel, too—admittedly difficult to understand—seems to see the process as a struggle between Spirit and matter, the former objectifying itself and then trying to recapture its alienation, a process in which humanity at least helps God or the Absolute Spirit achieve its ends. The distance between the two German giants may be less than some have thought. They simply chose to stress different sides of the dialectic. Recent attempts to Hegelianize orthodox Marxism have sought to rescue the latter from a sterile materialistic determinism by introducing more freedom and voluntarism. It is sometimes said that Engels, if not Marx, first construed Hegel as teaching a deterministic idealism and then "stood Hegel on his head" in an equally deterministic materialism, thus repeating the error, which passed into popular Marxism; whereas the true spirit of both Hegel and Marx is a genuine dialectic between idea and matter.

In any case, Hegel's exciting vision of human progress stimulated great interest in history. Later historians, more positivistic by temperament and disillusioned with Hegel's overly rational history, have disparaged him, but all historians probably owe their basic professional debt to Hegel. It was in Germany that the great historical profession of the nineteenth century began, with such contemporaries of Hegel as Leopold von Ranke and B. G. Niebuhr developing the "scientific" historical method (use of archival source materials, careful criticism of the documents). We cannot seriously become interested in history so long as it has only an antiquarian or storytelling value, however amusing it may be; to be elevated to the dignity of a leading professional study, history must be thought of as revealing significant truths about humanity and the universe. Bonald and Maistre saw in it the training school of politics; Hegel saw much more: nothing less than God's Will immanent in the world, the unrolling of a great purpose.

Hegel should be defended against certain criticisms of his history that are frequently encountered. He did not say that all events are logical or that the pattern of history can be determined without reference to the events. The actions of history are the outward expression of thoughts, and these thoughts form a logical, necessary chain of reasoning. We should study the actions, the empirical events, but we should not stop there; we should "think them through" to discover their inner logic. This still seems sound enough method, whatever mistakes Hegel made in his actual historical reconstructions. The mind of the historian, it is clear, must supply *some* sort of structure for the facts, which by themselves are without meaning. Hegel seemingly felt that there was a single objective pattern into which all would fit, a faith few historians find relevant to their tasks today.

The three main phases of history, according to Hegel, have been the Asiatic, characterized by absolute monarchy, followed by the classical Graeco-Roman, marked by individual freedom, and finally by the Germanic-European which fused the two earlier civilizations in a synthesis of freedom in the context of the strong state. Hegel's disciple F. C. Baur applied the dialectic to New Testament studies by finding the thesis in Jewish nationalism, antithesis in Pauline universalism, and synthesis in the mature Church which emerged in the second century. An eagerness to make the facts fit this framework led Baur into some serious mistakes. One may judge from him both how stimulating and how dangerous the Hegelian formula might be.

It is interesting and typical that Hegel defined his historical epochs in political terms. To Comte, the key lay in modes of thought, while Marx found it in the technological-economic sphere. Hegel's preoccupation with the political probably reflected the urgency of that problem in the Germany of his day, disunited and seeking to find its political unity. Hegel has been accused of an excessive nationalism, especially German nationalism, but in his time this was considered liberal and progressive. The key institution of the present age, Hegel felt with some justification, is the nation-state. He bequeathed to most German historians, and indeed to most nineteenth-century historians in all countries, a belief that the proper subject matter of history is politics; "history is past politics," in the definition of E. A. Freeman, the British master. While there was a subsequent rebellion against the narrowness of this definition, it might be defended on the grounds that the political order has usually given the distinctive stamp of epochs and peoples, from the oriental despotisms of earliest times through the Greek city-states, the Roman Empire, feudalism, and down to the age of the territorial state. If tomorrow should bring a world-state or even a federated Europe, this development would surely be so striking and significant that an epoch would be named for it. The "primacy of politics" is often a sound position.

In any case Hegel does not suggest that the process of change has come to an end. Process and organism are Hegelian keynotes. As opposed to the static formulations of Enlightenment thought, he has everything in motion, to be grasped only when its growth and development is understood; no one better reveals the nineteenth century's genetic, evolutionary outlook or contributed more to implanting it. And, though somewhat obscurely, Hegel believed that the universe was not like a machine but like an organism, a view closer to both the older and the newer conceptions than to eighteenth-century mechanism. His logical methodology was based on the organic approach: Nothing can be understood except by reference to the whole of which it is a part. With specific reference to the Kantian categories, Hegel held them to be bound together in a unity; not isolated and separate, but aspects of a single entity, the mind, which itself is a part of all the rest of reality. (That is why the real is rational and the rational real: Our minds and the universe are parts of a single whole, and hence obey the same laws.) We are almost back where we were before Descartes taught men to dissect, to break things down into simple components for purpose of analysis. Hegel was the philosopher of process and of organism.

All this may seem rather difficult. Many found Hegel hopelessly difficult. But the spirit of his philosophy, when one gets hold of it, hangs together and communicates a special vision, an excitingly new one in its day. We asked what some of its implications were and may resume that discussion. Belinsky, our Russian friend, drew from Hegelianism some highly conservative inferences: It seems to teach that whatever is is right, like all systems declaring the universe to be perfectly rational. With particular reference to history, it apparently requires the belief that whatever has happened is for the best: in the Lisbon Earthquake controversy, Hegel would assuredly have been on the side of Rousseau and the church against Voltaire's pessimistic protest. He has been accused of teaching that might makes right, and there is a certain truth in this, for "the hour strikes once for every nation" and whoever has the power at a particular moment of history is presumably in the right. Some nations are "world-historical" ones destined to contribute more than others to the pattern of history. And everything, including war, is a necessary part of the pattern. Hegel at times declared that individuals are the unconscious tools of the world-force; they have no wills of their own.

Yet this view of the past greatly encouraged historical research by inculcating a deep respect for each epoch of the past, which made its unique contribution and is therefore worth studying for its own sake. One did not demand that it conform to current prejudices and thus commit the sin of an excessive "present-mindedness," distorting the past by forcing it into a mold of recent construction. One studied each era of the past as if, in Leopold von Ranke's words, it was "equidistant from eternity"—just as much a part of God's plans as our own age. German historians like Ranke, who led a great nineteenth-century renaissance of historical studies, were not Hegelian metaphysicians, but they did broadly share this outlook which saw order and purpose in the events of history and hoped to lay bare the whole mighty plan by their industrious researches.

Politically, Hegel might best be described as a conservative liberal. An ardent Bonapartist in his day, Hegel's chief political work was a product of the reaction (*Philosophy of Right and Law,* 1821). He believed in constitutional government but preferred monarchy to democracy and opposed individualism. He shared some of the presuppositions of the upper bourgeoisie who greatly mistrusted the mob, though in a certain sense they were liberal. Certainly Hegel claimed to believe in progress through orderly government—progress toward freedom. But his version of freedom was the so-called positive one. Freedom, that is, was not to him the negative practice of just letting people alone. The proper definition of freedom is realization of possibilities, Hegel believed. This may be made clearer by the example of the child, whom we compel to go to school, though if given his will, the child would doubtless prefer the freedom of play. We are preparing this child to be truly free by expanding the possibilities of growth. (Rousseau's "forced to be free" will be recalled.) Ignorance is slavery; the savage who is "free" is really far less free than the modern individual who is bound by the rules of a state. No creature is absolutely free, but free only to realize its natural possibilities. A bird is free to fly, but not to swim. We, as creatures of reason, realize our freedom by developing our rational potential, and to do this requires making many sacrifices of our liberty of action. We must live in an organized state, obey its laws, and serve the interests of the community.

Hegel's stress on the state as the highest unit led on to social-welfare protests against extreme individualism (see particularly T. H. Green in England). When Hegel glorifies the State, we should understand that he uses the term in a rather special way. In his system it is the dialectical synthesis of family and civil society, or, in his jargon, the union of universal and particular in the "concrete universal." In more commonplace terminology, this means that the State (as an ideal) is the highest development of the community, the place where a perfect society would find its completest expression. Hegel, in brief, does not conceive of the state as a leviathan standing over against its subjects, ordering them about, and intimidating them; it is more like Rousseau's General Will—the common rational spirit of the whole community—made manifest. This view appealed to moderate liberals because it claimed not to sacrifice the individual completely to the state; nor was it socialistic. According to Hegel, it is only as a citizen that the individual becomes wholly free and possessed of rights. This feeling for association against individualism, though with a conservative cast, made Hegel a significant founder of the more moderate movements of social reform. And if Hegel was a conservative, his disciples do not show it. While some went to the Right and some to the moderate center, the "young Hegelians," including Karl Marx and Ludwig Feuerbach, became materialists and atheists. Belinsky, too, was a socialist or anarchist.

Hegel was apparently a Christian, but Kierkegaard, the Danish pastor who is now considered the chief founder of modern Christian existentialism, accused him of devitalizing Christianity by rationalizing it and making it abstract. There is some truth in this. Hegel's new version of scholasticism made reason and religion coincide, but the highest synthesis is philosophy; Christianity is the symbolic or mythical mode of expression presumably meant for minds incapable of philosophy. Christianity is done the honor of having its representations agree with Hegel's philosophy, though in a slightly inferior manner. If many Christians had their faith confirmed by finding that it agreed with the most advanced philosophy, others like Kierkegaard resented the relegation. One could easily, with Feuerbach and Marx, forget about religion and take the philosophy alone. Hegel was closer to the atheism of Marx than he may have realized. One finds, for example, that in Italy, Hegelianism was adopted by the anticlericals and laicists. The state represents the highest ethical ideal and is above the church, they held. The Roman Catholic Church, when in 1864 it produced its great Syllabus of Errors or list of modern heresies, included Hegelianism as a form of anticlerical liberalism. Actually, Hegel excluded religion from the historic sphere, regarding progress as social and political, not religious; in sharply separating private religion from public, political matters, he was in a traditional Lutheran scheme.

Hegelianism exerted so strong an appeal in good part because it was a complete system, an organic whole, an exceptionally unified, "total" philosophy. It was the first of several such in the nineteenth century—Comte's was another, then Marx's and Spencer's. Of these at least one, Karl Marx's, owed its basic traits to Hegel. It was an evolutionary system, thus incorporating the nineteenth century's most characteristic point of view. By comparison with Kant, the evolutionary or historical element stands out; Kant had failed to see, Hegel thought, that reason is not static.

Hegel's remarkable system of rational metaphysics based on historicism and dialectical evolution was hard to overlook; some have hated it, regarding it more as the scandal than the glory of the century, but like Marxism, its lineal descendant, it demanded attention and commanded allegiance because of the boldness of its stance as a complete reconstruction of human knowledge.

At the end of the century there was a decided reaction against the rigorous monism of Hegel's system. William James thought it a stuffy house with not enough air in it. In our time the "historicism" of Hegel, insofar as it meant a closed and deterministic system, has been assailed.[6] The enormous influence of Hegel is evident as much in his opponents as in his disciples. In protesting against Hegel, two giants of unorthodoxy in his time created movements of future significance: Schopenhauer and Kierkegaard, both of whom reacted against Hegel's cosmic rationalism and optimism to produce ideas of the irrational (Schopenhauer's "Will," a blind striving cosmic force) and of completely undetermined freedom (Kierkegaard's individual existent person). Today Kierkegaard's "existential" religion is more popular than Hegel's rationalized religion. But Hegel's vision of an organic rather than a mechanistic universe was prophetic, and his stress on process, evolution, development, has been basic to the modern mind. His influence can hardly be overestimated. Moreover, there has recently been a significant revival of interest in Hegel, chiefly on the Left.

Another novel and attractive implication of the many-sided Hegelian structure may be mentioned. In effect, very nearly, God is humanity, according to this philosophy—not the individual person, but humanity collectively in its historical evolution. The historic process is "the march of God through the world." The world spirit grows and develops through human history. From this one may derive a new explanation of the riddle of the human situation, with its lofty aspirations and its frustrations. Each of us possesses something of this universal humanity, whose nature is nothing less than potential perfection, the self-realization of the world. But each of us also is a particular person, bound to one time and place, destined to make only a tiny contribution to the splendid temple of reason that will someday be finished. Hence our soaring aspirations and our limited achievements. We can nevertheless do what our talents permit us to do in the confident knowledge that it does fit somewhere into the great plan. Nineteenth-century optimists who believed in progress found that Hegelianism fitted comfortably into their scheme of things.

---

[6]Karl Popper, in the important but argumentative book *The Open Society and its Enemies,* Vol. 2, 4th ed., 1962—the work of a modern philosophical analyst with a bias toward liberalism—attributes practically all the sins of the modern world to Hegel's baleful influence (pages 25–80). L. T. Hobhouse blamed the First World War on him!

Hegel inspired or reinforced a large amount of nineteenth-century nationalism of the messianic sort; perhaps a less appetizing outgrowth than some of the others—we can see what Hobhouse meant when he accused Hegel of encouraging war. As an example, Count August Cieszkowski (1814–1894), Polish nationalist and Hegel disciple, used the Germans (Herder as well as Hegel) to support his vision of a great Slavic state that would adorn the next and perhaps last stage in the evolution of mankind. Hegel's influence in Russia and other parts of eastern Europe was strong for a generation—about 1835 to 1860—and contributed somewhat to the great nationalist myth known as Pan-Slavism. Historicist messianism throve on a simplified version of Hegel, who taught that history has a goal toward which all is tending; and nationalism did too, since the philosopher had seen "historic peoples" and their states as the vehicles of historical destiny. This sort of Hegelian historicism is obviously deeply laid within the popular modern mind. In this study of a twentieth-century American politician, Henry A. Wallace, Dwight Mac-Donald noted the theme of an "American hour" in world history, prepared for by all previous happenings. God has brought forth the United States in due time to do His bidding in the cosmic drama of historic humanity. Each nation might, gratifyingly, find the god of history on its side.

To a generation confused by many new ideas and by drastic political and social change, Hegel offered an apparently satisfying unity that found a place for everything and discerned the order behind the baffling facade of events. Faced with the question of whether liberals, conservatives, or socialists were right, the Hegelian could answer, all are— each in its place and time, each a part of the final synthesis. Confronted by revolutions and counterrevolutions, wars and political turmoil, the Hegelian could hold that all these occurrences are part of a necessary pattern. Hegel also found a place for both reason and Christianity, which many had seen as locked in mortal conflict: just different ways of stating the same truth. Hegel's synthesis, which seemed to harmonize all things, was almost as impressive as that which Thomas Aquinas had offered at the peak of medieval civilization in the thirteenth century. It proved equally fragile. Some found it distressingly abstract, a mere house of words. Others converted it to materialism and atheism by discovering that there was no need to posit Hegel's spirit underlying the natural world. Still others used the idea of historical destiny to justify all kinds of revolutionary and nationalistic causes.

Hegel influenced practically all schools of thought in Germany, as well as British idealist philosophers of the later nineteenth century such as F. H. Bradley and Bernard Bosanquet who were dominant in the British universities for some time, the Italian philosophers Benedetto Croce and Giovanni Gentile, and many others. Socialists made use of

him, historians knelt at his shrine, both the religious and the antireligious seized on pertinent aspects of his thought for their purposes. He lent
authority to conservatives and radicals, reformers and foes to reform.
His ability to be all things to all people is perhaps an indictment of Hegel
as well as tribute to him.

Karl Marx in his youth belonged to a group known as the Young
Hegelians, who were all left-wing exponents of a modified Hegelianism.
Among these, Bruno Bauer and David Strauss showed a decided interest
in Biblical and religious studies—Strauss's critical biography of Jesus
being one of the century's most sensational books—while Ludwig Feuerbach treated the theme of religions in a more general way. All the Young
Hegelians believed that Hegel's thought represented the most advanced
creation of the human mind thus far. But they thought it needed restatement, a very sweeping sort of restatement, in a sense really the
abandonment of Hegelianism. For Hegel had been wrong in his
idealism. He should be turned over, "set right side up." Reality is actually
material, and ideas are only a projection of physical being. The idea of
God had been invented as a symbol for human ideals and goals; as such
it served a useful purpose, but may now, at a higher stage of self-
awareness, be abandoned. Theology becomes anthropology, in Feuerbach's words. We realize that "politics must become our religion": The
goal of our perfection through our own social action is to be explicitly
recognized.

Feuerbach was far from a great philosopher, but this somewhat
vulgar materialism, atheism, and (in the specifically modern sense)
humanism was extremely significant. Large numbers of moderns have
accepted it as their "philosophy." August Comte was, even then, pointing
out that the nineteenth century had witnessed the birth of the Positive
Age, replacing the ages of Theology and then Metaphysics. The new
God was materialistic science, the only goals practical, mundane ones.
The Absolute as well as God would have to be relegated to the realm of
fairy tales. It is remarkable that Hegel led in this direction, but in fact it
was possible to stand him on his feet in this way. (Hegel himself pointed
out that science was relegating art as well as religion to the sidelines in
the modern age.) Marx was the most celebrated of those who did so,
after Feuerbach.

The young Marx's intellectual life was immersed in the debates of
the Young Hegelians. He tended to define his position in criticism of
them, as for example in *The Holy Family* (1844) versus Bauer, and in the
Theses on Feuerbach (1845). In his early manuscripts, which remained
unpublished until recently, he also does incessant and rather obscure
battle with Hegel's *Phenomenology*. Marx remained strongly under the
influence of Hegelian concepts even as he struggled to go beyond the
master. Hegel, it should be noticed, instilled in his followers a desire to

surpass him just because they were his disciples. Had not Hegel taught that the dialectic goes on, and each age has its own statement to make? Hegel had made the ultimate statement for his generation; the next generation must say something else, something beyond this. The Hegelians of the years after the master's death in 1831 tended to think that he had brought pure philosophy, speculative thought, as far as it could go. What remained? To translate this thought into action, to change the world and not just understand it. The age of metaphysics had ended with Hegel, the age of humanism had begun.

The element of political ideology, then, in the seemingly metaphysical system of Hegel, becomes evident. The great object of knowledge is history, and especially political history; at the end, by a slight alteration in Hegel, we decide with Feuerbach that "politics must become our religion." The sole aim and interest of humanity is to discover and create the good society on earth, with the aid of scientific intelligence.

SOCIAL ROMANTICISM AND THE REVOLUTION OF 1848

The ideas of Fourier, Saint-Simon, and Owen, formulated during the 1820s, enjoyed considerable popularity in the 1830s and 1840s and were joined by others. The disciples of Saint-Simon tended to split up, but the movement nevertheless went on. As their 1830 manifesto stated, they rejected the equal division of property and accepted the "natural *in*equality of man," thus favoring a hierarchical society; but "each is placed according to his abilities and rewarded according to his works" by planning and coordination, property being held by the state and not individuals. (The one-time secretary of Saint-Simon, August Comte, who will be dealt with separately, probably cannot be classed as a socialist, though the influence of Saint-Simon remained on his thought in the form of a stress on authority and the subordination of individuals to the state.)

The most popular French political tract of the 1830s was probably the *Paroles d'un croyant* by La Mennais, or as he now called himself (the change is significant of a democratic shift) Lamennais. We may recall him as an enthusiastic disciple of the "reactionaries" a decade earlier. He now became an equally enthusiastic social democrat. The change is not so great as we might imagine, for most French socialists acknowledged some debt to Maistre and Bonald. The "words of a believer" came from one who was a Catholic priest but was not long to be, for the Church would not tolerate his left-wing views. His romantic eloquence made him the individual of the hour and enthusiastic followers proclaimed Lamennais the new messiah, while Metternich, the statesman in charge of keeping down revolutionary discontent in Europe, grumbled about "this anarchist... fool... abject being." No work had more to do with the revolution of 1848. In this and ensuing books, the Breton priest expressed a lyrical, if vague, awareness of a "tremendous revolution going on at the heart of human society," a revolution that was the march of "the peoples" and would produce a "new world." He denounced "wage slavery" and castigated the rulers of society for neglecting their responsibilities to society. "If you reject peaceful reform you will have reform by violence." The obvious British counterpart to Lamennais is Thomas Carlyle, whose electrifying prose called attention to the "social question" in an enduring classic, *Past and Present* (1843).

Lamennais and Carlyle represented a blending of romanticism with social reform in what has been called "social romanticism" or "political Messianism." The late romantic writers, Victor Hugo, Lamartine, and George Sand, were caught up in it. As David O. Evans observes in his little book on *Social Romanticism in France 1830–1848*, "*Les Misérables* was the culmination of a massive literature of social novels and dramas which flourished between 1830 and 1848," including those of Sand and Balzac, from which Friedrich Engels said he had learned more than from all historical and economical treatises put together. The ground was thus prepared for that remarkable revolution of 1848 of which the leaders were a poet, Lamartine, and a social theorist, Blanc. As one might expect from romantic poets and novelists, the spirit was rather more emotional than logical. The mood was messianic or apocalyptic; the "people" were on the march, tyrants trembled on their thrones or in their counting houses. A splendid new world would dawn after brave deeds by popular heroes and heroines had overthrown them. The French Revolution, heretofore unpopular, was rehabilitated by historians like Michelet and Quinet, not to speak of Louis Blanc. Had there not been something splendid, if terribly splendid, about that volcanic upsurge of the people? They had announced their arrival with an explosion that signaled the great revolution of modern times, the democratic revolution.

Lamartine and Hugo were not really socialists, as 1848 was to make clear. Under the impact of that event, a split developed between the republicans or democrats and the working-class socialists which helped doom the revolution. Prior to 1848 these two strains mingled in a chorus of slogans about social justice, popular rights, and the march of the masses. The young romantics made a cause out of Victor Hugo's defiance of formal literary conventions in his 1830 play *Hernani*, defending it against the taunts of traditionalists in a famous theatrical riot of that year. Romantic bourgeois youth was soon firing at broader targets. "Bohemians" with long hair and bizarre clothing created a surrogate society in the 1830s, featuring hard drugs, little magazines, spitting on the flag, unconventional morals, and much cursing of the bourgeoisie from which they sprang (nothing much has changed in a century and a half). In 1835, following an insurrection among the artisans in the silk industry of Lyon, the French government held a "monster trial" of 164 radicals, mostly young, and convicted 121 of them. A land weary of revolutionary bloodshed gave them little sympathy at that time, but the ferment continued.

In England there was something similar, if more restrained, befitting the national temper. There was nothing restrained about the Scotsman Carlyle or such working-class speakers as the Irishman Fergus O'Connor. The novels of Dickens and Mrs. Gaskell contain their share of social protest. The Chartist movement was a more impressive organization of the actual working-class people than anything in France. But Britain already had its liberal reforms and a national Parliament with deep roots in the national tradition. The great debate of the 1840s turned on the relatively concrete issue of free trade versus protection. During this struggle to repeal the tariffs on grains, Richard Cobden and John Bright organized the Anti-Corn Law League and carried political debate down to the grassroots level. Great Britain avoided revolution in 1848 and proceeded toward social democracy at a more moderate pace.

Democracy might now be observed in relatively successful operation in the United States of America. In the mid-1830s Alexis de Tocqueville returned from his visit there to write *Democracy in America,* one of the political classics of the century. Countless others went to America and wrote travel books, but Tocqueville's was a uniquely philosophical mind. He wrote against the background of a considerable discussion of democracy in France at this time. And he brought to the task the new ideas of a social-scientific methodology as proposed by Bonald, Saint-Simon, and Comte. Consequently, *Democracy in America* is a good deal more than a travel book; it is a work of systematic sociology. Highly praised at the time, it has retained a considerable repute ever since. It is a truly objective work, not a partisan one: Tocqueville was amused to find that some thought that he had written against democracy and others that he had written for it. A liberal noble, Tocqueville reminds us a great deal of Montesquieu; he had learned from Burke, too, as well as many others. The integrity, moderation, and wisdom of a book that nevertheless sparkles with ideas has earned high standing in the literature of politics and society.

The question in which Tocqueville was really interested was whether this new thing, democracy, which his historical sense told him was inevitably on the way, could be reconciled with liberty and with traditional European civilization. Was it a triumph of barbarism from within, a revolt of the blind masses certain to destroy culture? Would it lead to a new despotism? These things had been said. The social scientist in Tocqueville wished to test them by a method more fruitful than mere theorizing. So he went to the United States and observed.

Social scientist that he was, Tocqueville was not free from ideological influences. As a moderate, a liberal, he wished, he said, both to "allay the terrors" of the reactionaries and "calm the ardor" of the radicals. Perhaps Tocqueville found in America what he wanted to find—as it has been alleged. The charge is only partly true. He did find a mixture of good and bad. For example, Tocqueville allayed the fears that democracy meant wild instability, dictatorship, destruction of property, and irreligion. Here in the democratic United States, property was safe, religion flourished, and there was no fear of violent revolution. Give power to the people and they will become responsible, Tocqueville implied; democracy has its own safety valves. On the other hand, he found science and literature mediocre in the United States and the uncommon individual intimidated by the mass, and he feared that this was a law of democracies; he was among the first to complain about democratic conformism and the "tyranny of the majority." To some of his contemporaries in Europe he apparently taught that democratic society destroys liberty. But in the main his temperate and sympathetic appraisal helped the republican cause in France. Tocqueville himself, though by no means an egalitarian, served in the short-lived Second Republic born of the revolution in 1848 and never learned to love the despot who ended its life, Louis Napoleon. Liberty was Tocqueville's passion. He loved England, as Montesquieu had, and John Stuart Mill was one of his friends; thus he seems close to British liberalism.

His moderate note was unusual in France in the 1830s and 1840s. Among the new socialist voices of the 1840s was Pierre-Joseph Proudhon, himself a man of the people, whose chief message was to abolish unearned increment and unproductive property: "What is the producer? Nothing. What should he be? Everything." An enemy of statism, Proudhon suggested "mutualism" or farmers' and workers' cooperatives as the answer to economic injustice; he was an ancestor of the anarchist-syndicalists, and perhaps also of the populists and Henry George agrarians. But his revolutionary spirit appeared in his advocacy of class war, his call to the working classes to rise up and throw off their chains, as the *Communist Manifesto* of 1848 put it. Marx later ridiculed Proudhon for the crudeness of his thought, but he influenced Marx, being in the 1840s and 1850s the best known of the radical socialist theoreticians. Proudhon had no faith in democratic processes as such; "social reform will never come out of political reform, political reform must emerge from social reform." "Universal suffrage is the materialism of the Republic." But Proudhon seldom stayed long in one position; he seemed "determined that none should share his views." Marx was right about the shoddiness of much of Proudhon's thought. But he possessed a style, an aptitude for phrase-making, along with a burning sense of social injustice.

Paris was discontented and bored with the prosaic "bourgeois monarchy" of Louis-Philippe, which had come into existence in 1830. Though liberal enough to permit free speech and encourage education, its constitution denied representation to all but a few and its social philosophy was largely laissez-faire liberalism—its motto, "enrich yourself." The dominant class was the "grande bourgeoisie." In the cafes of Paris lesser men listened to Proudhon's call to revolution. When the revolution came he disagreed with it; "they have made a revolution without ideas," he declared. He laughed at the panacea of the influential socialist Louis Blanc: state-owned factories. To Proudhon the root of the matter was demand, not production. Leave the working class without adequate purchasing power and the state factories would stagnate quite as much as privately owned ones for want of a market. Proudhon's was the classical statement of the underconsumption theory of economic depression.

Proudhon's *What is Property?* (1841) had been preceded by Louis Blanc's *The Organization of Labor* (1840). At this time also, it may be recalled, Etienne Cabet's *Voyage to Icaria* appeared, with its message of utopian communism. Blanc, an indefatigable writer, produced a stream of works in these years, including a laudatory history of the French Revolution and a *History of Ten Years,* in which he cataloged the sins of the capitalistic Orleanist regime. Blanc stood for a blend of Jacobin democracy and socialism that perhaps lacked logical consistency but was proclaimed with great eloquence; it rejected Saint-Simonian authoritarianism in favor of a more democratic political order, yet was socialist in its attacks on private property in the means of production. Blanc did not, like Proudhon, call for violent revolution, or, like the intrepid Blanqui, socialist working-class leader, seek to practice it. He evidently believed that the people would freely vote for socialism if given a chance. The results of the elections of 1848 severely disillusioned him, and he appears then to have discovered for the first time that France was a country of peasants and not of Parisian left-wing journalists. At that time he retreated somewhat from democracy. Later, however (he lived well into the Third Republic), he continued to support a moderate, democratic, and "gradualist" socialism against Marxists and Anarchists.

Among other rebels and prophets who led the way to 1848, there was the Italian Giuseppe Mazzini, a passionate Genoese who as a youth joined the *Carbonari* and vowed his life to the cause of national liberation for Italy under a popular government. He spent most of his life as an exile in London but returned during the revolutions of 1848 to take part in those tumultuous events, presiding over the short-lived Roman Republic of 1848 to 1849. His prolific and eloquent pen gained him a place as one of the chief writers of this time and a great leader of the Italian *risorgimento,* which from 1860 to 1861 became the most exciting movement in Europe. If the gallant soldier of liberty, Garibaldi, was the most popular figure of the Italian national political revival, Mazzini was its spiritual leader. Belonging as it does to the generation of "social romanticism," the eloquence that so bedazzled his contemporaries may seem bombastic and hollow today, though on the whole it wears better than most of that sort. Mazzini, with Louis Blanc, belonged among the democratic socialists. Hostile to liberalism because it was too negative and selfish, he affirmed the value of both democracy and "association." He was equally against class war and individualism; all people should be brothers and sisters, there should be solidarity, and there should be religion, a religion of humanity. Mazzini quickly quarreled with Marx and Bakunin in the First International; he was too radical for Italian liberals, who fought him for control of the *risorgimento,* but too conservative for the left-wing proletarian rebels. Like Blanc, he called himself a republican and obviously derived from Rousseau and the French Revolutionary tradition; he was an Italian Jacobin. (Northern Italy had been as eager for the French Revolution as France; Mazzini's father had lived under the Ligurian Republic.) But his stress on national liberation and a social-democratic *mystique* put him in the center of nineteenth-century ideology.

Lamennais, Blanc, Proudhon, and Mazzini supplied a good part of the fuel for the engine of revolution that roared down the track, only to crash in 1848. Broadly speaking, they formed a family of social protest with generous ideals, but they failed to agree, and their thought was often vague. These limitations must probably be held responsible in good part for the failures of 1848. Nevertheless the ferment of social thought in this generation must be recognized as a powerful force in modern Europe. It produced most of the ideas, in embryo, on which social reformers of all sorts have been living ever since.

But the experience of 1848, a year that began with democratic revolutions all over Europe and ended with the confusion and discomfiture of these revolutions, caused a temporary reaction against all forms of "social romanticism." In general, the sad failure of the revolutions of 1848 was like a large bucket of very cold water poured on the slogan-intoxicated men who had begun them so hopefully. All over Continental Europe the sobering up was much in evidence; people felt that there had been too many daydreams and vague formulae, too little precise thinking. The reaction was toward realistic means and limited objectives. Like all reactions, it went far in the opposite direction. The feeling spread that power alone counts, and practical methods of politics are also significant. It was a German (evidently Ludwig von Rochau) who coined the word *Realpolitik,* but the same idea could be found from one end of

Europe to the other. Thus 1848 was almost a repetition of 1789 in that the ideals and ideas that inspired it turned out to be too vague and were held to have caused more harm than good because of this flaw: zeal without knowledge. The counterparts of Rousseau and Voltaire were Proudhon and Mazzini; although with more of romantic fire, they had as little of concrete social engineering. If Bonald and Maistre had suggested a more realistic approach, it was swept aside because they were conservatives; if Saint-Simon demanded science, he had in reality supplied only ideology. Evidently much yet remained to do before that ideal human society could become more than a vision or dream. Again there was a reaction away from utopias.

Not until the 1880s did the socialist movement really revive; only in the 1860s did it show any spark of renewed life. "Social romanticism" and indeed romanticism of all sorts went out of fashion among men and women of letters. The success of the Italian national liberation movement in 1861 might seem to be an exception to this, but in actuality this miracle was the work of realists and moderates, not of Garibaldi and Mazzini. During the French Second Empire, when another Bonaparte arose on the grave of the Republic, the reigning intellectual system was the austerely scientific credo of positivism.

But it is also true that bourgeois liberalism of the "classical" type became less harshly dogmatic. It too had had its heyday between 1830 and 1848; the uncompromising features of the *grande bourgeoisie's* political and social outlook had contributed not a little to do with bringing on that outburst of resentment, the revolutions of 1848. After 1848 the suffrage was less restricted, despite the apparent failure of that revolution. Even Napoleon III was careful to have his mandate affirmed and reaffirmed from time to time by universal suffrage, which has never ceased to exist in France, whatever the regime, since its installation in 1848. Napoleon ran something of a welfare state; the realistic conservative Bismarck installed sweeping welfare measures in Germany. *Realpolitik* turned away from romantic visions of utopia, but it also turned away in some measure from the absolute dogma of laissez-faire, equally visionary.

Whatever the final verdict, this generation from 1815 to 1848 must be granted primacy in the modern Western world, perhaps repaying close study more than any other one by those who wish to understand present-day problems, dreams, and outlooks. These ideologies—liberal, socialist, nationalist, conservative—are still the basic value structures for most people in Europe and its offshoots.

3

Classical Ideologies of the Mid-Nineteenth Century: Mill, Comte, Darwin

The history of the human race is the history of growth.

FREDERIC HARRISON

If there is the mob, there is the people also. I speak now of the middle classes—of those hundreds of thousands of respectable persons—the most numerous and by far the most wealthy order in the community.

LORD BROUGHAM

Nothing exists in nature, is born, grows, multiplies except by struggle. It is necessary to eat and be eaten for the world to survive.

EMILE ZOLA

THE MID-VICTORIAN ERA

After revolution and romanticism receded in 1849, Europe entered upon a period which could well be described as the classical age of the nineteenth century. It was the mid-Victorian era, with all the phrase conveys: middle-class domination, comfortable bourgeois virtues, industrialism and free trade, political stability with an undercurrent of working-class distress. Victoria, the personification of the bourgeois virtues, reigned only in Great Britain, but Great Britain led the way into the industrial age, and in other places, notably Germany and the Low Countries, "Victorian" phenomena could be observed.

In Great Britain at mid-century, the classical school of economics reigned, its laissez-faire injunctions only slightly modified by the post-Ricardian economists; by 1846 it had converted most statesmen. Along with it flourished the popular ideology of self-help, making perennial best sellers of such books as Samuel Smiles's *Lives of the Engineers,* the stories of poor boys who made their way to wealth and glory: Faraday was a blacksmith's son, Stephenson a collier's, Telford a shepherd's. George Orwell, the modern essayist and novelist, remarked that his father had read only two books in his life, the Bible and Smiles's *Self-Help*—probably a typical Victorian intellectual history. The powerful London *Economist* assumed dogmatically and without any question that the sum of private interests "is always the same as the public interest." Free trade conquered in the struggle concerning repeal of the Corn Laws (grain tariffs) in the 1840s. While the factory laws removed the worst abuses of child and female labor, the country having been stirred by Parliamentary investigations into this cruel scandal, there still remained no protection for adult male workers against the law of the market in wages; the trades unions had barely begun their long march to respectability and power in 1850. (They did not receive legal recognition until 1870 and were not a strong factor before the 1880s.) With government as well as wages cheap in this incredible paradise of private enterprise by modern standards (no taxes, no labor unions!), industry and invention flourished, the nation seemed to grow rich, and British power, influence, and prestige were never greater. Victoria came to excel even Queen Bess as a long-lived symbol of greatness.

This was the heyday of the middle classes, whose peculiar ethos permeated the era. Recently arrived through hard work and frugality, the middle classes radiated respectability. This was the "age of improvement," as historian Asa Briggs has named it. Some have spoken of a "mid-Victorian combination of Puritanism and Enlightenment." French morals were frowned upon (witness the reaction to Swinburne), as were those practiced by English romantics and lords in the Regency era just prior to Victoria's accession. Such magisterial organs as the *Edinburgh Review* dispensed the dogmas of "free trade and tight morals," high intellectual seriousness, and a robust common sense ("masculine sanity," G. M. Young calls it), along with a deplorable lack of taste and imagination in the arts. Indeed, the arts were often declared to be a waste of time. The middle class doubtless shared some traits all over Europe, but Puritanism and individualism were not so prominent elsewhere. In regard to Puritanism, it may suffice to recall that over in Vienna, on the banks of the beautiful blue Danube, the bourgeoisie at this time built a culture marked by its music, gaiety, and charm. Nor could the French bourgeoisie ever have displayed that egregious prudery found among the British middle classes, who (so we are told) segregated the male and female authors on library shelves.

Victorian prudery must not be misunderstood as an anemic rejection of the sexual impulse, however. As Walter E. Houghton points out, "The major reason why sex was so frightening to the Victorians was the glaring fact that . . . sexual license in England not only existed on a large scale but seemed to be increasing." The romantic cult of free love (Shelley, Byron) survived, and French socialism and bohemianism threatened from across the Channel. The Obscene Publications Bill of 1857 reacted to a large popular literature of pornography. The Victorians knew that sex was a potent force—in need of restraining rather than encouraging, Matthew Arnold observed. There was still a savage underworld of "dangerous classes" in Paris as well as London, respectable citizens thought, which it was best not to stir up. Dickens's Mr. Podsnap, whose standard in the publishable was whether it could bring a blush to the innocent cheeks of a "young person," might secretly sneak off to the company of one of London's scandalously numerous prostitutes. What later critics denounced as hypocrisy, the Victorians thought only common sense. The whole treatment of women, against which much of the twentieth century would rebel, later seemed the ultimate in hypocrisy; it was, in fact, as George Bernard Shaw noted, based on idealism:

> That sort of feeling that you must have something to adore, something to lift you up, gave them the curious notion that if they took the women and denied that they were human beings . . . if they set up a morality and a convention that women were angels, . . .[1]

they would then have a large congregation of angels to adore. And so if Shaw, as he relates, never knew until well into young manhood that women had legs, it was because the "angel in the house" was conceived of as belonging to a higher realm of being—some women, at least. It is well to remember also that the great crusade to gain equal rights for women—property rights in their own names, the vote, access to education—began in mid-Victorian times, above all with John Stuart Mill's essay on the subjection of women (1869).

The high seriousness and earnest moralism of the Victorians was a bond that stretched broadly from Samuel Smiles to Matthew Arnold, whatever other differences the merchant and the poet-intellectual had. The wish to edify and to improve, to overcome evil and to spread enlightenment, was at the bottom of it—no unworthy spirit, despite the

---

[1]G. B. Shaw, "Woman—Man in Petticoats," *New York Times Magazine,* 19 June, 1927. Regarding France, Theodore Zeldin in his *France 1848–1945,* vol. I (1973), Part II, Chap. 13, notes the "simultaneous idealization and repression" of women.

prudery into which it might stray. For all their blind spots, the British middle classes, strong and energetic, led the way to prosperity and success and wished to build a vigorous society in their own image.

On the other side of the picture, callousness, poverty, ugliness, and degradation caused Carlyle, Ruskin, and others to protest against the very foundations of this civilization, alleging it to lie in selfishness and materialism. Hazlitt had written that "the carriage that glitters like a meteor along the streets of the metropolis often deprives the wretched inmate of the distant cottage of the chair he sits on, the table he eats on, the bed he lies on." Shelley had burned with indignation at the factories of England and the suffering they imposed on the hapless creatures who labored incredibly long hours at work that was both body- and soul-destroying. Coleridge had declared that if society disclaimed all responsibility to the poor, as the economists and liberals preached, then the poor would feel no sense of belonging and would eventually rebel in a class war. In 1844 Disraeli wrote in his celebrated novel *Sybil* that there were indeed two nations in England, the rich and the poor, utter strangers to each other.

John Ruskin claimed that the ugliness of the factory towns, and the appalling lack of artistic sensitivity in the country generally, were a part of the social order, knit deeply into the outlook of the middle classes whose ideology was a blend of puritanism and utilitarianism, both absolutely hostile to all the arts. In *Unto This Last* (1860), Ruskin voiced an eloquent protest against the economics of irresponsibility and the social creed of selfish neglect—for which he suffered ostracism.

Dickens in *Hard Times* (1854) flagellated a society that had just finished congratulating itself, upon the occasion of the great Crystal Palace Exhibition, for its infinite progressiveness. It is a world made up of Bounderbys, greedy capitalists unscrupulously pursuing success, and Gradgrinds, who, aided by utilitarianism and political economy, have reduced life to statistics and forgotten its beauty. The city has become a place of loss of identity in the lonely crowd; the factory is a scene of ugliness and inhumanity; the bourse and marketplace erase human connections. And this society does not even deliver its one specialty, more and more material goods, for hundreds of thousands are in want and "hard times" may throw the whole economic system into confusion.

The protest voice, thundering indignantly like Carlyle's and Ruskin's and Dickens's, exposing the structure of exploitation as did, for example, Charles Kingsley's famous tract *Cheap Clothes and Nasty*, indicated a considerable Victorian social conscience. Carlyle became unbalanced in his hatred of the liberal orthodoxy and discredited himself by some of his later pronouncements, which have a fascist ring to modern ears. (Such were the abjurations against parliamentary "talking shops" and in favor of strong, silent dictators; the contempt for democracy; the worship of heroes; the scorn for humanitarianism, seen as shabby sentimentalism. The Tory socialist became more and more the Tory.) An incomparably vivid prose stylist, Carlyle was read by the Victorians, but they discounted his views as chronically wrong-headed, just as they thought their one-time favorite art critic, Ruskin, had gone mad when he began assailing the social order.

It would be unfair to suggest that the Victorians did nothing except let factory owners exploit the poor, and did nothing about social problems and evils. Apart from the fact that the great revolt against the negative state and social irresponsibility began in the 1880s in good part as a result of earlier spadework, there were heroic victories much earlier in some areas. In 1858, London confronted a grave crisis of public health threatening the very existence of the city, and surmounted it by purifying the Thames River. The appalling slums gradually receded before the advance of new avenues and street improvement, but this was less spectacular than the rebuilding of Paris in the time of the Second Empire (1851 to 1870), which also saw purification of drinking water and construction of sewerage systems. One cannot accept Ruskin's indictment of Victorian architecture at face value; even London was a bit more than "a ghastly heap of fermenting brickwork," all jerry-built for quick profits by stony-hearted Bounderbys. Today people yearn to preserve and restore many beautiful and solidly built Victorian buildings, whose craftsmanship in woodwork and masonry puts others to shame.

Eminent Victorian Thinkers

John Ruskin began as a student of architecture, making himself the Victorian oracle on this subject and prophet of the Gothic Revival with *The Seven Lamps of Architecture* and *The Stones of Venice* (1849 to 1853). He believed that all great art comes from a sound society; the Gothic, he thought, stemmed from the free medieval craftsworker not yet a degraded appendage of the machine. Ruskin carried on Carlyle's fierce hatred of modern industrialism and unregulated capitalism. Shaw said that Ruskin's jeremiads made Karl Marx sound like a Sunday School teacher. He increasingly thundered at modern soullessness and destruction of beauty; "we manufacture everything but men." In his later years he tried to create medieval orders dedicated to social service. With a prose that had the power to move people, he stimulated and influenced an incredible number of successors: William Morris and British socialism, Tolstoy, Proust, Gandhi, Frank Lloyd Wright. The historian of the Manchester School (W. D. Grampp) credits Ruskin with doing more than any one else to discredit and destroy the old laissez-faire creed. A little mad in his old age, he launched his diatribes like an Old Testament prophet and was increasingly ignored, but he seared the souls of a dedicated few. His stature today is recognized and his reputation as a great Victorian secure. Few have so influenced certain aspects of the modern mind.

Another eminent Victorian critic of society, Matthew Arnold, was a poet and critic who also branched off to political and social thought. Hardly a popular writer, he tremendously affected literate England, and no one better carried on the grand traditions of European culture in an era of bourgeois philistinism. He preached no panacea, but like John Stuart Mill aimed at a "certain temper of mind"—a civilized mind, broad, intelligent, critical, refined. Civilization, he reminded his progress-enchanted Victorian readers, does not consist of material things and mere numbers; it is a development of intellect and taste. In *Culture and Anarchy* (1867), Arnold rejected anarchy in cultural matters and asked for use of the state to promote the arts and letters. Like the French esthetes by whom he was much influenced, Arnold looked largely to literature for salvation: "The best poetry will be found to have a power of forming, sustaining, and delighting us, as nothing else can." The barbarians and Philistines of industrial Britain might, he sometimes thought, be converted to sweetness and light. Though savagely critical of their taste and manners, Arnold admired the energy and curiosity of the middle classes and did not entirely despair of their conversion. Arnold essentially upheld an ideal of high culture—the best of the great Western tradition from Homer to Baudelaire—as best he could in a time of cultural decay, as he saw it. No one felt more keenly the decadence of the modern, with its "sick hurry and divided aims," or longed more for some kind of healing faith to cure the disease of modern skepticism. He also besieged the parochialism of the English from his position as connoisseur of world literature, aware of the value of the modern European greats (German as well as French—Goethe and Heine were among his favorites) as well as of the ancient classics.

If Matthew Arnold, perhaps the most civilized of all the Victorians, was a critic of the narrowness of the bourgeoisie, the "philistinism" of the middle classes as well as the crudities of the landed gentry, the fact is that almost all the greater Victorian writers were critics of their society. The charge of complacency will not stick against Tennyson and Browning, the great Victorian poets, though they have been accused of it.

The most celebrated and symbolic thinker of mid-Victorian England was John Stuart Mill. His early career may be familiar to many from his well-known *Autobiography*. Brought up in the strictest Benthamite discipline, he rebelled and turned to Wordsworth and Coleridge for relief. His searching essays on Bentham and Coleridge reveal the patient catholicity of his fine mind, looking for the value in each figure while peeling off the dross. He became interested in Comte, finding in his discipline and social sense a corrective to British individualism, though there was much in that Frenchman he could not stomach. Indeed Mill, who lies buried with his wife at Avignon, always owed much to the French, something to be remembered when one sees comments on his "typically British" philosophy. He read the novels of Dickens; he formed a firm friendship with Carlyle for a time. Tocqueville's great work on democracy attracted him; Kant and Hegel mostly repelled him, being too metaphysical for Mill's essentially positivist mind. In the long run the mark of Bentham prevailed: Mill was essentially the rationalist and liberal. But his thought has been summed up as a series of compromises, and no nineteenth-century thinker read more widely and sympathetically than Mill.

What compromises did Mill suggest? Empiricist and positivist in his philosophy, he refused to say with the Kantians (as he construed them) that the laws of thought are merely mental categories; he held them to exist objectively, and he prepared a systematic treatise of inductive logic. A classic defender of the liberty of the individual, he showed some sympathy to Comte and French socialism up to a point; fearing the element of compulsion that lurks in every socialist scheme, he approved voluntary cooperation. In his famous textbook on the *Principles of Political Economy,* his foundation was individualistic capitalism, yet he was prepared to entertain exceptions to the rule wherever a sound case could be made—and the exceptions, it has been noted, grew with every edition of the *Principles,* so that Mill has been claimed as an ancestor of English socialism (Fabian). Skeptic in religion, near the end of his life he felt the bankruptcy of "scientism" and edged cautiously toward belief in a finite God; at any rate he recognized the human need for religious experience. He had always been willing to temper the narrower individualism of the Benthamites with some of Coleridge's feeling for the community. Doubting sometimes about democracy because of his love for liberty, he believed the strongest argument for it to be that it is a process of education; Mill always remained the optimist, feeling perhaps that all were potentially as rational as himself. British empiricism was deeply engrained in him, and a part of that tradition was an openness, including Locke's doctrine of a malleable human nature (Mill believed this strongly) and Hume's dislike of dogmas. He remained resolutely open-minded all his life, and thus has seemed the classic "liberal."

His strongest hatreds were of censorship, intolerance, conformity—anything that interfered with individual liberty. His best-known work, the essay *On Liberty* (1859), to which his wife, Harriet, contributed much, is the classic argument for the maximum of individual liberty. "The only purpose for which power can be rightfully exercised over any member of a civilized community against his will is to prevent harm to others. His own good, either physical or moral, is not a sufficient warrant. He cannot rightfully be compelled to do or forbear . . . because in the opinion of others to do so would be wise or even right." (Mill stressed that this was in a *civilized* community; "barbarians" would do best with an enlightened despot.) The goal and purpose of civilization, the only end worth striving for, was to Mill the complete development of the individual's powers to the highest possible point; he quoted Humboldt and remarked that "few persons, out of Germany" comprehend this, suggesting a Kantian or romantic source of his doctrine of freedom.

The argument of *On Liberty* then majestically unfolds for liberty of thought and discussion. The doctrine we suppress may be true, unless we assert infallibility for received opinion; or, if not true, it may contain *some* truth; or, even if it contains little or no truth, dissent is necessary to prevent intellectual stagnation; if we do not have to defend our creed, we will forget why we hold it.[2] Mill next makes it clear that under certain circumstances speech cannot be free, as when it is "a positive instigation to some mischievous act." Justice Oliver Wendell Holmes later observed that there can be no freedom to cry "fire!" in a crowded theater, and this is about what Mill meant. One always wonders when reading Mill how far agreement could ever be reached on the exact or even approximate boundaries of the limits he mentions. Holmes used the above principle to ban free speech in wartime by those who allegedly did not support the war, a ruling that others thought to be an outrageous violation of civil liberties. But Mill seemed to think that these boundaries can be made clear.

He believed at any rate that the liberty necessary to human dignity and growth was all too lacking in the modern world. He stressed the danger from the "tyranny of the majority," which had replaced regal despotism as a threat to liberty. "That so few now dare to be eccentric marks the chief danger of the time." Everything was becoming standardized, from shoes to ideas, and Mill complained, as so many have done since, of the mass culture that was stamping conformity and mediocrity on everyone. Reverting to his effort to defend the individual, Mill sought to meet the objection against his own criteria that, after all, everything we do *does* concern others. About all that Mill succeeded in doing was to reassert his position. When finished reading this extraordinary essay one is likely to feel that while Mill has presented an incomparable discussion of the issues and made an eloquent appeal for the free individual, he has not resolved the ancient dilemma of liberty versus authority, the individual against society. He has expressed a preference for the individual; but anyone who prefers to stress society's claims can easily turn most of Mill's formal arguments against him. (One such

---

[2]Mill's fellow Victorian, the great Roman Catholic John Henry Newman, adjusted his religion to liberalism by arguing, similarly, that heresy is necessary to faith. Unless error forces us to clear thinking, we do not perfectly know our creed.

Victorian answer to Mill was written by James Fitzjames Stephen, *Liberty, Equality, Fraternity.*) But this tract with its magisterial style and high seriousness remains one of the great Victorian period pieces.

Mill's social-economic views, while also fundamentally "liberal," were not complacent. He questioned in a well-known passage whether all the machinery thus far invented had yet lightened the toil of a single person, and said that "the restraints of communism would be freedom in comparison with the present condition of a majority of the human race." In *Principles* he defined property as what one has "produced by one's own exertions" (or received by legitimate gifts from one who did so earn it). But he held that the worker in the factory is not entitled to the whole of his or her produce, because machinery and materials are also involved. He often expressed sympathy for the ideals of socialism while doubting that it could work without compulsion in the present state of human nature. As noted, he was willing to make exceptions to the rule of economic individualism, and the list of these steadily increased.

But as the classic mid–Victorian liberal, Mill fought for such causes as votes for women (his essay *On the Subjection of Women* is almost as famous as *On Liberty*), Jewish admission to Parliament, freedom of the press, and freedom for the orators on soapboxes in Hyde Park, which he once saved by a filibuster when he sat as an independent member of Parliament. Mill may be credited with almost single-handedly giving liberalism the larger meaning it has since conveyed to the minds of Anglo–Americans, of "an attitude rather than a set of dogmas" (Theodore M. Greene)—the attitude of open-mindedness, dispassionate and skeptical consideration of all views, faith in a process, a method, a climate of opinion rather than in any particular creed. Liberalism had previously meant, much more nearly, the doctrines of atomistic individualism, hedonism, and also laissez-faire: the "economic man" of Adam Smith, the calculating pleasure-seeker of Jeremy Bentham. As such, it had been a somewhat narrow and barren ideology, if a potent one. Generous-minded individuals, filled with large visions of hope in human kinship, people such as Mazzini, for example, who despised what he knew as "liberalism," were repelled by it, declaring it to be selfish and materialistic. But Mill imparted to English liberalism his own catholicity and libertarianism, his steadfast faith in the free individual as something spiritually noble. "The saint of rationalism" has occasionally been seen as at heart a kind of narrow-minded fighter for his own particular set of preconceptions; but this view is unusual and the interpretation strained: Mill's typical spirit is quite the reverse. Under his influence even liberalism's deep-seated fear of the state could melt, for no dogma is sacred, only the individual is, and perhaps may be defended and strengthened by some forms of state aid.

Mid-century liberalism was represented in France, where it was weaker than in Great Britain but far from nonexistent, by Prévost-Paradol, whose *France Nouvelle* (1868) is a kind of Gallic *On Liberty*. (Both Mill and Prévost-Paradol, as a matter of fact, were influenced by Alexis de Tocqueville, perhaps the greatest liberal of them all and also French.) Prévost-Paradol regards democracy perhaps a bit more favorably than Mill, seeing in the people a check on Parliament, though he would have the popular will checked by an upper legislative chamber not popularly elected, an independent judiciary, and strong institutions of local government. This decentralization and pluralism carried echoes of the Ancien Regime in a France strongly centralized since Napoleon; antistatist and antisocialist, but libertarian and to a degree democratic (universal suffrage), Paradol's *New France* would indeed have been a new blend of ingredients in the French tradition and was not so far from what soon came into existence in the Third Republic. He wrote it in the last days of the Second Empire, when even Napoleon III was making his way toward the "liberal Empire." After his defeat in war and the subsequent shock to French pride, against all expectations a liberal-democratic republic arose from the ashes and gradually put down roots in France.

This tribute to the spirit of the age was matched by Great Britain's step in liberalizing the suffrage in 1867, after intensive debate and much lamentation from those who feared the death of liberty as well as stability at the hands of a mobocracy. These "Adullamites," as John Bright derisively christened them, led by Robert Lowe, contributed the most brilliant and enthusiastic speeches to the great debate. They had not changed from Macaulay's earlier liberal pronouncement that universal suffrage would be a new despotism "utterly incompatible with the very existence of civilization." So too in France, Benjamin Constant had believed that "unlimited popular sovereignty is an evil no matter in whose hands it is placed." The liberal statesman Thiers, a Voltairean, said that universal education would be like building a fire under a huge empty pot! But these early-century fears of the power of a still ignorant and brutalized plebs receded somewhat after mid-century. A new era of politics came in the wake of the Second Reform Bill, with new leaders and new issues. It was, for Britain, the decisive turning point of the century politically, the First Reform Bill of 1832 having not brought any marked change in the aristocratic tone and tenor of British political life. Whether the delicately balanced British political mechanism could really survive democracy, commentators as wise as Walter Bagehot honestly doubted; it was as much a gamble here as in France. But in both countries the feeling was that there could be no turning back, and for the rest of the century the task was adjustment to this potent force, mass democracy. Nothing influenced thought nearly as much.

Many dynamic processes were at work transforming Europe and the world in this epoch. Italy and Germany attained their national unification (1860 to 1871) in the most exciting developments on the Continent. Russia freed her serfs (1861) and began slowly to advance toward a modern industrial civilization. The 1860s was a crucial decade in modern history. The American Civil War, the Russian serf emancipation, the unification of Germany and Italy as national states, the fall of the Second Empire, and the beginning of the French Third Republic joined the 1867 Reform Bill in Britain as landmarks which shaped, or recorded the shaping, of their people's future.

Between 1858 and 1870 the intellectual landmarks were Darwin's *Origin of Species*, Marx's *Capital*, Bagehot's *English Constitution*, Arnold's *Culture and Anarchy*, Ruskin's *Unto This Last, Sesame and Lillies*, and *The Crown of Wild Olives*, Mill's essays *On Liberty* and *On the Subjection of Women* together with the late edition of *Principles of Political Economy*—to name only the most famous. The "higher criticism" came to England in 1860 with the publication of the jointly authored *Essays and Reviews*. Spencer, Acton, Newman were active; Dickens wrote his splendid last novels, George Eliot had become an oracle. The list could be much extended. These were vital times.

Spiritually, Europe was far from at peace; the surge of mid-Victorian prosperity carried in its wake grimmer phenomena, such as industrialism's bleak landscapes and exploited workers, or a bourgeois vulgarization of culture. It also brought the celebrated Victorian crisis of religious faith. But the classic age of the nineteenth century produced some classic ideologies. Among the most important figures were August Comte, Karl Marx, and Herbert Spencer, as well as Mill, all of whom might be described as synthesizers of social doctrine, creators of systems of secular ideology. Charles Darwin promulgated a scientific ideology for the age of science. Socialism, liberalism, and democratic nationalism assumed the stature of popular creeds by which people lived, with traditional Christianity's hold generally declining. Romanticism received a check, or at least a dilution. Literary realism and naturalism became prominent, bearing strong social themes—one is more likely to meet novels about working people or ordinary burghers than about exquisite souls or North American savages.

The mid-Victorian age has been categorized as an age of equilibrium. Its balance was between aristocracy and democracy, country and city, the old deferential, hierarchical society and a new one based, in a great Victorian's analysis (Henry Maine), on status rather than contract. In terms of ideas, the mid-Victorians were poised between ancestral religious belief and the new secularism of science and skepticism; it was their central preoccupation. Their great novelists—Dickens, Eliot, Trollope—were absorbed in the changing human relations of an industrializing and modernizing society. Their concern was indicated in the title of Thomas Carlyle's famous *Past and Present*. They did not always wish to leave past things behind and looked with some trepidation on an uncertain present, but on the whole they were optimistic. They had yet to look upon some of the more frightening features of the new society.

Standing out among the intellectual achievements of the era were social ideologies. The works of Comte, Marx, and Darwin hold rank as the classic statements of the middle third of the nineteenth century. These are the three giants of that century's noontime.

COMTE AND POSITIVISM

Comte's first writings go back to the early 1820s, when he was working under Saint-Simon; the crux of his positive philosophy appeared in six volumes between 1830 and 1842. Partly overlooked during the romantic revolutionary excitement of the 1830s and 1840s, positivism emerged, somewhat transformed, to become the reigning intellectual orthodoxy of the Second Empire from 1851 to 1870. Through John Stuart Mill principally, Comte's influence spread into England. It is recognized now as one of the leading systematic philosophies of the century. These vast edifices of thought that tried to subsume everything in one system seem incongruous today; they were the work of amateurs who assumed omniscience. But the intellectual energy that went into them cannot be denied, and for the nineteenth century they were the nearest thing there was to a new synthesis of knowledge. Basil Willey has commented that Comte was a nineteenth-century schoolman, basing his *Summa* "not on dogmatic theology, but on dogmatic science."

He did feel acutely the need for a complete reconstruction of ideas to replace the "intellectual anarchy" that was an aftermath of the French Revolution, a feeling he shared with Maistre, Saint-Simon, Hegel. As Saint-Simon's secretary he came to feel that the socialist count was too much in a hurry. He was right in seeking to found a new science of society based on the positive facts and scientific method, wrong in leaping to his conclusion about the shape of the new society. But when Comte branched out on his own, he showed himself quite as doctrinaire as Saint-Simon. Certainly the note of authority was strong in his plan for social reconstruction. Order must be reestablished in Europe, and having found the right foundation Comte proposed to make everybody accept it, by means of a suggested authoritarian social structure of which the high priests of positivism were to be the directors. Comte was as antiindividualist as any socialist, though he preferred to keep private property and the family. He was, if anything, more so. John Stuart Mill, who was attracted to some features of positivism, pronounced Comte's social plan "the completest system of spiritual and temporal despotism which ever yet emanated from a human brain, unless possibly that of Ignatius Loyola." Its hostility to representative government and approval of the Napoleonic dictatorship gave it its standing under the Second Empire.

Comte thought he had laid the foundations for social reorganization in his philosophy. The method appropriate to modern times is the scientific or "positive." Comte put forward his famous "three stages" theory of human development, according to which society passes from the theological to the metaphysical to the positive stage, based on the dominant mode of thought typical of each period. His history, like Hegel's, was highly speculative; it seems impossible to fit the actual facts into this scheme. For example, anthropologists no longer accept the progression within religion as postulated by Comte, from fetishism to polytheism to monotheism. Historians would have to point out among other things that science appeared as early as the ancient Greeks and metaphysics as late as Comte's contemporary Hegel. If the Comtean formula is reduced to the statement that primitive peoples are not capable of modern thought, it becomes little more than a tautology.

In brief, the same objections to so staggeringly oversimplified a scheme may be raised against Comte's as against other examples of this sort of thing: Marx's five stages, Hegel's three political epochs, and so forth.[3] Nevertheless, these "philosophies of history," if now outmoded, were exciting at this time, and the nature of their appeal may readily be seen. This was already discussed in connection with Hegel. Comte had at least this advantage over the German, that his historical system purported to rest on the facts and not on a speculative theory, and thus was attuned to the scientific age. So discriminating a critic as John Stuart Mill thought the three stages an illuminating and reasonably accurate key to the natural evolution of civilization.

Europe was now in the positive stage and needed to reconstruct its civilization on that basis. To Comte this meant, to repeat, a highly organized social order. The existing stage of liberty and laissez-faire he regarded as the interlude of anarchy between two eras, an anarchy he proposed to bring to an end as speedily as possible. The new scientific order would not be less organic and hierarchical than the older orders dominated by priests and metaphysicians.

Positivism means the method of observed facts handled with the use of hypothesis but refraining from any conclusions about the substantive nature of reality. Comte agreed with Kant that science studies only the phenomena. In his own words: "The human spirit, recognizing the impossibility of obtaining absolute ideas, renounces the search for origins and goals of the universe and the effort to know the innermost

---

[3]In Italy the "new science" of G. Vico, dating from the eighteenth century, came into its own at this time. Vico's phases of all civilizations were the religious (theocratic), heroic (aristocratic), and humane (democratic).

causes of things, in order to concentrate on discovery, by experiment combined with reason and observation, of the effective laws, i.e. their unchanging relations of succession and similarity." This was not exactly new, and Ernest Renan later reproached Comte with having said, "in bad French," what all scientific minds had known for two hundred years. This was not quite fair; it had really only been known widely and clearly since Kant, and Comte undoubtedly revealed some of its practical implications. He was perhaps philosophically more astute than those Marxists and others who assumed a dogmatic materialism which Comte knew was untenable: We are not justified in saying what the essence of reality is. (Marx held a low opinion of Comte, perhaps in part because he was a rival; "this is miserable compared to Hegel," he thought. Lenin would follow Marx in discarding positivism or phenomenalism for a direct-copy theory of sense perception which seems naive but permits a full-blooded materialism. The Marxists have seemingly felt there is something wishy-washy about positivism, inappropriate to revolutionaries.) Comte felt that we are not justified, either, in atheism, only in accepting the impossibility of having certain knowledge about God. Science is descriptive only; we should not even speak of "causes," only of "observable sequences."

In his *Course of Positive Philosophy,* Comte undertook to arrange the sciences in a logical order; his, obviously, was a mind delighting in tidiness. From the most abstract, mathematics, we proceed through astronomy, physics, chemistry, biology, and finally to the most concrete, sociology, a word of Comte's invention that has stuck in our vocabulary. Sociology, at last possible in the positive stage, steps forward to become queen and capstone of all the sciences. Of this last and greatest science Comte, of course, regarded himself as the discoverer.[4] It included what one should now call social psychology, economics, politics, history, and originally ethics. Later Comte put ethics and religion at the top, above even sociology, and gave the world the Religion of Humanity.

Comte seems hopelessly to have confused his multiple roles as social scientist, social reformer, and inventor of a new religion, though he believed he had unified them. As one of his British disciples, Frederic Harrison, observed, "Positivism is at once a scheme of Education, a form of Religion, a school of Philosophy, and a phase of Socialism." Could it be all these things at once, effectively? As a school of philosophy it has survived, though the English would be more apt to think of Hume as its founder. Sociology has survived as a discipline, but many others than

---

[4]It is to Comte's credit that he recognized that each of the sciences has to have its own methods; you cannot "reduce" social science to biological, or biological to mathematical. Certain sociologists who seem to wish to convert social phenomena into statistics are ignoring the warning of the founder of their science—that this sort of procedure often "disguises, under an imposing verbiage, an inanity of conceptions."

Comte have contributed to it, and its scope is much narrower than Comte conceived. The Religion of Humanity for a time showed a surprising vitality. Positivist societies were formed in England and France for the worship of great people; there were Comtean churches as far afield as Brazil. (Positivism had a considerable popularity in Latin America.) This was in George Eliot's mind when she expressed her poetic wish,

> O may I join the choir invisible
> Of those immortal dead who live again
> In minds made better by their presence.

Hero-worship had a considerable Victorian vogue in wider circles than Comte's disciples; quite evidently it "inherited the functions once fulfilled by a living Church" (Walter E. Houghton)—it was a substitute for religion. From Sam Smiles to Ruskin, many a Victorian author held up to admiration, for inspiration, the lives of great individuals. But as such, the Religion of Humanity fell far short of its author's expectations. Positivism served chiefly as a rallying point for the militantly antireligious.

In regard to positivism as "a phase of socialism," if defined as such, it never had much appeal. Comte's social utopia most closely resembled an iron dictatorship of social scientists, which is perhaps a fate to be avoided. In practice he sanctioned the ill-fated "democratic despotism" of Napoleon III. But it may be conceded that Comte did something to advance the cause of socialism by his criticisms of laissez-faire and by his belief that the social instincts evolve with humanity. The path of development is from selfishness to altruism, he taught.

Louis Napoleon's regime, established in 1851 on the ruins of the Second Republic, was much influenced by Saint-Simonian and Comtean ideas and undertook some interesting if inconclusive experiments in state socialism. Its economic and social policies were not failures, the collapse coming from an ill-advised foreign policy and defeat in war at the hands of Prussia. But its denial of representative government and full liberty caused its demise to be unlamented. Comte and most of his followers rejected individualism and democracy as the equivalent of anarchy.

If many of the details of Comte seem absurd, his central conception may be a valid intuition of modern humanity's problem. It is easy to agree with Comte that modern European civilization is "positivist." Is it possible to have a civilization on this basis, that is, without faith in God, without a metaphysic, with only science and technology, which supply our wants very well but give us no values, except to go on supplying more and more wants? Is modern society condemned to be "fissiparous," with no unity—soulless, with no values?

Many of Comte's successors were absorbed in just such problems. Positivism became extremely fashionable in France between 1850 and 1870. Its disciples included Emil Littré the lexicographer, Claude Bernard the psychologist, Hippolyte Taine, critic and historian, and Ernest Renan, one of the most brilliant and versatile French men of letters of the century. This group tended to reject Comte's dabblings in religion as an eccentricity and accepted only his scientific method. They distinguished themselves from atheists and materialists in the manner indicated: We cannot know ultimate things or essential qualities, only the observed phenomena. They evidently thought, however, that science does give certain knowledge, which a thoroughgoing phenomenalist (*vide* Hume) could hardly believe. They searched for a religion of science. Most of them finally became aware that science itself cannot give us values, ideals, goals. Insofar as we have these, they must come from outside science.

Renan, a passionate seeker, deeply troubled by his skepticism, looked long for a religion he could square with his scientific outlook. He rejected Christianity on the grounds of evidence (his *Life of Jesus,* his best-known work, shocked the orthodox all over Europe by its critical handling of the supernatural claims), and he rejected Hegelianism as too metaphysical. He occasionally came close to doing what some disreputable young poets were about to do, make a religion of art. Like Matthew Arnold, his British contemporary and perhaps kindred spirit, Renan felt the need for religious experience and suggested an esthetic equivalent. But a "religion of science" remained his lifelong quest and he failed to find it, ending in skepticism. He came closest to finding it in a positivistic version of Hegelianism, a theme of progress running through history which gives evidence of God.

In France after 1870 positivism suffered a decline. True, there were some eccentric survivors, especially the leader of the reactionary, nationalistic *Action Française* movement of the twentieth century, Charles Maurras, and also so vigorous a literary personality as Julien Benda. But strong forces in French thought rejected "scientism" and returned to metaphysics and religion in flat defiance of the positivists. (Compare Henri Bergson, or the Catholic revival, or more recently existentialism in literature, symbolism, and surrealism.) Intellectual France has never since felt much attraction for positivism, apparently having received a thorough immunization in the period from 1850 to 1870.

In Italy, positivism reigned as the leading philosophical school in the later part of the century, its chief systematizer being Roberto Ardigo. Comte's influence in nineteenth-century England (and the United States) was far from negligible. A British disciple was Richard Congreve, Oxford don in the 1850s, whose pupils included the leading publicist of English positivism, Frederick Harrison, and also E. S. Beesly. But Comte's influence extended to people who were not in any sense "disciples" but whose own independent thought received definite impulses from positivism: powerful voices such as Herbert Spencer and H. G. Wells. In Germany, Comte's direct influence was not great, but there was a parallel movement in the form of "back to Kant"—the positivist or phenomenalist Kant, in reaction against the romantic and Hegelian metaphysics; one might also include the materialism of the Young Hegelians. By and large, the period from 1850 to 1880 was uniquely "positivist."[5] Anglo-Saxon philosophy since World War I has been invaded by other forms of positivism (logical positivism) which owe less to Comte than to other sources, though there are affinities. This more recent theory in intellectual history will be handled later in Chapter 7.

In the broadest sense it might be said that modern Western civilization is positivistic in that metaphysical or religious modes are not congenial to it. This would be true of the average mind, the common person's, more so than of the intellectual's or artist's. Everyday life is so surrounded with the technological and the scientific, so extensively "rationalized," so conditioned to mechanical models and explanations that conscious mental life runs naturally and normally in grooves that can be called "positivist," that is, scientific, rational, nonmetaphysical, averse to mysticism or any truths not immediately verifiable by experiment or demonstration. For better or worse, that is the kind of culture in which most people live. "What grows upon the world is a certain matter-of-factness," Walter Bagehot wrote. He blamed it on business as well as science. So Comte, though far from inventing this feature or being the only thinker to express it, identified himself with a basic trait of modern civilization. And his belief in a tightly organized, hierarchical society ruled by the scientists may not miss by much the modern forms of totalitarianism.

LITERARY REALISM

The specific post-1848 atmosphere was, of course, highly conducive to a positivist reaction against the romanticism, idealism, and sentimentality of the previous generation. All over Europe, people in all walks of life felt what Napoleon III's minister, Emile Ollivier, expressed when he said, "We have collected in our hearts enough images, sentiments, aspirations, too many. . . . We must, to make these things useful, fill ourselves with practical facts." This was the generation of Cavour and Bismarck as well as of Pasteur and Darwin: the realistic, fact-minded

---

[5]James H. Billington in "The Intelligentsia and the Religion of Humanity," *American Historical Review,* July 1960, discusses the vogue for Comte among Russian intellectuals in the 1870s; the French positivist tended to supplant Hegel and to precede Marx as the leading influence from the West on Russian socio-political thought.

generation. The reaction extended into literature, which reacted strongly against romanticism by retreating to a realistic, even humdrum description of the ordinary. Romanticism had begun to fade by the 1840s and was almost fully out after 1850, despite lingering vestiges. In France the "art for art's sake" movement accused the romantics of sentimentality and sloppiness, demanded a greater sense of form and discipline, and also rejected romantic subject matter ("Deliver us from the Middle Ages!" cried Theophile Gautier, the leading spirit of this school.) "Art pour l'art" insisted upon more careful craftsmanship as well as less moralizing and philosophizing in literature. These French writers were disgusted with bourgeois society, retreated to a private world, became rebels and "bohemians," and thus began a literary attitude destined to carry on into the later period. Flaubert, the leading novelist of the 1850s and 1860s, practiced a severely objective, "scientific" approach to literature and dealt realistically with far from heroic people.

John Stuart Mill in 1873, as seen by the famous *Vanity Fair* caricaturist, "Spy." (*Vanity Fair*, March, 1873.)

The book of the hour was *Madame Bovary* (1857), which is among other things a savage satire on romanticism. Poor Emma, a lady of some spirit and intelligence, trapped in marriage with a clod in the provinces, dreams of Prince Charmings and a grand world but is led to destruction by her inability to grasp reality. Yet Flaubert includes a hatred of this stupid society in which Mrs. Bovary, a person of potential creativity, is trapped. She is Jude the Obscure and Tonio Kroeger and all the American "rebels against the village" of a half-century and more later. Flaubert, like the poet Baudelaire, was a bitterly alienated personality. For them art was a retreat from a most unsatisfactory world, an ivory tower: "Give me the highest one possible," cried Flaubert. A fierce hatred of the existing bourgeois society accompanied an extreme disillusionment with politics, associated with visionary romantic schemes and dreams. The thing about *Bovary* that most startled and upset Flaubert's readers was its amoralism. No edifying moral was drawn; it was a sad piece of life ending in tragedy and left at that. Even Sainte-Beuve complained that "the good is too much absent; not a single character represents it," while Ruskin contrasted such "foul" fiction, utterly demoralizing, with "fair."

The same lean, spare, detached style, using irony, "dry," shaped with fastidious craftsmanship, could be found in the poems of Baudelaire and in the writings of other great "realists" of this era such as Flaubert's friend, the Russian emigré Turgenev. Its detachment went with a mood of pessimism. The philosopher for this disenchanted post-1848 antiromanticism was, in its gloomier moods, the brilliant misanthrope, Arthur Schopenhauer. In his younger years Schopenhauer had challenged the great Hegel but failed to win adherents; in his old age, after 1848, he became fashionable. Philosophically, Schopenhauer asserted that the universe is not Hegel's Reason but is Will, a blind amoral striving expressed in us as wanting, desire, appetite. In seeing the world as an arena of power without meaning or purpose and in seeing reason as a tool of instinct, Schopenhauer's vision came close to Darwin's, though expressed in quite different terms. He recommended art as the only antidote to an intolerable existence—other than that extinction of the will to which Oriental philosophy aspired as the ultimate wisdom. In esthetic contemplation we can achieve a degree of disinterestedness and thus escape from the tyranny of the will. An interesting and highly readable philosopher, Schopenhauer appealed to this generation both in his elegant pessimism and in his estheticism.

The French writers shocked the English; but in Britain too there was an antiromantic reaction. The great Victorian novelists—Thackeray, Trollope, George Eliot—followed what might be called the cult of the commonplace; "the setting of tragedy moves to the abodes of the humble," observes Mario Praz, whose book on the Victorian novel is titled *The Hero in Eclipse*. A democratic art, celebrating the simple virtues of ordinary people, may be found here. The great poet Robert Browning examined humanity as it is. This Victorian literature differed as far as possible from the French in that it observed the Victorian reticence about sex and was highly edifying and morally earnest, as well as basically optimistic (though George Eliot was as aware of a crisis of faith as was Matthew Arnold). The exceptions, like the Francophile Swinburne, were scandals. But the same theme of realism may be seen in both, and it is in good part a reaction to the excesses of romanticism.

THE DARWINIAN REVOLUTION

The progress of science had continued at the end of the eighteenth century and into the nineteenth. More precise calculations on the moon,

Darwin and Evolution: A Contemporary View. (Washington, D.C., Library of Congress.)

planets, and comets perfected the Newtonian system. The discovery of the planet Uranus and the satellites of Saturn owed most to the German-born English astronomer, Herschel. Having measured accurately the distance to sun and moon and arriving at a notion of the fantastic distances of the stars, astronomers by the end of the century came upon the stunning fact of the existence of other *galaxies*. Herschel and Laplace formulated hypotheses concerning the origin of the stars and planets. The latter in 1796 summed up the *System of the World*, presenting it almost rhapsodically as a triumph of scientific method and a proof of the orderliness of nature.

There was also the breakthrough in chemistry. It is interesting that Coleridge, speculating about the influence of scientific ideas on other branches of knowledge, thought that the discoveries of Scheele, Priestley, and Lavoisier, "reducing the infinite variety of chemical phenomena to the actions, reactions, and interchanges of a few elementary substances," would affect philosophy and other fields of thought no less than Newtonianism had done in the eighteenth century. It did not quite prove so, but the influence was hardly negligible. It may be significant that Friedrich Engels, when illustrating the laws of dialectical materialism in the physical sciences, tended to use examples from chemistry.

The path of progress in electrical phenomena, from Volta and Galvani at the end of the eighteenth century to Michael Faraday's discovery of the generator in the 1830s, prepared for that mighty invasion of the life of individuals by electricity later in the century (electric lights, trolley cars, and so forth). But with all due regard for these celebrated achievements, destined to alter the lives of millions and contribute to their welfare, the most significant developments in the sciences in the nineteenth century, at least from the standpoint of thought in general, lay in the realm of biology, of life, especially its evolution. The Frenchman Pasteur has been called "the Galileo of Biology" because of his contributions to bacteriology and medicine; but in the history of ideas, by far the largest figure is Charles Darwin.

The road to Darwin's theory of biological evolution actually led through another science. The science of geology came into its own in the closing years of the eighteenth century. The Geneva geologist, de Saussure, seems to have been the first to use the term in 1779. It may be said to have attained full status in 1788 when the Scotsman, James Hutton, presented his "uniformitarian" theory. All during the eighteenth century there had been speculation about the meaning of fossils and about the earth, but it was often fanciful. The German mineralogist, A. G. Werner, proposed a hypothesis in 1780 that the earth was originally engulfed in ocean, which subsided, leaving behind the various formations, minerals, and fossils. This was the "catastrophist" or "neptunist" school, which had many followers, in part because it squared well with Biblical stories. Hutton then caused a sensation by proposing to account for the phenomena by the steady operation of the same natural forces over what then seemed immensely long periods of time. This was "uniformitarianism," and it stirred the wrath of some religious critics because it could hardly be adjusted to a literal reading of the Old Testament. Between the catastrophists and the uniformitarians a lively competition ensued—which is always good for the progress of a science. One would say today that both were partly right; but concerning the matter of the time element, Hutton was right, and this revolution in time constitutes on any reckoning one of the great changes in one's conception of this world. Coming between 1788 and 1830, this revolution is comparable in some ways to the seventeenth- and eighteenth-century revolution in astronomy: To the immensity of space, it has been well said, was added the immensity of time. "Oh, how great is the antiquity of the terrestrial globe," Lamarck, the French paleontologist, exclaimed. "And how little the ideas of those who attribute to the globe an existence of six thousand and a few hundred years duration from its origin to the present!"

There were those, during the period of conservative domination in England from 1794 to 1820, who attacked Hutton and his followers as dangerous subversives; so also Lamarck in France. But as data were collected, especially in the area of paleontology, rigid conservatism had to give way. The Reverend William Buckland, an Anglican clergyman, became a leading geologist and devised a sort of compromise between scriptural and geological views; he seemed to uphold the Deluge, yet the Bishop of Chichester noted his ambivalence in a witty paraphrase of Pope on Newton:

> Some doubts were once expressed about the Flood:
> Buckland arose, and all was clear as mud.

At this time geology, it has been said, became something like the favorite outdoor sport of the English upper classes; certainly it flourished there preeminently, though French scientists such as Cuvier and Lamarck made signal contributions.

It remained for Charles Lyell, from 1830 to 1833, to write the definitive geological synthesis. Lyell was a thoroughgoing uniformitarian, and he brushed aside religious objections as irrelevant. His geology formed an important part of the background for the biological discoveries of Darwin; "I feel as if my books came half out of Sir Charles Lyell's brain," Darwin once wrote. The time-revolution disposed of one obvious objection to an evolutionary theory, while increasing knowledge about fossils suggested its possibility. But Lyell was not an evolutionist.

He could not find in the fossils sufficient evidence for the transformation or progression of species, that is, one actually growing out of another. Indeed for many centuries this had been the invincible obstacle; it was a stumbling block to evolution comparable to that which the problem of motion had presented to the Copernican theory. As in the case of the slow acceptance of the Copernican hypothesis, one finds here that Biblical prejudices played a smaller part in delaying the evolutionary theory than is often suggested. The real difficulty lay in overcoming the dogma of constancy of species, which the biological evidence seemed to support. No examples of such change of species seemed to be found in nature; the evidence, notably the sterility of animal hybrids, showed the opposite.

Since the time of Aristotle, European thought had speculated about a "great chain of being," a logically complete range of life forms arranged in a hierarchy from lowest to highest. The chain ascending upward may suggest evolutionism to us, but it was always then conceived as a *static* hierarchy, a plan emanating from God's mind that was pleasing in its order and that was given for all time. Forms stayed as they were and did not change. The chain of being might be conceived as organically related, like a single great body or like an electrical circuit, and it could evolve into an evolutionary theory. But the traditional doctrine did not entertain any notion of evolution through time, of the transformation of species by gradual and natural means. Aristotle held that the world was created from all eternity and had no beginning—a most profoundly unevolutionary outlook. This is not to say that no one had ever proposed the idea of evolution. Among the ancient Greeks, who canvassed all ideas, Anaximander and Empedocles suggested it. As in the case of astronomy, Aristotle prevailed over their view.

The eighteenth century had shown an enormous interest in biology. Buffon was one of the most popular writers of the age, and other distinguished *philosophes,* including Maupertuis and Diderot, speculated on the origins of life and the nature of species, speculations quite natural in any curious age released from conventional explanations. Biology was somewhat of a factor in romanticism and German philosophy, suggesting organic to replace mechanistic images. Diderot and Maupertuis may readily be seen as anticipating Darwinism, but again, there seemed no convincing evidence for transformation of species, and the great authority of Buffon was, on the whole, it would seem, thrown against it. These stimulating writings did serve to arouse great interest in the question. It can be said that this period between about 1750 and 1850 was like the century that elapsed betwen Copernicus and Newton: The question had been raised, there was much interest in it and growing knowledge; eventually a master jigsaw-puzzle worker would fit all the pieces together.

The pieces to be fitted together came, in a fascinating manner, from many different areas of thought. Darwinism constitutes one of the most interesting of all studies in intellectual history because it shows how much science is a part of the "climate of opinion" of its day. The idea of "survival of the fittest," which Darwin was to turn to such good account as an explanation of biological evolution, was suggested to him by Thomas Malthus and Herbert Spencer. Reading Malthus's *Essays on Population,* which expounded the tendency of population to increase faster than food supply, Darwin saw that this must lead to a struggle for survival in which the less durable organisms would die and fail to reproduce themselves.[6] As for Herbert Spencer, this Victorian oracle preceded Darwin in setting forth a ruthlessly competitive natural order. The idea of natural selection through competition in a world where some must go under because there is not enough sustenance for all came first from the economists. It was "in the air" by the 1830s, and Darwin, a naturalist, picked up and applied it to his field of study. He had his hypothesis many years before presenting his proofs in 1858.

From 1800, Europe seemed to be grasping for the concept of evolution, though not until 1858 did Darwin (and, almost simultaneously, Alfred Wallace) cage the elusive idea. The romantic approach to science known as *Naturphilosophie,* an interest of some German philosophers, thought in evolutionary terms and sometimes believed in transmutation, but, not strictly scientific, its explanation was closer to what later became known as vitalism, that is, a life force immanent in nature that strives to fulfill itself. Schopenhauer, the interesting German philosophical pessimist, strongly believed that this life force appears as an instinct to live, which nature uses to trick us into striving for, so that the species may be reproduced; an outlook some of which may have worked its way into Darwinism. We hardly need to remind the reader how historical-evolutionary the popular systems of Hegel and Comte were; this undoubtedly conditioned men to think in terms of the genetic, developmental explanation of things.[7] So it seems that the century conspired to bring about the theory of evolution.

Already, before Darwin, the French paleontologist Lamarck had proposed a theory to account for the evolution of species. He believed that developed characteristics could be inherited. There are (to choose an example) Polynesian swimmers who have developed in the course of

---

[6]"It at once struck me that under these circumstances favorable variations would tend to be preserved, and unfavorable variations would be destroyed. The result of this would be the formation of new species."

[7]But Hegel, an evolutionist in his philosophy of history, was not so in his philosophy of nature. There is no temporal, only a logical relationship between humans and the lower organisms. "Nature and history are different things," and "Nature has no history" were Hegelian axioms. The cycle of nature is endless repetition from which nothing new evolves, contrary to the situation in human history.

generations an unusual lung capacity, enabling them to stay under water (so we are told) as long as six to eight minutes. Lamarck would have explained this as, perhaps, many people today might do unthinkingly: Each generation stretched its lungs by long practice and then handed on this lung power to the offspring. This is wrong, according to modern biologists, who follow Darwin; what happened was that people with unusually large lungs became divers and the others did not, or perhaps drowned. Darwin usually disparaged and ridiculed Lamarck, whom he accused of intruding desire or purpose into the picture, as if the bird's *wish* to fly gradually succeeded in stretching an organ into a wing. Evolution is simply the mechanical result of survival value, on Darwin's more "scientific" explanation. Some birds happened to have more nearly winglike organs and these survived, the process being repeated for many generations. Lamarck's theory, of course, rested on the vulnerable hypothesis of the inheritability of acquired traits, though to be sure Darwin did not entirely avoid this either.

In 1844, the Scottish encyclopedist Robert Chambers published, anonymously, *The Vestiges of the Natural History of Creation,* a work that substantially set forth the Darwinian hypothesis although without Darwin's careful accumulation of scientific evidence. It caused a considerable stir of controversy. Thus the state of the question when Darwin arrived was about as follows: The hypothesis of evolution, in the sense of the transformation of one species into another, all descending from one original form of life, was already familiar, but the evidence for it did not seem sufficient to overcome long-standing and apparently strong objections—chiefly, the seeming fixity of species, as attested by the sterility of hybrids, but also certain moral and theological prejudices. Geology and paleontology, however, had strongly suggested its possibility. The "climate of opinion" was favorable to the evolutionary outlook, and some economic writers had called attention to the struggle for existence. It was urgent, it seemed, to either prove or disprove the assertions of Chambers, which had aroused controversy. The Lamarckian theory was not convincing.

Rapidly developing scientific knowledge in a number of fields and far-ranging scientific expeditions over the whole face of the globe had produced much new data about life on earth. Darwin himself had sailed on the famous *Beagle* voyage from 1831 to 1836, studying and collecting zoological evidence. As a sickly youth, marked by few signs of genius, Charles Darwin had tried and failed to follow his father's profession of physician but had his life changed by a teacher at Cambridge who got him to apply for the *Beagle* post. He had no notions of overturning long-held and deeply cherished views when he set out; but as he gathered and observed specimens of flora and fauna, he found questions forming in his mind. As he observed the unusual forms of life on isolated islands, such as the giant turtles on Galapagos, he became convinced that species are not immutable; if so, why should different environmental conditions give rise to different plants and animals? Darwin had his hypothesis by 1835 and his theory, from Malthus, by 1838; he spent the next twenty years patiently assembling every possible strand of evidence with which to tie it all together. As early as Chambers, that is, 1844, Darwin had a manuscript, but he would not publish it until he had made it entirely convincing. By 1858 it had grown to one thousand pages, which he considerably abridged for publication.

Darwin assembled all the pieces and gave an answer that convinced most of the independent minds of his day. In so doing he wrote the most important book of the century, by rather general agreement, and took his place along with Galileo and Newton among the greatest of scientists, those who have altered the entire mentality of civilization. A poll of distinguished people taken at the end of the century to determine the ten most influential books of the century showed that *The Origin of Species* was the only book on every list. Today the story would hardly be different, though one or two others might also gain unanimous support. A.D.—after Darwin—all was changed utterly.

Darwin's achievement has occasionally been disparaged, because so many other people *almost* hit upon his idea, but while scientific discovery like technological invention is always a social product, no credit may justly be taken away from the person who has the genius to make that discovery. Darwin was a very plain and straightforward professional scientist without philosophical pretensions. His last work was on *The Formation of Vegetable Mould through the Action of Worms*! Subsequently, he was drawn into some philosophical issues that were perhaps beyond him. But the combination of scientific research and clear thinking found in *The Origin of Species* is very nearly up to Newtonian standards.

Darwin's views, even among scientists, did not prevail without considerable difficulty. His supporters alleged "a conspiracy of silence." Twelve years after the publication of *The Origin of Species,* a conference of French anthropologists found "no proof or even presumption" in favor of natural selection as a cause of transformation. The pace of acceptance varied in different countries; many French saw Darwinism as a kind of ideology of Anglo-Saxon imperialism—it was notoriously difficult to separate scientific from ideological elements in the consideration of Darwinism. Darwin himself noted "it is curious how nationality influences opinion." In the end Darwinism prevailed among scientists, as by and large it has continued to do since, so one must be sure one knows just what it was that Darwin alleged. It is important to note that he did *not* originate the theory of evolution. What he did do was (1) provide a wealth of evidence for it, that is, for the mutability of species and (2)- propose the theory of natural selection to account for it. Darwin convinced most people that evolution had occurred, and today scarcely any-body doubts it. Assembling data from paleontology, anatomy, experi-mental breeding, and other fields, the new view represented a triumph for thoroughness and collation of scientific research, a victory that rightly enhanced the prestige of science as a social institution. That is to say, it became clear with Darwin that scientific discovery is less the fitful inspiration of genius than the certain result of steady accumulation of data and the patient collation of it. Darwin had genius, but his warmest admirers confessed it was the genius of infinite pains rather than superhuman intelligence.

Darwin was persuasive not only because of the empirical evidence he drew together but because of the striking hypothesis he put forth to explain how evolution takes place. It is noteworthy that the two things were intimately connected: Darwin began his great twenty-year cam-paign of fact-collecting *after* he hit upon the theory of natural selection, from which we may infer that a good theory both stimulates and directs research. But it could be that the hypothesis was wrong as explanation, that evolution indeed has occurred but not in the way that Darwin imag-ined. The theory of natural selection has been modified since Darwin, principally by an understanding of the mechanism of heredity, which was not generally known until 1900.[8] Today few biologists deny natural selection's importance, but the function of mutation, including macro-mutation or the accidental production of extreme variants, has brought in an additional factor. The majority of scientists think that variations in heredity *plus* natural selection account for evolution. There are a few who question whether natural selection is really a *major* cause of evolution. (No one can deny that it occurs and plays *some* part.) It should be noted that Darwin was wrong insofar as he proposed slow and gradual evolutionary change, declaring that "nature makes no leaps." Modern mutation theory stresses the sudden leaps. The giraffe did not get his long neck inch by inch, as Darwin thought, but by monsters of long-neckedness that sporadically appeared and proved to have survival value—so runs the current view, roughly, as against original Darwinism. Darwin's view that offspring blend the characteristics of their parents rested on ignorance of the mechanism of heredity (as he knew) and entailed difficulties he could not solve. If a slightly longer-necked giraffe did appear, by mating with an ordinary one, the effect of the mutation would be partly lost, on Darwin's supposition. Modern genetics has es-tablished that heredity does not work by simply blending the parental traits; in the genes all traits are preserved and may appear unimpaired in some later individual.

[8]The Austrian monk Gregor Mendel published his pioneer findings in 1866, but they were ignored by scientists until 1900.

All this may be studied in textbooks of biology or zoology. Clearly Darwin was the founder of large and important areas of modern biological science, whatever modifications of his original theory new knowledge has made necessary. The main interest is in his impact on wider areas of thought and in the sharp moral and religious controversies that ensued.

REACTIONS TO DARWIN

"With the one exception of Newton's *Principia*, no single book of empirical science has ever been of more importance to philosophy," Josiah Royce wrote. Equally important to social and religious thought, and soon brought into the hustings of popular debate, Darwinism eventually affected just about everything in the modern world. It was immediately controversial, as Darwin had foreseen. Most epoch-making books have been greeted in total silence and had to wait years to be accepted as important: Marx, Freud, and Nietzsche, for example, all took about twenty years to gain recognition. *The Origin of Species* sold out on its first day of publication and made its author immediately famous. Many were dismayed, a feeling not confined to the clergy and little old ladies, shocked at the refutation of Genesis. Some of the keenest minds of the age, and some of the least orthodox, joined in the dismay. George Bernard Shaw wrote, "If it could be proved that the whole universe had been produced by such selection (Darwin's "survival of the fittest"), only fools and rascals could bear to live." Von Baer, the distinguished German scientist, refused to believe in a theory that made humanity "a product of matter" and debased it to the level of animals, while the Professor of Geology at Cambridge, Adam Sedgwick, declared that acceptance of Darwinism would "sink the human race into a lower grade of degradation than any into which it has fallen since its written records tell of its history." Was not Darwin another Schopenhauer, his science teaching that only accident and blind will rule the universe, or, if gods, "gods careless of our doom," as Matthew Arnold put it? Apart from the fate that might overtake orthodox Christianity, were *any* moral values possible in a Darwinian world? The implication that we are not unique children of God endowed with souls, but rather offspring of the amoeba by way of other animals, was disturbing; so was the apparent view of life as an amoral struggle, "nature red in tooth and claw," filled with pain and death, the sacrifice of countless individuals to the species. Still more so was the indication that the universe is nothing but chance and luck.

Though Darwin made some gestures of appeasement in his book to the religious, he was not a religious person and steadily grew less so. In his *Autobiography*—the undeleted version—he explains how he first rejected Christianity about 1840 and later also dropped the "theism" that appears in the last two pages of the *Origin*. He undoubtedly shared the position popularized by his vigorous proponent, Thomas Huxley, as "agnosticism." The acrimony with which the war between science and religion soon began to be waged owed much to the belligerence and even arrogance of Huxley, as well as to the blindness of his most famous adversary, "Soapy Sam" Wilberforce. Huxley and Bishop Wilberforce met in a debate in 1860 on which occasion a famous exchange of insults took place—the clergyman observing that he would rather not claim a monkey for an ancestor and Huxley retorting that he would rather be descended from an honest ape than from one who, though endowed with brains, refused to use them! These two were hardly typical specimens. Huxley was driven by a rage against the clergy that led him to write privately of an urge to "get my heel into their mouths and sc-r-unch it around"; he made the wholly inaccurate statement that "extinguished theologians lie about the cradle of every science as the strangled snakes beside that of Hercules"! Not all clergymen rejected Darwinism—some soon began to find it agreeable to theism—while its foes included many nonclergy, scientists among them. Roman Catholics were more inclined to accept, or at leat to tolerate, Darwinism because they were freer from Biblical literalism.

But Darwin undeniably moved away from religion. His life story reveals one who earlier was quite pious but whom Lyell's geology led away from Biblical Christianity; then the hypothesis of natural selection destroyed in his mind the classical arguments for natural religion, drawn from the evidences of design and purpose in organisms. His concluding paragraphs in *Origin* point to a theism that was in fact quite widely adopted: It is not less wonderful, but *more* so, that God chose to plant the seeds of all life in a few simple forms rather than create each species separately. But Darwin abandoned this position, as a study of his letters and subsequent published writings reveals. There was too much chance and too much evil in the biological world he saw to permit him to believe in a benevolent plan. "I cannot persuade myself that a beneficent and omnipotent God would have designedly created the Ichneumonidae with the express intention of their feeding within the living bodies of caterpillars, or that cats should play with mice." It was the old problem of evil that destroyed Darwin's faith, along with the muddle and untidiness of the evolutionary picture that went so far to discredit the notion of an orderly plan. Darwin was certainly not, like Huxley, a naturally irreligious man. He simply was driven by the evident facts to lose his faith in a "beneficent and omnipotent God." If reproached for destroying religion, he could only answer that he did not invent these harsh facts; they existed.

The thought also struck him, later, that the mind of humanity itself is a product of the evolutionary order, thus merely a tool of survival. This same idea was to jolt others. The result was evidently to dethrone intelligence or soul as a separate principle, making it merely a factor in evolutionary adaptation. Oddly enough, this would seem to destroy science along with theology as having any higher validity; everything would have to become just a weapon in the struggle for survival. At any rate, Darwin's somewhat confused speculations mirror those of many others; all had been thrown into disorder by this amazing new knowledge. Unwilling to be dogmatic, Darwin called himself an "agnostic," though a careful study of his religious views concludes that it would not be too unjust to equate them with atheism. Darwin found absolutely no evidence for a divine creation and providence; that he was not an atheist was owing only to his reluctance to be dogmatic about anything. Perhaps—who knows?—such evidence might appear in the future. Darwin did not find it.[9]

THE AFTERMATH OF DARWIN:
EVOLUTIONARY CONTROVERSIES AND
PHILOSOPHIES

I find no hint throughout the Universe
Of good or ill, of blessing or of curse;
I find alone Necessity Supreme;
With infinite Mystery, abysmal, dark,
Unlighted by the faintest spark
For us the flitting shadows of a dream.

So wrote James Thomson in "The City of Dreadful Night." Thomson was by nature a pessimist, but he was not alone in drawing gloomy conclusions from Darwin and science. At a time when belief in the divine inspiration of every line of Scripture was still regarded as the sole foundation of Christianity (Gladstone, the great Oxford-educated liberal statesman, so argued in 1865), and Christianity was regarded as the foundation of the social order, the discrediting of Genesis was no small matter, and the blows that came from Lyell and Darwin fell on a body already bruised by those of the positivist historians and the schools of Biblical criticism. The theological-Biblical debate has today lost its importance, for most Christians no longer construe the Scriptures so literally; but as late as 1925 in the United States (the Scopes trial) it retained considerable power to arouse emotions. Wider than this was the moral debate, concerned with the question of whether Darwinism did not de-

---

[9]The disciples of Darwin have continued to be militantly antitheist. Thus wrote Julian Huxley, grandson of Thomas Huxley and distinguished twentieth-century biologist: "Newton's great generalization of gravitational attraction made it possible and indeed necessary to dispense with the idea of God guiding the stars in their courses; Darwin's equally great generalization of natural selection made it possible and necessary to dispense with the idea of God guiding the evolutionary courses of life" (*On Living in a Revolution,* 1944). Huxley's comment on Newton is inaccurate in that eighteenth-century thinkers did not so construe Newtonianism.

stroy all values by eliminating purpose and design from the universe; many who were not at all orthodox Christians joined in disapproving a creed apparently consistent with no sort of belief in rational order in the world. In one of his books the Victorian author Winwood Reade told of a young man's suicide, under the impact of Malthus and Darwin, whose books he placed, bound in somber colors, on the table in his room, the *Essay on Population* labeled "the Book of Doubt" and *The Origin of Species* labeled "The Book of Despair." Yet others were able to accept Darwinism as meaning progress.

The great debate went on with endless ramifications. A classic story is that of P. H. Gosse, lay minister and naturalist (father of Edmund Gosse, whose *Father and Son* is a Victorian classic), who, struggling to reconcile his Christian faith with his science, hit upon what he regarded as a brilliant answer: God had created the world "prochronically," at a particular and arbitrary moment in its life, *as if* its past history had existed (*Omphalos: An Attempt to Untie the Geologic Knot*). He was laughed out of court. By 1872, Darwin could write that "almost every scientist admits the principle of evolution" and also the theory of natural selection as its means of operation. Yet Louis Agassiz, the famous American (Harvard) naturalist, would not accept Darwin and spent the rest of his life laboring to prove this "monstrous" theory false. Samuel Butler, Victorian freethinker and critic of religious orthodoxy, began by admiring Darwin but came to think that the Cambridge scientist was a deceiver who supplied the wrong explanation; Butler accepted evolution but not natural selection and was led back to Lamarck via St. George Mivart, the Roman Catholic biologist, author of *The Genesis of Species* (1871). In *Evolution Old and New* (1879) Butler attacked the scientific establishment as more bigoted than the religious. Bernard Shaw also became a neo-Lamarckian, but moralists found this more appealing than scientists.

There were harmonizers and accommodators who sought to show that even Darwinian evolution is consistent with divine purpose. Was there not something sublime in the ascent of humanity through the eons from primeval slime to intelligent and spiritual being (Henry Drummond)? Admitting the cruelty and suffering, one still had as an undeniable fact the grand result.[10] Asa Gray, the American naturalist, complimented Darwin for having *restored* teleology to nature. There was design, if "on the installment plan": Darwin himself had once been reduced to awe at the greater wonder of God contriving to draw all life from a single simple beginning. In any event, as Mr. and Mrs. Carlyle had observed, whether we are or are not derived from the amoeba is

---

[10]"Red in tooth and claw" was somewhat overstated; survival depends more on the struggle against nature than between organisms, and cooperation may be a help to survival. "Strength," indeed, may be less important than efficiency, energy, intelligence.

irrelevant to our spiritual life. Josiah Royce, the distinguished American philosopher, held to an evolutionary idealism and pointed out that the human mind does seek values, is not animallike: These are facts as incontrovertible as Darwin's, if puzzlingly different from them. Darwin had not and could not make us brutes. He had given us new and puzzling knowledge, but so long as human consciousness exists it will rise above matter to seek understanding and the good.

There were also vitalist approaches to evolution that pointed out that Darwin had not addressed himself at all to the important question of what really (in a final sense) causes the evolutionary process. Granted that natural selection does take place and with an apparent blindness and cruelty (millions of individuals, whole species even, may perish because of some accidental change in their environment), it would seem that other factors are present, too, including an intelligence that runs through all life. The behavior of organisms is often so remarkably purposive that one has difficulty in attributing everything to a mechanistic process. At any rate, can natural selection account for the emergence of life itself? There is also running through life a will to live, as Schopenhauer and Bergson noted. Can this inextinguishable vitality be the result of a mechanical process? It must have been there to begin with, though strengthened by natural selection. Perhaps this life force is really the "cause" of evolution, natural selection only one means it uses. If we see a large group of people running a long race and notice that some of them fall or drop out while a few run strongly and forge to the front, it would seem odd to say that the cause of the winning of the race (evolution) is the fact that some drop out from unfitness (natural selection), without raising the really interesting question, why are they running? Why do they bother with this rigorous competition at all? Why do they not all sit under a tree and rest? Darwin pointed out that there is competition in nature and refrained from speculating about the reason. This is good; but was he justified in implying that the question has no importance and need not be raised? If natural selection is made into a dogma, it may divert our eyes from other questions of great moment and distort our outlook on nature. So, at least, Henri Bergson was to argue.[11]

The outcome of all these efforts at accommodation with evolution was perhaps uncertain, but in general people learned to live with it, sometimes by making a separation between animal world and human world, nature and value. On this view a great change had taken place in "nature." "Nature" to the eighteenth century had suggested order, harmony, benevolence, indeed something to be imitated, an agreeable model for humanity. After Darwin nature might be thought of as fas-

---

[11]There were other French vitalists—Vandel, Mercier, Varagnac, and more recently the celebrated Jesuit father, Teilhard de Chardin.

cinating, but it was in part terrible and it was not a proper model for human beings. But on the other hand, there were those who embraced the new "naturalism" that placed humanity in the setting of the natural order and did not separate us so sharply from it as had, for example, the Cartesian or Kantian dualism. Darwinians were "monists" (their foes said materialists) who could not accept any mind-body dualism, and separation between the physical world and the mental. The human animal is an organism like any other, responding to its environment and in part shaping it while responding. Humanity became a part of the biological natural order as it had not been before.

If some of the more thoughtful drew pessimistic or tragic conclusions from evolution, most people probably integrated it casually with the reigning belief in progress. Constant and inevitable progress does take place on Darwinian terms, progress of the species or race if often at the expense of individuals. Organisms adapt to their environment and grow steadily more efficient; if the unfit perish, the fit live, and life evolves from lower organisms to higher. It was one version of the "idea of progress" for which Victorian stability and economic prosperity provided a favorable atmosphere.

Philosophically, Darwinism helped discredit idealism or intellectualism. Young philosophers like John Dewey abandoned Hegel for some more naturalistic outlook. Mind, it seemed, must be a product of evolution, ideas of natural selection. Mind could hardly be detached from the organism and erected into a separate principle. If we even believe that the universe makes sense, as Nietzsche was fond of saying, is this not just because those of our ancestors who could not make sense of it failed to survive, and natural selection bred those who did? An instinct, will, or life force may throb through the universe, but intellect is its tool; reason is a survival trait. A character in a Shaw play remarked that the modern view is not "I think therefore I am," but "I am therefore I think." A new reason for distrusting reason had appeared: Reason is a product of the nature it purports to understand. If I believe in God, or say that the universe is orderly, I may be doing so because of traits bred into the intellect by the struggle for survival, and if I am tempted to assume the absolute truth of these beliefs, I am caught up by remembering that my mind itself is an evolutionary product, hence essentially a survival tool, like the monkey's tail or the giraffe's neck! This "irrationalism" might take various forms: Pessimistically, it could be presented as grounds for despair with blind will and instinct ruling the universe; optimistically, it might be said that human intelligence is no less a creative tool for being a part of the natural order. But there remained a fundamental difference between all the new thought and the old, in that for many it was no longer possible to set the human mind *outside* nature. Being a part of nature, the mind had to give up its proud claim to be able to understand it as one understands something from which one is detached. The mind is just that part of our organism that participates in a certain way in the great game of life. Humanity was no longer Pascal's "thinking reed," its intelligence set against the world.

The implications of Darwinism are too numerous to be recorded. "Evolutionary views have deeply penetrated our present thinking in almost every conceivable field. . . . It has become regular procedure to study phenomena in terms of their development. . . . Interest in evolution has moved out of academic circles even into the field of commerce and industry."[12] Perhaps this judgment attributes too much to Darwinism as such, for the bent of the nineteenth century toward historical explanations and the idea of progress was rather more general; Darwinism may be seen as only a part of this larger pattern, which included such independent forces as Hegelian philosophy, Burkean political thought, aspects of Comteanism, and the maturing profession of historiography. But it is interesting to note that John Dewey, in his famous assessment of Darwin's impact on philosophy (*The Influence of Darwin on Philosophy*, 1909), attributed to him the enthronement of "the principle of transition," or seeing things as involved in processes of change rather than as Platonic "eternals." Clearly Darwin did exert the greatest force in this direction. Unlike Hegel and Comte he seemed truly scientific. Dewey added that Darwin had shattered the closed metaphysical system of Hegel in favor of a pluralism and experimentalism. One did not simply postulate movement here, one *studied* it, looking closely at every natural object with the eye of the scientist, but looking at it in motion, in process. Thus to many living in the later nineteenth century a whole new vision of things opened up, and evolutionism seemed a refreshing breeze blowing over the somewhat desiccated landscape of idealism.

The rise of science as the prevailing mode of thought, predicted by Comte, owed more to Darwin than to any other one figure. Many noted this change at mid-century. Mark Pattison dated it between 1845 and 1850. Oliver Wendell Holmes, Jr., the great American jurist, reminiscing many years later, thought that of all the intellectual gaps between generations, that between his own and his parents' (about 1865) was the greatest: "It was the influence of the scientific way of looking at the world." He mentioned, in addition to *The Origin of Species,* Herbert Spencer and Henry T. Buckle.[13] Buckle was an amateur historian, author of a multivolume *History of Civilization in England* (from 1857 to 1861), the Toynbee of his day, whose volumes lined the shelves of many a Victorian library and who sought to reduce history to an exact science. More famous yet was the apparently omniscient Herbert Spencer, who

[12]Walter J. Ong, in *Darwin's Vision and Christian Perspectives*, 1960, pp. 1–2.
[13]Leonora C. Rosenfield, *Portrait of a Philosopher: Morris R. Cohen*, 1962, p. 321.

did not confine himself merely to human history but claimed to have reduced the whole of the cosmos to an exact and evolutionary science.

Spencer, the most celebrated of mid-Victorian philosophers, was a sort of combination of Comte and Darwin. Like the former, he was a tremendous synthesizer of every field of knowledge under the general rubric of a scientific or positivistic method—a synthesis that greatly impressed his contemporaries, eager for an integration of thought, but which has since considerably depreciated in value. Someone has called him "the Marx of the middle class"; he could equally well be called the British Comte. A distinctive feature of his philosophy was its stress on evolution, a stress indeed not lacking in Comte, Hegel, and Marx, but which in Spencer is even more pronounced. Influenced by Lyell and von Baer, he popularized "survival of the fittest" before Darwin. Unlike the Cambridge scientist, Spencer proceeded to set about creating a full-scale philosophy of evolution. While Darwin was largely content to nail down the lid on evolution with a large supply of experimental facts, Spencer assumed the case closed and set off on cosmic speculative adventures with it.

The entire universe obeys the same laws of evolution, Spencer affirmed. He wished to show that the evolution not only of life but of the physical cosmos and human society could be reduced to the same laws—an exciting idea, indeed. Spencer found that things invariably evolve from (1) the homogeneous to the heterogeneous, (2) the undifferentiated to the differentiated, and (3) the unintegrated to the integrated. "From a relatively diffused, uniform, and indeterminate arrangement to a relatively concentrated, multiform, and determinate arrangement," so ran his formula. The cosmos began with separate, simple atoms uniformly dispersed through space and will end, presumably, with highly organized structures working together in a single complex system (rather the reverse of the "primeval atom" theory later popular). Human society began with isolated individuals performing simple tasks without specialization and proceeded towards an order at once more diverse, specialized, and interdependent. Writing voluminously with an encyclopedic knowledge few could match, Spencer tended to bowl over opposition by the sheer weight of this formidable erudition. Darwin called him "about a dozen times my superior" and said Spencer would go down as the greatest thinker of the century. He was certainly the most popular of all serious thinkers, to judge by the sale of his books. "Probably no philosopher ever had such a vogue as Spencer had from about 1870 to 1890," wrote the American publisher, Henry Holt, who had the enviable privilege of selling Spencer's books in the United States. (Between 1860 and 1903, some 368,000 copies of Spencer's various works were sold in authorized editions in the United States, countless others in unauthorized ones.)

Spencer combined with his evolutionary outlook a Comtean positivism (it came to him from more native sources) that insisted that scientific laws are descriptive statements only, telling nothing about essential natures or origins. The latter doubtless exist but are "unknowable." Like Kant, Spencer invites a certain sense of awe before this realm, but one can have no real knowledge about it. Positivists have generally been divided between those who say that there is no point in even talking or thinking about what we cannot know and those who would not rule out our speculations and intuitive insights into it provided we do not confuse these with knowledge of a scientific order. Spencer belonged to the latter group; he does not forbid us from speculating about the unknowable. Still, faithful Christians classed him among the "agnostics" who did so much to undermine religious faith. At the same time, it is obvious that (like Marx) he really offered a sort of religion in the trappings of science.

But in time many of his generalizations came to seem rash, founded on inadequate evidence, made by one who was determined that the facts prove his theory. A Victorian giant, Spencer's reputation has fallen perhaps faster than he deserved. But he was certainly guilty of letting his speculations outrun the facts on which they were supposedly based. Little if anything now remains standing of his vast intellectual edifice.

SOCIAL DARWINISM

By far the most notable feature of Spencer's exuberant thought was its application of evolutionary ideas to human society; and of all the speakers for what was termed "social Darwinism," he was the most renowned. There is some irony in Spencer being known as *the* "social Darwinist" since his conception of biological evolution (which he formulated before Darwin's was published) was more Lamarckian than Darwinian: He believed in the inheritability of acquired characteristics. On the other hand, he fully accepted the Darwinian notion of a struggle for existence as the key to evolution. "Survival of the fittest" was his term. An editor of the *Economist* at one time, Spencer knew the tradition of laissez-faire liberalism before he turned to evolution and shows us the intimate connection between the two. John Maynard Keynes, the modern economist, wrote that "the principle of the Survival of the Fittest could be regarded as a vast generalization of the Ricardian economics." Typically British, the principle of individualism remained powerful in his evolutionary synthesis. While society grows more complex with progress, it also grows freer and more diverse. The evolution of the individual is toward greater freedom and less constraint. Competition is the key to progress. Spencer's complacent identification of the poor with the unfit who may safely be left to die out is in good part responsible for the later dislike of his whole philosophy. The oft-quoted passage in *Social Statics* (first published in 1851, revised in later editions but not changed in any significant way) argued that "to prevent present misery would entail a greater misery on future generations"; "When regarded not separately but in connection with the interests of universal humanity," individual suffering is seen to be for the best. Spencer was sure that "as civilization advances, government decays"; in this opinion, he was as far as possible at odds with Comte, whom in some other ways he resembles. He takes us back to the Godwinian anarchists at the beginning of the century. He was the principal source of a revival of radical antistatism in Victorian England, against which however there was to be a strong reaction after 1880.

"Social Darwinism" has been a loosely used term. There are in fact several different ways of applying the formula of evolution via natural selection or "survival of the fittest" to human social development. Spencer sometimes mixed them up. One could postulate a competition, first, between whole *societies,* perhaps between nations or states, which compete against each other peacefully and sometimes go to war against each other. Applied here, a social Darwinian might hold that such competition is healthy, even that war tests the character of a people (Hegel as well as Spencer occasionally said this), that out of this struggle for survival between social units we get increasingly efficient societies. Spencer presented this sort of social Darwinism at times, declaring that societies are organisms akin to individual bodies, being functionally organized and experiencing growth; they are tested by their environment and evolve from small and simple to large and complex types.

Or, again, evolution via competition might be said to occur among specific social *institutions* such as the family. As E. B. Tylor, another social evolutionist, put it, "the institutions which can best hold their own in the world gradually supersede the less fit ones, and . . . this incessant conflict determines the general resultant course of culture." Finally, competition with resultant progress could be applied to *individuals*—the form of social Darwinism most often associated with Spencer. Here, there is perhaps a logical distinction to be made (Spencer sometimes confused them) between *biological* competition—the sickly dying off, the healthy surviving—and *economic* competition. In any case, the competition between individuals *within* a society is clearly a different thing from the competition *between* societies, and some have thought Spencer guilty of inconsistency in holding both ideas. But he thought, more or less consistently, that free competition makes for the best society and the best humanity as well as the best individuals ("best" meaning most efficient, best adapted to the challenge of the environment).

Beyond any doubt, Spencer freely mixed ideological elements into his alleged science of society. He owed much to the tradition of liberalism, reaching back through the Manchester School to Locke and Hobbes, and he perhaps owed something too to the school of Burke, which had tended to see society as an organism too complicated to tamper with safely. Spencer's world view betrayed his own time and place, just as Comte smuggled his Saint-Simonian predilections into a system supposedly scientific. Yet Spencer gave a great boost to the supposed sciences of sociology and anthropology. The latter rather clearly dates from Darwin and Spencer; it was born under evolutionary auspices. It was assumed that "primitive" peoples represent the first stage in a ladder of development, comparable to the biological ladder; they are our ancestors in the same way that simple forms of life are the ancestors of the human race. There are universal stages and laws of development. For example, in religion animism always comes first, monotheism last, in a single straight-line path of evolution. Today these views have been discarded or enormously qualified, but the study of different societies gained its initial impetus from an expectation that research would uncover simple laws of development. Thus E. B. Tylor, less dogmatic and more empirical than Spencer, nevertheless expected that in time the laws of development would be revealed; "human institutions like stratified rocks succeed each other in series substantially uniform over the globe." Skepticism about such grand laws of evolutionary succession appeared by the end of the century, when anthropologists tended to find that each primitive society is unique and can be fitted into no schematic pattern. But for the English-speaking peoples, Spencer was the fountainhead of both anthropological and sociological science. And the fact that sociology failed to become an important academic discipline in England until the 1950s, suffering a severe setback in the first half of the twentieth century, is due in part to the discrediting of Spencer about 1900.

Spencer's brand of "social Darwinism," with its sanctioning of a ruthlessly competitive social order ("root, hog, or die" is the law of life, the American social Darwinian William Graham Sumner bluntly put it), created something of a dilemma for other Darwinians, less inclined to grant indulgent smiles to a capitalistic society. In 1893, Thomas Huxley, the aggressive champion of Darwinism, argued in a well-known series of lectures that in human affairs natural selection is *not* the rule to follow. Progress, he said, consists in working *against* nature and evolution, "checking the cosmic process at every step." He could agree with Matthew Arnold that

> Man must begin, know this, where Nature ends;
> Nature and man can never be fast friends.

"It is an error to imagine that evolution signifies a constant tendency to increased perfection," Huxley wrote. What survives, because it is the best adapted, is not necessarily or usually the best in an ethical sense. Unguided evolution may well lead to moral regression and social failure. Thus did Huxley in part withdraw his faith in evolution.

Clearly this must be so. Victorian social Darwinians usually wished to approve a fairly civilized process of competitive economics against any sort of state socialism. But if one applied Darwinism to human society literally and thoroughly, one would evidently revert to the prehistoric jungle. The biographer of Adolf Hitler (Alan Bullock) tells us that the only idea the infamous Nazi dictator held to was "a crude Darwinism." To Hitler this meant that only power counts, individuals may be ruthlessly sacrificed, the ill and injured put to death, whole races wiped out because allegedly less biologically fit. Anyone stupid or evil enough to take this sort of social Darwinism at its full value would seem to find in it sanctions for the law of the jungle applied *à outrance*. Though nature might be "red in tooth and claw" in the animal world, no sane person could wish to reduce human society to such a condition.

There were those who pointed out that even in the subhuman biological realm conflict is not the only rule. Cooperation also exists as a means of biological survival, as numerous examples of symbiosis and social organization in the animal world testify. Moreover the will-to-power, the life force, the instinct to survive that pulses through all living things, can be "sublimated" so that it works for good rather than evil. Humanity, in particular, evolves by inventing new modes of social cooperation; it has passed to a higher phase of evolution, *rational* evolution, involving the use of brain power rather than brawn. Animals do this to some extent; humanity has made it supreme. Why should "natural selection" mean physical strife and bloodshed? There is more survival value in the intelligence that organizes peace and social welfare. It was possible in this way to turn the argument against Spencer's cult of dog-eat-dog competition. And, in fact, after 1880 western Europe turned rapidly toward social-welfare modifications of the competitive economic order.

In "Why Darwin Pleased the Socialists," G. B. Shaw made the point, half-seriously as usual, that it took the capitalists down a peg to be told that they were rich not because of their virtue or the design of providence, but simply by accident. Darwinism's hostility to religion, along with its reinforcement of a naturalism that looked squarely at harsh social facts, rendered it pleasing to the Left. The most notable literary offshoot, the naturalist school of Emile Zola, Jack London, and others of the sort, was daring, brutally frank, and much interested in the lives of the lower classes. Zola was not really a socialist since he thought, consistently enough with a naturalist outlook, that no one was to blame and everyone was a victim of circumstances, the capitalists no less than the workers. But no one is likely to read *Germinal* without acquiring a good deal of sympathy for the coal miners. So "social Darwinism" did not always mean rugged individualism of the sort most pleasing to expectant capitalists. Careful research has revealed that Darwinism was much less frequently employed by businesspeople to justify their acquisitive instincts than used to be thought. Marx and Engels admired Darwin, though it is now known that Marx did not, as once was claimed, try to dedicate *Das Kapital* to the author of *The Origin of Species*. Socialists sometimes tried to appropriate Darwinism. In his preface to an 1894 book on socialism and science, the British socialist Ramsay MacDonald asserted that "Darwinism is not only not in intellectual opposition to socialism, but is its scientific foundation." That struggle is the law of life; that conditions change and institutions must change too were principles easily bent to radical usages. It may be relevant to add that Darwin, Huxley, and Spencer were all compassionate people shocked at human suffering and hopeful of alleviating it, and that they all believed progress possible. Spencer was a vigorous antiimperialist who also believed that war was obsolete in the modern world. He deeply influenced radicals as well as conservatives and, in fact, was by nature much more a rebel and an outsider than a member of the British intellectual establishment. So one would be wrong to think of "social Darwinism" only as a creed congenial to the successful. It revealed what Nietzsche called "that Janus-face possessed by all great ideas."

THE IDEA OF PROGRESS

At least one substantial common denominator in all these nineteenth-century ideologies was progress, that idea the nineteenth century so generally bowed to. "The history of the human race is the history of growth," the English Comtean historian Frederic Harrison proclaimed as "the meaning of history." The Hegelian, holding that the spirit of God dwells within the historical process and guides it to ultimate completion, and the positivist, refusing to acknowledge such a metaphysical hypothesis as God or Absolute, were equal sharers of the optimistic world view that found in history a steady advance from one beginning to one end, and that a glorious one. One thought that progress worked through the Absolute without man even being aware of it; the other believed that only in rejecting the Absolute and becoming conscious of his human powers did humanity learn to advance; neither doubted the existence of progress. Marx, next to be considered, inherited the Hegelian spirit; Comte's lived on in many bourgeois versions, liberal or conservative, of the idea of progress. (J. B. Bury, in his classic study of this idea, wrote that Comte did more than any other thinker to establish it as a permanent fixture on the mental landscape.) Mill agreed with Comte on this, and Darwin taught most people that incessant advance is the law of life, though doubtless they mistook him if they thought he believed in a purposeful progress. Spencer's incredibly popular evolutionary ideology proclaimed a steady advance, onward *and* upward. A disillusioned post-1919 critic, Emil Brunner, called the idea of progress "an axiomatic belief which needed no proof nor could be disproved ... a pseudo-religious creed, which to negate was a kind of blasphemy." One can round up some doubters, but there were not many at the high tide of Victorian optimism, and as late as 1908 the distinguished statesman-philosopher of Great Britain, Lord Balfour, proclaimed that "there are no symptoms either of pause or regression in the onward movement which for more than a millennium has been characteristic of Western civilization." What seems remarkable is that these beliefs in progress assumed not only a steady onward and upward movement, but a movement of the entire society. One would be inclined to say today that some things doubtless "progress," if the term is defined in certain ways— technology becomes more efficient, scientific knowledge accumulates— but other phases of life remain much the same and some deteriorate. It would be a rash person who would claim that art, morality, even political wisdom have advanced. The nineteenth-century optimists supposed that society is a unit which progresses as a whole, so that every part of it is engaged in constant improvement.

What Georges Sorel later called "the illusions of progress" did not escape some nineteenth-century spirits. Writing in the bitter disillusionment that followed the failure of the 1848 revolution, the Russian emigré Alexander Herzen asked:

> If progress is the end, for whom are we working? Who is this Moloch who, as the toilers approach him, instead of rewarding them, only recedes, and as a consolation to the exhausted, doomed multitudes, can give back only the mocking answer that after their death all will be beautiful on earth?

Poets and artists had occasion to comment that in these really important areas there is no "progress"—nor, Theophile Gautier added, in lovemaking! Such voices were a distinct minority, often a fleeting one, before the last quarter or so of the century. Those thrown into despair by Darwin have been mentioned, but the general temper of the first half of the century, filled as it was with the excitement of meaningful change for perhaps the first time in human history, was generally optimistic. In his book on Charles Dickens, G. K. Chesterton wrote that "the first period [of the nineteenth century] was full of evil things, but it was full of hope," while the last part, full of good things, lacked hope.

This optimism, fed by a steady procession of technological gains, in Britain a newfound political stability, a general prosperity, and the conquest of some social evils, survived the Darwin-induced crisis of faith. It is a tribute to it that even the greatest critic of Victorian society, Karl Marx, embraced the creed of optimism too, in his way. It was a significant point of contact between high thought and low, philosophers and common people.

4

Nineteenth-Century Ideologies: Marxism

If previously the gods dwelt above the earth, now they have become the center of it.

KARL MARX

The fundamental problem of social science is to find the law of motion according to which any state of society produces the state which succeeds it and takes its place.

KARL MARX

The curse of all art is that the disciples are always more certain than the master.

KIPLING

FOUNDATIONS OF MARXISM

A native of the city of Trier on the French border, Karl Marx first became acquainted with Friedrich Engels in Paris whither he had gone in 1843. Prior to this, attendance at the University of Berlin had exposed him to the school of Hegel, though the great philosopher had died a few years before, in 1831, and this was a lasting and significant influence, much though Marx might disparage certain aspects of Hegelianism. Marx obtained his Ph.D. at Jena with a dissertation on the ancient materialists, Democritus and Epicurus—an appropriate topic for him in view

Karl Marx (Washington, D.C., Library of Congress.)

of his long commitment to philosophical materialism. A career in the German universities might have been in the offing for the brilliant young man, as it had been for Hegel and would be for Nietzsche; but Marx was always uncompromisingly radical. He had adopted the atheistic and naturalistic views of the young (left-wing) Hegelians of whom the foremost was Ludwig Feuerbach. Outspoken impiety doomed his chances for a professorial post.

The young Marx thought in Hegelian concepts, though by 1845 he had rejected Hegel and German idealism as an inversion of reality, putting spirit before nature rather than vice versa. Left-wing Hegelianism led him to a concern with religion, influencing Marx to see God as really only the alienated (externalized) essence of human nature. He continued to struggle with Hegel through much of his early, formerly unpublished writings, especially the 1844 "Paris Manuscripts."

Practically unknown for more than half a century after his death, these writings reveal a rather different Marx than the tough-minded "social scientist" on which his disciples had long drawn. They make extensive use of the "alienation" idea, almost missing in the later works, and are more concerned with the individual personality in a complex society than the later treatises; for that reason, along with their less dogmatic tone, they have attracted more interest in recent years than the "classical" Marx-Engels texts that had seemingly led to totalitarian dictatorship. Changing Hegel's "alienation," which was Spirit externalizing itself in nature, Marx used it to analyze what happens to the worker when excessive division of labor, along with ownership by others of what is produced, deprives the individual of the satisfactions of creative labor. Under capitalism, the workers are alienated not only from the product of their labor, but also from themselves and their fellow workers. Later Marx talks of labor as a commodity and of the "fetishism" of money, an alien power objectifying and masking a human relationship; this is a link with the "alienation" theme.

Marx left Germany in disgust in 1843 after battling censorship for a time as a journalist.

In Paris he breathed the intoxicating air of that intellectual capital in the giddy forties, when the socialist ideas of Fourier, Saint-Simon, and especially Proudhon were being discussed. Here also came colorful Russian revolutionaries such as Michael Bakunin. The meeting with Engels resulted in a friendship for life, bringing to Marx support, both financial and intellectual, on which he was often to lean. The two men seldom disagreed, an unusual partnership and one of considerable moment, for without Engels, a man of some means, Marx could surely never have spent his life writing books that few bought. For Marxists it would seem to be an awkward fact that the proletarian theory owes its existence to the money of Engels, a capitalistic factory owner. (Engels

Marx's fellow socialist and sometime rival, Pierre-Joseph Proudhon, as seen by the great French caricaturist Daumier. (P. J. Proudhon (B-6230) Honore Daumier National Gallery of Art, Washington, Rosenwald collection.)

was the son of a German textile manufacturer, manager and part owner of a branch his father set up in Manchester, England, ultimately inheriting the business on his father's death. Marx himself was of bourgeois lineage, son of a moderately well-to-do lawyer.)

Marx eagerly imbibed socialist ideas in Paris. Soon came the revolutions of 1848 and the *Communist Manifesto,* a brief work written by Marx and Engels for a left-wing organization, which had little influence on the events of 1848 but was destined to lasting fame as the most concise and eloquent statement of the Marx-Engels position. (The first draft of the *Manifesto* had been made in 1847, before the revolution.) For by this time the main contours of Marx's thought were pretty well set. Like Darwin, he had his thesis and would spend the rest of his life supplying the documentation. The excitement of 1848 probably never left Marx; he spent the rest of his life preparing for other revolutions, which never came. Marx returned to Germany to edit a newspaper in Cologne for a time, but to his disgust the revolution failed and he was forced to leave the country. He came to London in 1849, home of all refugees, and lived there the rest of his life, happily married[1] but perennially poverty-stricken until the last twelve years of his life (he died in 1883 at 65). He would not adopt the suggestion of his mother-in-law that he write less about capital and make more of it! He burrowed in the British Museum library, wrote, and organized Communist associations. As an organizer he left something to be desired, the famous First International of 1864 amounting to little at the time. His chief opus was *Das Kapital,* the first and only completed volume of which appeared in 1867, written in Marx's native tongue. A second and third volume were edited after Marx's death by Engels from his fragments, a fourth later by Karl Kautsky. Marx's failure to finish his *magnum opus* perhaps indicated problems in his theory he could not solve. There were other tracts, polemical, journalistic, or theoretical. He died and was buried in relative obscurity in London, though his fame was beginning to spread on the Continent in the last years of his life. He was surrounded by a faithful corps of German socialists.

His intellectual background was an unusually rich one. He had experienced the best of German, French, and British thought. Having gotten philosophy virtually from the mouth of the great Hegel, he then drank up socialism in the cafes of Paris at a vital moment and went on to study economic theory and economic history in London, where he laid the great library of the British Museum under heavy contribution. He kept abreast of current thought in this age of ideas and proved to be one

---

[1]The picture of Marx's happy marriage must now be somewhat tempered by the account of his fathering an illegitimate child, a family scandal suppressed in good Victorian manner. In their later years the Marxes were far from congenial.

of the ablest of all synthesizers. He blended German philosophy, French social doctrine, and British political economy in a system that could well claim to have drawn on all the best minds of the nineteenth century and forged them into a harmonious unity. Marx's range of reading was wide and deep, stretching from the classical Greek dramatists, whom he adored, to great contemporary novelists like Balzac, whom he admired despite the latter's right-wing political views. Marx's immense intellectual curiosity and essentially critical mind led him to start vast projects he could never finish. Often the task of putting them in shape for the printer was left to the alter ego, Engels, a shrewd man with a facile pen but much less profound than Marx; some of the problems of "Marxism" arise from this fact.

On his death, Marx left a movement organized as the Social Democratic Party, which soon was the most vigorous and successful socialist group in the world. The Communist party was a subsequent offshoot of this movement. The success of these parties, as well as their failures perhaps, could be traced to the vigor and clarity of Marx's thought. Yet it is somewhat problematical whether their leaders really spoke for Marx. "Thank God I am not a Marxist" was one of his late pronouncements! One need only instance the Russian party's conversion of Marxism into an iron dictatorship, based on very slender foundations in Marx himself and, according to experts, entirely foreign to his spirit.

Despite the harmonics of what was made into a Marxist "system," there were many tensions in Marx's thought, especially that between an intellectual, philosophical theory of society and a revolutionary, political ideology. Marx's disciples in the organized socialist movement—a common fault of disciples—in combining these two functions drastically simplified and dogmatized his thought, converting it into a kind of secular church—militant marked by the trappings of religion, including a scholastic theology. In part this was Marx's own fault, for he had insisted that his thought was not merely speculative but practical. Philosophy had heretofore only understood the world, now it must change it, he proclaimed. Hegel had brought speculative philosophy as far as it could go; the next step, taken by Hegel's successor, was to convert this knowledge into actuality. Marx's whole dialogue with Hegel, dating from seminal works of 1845 such as *The German Ideology,* was based on the proposition that the Berlin professor, sharing in the German weakness for theorizing,[2] had gotten the whole equation of historic development backwards, making the child beget the parent, the effect precede the cause. The Spirit did not beget human affairs, but vice versa. "It is not the consciousness of men that determines their being, but, on the contrary, their

---

[2]Perhaps Marx recalled the saying of his friend, German poet Heinrich Heine, that the English were lords of the sea, the French of the land, and the Germans of—the air.

social being that determines their consciousness." The individual working, struggling, acting comes first, ideas are a product of this activity; history is nothing but the actions of real, sentient people in pursuit of their ends. Ideas are engendered from this process and, in turn, exert an influence; Marx was no crude "economic determinist." But in the end it is "the economic structure of society" that determines thought, not vice versa, according to Marx and Engels.

It therefore seemed necessary that Marxism be understood by the masses, and leaders of the Social Democratic parties produced simplified catechisms: The workers are exploited, they must break the mental as well as physical chains of capitalism, the great revolution is inevitable and will usher in a classless society, the last, millennial state of humanity completing its long journey through five stages from slavery to freedom. It was a thinly disguised version of the Judeo-Christian eschatology but it rested also on the allegedly scientific economics of Marx. These disciples knew little or nothing of the early writings, but rested their faith chiefly on the analysis of capitalism contained in *Das Kapital.*

DIALECTICAL MATERIALISM

Most people associated Marxism with either (1) the economic analysis of capitalism, purporting to show its inevitable destruction from its own "contradictions" and replacement by socialism or communism or (2) the broader materialist interpretation of history, which alleges that the fundamental causal factor in social change at any time is the technological or economic. But classical Marxism based both of these on the philosophical framework of *dialectical materialism.* "Materialist in substance and dialectical in manner," this philosophy sought to combine the Hegelian dialectic with a materialist view of reality, in effect, to combine a scientific with a metaphysical outlook. In many respects, Marx was hardheadedly empirical or positivistic, that is, he would not accept knowledge that was not evident to the senses. In his mature years he shared the outlook of Comte and Darwin and ridiculed "speculative idealism." Nevertheless he silently retained Hegel's dialectical *method,* the formula of dialectical movement. When we look at nature or history we find that everything exhibits in its activity and development a dialectical pattern of action and reaction. The dialectic is a characteristic of matter. "Dialectics," Engels wrote, "is nothing more than the science of the general laws of motion and development of nature, human society, and thought." It is important, but difficult, to know whether Marxists assert this as an empirical observation, which in that case might not always be true, or as a dogma beyond criticism.

It does not seem that Marx himself used the term "dialectical materialism." This name for his "philosophy" came from Engels and from the

Social Democrats of the period from 1880 to 1914, including Plekhanov in Russia, Karl Kautsky in Germany, and Jules Guesde, aided by Marx's son-in-law, Paul Lafargue, in France. Lenin defended materialism against an "empirio-criticism" which he suspected of idealist tendencies, and the cruder-minded Stalin made it the Communist orthodoxy.

As stated by Engels the three laws of the dialectic are (1) the transformation of quantity into quality, (2) the interpenetration of opposites, and (3) the negation of the negation. These rather mystifying formulae may perhaps be clarified by the following examples. (1): Water suddenly becomes ice at a certain point of coldness, thus a qualitative change takes place as a result of a series of quantitative changes. Or, a revolution finally takes place after years of cumulative pressures. Pile one thing on another and at a certain point you cease to have just a pile of the same things, you have something entirely different. A humbler and possibly facetious example might be the inflating of a tire: Keep putting in air and finally, at a critical juncture, you get not a tire but an explosion. (2) and (3): Change is the rule of nature because everything contains within it its own opposite, which negates it and in turn will be negated. The seed contains within itself the plant into which it will turn; the plant will decay, giving rise however to new plants. A social order, such as capitalism, creates out of its own body the socialism destined to destroy it. Socialism thus interpenetrates capitalism and negates it. Struggle and conflict punctuate this process: The old organism produces its violent destroyers.

As applied to the sciences, it has seemed to critics that the dialectical method does not mean much or, if insisted upon as a dogma, is harmful to science. Soviet scientists work like Western ones. Whenever (as happened on one or two occasions, notably in the Lysenko case) there has been an effort to force on Russian scientists a Marxist scientific orthodoxy, the results have been unfortunate for science. Either dialectical materialism is so commonplace that even "bourgeois" scientists follow it without knowing that they are doing so (like Molière's M. Jourdain talking prose!), or else it is a failure. The attempt to distinguish a Marxist science from a bourgeois one, with the former being superior, clearly has failed. Nevertheless from Engels down to Stalin, Marxists insisted that dialectical materialism is the distinctive foundation of their science, and the famous analysis of capitalism is meant to be but a special application of it. Under Stalin, scientists in the Soviet Union suffered pains and penalties because they appeared to stray from the dialectical path. Not only human affairs but the natural sciences are expected to conform to dialectical principles. To be a Marxist, one must be able to enter into the spirit of the dialectical universe and visualize things in motion and in contradiction, giving birth to their own opposites, negating and renegating, occasionally bursting through the barriers of quantity to create a new form. A vision not unlike this is to be found in the more recent school of Emergent Evolutionists, who in other ways do not resemble Marxists, however. They stress the freedom and unpredictability of life, ever proliferating in unexpected ways, whereas Marxism is deterministic, though to be sure there is a Marxian problem in this regard.

Many of the examples given by Marx and especially by Engels are from the natural sciences (the freezing of ice and the sprouting of the seed are theirs). But no one associates these German worthies with a revolution in chemistry or biology.[3] Many do associate them with a revolutionary new conception of the historical process, as well as with the first effective socialist economic analysis. They applied the dialectical method to these areas more consistently and successfully. It is well, though, to remember that this method was the tool of thought they always used, and that they held it to be of universal validity, *the* scientific method.

The dialectical method was after all Marx's distinctive contribution. Today, because he is the most famous socialist or Communist, he is often thought of as the person who invented socialism, but this, as we know, is not so. The protest against the suffering of workers under capitalism antedated Marx, as did the idea of social ownership of industry as a remedy for the evils of "capitalism." The Chartists, Robert Owen, Saint-Simon and Fourier, Proudhon, Blanc, all came before him. We have previously discussed these pioneer socialists. In Rousseau's vision of an original state of primitive communism, when there was no wickedness and exploitation, followed by the Fall due to eating the apple of private property, there is much of the basic vision of Marx, too, the latter more sophisticated, spelled out in greater detail, but in its archetypal essence quite similar. Engels, indeed, once said that Rousseau's *Essay on the Origin of Inequality* contained all the germs of Marxism. Marx respected the pioneer socialists, Owen and Saint-Simon, from whom he learned his socialism, and in calling them "utopian socialists" meant only that they lacked realistic notions of how socialism was to be established; they innocently assumed it had only to be proclaimed.

Likewise, other concepts associated with Marxism such as the class struggle and the class conditioning of morality and thought were hardly original. "Of all maxims none is more uncontested than that power follows property," Joseph Addison remarked early in the eighteenth century, an idea which may have come to him from James Harrington. John Stuart Mill, in *On Liberty,* a contemporary work (1859) but one not influenced by Marx, whom Mill at that time had probably never heard

---

[3]Marx and Engels knew about Darwin, of course, and regarded him as possibly congenial to their system. Engels claimed in his funeral address on Marx that Marx had done for the social sciences what Darwin did for the biological. But the attitude of Marx is indicated in his request to Engels to "study Darwin and see if there is anything there we can use"!

of, observed (parenthetically) that "wherever there is an ascendant class, a large portion of the morality of the country emanates from its class interests and its feelings of class superiority." Mill could have found this in the ancient historian Thucydides, among others. As any sociologist must, Herbert Spencer had also confronted the problem of the role of ideas in social change and had concluded that ideas are *largely* a product of "surrounding conditions" including "the social state." Spencer was concerned to stress the emotional determinants of rational processes: "Ideas do not govern and overthrow the world; the world is governed by feelings, to which ideas serve only as guides. . . . Though advanced ideas, when once established, act upon society and aid its further advance, yet the establishment of such ideas depends on the fitness of society for receiving them." Though a reasonably crude and confused statement, Spencer's is at least as adequate as Marx's thoughts on the subject.

Marx of course took no credit for discovering the concept of social class, which would have been absurd; he mentioned the historians Guizot and Thierry, and the political economists (Ricardo, it will be recalled, had stressed the opposing interests of manufacturers and land-lords in a famous tract written before Marx was born) as his predeces-sors, and he could have mentioned many others. Where he thought his originality lay was in explaining the origin of classes: a product of the contradiction between the forces of production and the *relations* of production—between, in substance, technology and social organization. Though popular ideologists developed "class struggle" into the essential element of Marxism, Marx himself never got around to making any thorough analysis of social stratification—one of a number of places where his genius lay in starting a discussion, not finishing it. The irony is that the great proposer of ideas found his suggestions fossilized into rigid dogmas by his organized disciples.

Also, the labor theory of value, on which Marx based his famous analysis of capitalism, came to him from Adam Smith and David Ricardo, while socialists such as Thomas Bray had already, before Marx, claimed that "by a fraudulent system of unequal exchange" the worker's just wage is taken away by the capitalist.

Of all these ideas Marx made a unique and powerful synthesis. The dialectic enabled him to tie them all together, much like Hegel. There is a plan and a purpose to history, Marx claimed; and moreover there is a method, the understanding of which enables us to decipher the meaning of history and thus collaborate with it in its purposes. He claimed to have provided this key that unlocks the golden gates of social science and shows us how every event fits into its place.

One might think that a dialectical philosophy would stress freedom and not determinism, for it is expressly opposed to a mechanistic outlook on nature, holding rather that the world is not static but like a developing and proliferating organism or like a conversation. One can scarcely predict the results of a dialogue in which a statement is made, is contradicted, restated, again objected to, and so on. This may be a good way to knowledge, but it is hard to see how the outcome could be known in advance.[4] One could argue that God does; but Marx, of course, did not believe in any God. Some critics of Marxism have wondered how Marx could exclude God or the Absolute yet insist on a rational, purposeful world, obeying regular laws. Or is Marx a pantheist, like his fellow apostate Jew, Spinoza?

All that can be said is that Marx shared to the full the positivist bias, that is, he wished to be scientific, to believe only in "facts," to dismiss such nebulous abstractions as God or the Absolute. He got this from the materialists of the eighteenth century as well as from the scientific atmosphere of his own time. But he married it to the very different system of Hegel. The marriage may have been incongruous, but it produced some lusty children.

Historical Materialism

Marx's theory or philosophy of history occupies the central place in his thought. He was strongly impressed by the "historicism" of Hegel and often spoke of the processes of history as operating independently of humanity's will. The historical process is an "it" that sweeps people along without regard to their wishes; one thinks of Thomas Hardy's phrase, the "immanent unrecking." This conception of a world-historical force was strong in Marx and even stronger in his disciples; that is why Soviet leaders were so sure capitalism is doomed and communism will triumph—this is not just a matter of probability or possibility but a certainty, decreed by the iron laws of history. Marx did not wish to think of the "laws" of society and history as merely descriptive of trends or tendencies, in the positivist sense, but rather as decrees imposed for all time, existing objectively and requiring all to conform to them. Nor did he wish to think of many small areas for social investigation, but of one great pattern sweeping through all history—a romantic and apocalyptic vision.

On the other hand he also had a considerable feeling for the active participation by people in shaping the historical process. This activism appeared in Marx in his famous statement that philosophers must not

---

[4]Neither inventions nor scientific theories can be entirely predicted, and these are what Marx regards as the basic factors; much less can future political and economic developments be foreseen. Prediction in general is possible only for a very short time ahead and for very general things. These points have been most fully established by present-day philosophers, especially Sir Isaiah Berlin (*Historical Inevitability*, 1954) and Karl Popper (*The Open Society and Its Enemies*, 4th ed., 1962 and *The Poverty of Historicism*, 1957).

merely describe the world but must help change it, in his own career as organizer of the First International and participant in other political movements, and in his statement that with the arrival of his philosophy people passed from the "kingdom of necessity" to the "kingdom of freedom." Marxists have of course made their great place in the modern world by this sort of dynamic revolutionary activism. Is this inconsistent with a deterministic outlook?

Whatever the possible discrepancies in logic, such a combination of activism with determinism produces a potent psychological stimulus; a similar combination was found in Calvinism. Adherents of Marxism feel that history is on their side and so they are bound to win, as well as serve nature's purposes; yet they can collaborate with nature, helping to make history by understanding its laws. Marx probably meant that (1) history is only determined within broad limits, leaving scope for variation in the particulars and in the pace; like a very large boulder bouncing around in a large and uneven chute, it will eventually reach the bottom but may pursue an uneven course and may be temporarily delayed. Present-day Communists assume that capitalism will eventually be destroyed but do not specify time or place; it might be now or in two hundred years; the process might move next in Vietnam or in England. In this way a general determinism can be reconciled with a practical voluntarism. (2) As in all social determinism, one must concede that people are a part of the social order and in acting and willing they play their part; fatalism is not the same thing as necessitariansim.

Here as elsewhere, Marx was somewhat impatient of finespun theoretical discussions, though theory was important to him. It has been pointed out that Marx uses terms like "condition" and "determine" (*bedingen* and *bestimmen*) much too loosely and indiscriminately. They do not mean the same thing, obviously. There is a significant difference between saying that human intelligence is conditioned (influenced) by society and saying that it is determined. No one would deny the former, almost everyone the latter. There is a characteristic flavor of rhetorical exaggeration about much of Marx's thought. In his materialistic explanation of history, that is, the theory that "material" factors (technological, economic) are "basic" in history while other factors may be relegated to a secondary role, such confusions of terminology and thought appear in profusion. Yet nowhere did Marx prove to be so stimulating and provocative as here.

Marx differed from Hegel, of course, in finding the motive forces of history in material factors, in the "productive forces," by which he evidently meant tools and the economic relations derived from them. Strictly speaking, the motive force of history is the class struggle ("All history is the history of class struggle"), but the techniques and modes of production of any given period determine the class structure. The windmill, said Marx, gives us feudalism (he would have been nearer the mark, according to modern economic historians, had he said the plough and the stirrup). He went on to claim that all the rest of civilization and culture depends on this economic foundation. In his speech at Marx's funeral, Engels put it this way: "The production of the immediate material means of subsistence and consequently the degree of economic development attained by a given people or during a given epoch form the foundation upon which the state institutions, the legal conceptions, the ideas on art and even on religion . . . have been evolved, and in the light of which they must, therefore, be explained. . . ." Marx, he claimed, had been the first to notice this "simple fact." This is the "materialist interpretation of history."

Here we encounter difficulties. If Marx and Engels are saying that people cannot think, write, worship, and so forth, without first finding some means of sustenance, then they are asserting an obvious truth, surely not original, to which no one would object. If they mean that the mode of production and the economic relationships of society influence or condition modes of thought in significant ways, it is also difficult to disagree with them, and once again the idea is hardly original, though Marx surely gave it more striking expression than any other writer one can recall. If however it is claimed that (1) all ideas and institutions are determined by the economic "substructure" and (2) play no real part or independent part in life or history, the claim appears almost self-evidently false. The saints may have been deluded, but they gave up their possessions to follow a religious ideal; others, including philosophers, adventurers, soldiers, political reformers, scientists, have followed their gleam without significant reference to capitalism or any other economic order. Marx himself is a classic example of one possessed by ideas to the exclusion of pecuniary motives, and the system he created is a prize instance of the power of an ideology. In this respect he is not a unique case, as he may have implied, for history is filled with the prophets crying in the wilderness, philosophers teaching in the marketplace, angry young individuals (and some old ones) denouncing the existing "establishment." There are manifestly human drives of a very fundamental nature other than the desire to rule and the desire for gain: drives sexual, esthetic, intellectual, spiritual. It strains our credulity to believe that Beethoven and Brahms wrote their music to serve the bourgeoisie and cover up their shameful exploitation of the workers, yet this is what crude Marxism requires us to believe. Engels and Marx conceded that this might be done unconsciously, without the individual being aware of it; but that is *really* the motivating force, nonetheless.

The "superstructure" consisting of all that is not economic is said to be only a "reflection" of the economic "substructure." Social change can take place only in the latter, the former following along in its wake. Also, "the ruling ideas are those of the ruling class." It is clear, though, that Marx was no crude economic determinist (such as would, for example, explain Milton's poetry by his occupation), and also that he granted at least some ideas a powerful place in history. He undoubtedly knew too little of the history of human thought and action to support his bold generalizations, and he tended to conceal by vague language some difficult problems. At the same time he was onto something in proposing an investigation of the origin and social relations of religions and philosophical systems. Nor can it well be denied that there are such things as ideological systems designed to support political regimes—that, indeed, institutions excrete ideologies as a normal function. The situation was much more complicated than Marx imagined, but he opened up fruitful fields of inquiry.

Marx's singular allegation, then, is approximately as follows: Ideas and ideologies of all sorts, legal and political institutions and processes, artistic and literary expression, all of religion, culture, and politics, all except the technological or economic comprise the "superstructure" and are ultimately dependent on it. Changes in the superstructure do not take place without prior changes in the economic foundation to which they respond; or, if such changes take place, they are not significant. Marx evidently asks to believe not only that Christianity is a tool of the ruling classes to divert and pacify the masses (not necessarily a deliberate tool, for remember that Marx holds that this process may be and indeed normally is unconscious), but that all other phenomena in some sense are the same. The class structure cannot be escaped. The bourgeois judge who thinks that perfect justice is administered is really doing so within the boundaries of the capitalist order and so engaged in defending it. Presumably Stravinsky wrote capitalistic music and Cézanne painted bourgeois pictures, much though these artisits themselves despised "bourgeois" culture. Marxist literary criticism has applied much ingenuity to exactly this sort of demonstration. Freud was a capitalistic psychologist, according to recent Soviet orthodoxy—a view that certainly would have surprised him. Though this is the evident import of Marxist theory, it should be pointed out that Marx himself did not conform to it: He was a great lover of classical Greek drama, which evidently had for him a value independent of its function in the class struggle.

Most people today are inclined to listen sympathetically to claims for the primacy of technological or economic change because they know what a dynamic agent it has been. The most common sort of "cultural lag" is perhaps the sort caused by a rapid advance in technology to which ideas and institutions have not adapted, though such adaptation is required. One might instance national states in an age of nuclear weapons. But this is not the only possible kind of "lag," and the reverse might be true. One might come up with a new idea or theory that will force changes in physical equipment. Freudian psychology has modified teaching practices and resulted in a new profession with at least some physical equipment (couches!), for example. A new theory of military strategy causes a government to build different types of weapons, abandoning others. Karl Popper presents an interesting example: Suppose, he says, that all the existing physical plant and scientific apparatus were destroyed, but the knowledge behind it, in books and human brains, were left in existence—the physical apparatus could be rebuilt, though no doubt with great expense and difficulty. But suppose the plant were to remain and the knowledge lost—as might happen if primitive savages suddenly replaced modern civilization and had no knowledge of modern technology. Then the machinery would fall into disuse and perish. In this sense, Popper concludes, knowledge, ideas, seem more "basic" than physical equipment, tools. What his example really indicates, however, is the impossibility of ever separating tools and brains; what he postulates could not happen. Since the beginning of civilization, tools and knowledge have evolved together in intimate association as aspects of the same process. We could not have brains without tools nor tools without brains. The skillful hand and the contriving brain (to borrow a phrase of James C. Malin's) go together. The experimental laboratory and the theorizing intellect must collaborate to make science and technology possible. Marx erred in attempting to separate the two things and make one of a different order than the other. As a matter of fact, he wavered in his view of scientific knowledge, sometimes putting it in the superstructure and sometimes in the foundation—a significant ambiguity.[5]

It seems especially important to recognize the sense in which the strictly *political* element may be primary. The story of some of the new nations today underscores the fact that economic development can scarcely take place until stable government has been secured. Until a political unit is secure both internally and externally, investment, trade, and labor can hardly function in any successful way. Unwise political decisions may cause deterioration of the entire economy, as has apparently happened in some South American countries with great economic potential but poor political foundation. The political process is often, it would seem, more "primary" than the economic. If people have to eat before they can live, they also have to cooperate in social units before they can eat or, at any rate, live much above the level of the beast.

[5] Josef Stalin himself, ironically, was responsible for detaching some fields from the substructure-superstructure zone when in 1951 he intervened in a debate about language to ridicule those solemnly orthodox Marxists who claimed that languages are part of the superstructure, that is, they will change when society changes and the Russian language could be expected to disappear under communism. In the Soviet Union today mathematics, logic, and other tools of thought have widened the breach opened up by the Marxist tyrant himself and successfully claimed a transcendent nature.

Anyone with much experience of the world knows that political processes exist in their own right, independent of economic ones. The fact that history is often divided into epochs based on politics is an indication of this political primacy. The age of the Roman Empire, the age of feudalism, the age of the national state—and, if such evolution took place, the age of the world state—unquestionably suggest politics as the decisive factor. These political classifications have at least as much claim to primacy as the age of slavery, of manorialism, and of capitalism. Political processes are acted upon by economic ones, but then the reverse is also true.

In sum, the "hard" version of Marxian economic determinism, which assigns everything to the economic foundation and denies any causal efficiency to the cultural "superstructure" of ideas, customs, noneconomic institutions, and so forth, has to be given up as obviously erroneous and has been given up in recent times by Marxists themselves, even in the Soviet Union. It was not held by Marx and Engels themselves.[6] A "soft" version, which does not see the "superstructure" as a product *only* of the economic structure or "mode of production," and which grants also that once created the elements of the superstructure can in turn exert causal influence in a significant way on human history, tends to decay into a rather meaningless statement, devoid of any real explanatory value.[7] One does better to agree that the world is multidimensional and many different kinds of autonomous processes act and interact in human social affairs.

One of Marxism's most startling failures was its inability to mark off any significant difference between the various *national* cultures. France, Germany, Great Britain, and the United States must all be substantially alike, except insofar as they are in slightly different stages of capitalist development, because they are all "bourgeois capitalist" stages; but it is obvious that in important respects these nations differ because of the role of tradition, that is, because of their different historic experiences. The Marxists expected socialist revolution to come first in Britain because capitalist development had proceeded farthest here. They overlooked the potent reasons why revolution was *least* likely in the land where, due to a complex variety of historical factors, the political constitution was the most stable in Europe. With their eyes fixed on only one set of forces, they were blind to the central facts of British history.

---

[6]Engels, in some letters on historical materialism written late in his life (between 1890 and 1894), complains that stupid people have written "fatuous notions" that "twisted" his and Marx's views; they meant nothing so absurd, he says, as that economic factors determine every last, petty detail. He tried to save the primacy of economic factors "ultimately" and "in the long run" but did not make this very clear.

[7]For illumination of this point see the article by James P. Scanlan in *Studies in Soviet Thought,* June 1973.

Marxists were disgusted with the failure of socialism to take root in the United States and could only declare that somehow, for unknown reasons, the American workers were hopelessly "petty bourgeois" in their outlook. Again, Marxists least expected revolution in Russia—a country for which Marx often entertained the deepest disdain—because it was economically backward.[8] This is not to say that some investigators did not creatively pursue answers to the interesting question why these various peoples utterly failed to conform to the Marxian theory.

Marx must be given credit for stimulating much fruitful inquiry, though it was necessary to go beyond his system to find the answers. He presented the first approximation of a theory on which subsequent historians and sociologists such as Max Weber, Karl Mannheim, Karl Popper, and others were to work.

According to Marx the dynamics of history spring from the inner contradictions of society, issuing in class conflict and revolution. The dialectical principle expresses itself in this process of clash and conflict, with one order emerging from the womb of another. The oppressed class or classes represent a negation or counterstatement destined in time to destroy the old society. Feudalism brought forth bourgeois capitalism from its own contradictions; capitalism in the same necessary way gives rise to the proletariat and to socialism. "The material powers of production, at a certain stage in their development, come into conflict with the existing relations of production. . . . Then comes the period of social revolution." In general, people are the unwitting instruments of historical destiny. The bourgeois does not want to create socialism but cannot help it; it arises from the very things that must be done.

Marx's vision of the historical process made a powerful appeal to the imagination. History not only has a plan and a meaning, but it is tremendously dramatic. Something of his Jewishness surely emerges in this essentially apocalyptic account of humanity's journey through time to reach a mighty climax at the end. For at the end, we are given to understand, and with the triumph of the proletariat over the capitalists, we reach the end of history.[9] There are now no more classes to create

---

[8]In 1848, at the time of the Slavic conference in Prague that confused the German and Austro-Hungarian revolutions, Marx and Engels wrote in their newspaper that the Slavs should be exterminated, "wiped from the face of the earth," since whole peoples may be "reactionary" and the Slavs are such a race. Many years later, however, Marx agreed with some Russian populists that the world revolution might perhaps begin in Russia.

[9]Condorcet had placed human history near the end of its days, and so apparently had Hegel; in 1841 so judicious an intellect as Matthew Arnold declared, in his Oxford inaugural address, that the modern age bears all the marks of being "the last step" in the human story. This somewhat curious finalism can be traced to several sources, but chiefly would seem to have rested on observation of the tremendous growth of modern Europe, in political units, population, extension of power, increased popular participation. Could one imagine anything larger than the nation-state, except the world state, an obvious finality? Or any further extension of democracy except to the lowest class, the proletariat?

another negation and another turn in the great cycle of history; this last victory of the submerged ushers in the classless society. History has come full circle from primitive communism to communism as the highest stage of human society. In the last phase human nature is cured of all those defects that were the result of its being "alienated" from itself and is whole again, a harmony rather than a discord. Such a vision clearly partakes more of faith than of science; it was the cogent restatement of an old and powerful myth.

MARX'S ANALYSIS OF CAPITALISM

In his *magnum opus, Capital*, Marx sought to apply his method in detail to the existing social situation. Here he drew on Ricardo and the classical economists as well as on socialism and the dialectic. Marx stumbled upon difficulties and failed to complete his book, but he left a deep impression upon the budding socialist movement with his major effort of economic theory.

Prior to Marx many less weighty socialist theoreticians had charged that the factory owners exploited, in other words, cheated, their employees. Indeed, this had emerged for all to see in the famous Parliamentary investigations of conditions in the textile factories and mines in England—on which Marx and Engels drew heavily for their ammunition, though their philosophy would seem to deny that these bourgeois bodies could be capable of such exposures.[10] The revelation of brutal long hours and pitiful low wages, frequently using child labor, while the owners drew large profits, had projected the "social question" (in Carlyle's phrase) onto the conscience of Europe when Marx was still a juvenile. The notion quickly grew that the wage system was a method of exploitation. A workers' jingle current before the *Communist Manifesto* was written (1847) made the point:

Wages should form the price of goods
Yes, wages should be all,
Then we who work to make the goods,
Should justly have them all.

This was a crude statement of the labor theory of value on which Marx erected his economic analysis.

The labor theory of value may be traced a long way back; it was forcefully stated by Adam Smith and adopted by Ricardo, where Marx found it. Later economic theory was to discard it, but Marx seized upon it and attempted to work out all its implications. It was still partly eco-

---

[10]Engel's *Condition of the Working Class*, 1844, made extensive use of the testimony before the Parliamentary committees.

nomic orthodoxy in Marx's time, though the "bourgeois" economists did not put it to the uses Marx did, needless to say. Value to them was "cost of production," which included materials and the natural reward of capital (the result of "abstinence" from present consumption) as well as labor. Senior had pointed out that some things have much value without any human labor at all: the pearl I chance to find in my oyster, for example! Yet remnants of the Ricardian labor theory of value existed in classical economics as represented most popularly by J. S. Mill at this time. The clean break with it was not to be made until Alfred Marshall and W. S. Jevons, about 1870.

The labor theory of value, plus the subsistence theory of wages, suggested to socialists that labor does not get its full and just price because wages are determined in the market, by the principle of supply and demand, whereas the products are sold for their "true" price, based on the amount of labor put into them. The difference was said to represent a surplus of value appropriated by the capitalist. Robert Owen had tried to change this pernicious system by using a currency reflecting units of labor, so that the price of a product would be exactly the amount of labor put into it. This naive idea proved entirely unworkable. Agreement could never be reached on just how many labor units commodities are worth, a major objection to the labor theory of value being that labor values submit to no accurate quantitative measurement. One carpenter might make a table in half the time another took; and how could one compare highly skilled labor to unskilled—how many hours of carpenter labor is one hour of an expert surgeon's time worth? Marx attempted to meet this objection by postulating a "socially necessary" amount of labor for every commodity, but this hardly removed the problem. In practice, the market price based on supply and demand would prevail anyway. The only alternative would be an elaborate system of administrative pricing based on the arbitrary decrees of a state bureaucracy, a system with many disadvantages and few advantages.

Marx ridiculed the labor-exchange idea. He believed that only the abolition of capitalism—of private property in the means of production—would solve the problem, and he used the labor theory of value not to support labor-exchange or social-credit schemes but rather to demonstrate, as he thought, the dynamics of capitalism as it worked towards its self-destruction.

Among the features of capitalism that seemed alarming were the periodic panics or depressions that afflicted it, tendencies toward monopoly, and of course the low wages and deplorable working conditions that frequently were the lot of the factory hands, to which one might add the demoralizing separation of workers from their tools and products, as they worked with machinery owned by others to produce goods that were not theirs to sell. For all these observable features of the nineteenth-century economic order in western Europe, Marx tried to supply explanations. The whole of his argument was designed to show that capitalism is a doomed system because it is unavoidably digging its own grave. The labor theory of value is the foundation stone for Marx's concept of the *falling rate of profit,* which is chiefly how he explained crises, consolidation, and the increasing misery of the working class.

Profits must come out of labor. Therefore the increasing use of machinery forces the capitalists to exploit their workers ever more mercilessly. They are forced to adopt machinery because of technological advances and competition; but as they increase the proportion of this "constant capital," as Marx called it, they have less and less of labor power or "variable capital" from which to make profits. Today it seems odd that Marx should have supposed that mechanization destroys profits by displacing human labor. One should assume that it would be more likely to *increase* profits, by cutting down the wage bill or stepping up efficiency of production. But he had his eye fixed on the labor theory of value, from which his conclusion seems to follow logically. This is the chief of the "contradictions" of capitalism according to Marx: that as it progresses, measured by the use of advanced machinery, it must intensify the misery of the working class, for profits must be squeezed out of human labor power. The more machinery used, the lower the wage of the worker has to be.

Strive as they will, the capitalists cannot, however, prevent their profits from declining. Of this unhappy fact another result is that some manufacturers are driven to the wall and fewer and fewer capitalists exist, holding bigger and bigger enterprises. This, too, unwittingly prepares for socialism; the huge industrial concern is already socialized, and at the last there are scarcely more than a handful of capitalists left to be taken over by society.

"In proportion as capital accumulates, the lot of the labourer . . . must grow worse." Marx evidently abandoned his early theory that wages must fall to the level of bare subsistence, and in other writings spoke of spiritual rather than economic impoverishment, or a relative impoverishment: workers may be better off but the employers are even more so. The fact is that absolute impoverishment of the working class was not happening; the evidence clearly indicated rising real wages through the later nineteenth century, not falling. So Marx often stressed the moral degradation of workers, through being made "appendages of a machine" and subjected to humiliating conditions of toil. He continued to insist that in some sense the workers became ever more miserable under capitalism, but this was not necessarily, one gathers, from material impoverishment. Marx is rather slippery on this vital point, one may find.

The labor theory of value on which Marx leaned so heavily was soon to be abandoned by economists, and today most of them think that it will bear little or none of the weight he put on it. His explanation of depressions, then, along with his theory of profits and wages, seem invalid. As for his predictions that small business would succumb entirely to big, and that with the advance of machinery people under capitalism would be worse off and not better—the doctrine of the declining rate of profit and the increasing misery of the working class—these things have not come about, though at times they may have looked plausible. By the end of the century workers were better off in material terms, not worse; the long-term effects of technology were to increase the whole national income greatly, though unevenly; and (it has been persuasively argued) the belief that the proletariat was growing ever more miserable was an illusion fostered partly by novelists, partly by that familiar phenomenon known as "relative deprivation"—we can think we are worse even when in absolute terms we are better off, because we perceive more things we want and do not have. The capital that Marx saw (under capitalism) as pushing the workers under was actually elevating them, gradually, unevenly, unequally, it is true, but in the long run, steadily. In his formula of exploitation, Marx had overlooked the enormous extent to which machinery raises the productivity of labor.

Many of Marx's own followers finally came to feel that a wholesale revision of his economic theories was needed. The main stream of economic analysis travelled away from Marx, and in later times John Maynard Keynes unquestionably spoke for professional economists of virtually all schools in calling *Das Kapital* "an obsolete economic textbook." But Marx's doctrines have of course exerted an enormous influence on the Soviet Union since its revolutionary birth in 1917. Still, economic practice even the USSR does not owe much directly to Marx, who failed to describe in detail the economics of socialism. He thought he had charted with scientific accuracy the last fatal illness of capitalism, and all Marxists continue to believe that "capitalism is doomed."

Perhaps it is, but apparently not for the reasons Marx gave. Sometimes it is suggested that Marx was a good prophet in a general sort of way, though he missed many details; for has not the economic order, even in the West, travelled a long way from the unregulated individualism of the nineteenth century toward a "welfare state" system which is in the broadest sense socialistic? It has indeed, but it should be noted that Marx has not really proved a good prophet here. The welfare state or "interventionist" economy (the French have a word *dirigiste*—directed—which is useful) was not really what he had in mind. Marx believed the state would die; his vision of the future was essentially anarchist, or perhaps utopian. Social ownership of the means of production did not mean to him statism.

Classical Marxism expected the middle class to be ground to bits, the class struggle to become more acute, the factory workers to grow ever unhappier until they rebelled, and the capitalist order to end in revolution, with private property in the sector of production disappearing. In all these respects he proved a poor prophet. It took a disastrous war to bring socialist revolution to Europe, and then it came to a backward, almost precapitalist society, quite contrary to the expectations of most Marxists.

Even as Marx was writing *Das Kapital,* economists such as Stanley Jevons were criticizing the labor theory, doing away with the mystical idea of a true or inherent "value" of a commodity that is not the same as its market price. They substituted a sophisticated version of supply and demand, the marginal utility theory.[11] Others pointed out that Marx's surplus value would not do; why should competition not cause it to disappear? It was argued that capital is more productive than Marx thought. But if in the eyes of experts not much was left of Marx's elaborate theorizing in his *magnum opus,* which he left unfinished, it remained a compelling document. In many portions of the book Marx abandoned the pretense of scientific objectivity to emit thunderous indictments of working conditions in the factories and the iniquity of capitalism. And the whole seemed an impressive vindication of the larger dialectical philosophy. Apparently Marx had shown in detail how capitalism destroys itself and in the process creates socialism, its "negation" that had always been included in itself. Socialism emerges out of the very womb of capitalism, as the dialectic predicts. Capitalism brought into existence the working class, forced it into the factories, and reduced the number of capitalists, thus inadvertently "socializing" the economic order and the technological system; it created advanced machinery, broke down parochial social units to create the national and even international economy, and also accustomed individuals to a rational, materialistic outlook. According to Marxists, capitalism had an indispensable historical role to play, and until Lenin they practically all felt that every society must work

---

[11]Developed almost simultaneously by Carl Menger in Austria and M. E. L. Walras in Switzerland along with Jevons in England, marginal utility analysis represented on charts the curve of diminishing utility as an individual—or, by extension, a nation—acquires successive units of a commodity. To a hungry person the first loaf of bread is extremely valuable, but each successive one decreases in its value to that person. The final increment, the marginal one, determines exchange value. "Commodities exchange at ratios such that their marginal utilities are equal" (Edmund Whittaker). The student may consult textbooks of economics for full understanding of the principle. Employed by the influential economists Alfred Marshall in Britain and J. B. Clark in the United States, marginal theory tended to dominate academic economics in this "neoclassical" phase. Marshall's *Principles of Economics* supplanted Mill's as the standard textbook.

its way through capitalism before it is ready for socialism. There was an ambiguity here, to be sure, revealed in the later history of the Marxist movement. One might choose to dwell on the horrors of capitalism, the misery it caused the workers, the need to destroy it; or one might point to its inevitability and the things it achieved to prepare the way for socialism. But it is the latter that is most characteristic of Marx as opposed to the mere moralists whose outlook he despised because it was not "scientific."

Perhaps the leading source of confusion in evaluating Marxism has been its enthusiastic believers' insistence upon the scientific, rational character of their creed, whereas they seem really to have committed themselves as an act of faith to a kind of religion. However fine and courageous a thinker Marx was, his overly ambitious system contains so many contradictions that, as Karl Popper (a sympathetic critic) observes, and as is known all too well today, those who remain dogmatic Marxists, like the Communists, "must become mystics—hostile to reasonable argument." They repeat the formula by rote and refuse to listen to objections; they ignore the real world and live in a dream world. It has become increasingly clear that theirs is a form of faith that has taken on the outer trappings of scientific positivism while preserving the inner structure of an emotional ideology. Many have pointed out the startling resemblance of Marxism to the psychological structure of religion, especially the Judaic-Christian framework transposed into secular terms. It has the original innocence of primitive communism, followed by the Fall (private property), the coming of the doctrine of salvation, the nature of evil and the struggle against it, and finally the apocalypse and last state of blessedness. It is clear that this secular religion was in the making before Marx, for Rousseau and the romantics contributed much to it; he gave it final form and further equipped it with enough intellectual content to satisfy a rational age. In a fine phrase of Professor J. Herman Randall, Jr., "Marxism is the last of the great Romantic faiths, lingering on in a scientific world."

Anglo-Saxon empiricism has typically accused Marxism of being, as Bertrand Russell put it, an "irrational dogma," which Marx took *a priori* from the speculations of Hegel and then found facts to fit, rather than proceeding in true scientific manner. Scientists, to be sure, must use hypotheses, but these are held tentatively and modified where experiment indicates. Most Marxists have held their beliefs as a sacred dogma beyond fundamental alteration, any "revisionism" being treated as dreadful heresy. Since Marx said he was not a Marxist, one perhaps cannot fairly blame the sins of his disciples on him. There is a sense in which it is logically impossible to be a "Marxist." Marx held that thought changes with the conditions of life, which are in perpetual change; thus no thinker is valid beyond his or her own time, and Marx, if he were alive today, would think quite differently than he did. Acceptance of Marx's central thesis rules out the permanent validity of any body of thought—including Marx's! Marx's essential characteristic was a critical mind, despite his occasional tendencies toward dogmatism and even intellectual arrogance noticed by some critics. The Communist party of the Soviet Union in Stalin's era colors this view of Marxism; but Marx would certainly have disapproved of Stalinism—many of his disciples among, for example, the Trotskyites have said as much. In recent years Marxism has become much more flexible and varied, with all kinds of "revisionists" participating in a renaissance of Marxist studies.[12] Marxism has intereacted with existentialism and with Christianity in a series of dialogues. It does seem to be much more a religion than a science. As such, it has displayed a remarkable vitality, indicating that it possesses much relevance to the modern situation. Yet, deprived of its monolithic structure of authority, it has tended to dissolve and lose its unity.

Marx represents a blend of simple, emotional faith with a critical and rational intellect. Often he ridiculed the simpler variety of socialist as "utopian" or soft-headed, wooly-minded. Yet he himself appears in some respects simplistic and utopian. Despite his protests he was essentially not scientist, but prophet. Judged in this light, he has recently received praise from some who have rejected his philosophy as meaningless and his economics as outdated. As a moral critic of capitalism, voicing a protest against its alienation of the worker from his or her work, its destruction of esthetic values and human dignity, Marx adds his powerful bass to a whole chorus of such nineteenth-century indictments. He would have indignantly rejected the classification of his thought as ethical, but his moral criticism seems to have survived his pseudoscientific theorizing through most of the Western world. He was the founder not, as he thought, of the social sciences but of the greatest religious movement of modern times.

Marxism is for millions in some parts of the world today a faith to live by, and one may well ask why—wherein lay its peculiar potency as a religion? The answer would seem to be in its strong combination of emotional-ideological with rational-scientific factors, a combination, if you like, of the Enlightenment and romanticism; or a new *Summa*, like St. Thomas's, blending faith with reason. If today the inclination is to "see through" the allegedly rational and scientific portions of Marx, this is not to deny that they were there and could carry great conviction for all but the most searchingly critical intellects. One way in which Marxism seems curiously old-fashioned today is in its absence of any sense of the irrational or nonrational factors in humanity. Marx scarcely has a psychology, and modern Marxists have usually strongly resisted Freud, Jung,

[12]On recent Marxism, see pp. 321–25 in this book.

and the existentialists, calling them bourgeois and decadent. Likewise Marxism contributed little to the study of politics as such, a rather strange neglect for a political creed. Politics is the mirror of economic-class interests, which are clear and calculable, without separate identity of its own, according to Marxism. All this testifies to an old-fashioned, Enlightenment rationalism in Marx.

The religious features gave expression to a powerful ethical imperative: One's duty was to advance the course of history by assailing the evil of capitalism and thus to prepare the way for the final kingdom of righteousness. Like Calvinism, socialist historicism made you feel that the fates were fighting on your side and thus was a great energizing factor. So in many ways this was the "religion of science," or the scientific religion, for which Comte and Renan had searched. Those who adopt Marxism may well feel that they understand the world, and from this they see what they must do to serve the good cause.

It may be unnecessary to add that this Marxist religion, an intolerant one, could lead to ruthless behavior. Lenin's pronouncement is well known: "Morality is what serves to destroy the old exploiting society." Hegelian historicism encourages the morality of being on the winning side; to this Marxism added a ferocious hatred for the old "exploiting society" and a keen desire to hasten the coming of the revolution. The Communist followers of Marx and Lenin were prepared to employ cruelty, force, treachery, and deceit, so long as these weapons were used against the bourgeoisie in behalf of the socialist revolution. These features were more evident in the Russian followers of Marx than among the milder Social Democrats of the western countries, but they are easily drawn from his doctrines.

In many ways the social ideologies now being considered, though they were tremendously influential, were out of touch with realities in their age. Of Comte, Marx, and Spencer alike, A. D. Ritchie has observed that "all three smell of the midnight oil and the ivory tower. They none of them have the proper smell of places where collective or public human action occurs, where discussions go on and decisions are made." It is difficult to object to this characterization. Few more pronounced "outsiders" ever existed than Comte and Marx, impoverished obscurities in their lifetimes, writing books nobody read until some years later. But not so unusual (Bentham is a good example, Rousseau another) is the phenomenon of the eccentric recluse-philosopher who proves to be a fountain of ideas destined to the utmost importance when taken up by others. These ideologies found emerging from the nineteenth century answered some great need. They all thought they were sciences; but clearly today one must see them as more nearly "miscellaneous prejudices dressed up to look like science." They did not serve any useful purpose in meeting practical problems of the day, such as officials and businesspeople faced in their daily affairs. Some Marxist historical works unto this day have the curious quality of spending much of their space lamenting that things did not happen as they were supposed to. Instead of conforming to Marxist theory and working tirelessly for the social revolution, nineteenth-century workers accepted capitalism, formed trades unions, were incurably "reformist." And practically all the Marxian revolutionaries were intellectuals and offshoots of the bourgeoisie, like Marx and Engels themselves, like Lenin and Mao Tse-tung later. Some writers early in the twentieth century developed the theory that Marxism was in fact the ideology of the bourgeois intellectuals, a credo for the workers of the brain or for a declassed element increasingly identifiable as a special group—*les intellectuels* (a term evidently first used in a prominent way at the time of the Dreyfus Affair in France, from 1894 to 1900).

Yet the writings of these nineteenth-century ideologists, presented usually in bowdlerized and simplified form, were very popular.

Nobody now reads the works of Comte or Spencer, yet a century ago "Spencer's books were read all over the world in many languages by thousands of devoted disciples." Marx's still are. The reason for this is that these imposing systems of thought offered to restore to the European the lost vision of an integrated universe, the source of values. In brief, they substituted for religion and for the metaphysical systems of the past. Comte was right in divining that the modern individual had lost the capacity for traditional Christianity and metaphysics. Humanity had not and could not lose its need for religion in the broader sense—as a fairly simple, comprehensible, satisfying picture of the world revealing its structure and purpose. Walter Marshall Horton has defined the human needs that faiths satisfy as three: "the need for an ultimate object of trust and devotion; the need for a final goal of hope and endeavor; the need for a concrete connection between trust and hope . . . ," in other words, a way of salvation. The increasingly numerous and somewhat disoriented masses of modern life, often uprooted by industrialism from traditional societies and cast into the maelstrom of anomic cities, have urgent needs of this sort. They may cling to traditional religion, but increasingly they have adopted substitutes. No doubt this explains the significance of the nineteenth century's classical ideologies.

OTHER FORMS OF SOCIALISM

Not well known in Europe until the 1880s, Karl Marx's formidable theories thereafter tended to mold and dominate Continental socialism but never had that kind of success in Britain and never monopolized the field anywhere. Socialism was far broader than Marxism. It ranged, taking the term in its largest dimensions, from a fairly conservative bourgeois right wing, including Christian socialism and moderate welfare-state reformism, to a revolutionary far left that by the 1880s had come to be designated "anarchism." In between lay many species in rich variety. Marx's contemporaries included Michael Bakunin, the Russian revolutionary, with whom he did many a battle; Louis Blanc, in exile in England after 1848 but tough enough to outlive the Bonapartist regime and return to France in 1871; Mazzini and Garibaldi, the Italians who became internationally famous in 1861; and the American, Henry George, whose book *Progress and Poverty* exerted a remarkable influence in Britain and parts of the Continent. Then there was William Morris, Ruskin's as well as Marx's disciple, poet, and craftsman, who popularized "guild socialism," a return to the spirit of medieval artisans. Proudhon, the French "mutualist," long retained a strong following in France, and the First International of 1864 produced quarrels between the Marxists and Proudhonists. In Germany, Ferdinand Lassalle, a romantic figure who disagreed with Marx on some matters, was a more important leader in the 1870s than the latter. In Russia, "populist" revolutionaries arose in the 1870s.

Then, within a few years after the major reception of Marxism and its success in the 1890s in capturing the strongest socialist groups on the Continent, came a major effort to "revise" Marx in the light of new developments; while in Great Britain the important Fabian movement rejected Marxian theory to build a more eclectic brand of reformist socialism. All this and more is part of the rich history of socialism and social reform in these latter decades of the nineteenth century, when Europe moved rapidly toward an order more urban, industrial, and democratic. A brief review of this long story follows.

Revolutionary socialism, or working-class socialism of any sort, sank almost out of sight after 1848 for some time, suffering from repression and disunity. The Second Empire in France jailed Proudhon, exiled Blanc, and stifled press freedom while "buying off" the workers with its great public works projects. With the softening of Louis Napoleon's regime in 1860, socialism revived somewhat, only to be crushed again in the gripping episode of the Commune of Paris, 1871. Working-class socialists were accused of fomenting class war in Paris and the reaction again brought severe repression. This phase of French socialism was Proudhonist. Under the banner of "mutualism" these followers of the Besançon-born working man, who died in Paris in 1865, manifested a hatred of the state and centralized power that marked them off sharply from other socialists. They thought proletarian revolution should lead to a decentralized, "federal" political structure, for Proudhon could see no purpose to the existing state except militarism and the repressive defense of property, both of which would vanish with the bourgeoisie. The economic order would be one of cooperatives, the workers in each factory, farm, or store jointly managing it. Somewhat fuzzy and inane, Proudhon's utopia had the merit of upholding liberty; he accused Marx of fomenting a new tyranny while Marx sneered at the simplicity of the Frenchman's economic ideas. In this respect Proudhon repeated the charge brought by the celebrated Russian revolutionary, Michael Bakunin, against Marx: His ideas would lead to a new state tyranny. For, though Marx and Engels expected the state to "wither away" (Engels's term) after the socialist revolution, they advocated seizing it and using it in the interlude between this revolution and the final achievement of communism. With considerable accuracy the anarchists predicted that the Marxists would be corrupted by the state power as they used it. The revolution, in the anarchist view, must be made outside the state and must immediately destroy the hateful monster.

In 1871, when the Parisians decided to secede from the rest of France after the abdication of the Emperor Louis Napoleon (defeated by the Germans in war), they were acting in large part on Proudhon's ideas. (Communes were proclaimed in several other French cities.) There were to be sure, other kinds of socialists, including the extremely romantic revolutionary followers of Blanqui, the legendary insurrectionist. Blanquists, Proudhonians, and other socialists and radicals formed a decidedly inharmonious group among the Communards, whose defeat might be blamed in part on this dissension. The defeat of this revolt, and the brutal reprisals, caused the death or banishment of some twenty thousand Communards and crushed French working-class radicalism to earth for another generation. One of the casualties was the First International, organized in 1864; always a scene of contention, it split, with the "Federalists" or "Anarchists" (Proudhonists) taking over what was left of it for a while, only to see it die in 1877.

From the shattering defeat and civil strife in 1870 to 1871, France headed slowly toward the Third Republic, under which freedom would revive and a new socialist movement gradually reappear. In Germany laws against the socialists were enforced in the seventies and eighties, while at the same time Bismarck tried to alleviate the lot of the workers with Europe's first state-administered social-welfare system, including old-age pensions and insurance against sickness. But the German Social Democratic party, now firmly Marxist, survived the persecution, developed able leaders and a magnificent organization, and after being legalized in 1890 following Bismarck's removal from power, went on to become one of Germany's largest political parties (*the* largest by 1912) and the dominant force in the Second International. The latter world organization dates from 1889 to 1890 and enjoyed considerable success until 1914, with its international congresses and its annual May Day demonstrations being impressive. It counted twelve million members by 1914; the war destroyed it.

The 1880s and particularly the 1890s saw a widespread interest in social legislation on all fronts; it is the watershed for the change of direction from laissez-faire economic liberalism to a more socially conscious, state-interventionist order. There were many signs of this change and many versions of it.

In Britain, the prosperity and stability of the period from 1850 to 1870 washed away Chartism and Owenism, marking the high tide of liberalism in its individualist, antistate phase. But the eighties brought a significant change. In 1881 the philosopher T. H. Green began at Oxford University a school of social thought influenced by Hegel and stressing the social origin of rights, the social responsibilities of property. The rapidity of change in outlook may be judged from a comment of Lord Milner: "When I went up to Oxford [in the early 1870s] the laissez-faire theory still held the field. . . . But within ten years the few men who held the old doctrines in their extreme rigidity had come to be regarded as curiosities." This was a respectable revolution. Green borrowed from Hegel a feeling for the claims of society and the positive role of the state, without any admixture of revolution or violence. At University College, London, economist Stanley Jevons undermined dogmatic laissez-faire by simply asking for scientific, empirical investigation in particular areas to determine "where we want greater freedom and where less," a solution of problems piecemeal, rather than in accordance with some general formula. This was the path taken by the Fabian socialists. It was a reaction against the dogmatic individualism often proclaimed by Victorian liberals (for example, Auberon Herbert and the Non-Interference Union), as much as against dogmatic socialism.

In 1887 the young Irish critic, essayist, orator, novelist, and playwright George Bernard Shaw introduced Marx (as he was soon to introduce Nietzsche) to the British public. But the sharp-witted youths with whom Shaw joined to form the Fabian Society at about this time soon rejected Marx's labor theory of value and with it the rest of his economics: They retained only his moral indignation at the alleged stupidities and wrongs of a capitalistic, acquisitive society, and this they got from others besides Marx—from Carlyle, Ruskin, Mill, Morris, Nietzsche. The Fabians emerged from the chrysalis of something called the Fellowship of the New Life, founded by a remarkable Scotsman, Thomas Davidson, in 1882. The Fabian Society broke away from Davidson's group in 1884. Shaw joined it in 1885. He had turned socialist after listening to Henry George. Fabianism was eclectic in its origins, not imprisoned by a dogma, and permeated with the spirit of British empiricism. Initially, after Jevons and Alfred Marshall had discredited the Marxian labor theory of value in favor of a marginal utility theory, the Fabians tried to elaborate a general theory of exploitation on this basis, using the Ricardian theory of rent. But before long they decided that "abstract economics" was not of much value.

A mentor of Fabian founder Beatrice Webb was Charles Booth, author of an exhaustive pioneer social study of *Life and Labour of the People of London* (9 volumes, 1892 to 1897). "The *a priori* reasoning of political economy, orthodox and unorthodox alike, fails from want of reality," Booth wrote. Booth had been influenced by Comte and by the German historical school of economics (Schmoller). The result was an economics mainly historical and descriptive; the chief works of the Webbs were massive historical studies of local government, trade unions, and poor relief. Problems should be tackled piecemeal with the aid of thorough factual documentation, they believed. Fabian pamphleteering was often hard-hitting and bitterly critical of bourgeois society. But the movement's enduring importance lay in the patient accumulation of facts and ideas directed at particular abuses, under the guidance of the industrious Sidney and Beatrice Webb.

Clearly a faith was at work here: The Fabians did not doubt that socialism was a higher form of human society, the next rung on the ladder of social evolution, and they worked for it with a missionary spirit. The following statement by C. E. M. Joad may suggest something of the mood, as he recalled it in later years:

> England before 1914 was a land of gross social and economic inequality, in which the poverty and misery of the many were outraged by the luxury and the ostentation of the few. Under Socialism we believed the poverty and misery would disappear and the inequality be rectified. This was the first, fresh springtime of the Fabian Socialism, and we saw ourselves marching in irresistible procession with Shaw, Webb and Wells—slightly out of step—in the vanguard, to the promised land of State ownership of the means of production, distribution and exchange which we believed lay just around the corner.[13]

In their early days at least, the Fabians were not too scholarly to take part in demonstrations and harangue working-class audiences. On November 13, 1887, Shaw, William Morris, Annie Besant, and other intellectual socialists were roughed up by the police at a demonstration in Trafalgar Square. After this they chose the path of gradual change by parliamentary means, their duty being to furnish the politicians with the facts of industrial life so fully and plainly that even a politican could not do otherwise than recognize the necessity of social legislation. In this they were remarkably successful. If, prior to World War I, there was in

---

[13]"What I Still Believe," *The New Statesman and Nation*, May 19, 1951.

Britain no very large Labour or Socialist party (there was a small Labour party, not Socialist until 1918, with less than 10 percent of the seats in the House of Commons),[14] this was largely because the older parties, especially the Liberal party, had been quietly infiltrated by a good deal of social-welfare doctrine.

If they rejected Marx's economic theory, the Fabians agreed with his faith in the future of socialism. It was, they thought, evident that socialism was the wave of the future. But it would come gradually, was coming everyday, rather than all at once in one great revolution. Parliamentary democracy and other institutions of self-government would ensure its peaceful adoption. The Fabians placed great stress on local government; contrary to a common opinion, they did not propose the nationalization of all industry, but at this time (pre-1914) hoped that the county and borough councils, recently established in Great Britain, would own and operate a great deal of it. They did believe in public ownership as a panacea that, by driving the landlords and capitalists out of business, would increase the workers' share and lead to an era of plenty for all. In this they were often quite naive.

But Fabian tactics helped ease the way to acceptance of social-welfare principles by moderate men in Great Britain. Under conservative auspices, paternalistic perhaps and including such things as municipal ownership of utilities ("gas and water socialism") and state-run health insurance or old-age pension plans, it could attract broad support; in 1889 a British peer remarked that "we are all socialists now." The sheer facts of life in a complex, interdependent industrial society forced people to modify laissez-faire capitalism. Bismarck declared in his great speech to the German Reichstag on social-insurance legislation that the modern state could not disclaim all responsibility for the welfare of its working-class citizens; if it did, it would invite revolution. More modestly, Birmingham industrialist Joseph Chamberlain found that the upper classes could not ignore sanitary conditions among the lower classes in a modern city, because cholera germs were no respecters of class lines.

Also, trade unions became accepted and respectable and gave the workers a modest voice in the affairs of industry and the state. They were at least a force with which to be reckoned, backed by the weapon of the strike. In the 1900s, British trade unions overcame the Taff Vale decision, making them responsible for damages in a strike. Bitter strikes swept France and Italy as well as Britain in this decade. While in France "syndicalists" dreamed of accomplishing the revolution by a great gen-

---

[14]The parliamentary Labour party was born in 1900. On its doctrinal side it owed something to the rather eccentric Marxism of H. M. Hyndman and rather more to William Morris's Socialist League, as well as a little to the Fabians, but it was much more motivated by practical trade-union goals prior to World War I.

eral strike, trade-union leaders were apt to scorn the socialist intellectuals who preferred theoretical argument to "practical work inside the labor movement." Orthodox Marxism deplored the "opportunism" of trade unionism that aimed at nothing more than getting some workers a bigger slice of the rewards without "changing the system." But in Germany the unions and the Marxist Social Democrats struck a close alliance. (The French unionists, by contrast, rejected such a relationship.) By 1906 it was the unionists who had the stronger position, but they accepted the SDs as their political arm. In all the countries of western Europe, the unions, growing rapidly in the 1890s, were strong in the 1900s.

"Socialism" in this sense, as a pragmatic modification of laissez-faire capitalism in trade-unionist and state-welfare directions, became an accepted part of the late Victorian political landscape, though not without its bitter controversies: As late as 1910 in Britain the Lloyd George budget, including an income tax for social insurance financing, inspired an opposition that ended only in the "swamping" of the House of Lords and the passing of a Parliament Act sharply reducing the power of the peers to block legislation. There followed what an English newspaper called "the greatest scheme of social reconstruction ever attempted"— the National Insurance Bill of 1911.

MARXIST REVISIONISM

Quite different was the situation in Germany, where a strong Marxist party developed, by far the strongest and best-organized one in Europe. The German Social Democrats won great prestige by their success against Bismarck's efforts to destroy them. After 1891, save for one brief period, this party thrived on legality, having shown it could survive illegality. It was a well-disciplined mass organization, publishing its own newspapers, and led by educated Germans of the caliber of August Bebel, Wilhelm Liebknecht, Eduard Bernstein, and Karl Kautsky. Entering into close association with the trade unions, in 1912 it was the largest single political party with one-third of the electorate. The Social Democratic leaders accepted the possibility of overthrowing capitalism by peaceful, democratic means. In the meetings of the Second International they opposed the radicalism of the anarchists and preached the inevitability of socialism on the basis of Marx's theory of the self-destruction of capitalism, the dialectically necessary triumph of socialism. Unlike the Fabians they did not view socialism as a piecemeal program but awaited the day when the entire capitalistic system would crumble, meanwhile generally refusing to collaborate in government with the "bourgeoisie."

Bernstein went further in the direction of reformism. His efforts to "revise" Marx touched off a battle of words within the SPD in which revisionism was finally rejected. Bernstein believed that Marx's prophecies about the decline of capitalism and the increasing misery of the working class had proved false. Small and medium properties had not disappeared but were even increasing; the working class was getting better off, not worse off; the class struggle had become less acute, not more so. Drawing conclusions from this, he suggested a reformism not far in spirit from British Fabianism. He held that political democracy, having arrived in western Europe, made it possible to establish socialism by parliamentary means. "In all advanced countries," he urged, "we see the privileges of the capitalist bourgeoisie yielding step by step to democratic organizations." The party refused to accept this gradualism in theory, remaining officially committed to the winning of the proletarian revolution by means of the class struggle. It would not participate in governments in collaboration with the "bourgeois" parties. It almost read Bernstein out of the party, though he was an old and dedicated servant. But while rejecting gradualism, the large majority of the party accepted legalism. Engels himself, living on into the 1890s, announced that "the time of revolution carried through by small minorities at the head of unconscious masses is past." The path to the revolution would be a democratic and parliamentary one.

Similar issues agitated the French Socialist party which, rent by schism, managed to achieve unity in the 1900s but not unanimity. In 1899, after the socialist Millerand had accepted a post in the government headed by the leftist republican Waldeck-Rousseau, the French socialists earnestly debated this policy, and it was the occasion for exchanges between their two outstanding leaders, Jules Guesde and Jean Jaurès. Jaurès argued that it was good to penetrate bourgeois positions in this way, for would not the capitalist regime fall little by little, and how could it fall if its outposts were never occupied? But Guesde carried the day, by a narrow margin, with an eloquent exposition of socialist orthodoxy— the doctrine of the class struggle, of the solidarity of the working classes, of the utter incompatibility of socialism and capitalism: There could be no "mixture" or in-betweens, it was a matter of either-or. In the 1914 elections the party won about one-sixth of the seats; like its German counterpart it refused to take ministerial posts in any government in which it would share power. Right-wing–left-wing tension still existed, with unity maintained only at the cost of a rather imprecise program. French socialism was complicated by the presence of strong traditions other than Marxism. If Guesde, "Torquemada in lorgnettes," was a rigid Marxian dialectician, Jaurès, the greatest individual in the party and one of the great Frenchmen of his generation, was a deeply civilized humanist who drew from many other sources than Marx. For Jaurès, Leon Blum later wrote, socialism was "the summation, the point of convergence, the

heritage of all that humanity had created since the dawn of civilization. . . ." Proudhonist and other elements still lingered on in France
despite a strong Marxian incursion.

Similarly in Italy there were reformist, revisionist speakers (for
example, Filippo Turati) arguing that democracy had rendered revolution obsolete but finding bitter opponents on the left to whom this was
dangerous illusion.[15] In Russia the Marxist debate took a not dissimilar
turn. Marxism entered Russia via the remarkable intellect of G. V.
Plekhanov, a self-educated but exceedingly well-educated man who,
exiled like so many other politically conscious Russians, lived and wrote
for many years in Switzerland. In the 1870s the political faith of revolutionary Russians was populism, a courageous, self-sacrificing but intellectually not very clear movement, based on a belief in the uniqueness
of Russia and especially of her communal peasant population. The "big
three" of earlier Russian socialism had been Belinsky, already mentioned
as a Hegelian; Bakunin, the fabulous revolutionary who, influenced in
Paris by Proudhon, became an anarchist and attacked Marx for his
statism; and Alexander Herzen, the powerful publicist who came to
Paris in 1848 to receive a shattering blow from the "June Days" when the
workers' insurrection against the Republic was savagely repressed. With
the aid of a German historian, they discovered in the *mir* or Russian
peasant village an allegedly natural foundation for Proudhonian
mutualism. Subsequently somewhat discredited, Bakunin and Herzen
nevertheless deeply influenced the populist movement of which the Social Revolutionary party was the political offshoot. In the 1860s the *mir*
socialists, though not a violent group, were repressed by the tsar's government; Chernyshevsky and Pisarev were imprisoned, Moscow University closed in 1868. The result was the famous "To the People" pilgrimage of young idealists in the 1870s, which suffered rude disenchantment
and brought about the arrest of hundreds; and then, in desperation, a
wave of revolutionary terrorism. This too led nowhere; and in opposition to the romantic excesses of populism, which resorted to assassination, climaxed in the killing of Tsar Alexander II in 1881, the cool,
analytical approach of Marxism was welcome. Marxism in Russia in
the1890s had the effect of turning minds from illegal revolutionary
pamphlets to the systematic study of economics, sociology, and history;
the stress was on a well-grounded intellectual outlook, careful planning,

[15]Other Italians involved in a very extensive canvassing of Marxist issues included
Antonio Labriola, a professor who became a leading Marxist theoretician whose distinctions were a bit too subtle for popular consumption; Achille Loria's crudely positivistic,
deterministic Marxism; and the great Benedetto Croce who was drawn to Marxism along
with most other young Italian intellectuals in the 1890s, only to become its critic in the next
decade. To Croce, as to his friend Georges Sorel, Marxism came to seem a myth rather
than a science.

no childish adventurism. Marxism even allowed some to accept the progressiveness of capitalism. It was a weapon against agrarian populism with its revolutionary terrorism.

A civilized, even fastidiously esthetic intellectual, Plekhanov believed in the Marxist laws of historical evolution and counseled waiting for a democratic revolution which would come about spontaneously after Russia went through a capitalist phase. Instilling Marxist precepts into a generation of Russian revolutionaries, Plekhanov found some of these disinclined to wait. In 1903, Lenin proposed the creation of an elite of professional revolutionaries, trained to seize power. To Plekhanov's orthodox Marxism this was little less than Bonapartism or Blanquism. The majority of the Russian Social Democratic party followed him and a split occurred. Lenin's "bolshevik" group was in fact in a small minority most of the time, the "mensheviks" a more numerous and prestigious group. Victory and fame would come to the stubbornly independent Lenin in 1917: prior to that he was thought to have departed widely from Marxian orthodoxy and was isolated at the far left of the socialist spectrum.

To sum up the Marxist debate: On the Continent, though not in England, Marxism prevailed as the reigning orthodoxy in the socialist or social democratic parties, which were well organized and gaining adherents, on the eve of 1914. But within the parties sharp debate took place centering on the issue of whether class struggle, revolution, and the complete destruction of capitalism at one stroke had not become an obsolete program in the era of democratic politics, trade unionism, and welfare capitalism. The usual answer was to refuse to abandon Marxism for Fabian gradualism (Bernstein) but also to reject stress on violent revolution through illegal or conspiratorial means (Lenin). The majority of socialists held to their faith in an apocalyptic revolution that would change the entire system but thought this could come peacefully as soon as their political party won a majority of the electorate, and they refused meanwhile to take any share of power. Their rate of growth between 1890 and 1914 held out some hope that this might happen. But this compromise was an uneasy one and gave rise to a degree of internal tension. Between Albert Thomas and Jules Guesde in France, Eduard Bernstein and Rosa Luxemburg in Germany, or Plekhanov and Lenin in Russia, one found a considerable ideological and psychological distance. This ambivalence can be directly related to unresolved dilemmas at the heart of Marxian doctrine; particularly between voluntarism and determinism, elitism and democracy, revolution and evolution. On one side there was the call to action, to an uprising of the downtrodden led by revolutionary leaders; and on the other there was the belief that the objective laws of historical development were fast preparing the way for the inevitable triumph of democratic socialism.

Viewed more broadly, Marxism itself was a kind of center between a right and left wing of the entire "social" movement. To its left lay the anarchists, who seldom could be contained in the same party with the socialists though the congresses of the International provided a place for a less than friendly exchange of views. (The socialists passed resolutions against the anarchists at the International and told them they were not welcome, but, as trade-union delegates, some anarchists always got in.) Anarchism was weak in Germany (though sometimes spectacular), stronger (as "anarcho-syndicalism" or direct action through the trade unions) in France, still stronger in Italy and Spain, where the condition of the lower classes was more desperate and industrialism was less advanced. An "anarchist" might be a peace-loving enemy of centralization, a Proudhonian friend of liberty and cooperation; but in the 1880s and 1890s a much more familiar type resorted to assassination and other violent actions. They all disbelieved in the value of political action through elections and parliaments. Some of them were Marxists or partial Marxists: What they had learned from the master was that economics determines all, that representative legislatures are a sham to cover the dictatorship of the bourgeoisie (this from Proudhon, too), and that capitalism owns the state and always will until smashed in the proletarian social revolution. After the revolution there would be no more parliaments or states anyway, anarchists held; there would be the pure freedom of the classless society—no government at all. Most anarchists were inclined to be far out on the voluntarist wing of Marxism, so far as to be beyond the pale of party orthodoxy. They stressed the freedom of individuals to change their situation by acting; nothing is predetermined. They might go as far as Georges Sorel in deciding that socialism is simply a myth, a religion, not a science at all. Sorel found Marx most unimaginative and the social democrats exceedingly dull—even bourgeois! A good example of such trends within socialism is Arturo Labriola, the Italian anarchist; a little later, Henri de Man, the Belgian.

The rapid growth of trade unions as an indigenous, spontaneous process encouraged some social thinkers to believe—as the Russians had believed about the *mir*—that here were "the units upon which the future society will be built" and others to theorize that the revolution would come about not through parliaments but by means of the general strike, when all the workers simultaneously would put down their tools and bring the economy to a halt. Sorel was identified with this position for a time, until he became disillusioned with the trade unions as agents of revolution.

Many varieties of anarchism existed, and indeed by their very nature these individualistic radicals could not be regimented into any one creed. But significant numbers of them tried to foment revolution, preparing the workers for it by sermons or, better, by action. Ultra-anarchists engaged in a wave of assassinations in the 1890s that shocked not only the bourgeoisie but also the social democrats, who denounced them furiously. Others dreamed of the general strike as a revolutionary weapon and meanwhile tried to stir up all the strikes they could to give the workers practice.

It is depressing to record so much hate, but the anarchists were idealists; many of them had known the suffering of the most deprived classes in the community. Their intellectual antecedents were vague but plentiful: all the denouncers of injustice and leaders of revolt from Spartacus to Marx, all the haters of ruling-class sham from Lucretius to Baudelaire. If they were educated they knew these; most were not, except for scraps of secondhand learning. They were the extremists of a revolution, the Black Panthers of the nineteenth-century proletariat. Much of their spirit got into the Russian Revolution that, nominally Marxist, was led by those who shared a good deal of the anarchist *ésprit*. But during the Revolution the anarchists were to be ruthlessly destroyed by the victorious Bolsheviks.

If the anarchists stood to the left of the Socialists or Social Democrats, there were many on the Right, among them the Fabians, simple trade unionists, and bourgeois upholders of the welfare state. British "Lib-Labs" or trade unionists often seemed highly out of place at International meetings taken up with debates between German Marxists and Italian anarchists. Lord Harcourt, needless to say, who had said "we are all socialists," would hardly have been welcome there at all. Conservative upholders of the status quo, pillars of society, might show an interest in mild socialism. Bismarck, as well as England's Disraeli and Joseph Chamberlain, and Italy's Giolitti,[16] held that some concessions to the workers would keep them from following lunatics into violent revolution; if to conserve is to preserve, preservation demanded an end to the irresponsibility of laissez-faire. In 1890 the emperor of Germany, Kaiser Wilhelm II, having just fired Bismarck and repealed the antisocialist laws, called an international conference to consider "international labor legislation." In France, following the turmoil of the famous Dreyfus Case, the bourgeois left wing (Radicals, and soon Radical Socialists) flirted with socialism: Basically Jacobin-democratic, people like Aristide Briand and Georges Clemenceau were prepared to tax big property for the benefit of small, and the government budget of expenditures on welfare rose sharply. The *Solidarisme* of politician-intellectual Leon Bourgeois found nature as well as society filled with cooperation and

---

[16]Giolitti, according to Denis Mack Smith "had studied *Das Kapital* with application and profit." He was the almost perennial Italian prime minister between 1900 and 1914.

interdependence, rather than dog-eat-dog competition. At the same time these Radicals showed no sympathy toward anarchist violence and used troops to break strikes.

Of these varieties of socialism, one more at least needs to be mentioned: Christian socialism. The great papal encyclical *Rerum Novarum,* 1891, was the most famous pronouncement here, though there were Protestant versions also. It was not difficult for the Church to approve a kind of socialism. Christian dislike of materialism and selfishness, the doctrine of stewardship by which the rich should aid the poor, the deeply implanted Christian concern for the meek and disinherited, all might be turned in this direction. Catholic social doctrine gained prominence earlier in the century from the writings of Lamennais, but the Breton firebrand had run afoul of orthodoxy. Albert de Mun and La Tour du Pin subsequently brought to Catholic social doctrine an interest in the corporate economics of the Middle Ages; politically, they were conservatives. W. E. von Ketteler was a pioneer of social Christianity in Germany; the Mainz priest tried to bring the working-class issue to the attention of the Frankfurt Assembly in 1848. The trouble with this by no means insignificant tradition of *caritas* was that it shunned class conflict and hoped to convert the wealthy rather than organize the poor.

Pope Leo XIII was deeply interested in the cause of regaining the working class for Christianity. *Rerum Novarum* opposed modern capitalism and, while rejecting "materialistic socialism," called for a fundamental reorganization of economic life to correspond with Christian principles. In France, Germany, and Italy Catholic trade unions were organized, many priests devotedly dedicated service to working-class education, and there were individual examples of capitalists (like Leon Hormel) moved to experiment with "the Christian factory," but it is doubtful if the Catholic social movement achieved very much. In England, an unusual group of Christian socialists had emerged in the 1850s, including notably Charles Kingsley, F. D. Maurice, and John Ludlow; this died out for a time but there was a revival toward the end of the century, which tended to merge into the broader movement of social reform (T. H. Green, the Fabians, and so forth) without achieving much identity. Christianity had lost most of the proletariat to the secular religion of socialism. Karl Marx was its new prophet.

By the 1900s, there were those who thought this secular socialism was dying of dogmatism and an obsolete, simplistic set of *idées fixés.* (See the remarks of Benedetto Croce, in *Cultura e vita morale,* 1911; or the view of Charles Péguy, leading French writer of the 1900s who broke with the Marxists to become a kind of Christian socialist.) In western Europe, considering the subsequent history of social democracy of all sorts, this was probably true. One need not be reminded that there were other parts of the world where it had quite a role to play. For western

Europe, the later nineteenth century was the great age of this secular religion or ideology: the Age of Marx.

THE RISE OF HISTORICAL STUDIES

As a footnote to Marx's exciting if controversial historical scheme, we note that history was of serious interest to many in the nineteenth century. Despised in the seventeenth and developed only in rudimentary ways in the eighteenth, it received its philosophical certificate of legitimacy from Burke, Herder, and Hegel and became a respectable academic citizen in the mid-nineteenth century. For example, a chair of modern history was first established at Cambridge University only in the eighteenth century and for long after that amounted to little but leaped to the front in the era of Lord Acton. The great historians—Voltaire, Gibbon, and on to Macaulay and Michelet in the earlier nineteenth century—had been amateur *literati,* more noted for their literary gifts than any professional competence, though often they did do capable research; now, beginning in Germany (especially at the University of Göttingen), history came of age as a specialized profession marked by the "scientific" use of materials and careful research in the primary sources, with thorough criticism and collation of knowledge. Making possible this advance was the collection and organization of historical materials in the great libraries, archives, and museums of Europe, something that was accomplished only toward the end of the eighteenth century.

The romantics stimulated imaginative interest in the past; German philosophers saw it as the unfolding of Truth, Burkeans as the school of political wisdom. It became possible to widen the range of historical studies to include social and economic history; this was partly a matter of having access to the sources of such knowledge, such as the records of medieval manors, but also partly the perspective of an age acutely aware of economic and social issues. In general, with the retreat of confidence in religion or metaphysics to answer the big questions about the meaning and conduct of life, people turned to history. There one found a repository of wisdom and experience, a treasure-house of knowledge throwing light on the present human situation. Darwin and other evolutionary thinkers popularized explanation of a genetic sort. With the arrival of professional methods and the organization of materials, history seemed to be passing from the realm of conjecture and opinion to the status of a genuine science. Quite a few others in addition to Karl Marx had the idea that a real science of history was now possible. Henry Buckle was dogmatic about it in England, Mill thought so more cautiously; the German scholars, doing their arduous detailed research, felt that some day, somehow, the fruits of painstakingly accurate spade-work would be gathered in the form of a universal synthesis.[17] French positivists agreed.

The belief in a science of history in this sense—the sense indicated by historian J. B. Bury when he declared in his inaugural lecture as Regius Professor at Cambridge in 1902 (succeeding Acton) that "there will no longer be divers schools of history," only one, true history, since history is "simply a science, no less and no more"—has almost died since then. But the nineteenth was, byond question, an historical century; Bury was not wrong in asserting that "in the story of the nineteenth century, which has witnessed such far-reaching changes in the geography of thought and in the apparatus of research, no small or isolated place belongs to the transformation and expansion of history." The leading ideologies, as noted, were historical—Hegel's, Comte's, and Spencer's as well as Marx's. Among the great intellectual figures of the century whose interest in history was much more than incidental one could list in addition Tocqueville, Renan, Mill, Arnold, Newman, and many others.[18]

And the reason for this "historical revolution" was that investigation of the past had become not just the indulgence of idle curiosity or trivial antiquariansim but something charged with the deepest meaning because it could explain the fate and future of mankind. It could reveal the great laws of development, the cycles of growth of the human race from earliest times to today—and tomorrow. All the great nineteenth-century theories of history posited an ascent from lower to higher, in one way or another. Bitter critic of capitalist society that he was, Marx was as optimistic as any Victorian in the long run: One more turn of the wheel of history and the millennium would be reached.

---

[17]There is the marvelous story of Leopold von Ranke, dean of the German school of academic historians, who had brought exacting source criticism and the seminar method to the study of history and had written scores of volumes in medieval and early modern history, embarking at last upon his "universal history" at the age of ninety! One is led to reflect that had Marx been this cautiously empirical, he would never have penned his exciting theories.

[18]Acton, together with his German friend the Munich professor I. Döllinger, dedicated historians as they were, formulated an historical theology of Catholicism according to which the Christian truth gradually revealed itself in history through the medium of the Church. Unfortunately the Vatican could not accept this because of its implications that individual popes might have erred (did not have the full truth in the past). It remains an interesting example of the impact of history on the age. "Metaphysics could not be relied upon to promote religion—that could be done only by history," as Acton reported the view of Döllinger.

5

The Crisis of European Thought: 1880–1914

[*With*] *the development of intellectualism and the rationalization of life.... Art takes over the function of a this-worldly salvation.... It provides a salvation from the routines of everyday life, and especially from the increasing pressures of theoretical and practical rationalism.*

MAX WEBER

It will no longer be a despot that oppresses the individual, but the masses. ... I shall return to the Bedouins, who are free.

GUSTAVE FLAUBERT

Our intellect—what a very small thing on the surface of ourselves!

MAURICE BARRÈS

It is common to mark off a new period of European history beginning in 1870 or 1871. One obvious landmark was the Franco-Prussian War, which brought to an end the Second Empire in France, led to the Third Republic there, and introduced Germany's Imperial Reich as the greatest state in Europe. The unification of Italy was also completed at this time with the annexation of Rome and the ending of the pope's temporal power. There were other landmarks: In 1867, Great Britain made a further extension of the suffrage and followed it within a few years with other reforms, in education, the army, the civil service, which constituted a significant turn toward political democracy. After the victory of the unionists in its great Civil War in 1865, which had some influence on the turn toward democracy in England, the United States experienced a vast economic boom that contributed not a little to Europe's, while Germany also waxed prosperous on its new unity, beginning a classic period of international trade and development. Also, one can trace the beginnings of the "new imperialism" to the 1870s.

But periodization is often arbitrary, and it is just as easy to make the break a little later. Neither imperialism nor democracy really got into high gear until the 1880s: Witness the Third Republic which was not firmly established until this decade, or British politics where Gladstone's Midlothian campaign of 1881 stands as the first really popular election. It is from the 1880s that the rise of trade unions and socialist movements date, as the last chapter indicated; there is general agreement that this was the critical decade for the turn away from laissez-faire liberalism. Moreover it was the 1880s which introduced electricity, the automobile, and other miracles of technology, though no decade in the nineteenth century was without its contribution to this process. Technology inspired daily gasps of wonder, and practical science almost monopolized public attention, for this was the age of Faraday and Edison, Gauss and Siemens, Pasteur and Hertz. The national cultures of each European state came of age as popular education and patriotic history held up to admiration the success story of each people: England from Alfred to Victoria, France from Capets to the Republic, accounts of slow but inevitable growth.

For the intellectual historian, some time in the 1880s is preferable as a turning point. This decade produced not only Nietzsche, Freud, and Bergson, in addition to the important social thought just referred to, but also such things as the beginning of a new trend in science, dateable from the Michelson-Morley experiment of 1887, and a revolution in the arts—a revolution best placed here, it would seem, though it straddled the whole period from 1870 to 1914. Involved are such writers and artists as Ibsen, Zola, Dostoyevsky, Tolstoy, the symbolists, and the impressionists. From the other end, one can hardly avoid seeing the 1870s as the evening of the mid-Victorian day, not yet quite done, its great figures still alive. One thinks of Mill, Marx, and Darwin in ideology, of the writers Tennyson, Browning, Carlyle, Ruskin, Arnold, and other "eminent Victorians." Of these, all except Mill lived into the '80s.

One cannot be precise in such matters. The 1870s, the 1880s, the 1890s, the 1900s, each brought forth its novelties and its men and women of genius. What no one doubts is that 1914 was an epochal date, the huge war that settled its gloomy cloud over Eurpoe in that year marking the end of an era in everyone's chronology. It is beyond doubt also that the years just before 1914 bore unmistakable signs of being critically disturbed ones. An unusual number of old truths became uncertain, an unusual number of strange creeds and novel doctrines appeared. This was true in the sciences, where verities not challenged since Newton were overturned in a new scientific revolution. It was true in philosophy, in the arts, and in social studies. It was no less true in religion. It is possible that these years were the critical ones for the future destiny of Western civilization. Intellectually, they are the most exciting years of all, to one living in the twentieth century, for the ideas born here have largely shaped the mind of that century—something rather comparable to the way the period from 1688 to 1720 set the directions of Enlightenment thought.

NATIONALISM

This was the time of Western civilization's spectacular conquest of the outer world, when the continents of Asia and Africa were forced to submit to the domination of the aggressive Europeans. This vast process was in the widest sense a tribute to the amazing success of Europe, its higher technical skills, and also its organizing genius. But it brought evil with it, and to many thoughtful Europeans it was a dismaying moral lapse, perhaps a symbol of decline and fall. The average person certainly found it gratifying; but eventually it would produce revolutions against Western domination on the part of Asiatic and African peoples. For the time being what it most notably produced was an inordinate pride and boastfulness, the jingoism that helped fan the flames of war in 1914.

The outbreak of the worst war in history lay ahead, constituting a terrific moral setback for a civilization that had believed itself on the high road to humanity's greatest success. In some ways the war reflected the conquest of nineteenth-century Europe by the sentiment of nationalism. Nationalism appeared in the wake of Napoleon's attempt to impose French domination on Europe; Fichte's "Addresses to the German Nation," written when Bonaparte invaded Prussia, might be called its manifesto. It went on after the Peace of Vienna, which tried to ignore it; and it played a prominent part in the revolutions of 1848. Thereafter it was to emerge truly into its own in the era of Italian and German unification, when Mazzini was Europe's leading prophet. It was still potent in the years before 1914 and was a basic cause of the war explosion of that fateful year.

Nationalism was not absolutely new, but its intensity and dominance in the nineteenth century made it a force as never before, "The outstanding feature of European history in the nineteenth century is the growth of nationalities," it has been aptly claimed. Nation-making in Europe goes back a long way, ultimately to the earlier Middle Ages. National consciousness, a different and later thing, may be found at least as early as Elizabethan England and Lutheran Germany. But other loyalties competed with that paid to the state or national group. Throughout the Middle Ages, a person was a Christian first, then a native of the home district, and only after that (if at all) French or German. The Church was universal; so, in theory, was the state, for a long time. Actually strongest were dynastic and feudal loyalties based on a personal and not a territorial loyalty. Only gradually did the future nation-states become clearly defined; but for an accident or two, indeed, there might be Burgundians today instead of Frenchmen. And in Germany the territorial duchies (Bavaria, Saxony, Swabia, Franconia) remained the focus of patriotic sentiment until fairly recent times.

The creation of national societies and cultures was a long-term social process, begun long ago—historians delighted in tracing the origins back to the early Middle Ages—and scarcely completed even well into the nineteenth century. A recent study of "the nationalization of rural France" (by Eugen Weber) finds the traditional village culture still immersed in customs and beliefs primordially old, even towards the end of the nineteenth century—just then beginning to yield to the assault of roads, railroads, urban influences, capitalism, modern communications, mass education. The village, Weber notes, ignored the Dreyfus Affair which, one reads in the textbooks, was tearing apart "all of France." Another study of a medium-sized German city around the turn of the century discovers little departure from old habits of following one's ancestral line of work in an essentially static society.[1] "Modernization" in some ways was just beginning its sweeping of traditional communities into the urban megalopolis, dissolving the small local units into one "great society." And if localism still stubbornly persisted, there was on the other hand among the thinkers and writers a persisting, cosmopolitanism which saw humanity as much the same everywhere and ideas essentially spaceless. The eighteenth-century Enlightenment was quite cosmopolitan. Though the work of knitting together the larger states of Europe administratively and economically went steadily on, the fashion in ideas did not then encourage the growth of nationalistic sentiments. The French Revolution and romanticism did contribute to nationalism, it is known, and yet there remained a substantial element of international feeling among men and women of letters and learning in the first half of the century. Writing to Thomas Carlyle in 1826, Goethe in his old age rejoiced that "for some time past the best poets and writers of all nations have aimed at what is common to all men" and hoped that this might aid the cause of international peace.[2] There were many trans-

---

[1] David Crew, "Social Mobility in a German Town, 1880-1901," *Journal of Social History*, Fall, 1973.

[2] *Letters from Goethe*, translated by M. Herzfeld and C. M. Sym, introduction by W. H. Bruford, 1957.

national European phenomena at this time. Not only were such secular creeds as liberalism and socialism much the same everywhere, but the arts, as well as the sciences, recognized no national boundaries. For example, in music Berlioz was an idol in Germany, Wagner in France—more so than either was in his own country! "The civilized world is to be regarded as now being, for intellectual and spiritual purposes, one great confederation, bound to a joint action and working to a common result," Matthew Arnold wrote.

But powerful forces were making for nationalism, and writers, poets, philosophers were to get involved. So were historians. The march of nationalism in the nineteenth century accompanied the advance of democracy. The German nationalist movement produced such popular figures as "Father" Jahn, who preached the kinship and equality of all in the *Volk*—"Freies Reich! Alles gleich!" sang the *Turnerschaften*. The *Volksstaat* or people's state knew no privileged orders, only citizens under the nation, all equal.

Dangerous though it might be, nationalism in the nineteenth century offered a wider sense of community, along with material advantages, to the masses of people. In the exhortations of such prophets as Mazzini, nationalism took on the attributes of a religion, in the same way socialism did, equipped with regeneration, rebirth, and salvation symbols. Born of a spiritual revolution, the national people achieve a sacred bond, which is their destiny and their salvation, and then they go forth to redeem the world. "Nationality is the role assigned by God to each people in the work of humanity; the mission and task which it ought to fulfill on earth so that the divine purpose may be attained in the world." Nationalists talked of universal unity, ("He who wants humanity wants a fatherland"); but typically they saw their own country as just a bit more privileged. Jahn pointed out that the Germans were the central people, the keystone of the West. In different accents but with a similar message, Mazzini reminded his country's people of their ancient Roman heritage of ruling and civilizing Europe. So did the Pan-Slav mystagogues.

The rise of popular nationalism in the nineteenth century can be illustrated by the creation of the Joan of Arc cult in France. The "virgin, heroine, and martyr to the State, chosen by Providence to reestablish the French monarchy" (to quote the subtitle of a 1753 book) had of course lived in the early fifteenth century; but her deeds excited little interest at that time and for several hundred years after. Bishop Bossuet's history of France granted her but a few lines, and Voltaire, singularly enough from a later point of view, treated her as rather a ridiculous figure in his play *La Pucelle*. A few always kept alive the story of the Maid's bravery and devotion, but until the nineteenth century she remained fairly obscure. Napoleon, in 1803, referred to Joan as a symbol of French unity against English invaders. The romantics of course were interested in the

Middle Ages, unlike the Enlightenment, and one finds the British poet Robert Southey as well as the German dramatist Schiller using Joan as a literary theme. Schiller's *Maid of Orleans* (also 1803) was indeed a key document: A German helped give the French their national heroine.

But it remained for the great nationalist historians of the nineteenth century to project the Maid as an image of French patriotism. Of these, Jules Michelet was the foremost, and Michelet depicted Joan in eloquent prose as the mother of the French nation. The legend of Joan grew. Finally she was canonized in 1920 as a saint of the Church. Her canonization in French nationalist hagiography had occurred earlier. A notable worshipper at her shrine was the distinguished writer Charles Péguy (who died in 1914 at the Marne). Charles Maurras and the conservative *Action Française* made much of her; but so did socialists and liberals, anticlericals as well as clericals: Joan was the symbol of national unity. Conceivably it was because the French lacked a monarch that they settled their common loyalty on an almost mythical figure from the past. For the British public, of course, the figure of Queen Victoria functioned as a living mother-image and symbol of unity through much of her long reign (1837–1901).

The poet and the historian both participated in this shaping of national consciousness. "A nation," wrote Ernest Renan in a famous definition, "is the common memory of great things done jointly by our ancestors, along with the desire to remain united in order to do yet more of them." The nation, in brief, is a literary creation. The Italian nationalist movement began with Alfieri (1749 to 1803), who reminded Italians in romantic writings of their past glories. Koraïs performed a similar service to Greece, and an American named Smith is credited with beginning the "Arab Awakening"—so says the distinguished scholar George Antonius—when he revived the study of the Arabic language and literature midway in the nineteenth century. The Irish, who had almost lost their ancestral tongue, tried to revive it, or at least some of the literary and Irish nationalists did; the Gaelic revival accompanied the Irish nationalist movement. A revival of Catalonian nationalism in Spain dates from the 1880s; so does Ukrainian separatism in Russia, while in southeastern Europe an upthrust of nationalism threatened to blow up ancient multinational empires and destroy Europe's shaky balance of power.

In 1896, Theodor Herzl's book, *Der Judenstaat*, laid the foundations of the Jewish revival and focused on the establishment of a modern Jewish state in the ancestral land of Palestine; the Zionist congresses began in 1897. The Dreyfus case in France and the ferocious persecution of the Jews in Russia, as well as anti-Semitic stirrings in Germany, had brought home to the Jews the fact that Europe was again in the grip of intolerance. Medieval anti-Semitism, the result in good part of religious emotions, had all but disappeared in the tolerant eighteenth century. Now toward the end of the nineteenth, intolerance reappeared in the guise of nationalism. (It also had enonomic, anticapitalist overtones; the myth of the Jew as the sinister international banker made its appearance. But the main charge against the Jews in the Dreyfus affair was that they lacked loyalty to France.)

Nationalism reached its apogee or nadir in the fateful epidemic of jingoism that accompanied the imperialist movement of the 1890s and preceded the great war of 1914 to 1918. A powerful social process involving all aspects of history, it cannot be left out of intellectual history, for many writers contributed to it. Of these, historians and novelists, thrusting into consciousness the past traditions of the people, were the most prominent. In addition to Michelet, the German historian Heinrich Treitschke, the American George Bancroft, the English Thomas Macaulay come to mind, by modern critical standards rather lacking in strict accuracy, but eloquent and inspired in their evocation of the national story of their respective lands in whatever guise they saw it. Never was history so popular as in this period when it dwelt on the rise of the nation and the destiny of its people.

Social Darwinism contributed its bit to the nationalist mixture. It is interesting that Herbert Spencer was a staunch antiimperialist, a relic perhaps of his Cobdenite days; but the view that peoples and cultures are in competition, with the strongest or more efficient rightly surviving, was hard to dissociate from popular social Darwinism. H. G. Wells provides an example of a highly intelligent man and influential writer, moreover, a leftist socialist and rationalist who nevertheless believed that Darwinian science had "destroyed, quietly but entirely, the belief in human equality." Some peoples, and some races, are inferior to others; the inferior peoples, "these swarms of black, and brown, and dirty-white, and yellow people, who do not come into the new needs of efficiency," will have to go; "it is their portion to die out and disappear." That international life is a struggle, that those nations not prepared to compete in the arena of power will go down to extinction and will deserve to do so was a widely shared article of faith around the turn of the century; it swept even the United States in the Teddy Roosevelt era and was entertained by quite sophisticated minds. For example, John Davidson, the British poet, influenced by Nietzsche toward the view that "the universe is immoral," enthusiastically supported British imperialism, which he regarded, *à la* Rudyard Kipling, as having a sanction to rule and rule vigorously over the lesser breeds. The British scientist and mathematician, Karl Pearson, was taught by social Darwinism that races and nations, as well as individuals, are in a ruthless competition for survival from which progress results.

Nationalism rose to an almost frenzied peak in the years just before

1914. Gabriele D'Annunzio, famed flamboyant Italian writer, a weather-vane who had adopted almost all possible positions just for the fun of it, became a fierce nationalist about 1909, calling on Italians to sharpen their sword on Africa and then advance on the world, phrases which found an all too frenzied response. The *Alldeutscher Verband,* or Pan-German League, entertained fantasies of German domination of all Europe. In France, Charles Maurras's significant *Action Française,* popular among students, was anti-Semitic and anti-German, militantly patriotic, and militaristic. In Russia, and throughout the east of Europe, there were various versions of Pan-Slavism. In the 1870s, Danilevski had argued that the next turn of the wheel of history would put the Slavs on top, the Latins and Germans having had their turn. Russia, the Pan-Slavist Fadeyev declared, must either advance to the Adriatic or retire behind the Urals; it was Russia's destiny to unify all the Slavic peoples of Europe. The personification of nations as having "destinies" was common; no doubt this was what the British philosopher Hobhouse had in mind when he blamed the war on Hegel, this sort of thinking being obviously related to a vulgarized Hegelian historicism. Seeley told the British about their imperial destiny, and according to Esmé Wingfield-Stratford, "The Press reeked with blood and reverberated with thunder" *(The Victorian Tragedy).* "Every important nation had become acutely and aggressively race-conscious," the English historian adds. It was one of the most apparent causes of the first world war.

DEMOCRACY

The accompaniment of nationalism was democracy. Here again the preliminaries reach far back, but no previous European age had felt the impact of the ideology and the practice of democracy as the one from 1880 to 1914. Most liberals of the earlier nineteenth century stoutly opposed universal suffrage. "Because I am a Liberal," wrote a member of Parliament and editorialist of the *London Times* in 1867, "I regard as one of the greatest dangers with which the country can be threatened a proposal to . . . transfer power from the hands of property and intelligence, and to place it in the hands of men whose whole life is necessarily occupied in daily struggles for existence." Tocqueville and Mill mistrusted democracy because they feared the degradation of intelligence and quality by the imposition of vulgar standards. Comte, as well as Bonald, equated democracy with anarchy, the absence of social order. Spencer wrote that the divine right of popularly elected parliaments would have to be resisted as firmly as the divine right of royalty if it should threaten liberty. Many of the socialists scorned political democracy as a fraud, designed to deceive the working classes, who could only win their freedom by a social revolution.

Yet throughout the century there was a democratic thrust, which the generation of Tocqueville and Chateaubriand had felt and which became irresistible after mid-century. It was associated with the economic revolution; it followed necessarily from the bourgeois revolution. Political rights could not be withheld from the masses once political authority became a matter of convenience, not sanctity, and when wealth became more widely diffused. Throughout the century illiteracy declined—in France declining from 39 percent to 18 percent by 1878 as measured by conscript soldiers—while the press became increasingly free and increasingly cheap. In 1870 the Education Act established free primary schools in Great Britain, compulsory within a few years after that. The "penny daily" made its debut about the same time. These are landmarks without equal in popular intellectual history.

In 1867 and 1884, Great Britain took steps towards full manhood suffrage, and by 1910 women were agitating for it. France never actually lost universal suffrage after 1848, but under the Second Empire it was managed and manipulated in a way that deprived it of much meaning; after 1874, however, the Republic came back. Imperial Germany had a Reichstag elected by universal suffrage though it lacked responsible powers. "An assembly of 350 members cannot in the last instance direct the policy of a great power today," Bismarck held. Perhaps it could not, but in Britain, at least, the system of government by a cabinet drawn from and responsible to the House of Commons found success in these years. All governments had to pay more attention to public opinion— which might or might not be a good thing, critics noted, depending on how enlightened public opinion was. In the realm of foreign affairs, it was all too likely to be xenophobic, shrilly nationalistic, disdainful of the rights of foreigners. At home, those unconverted to democracy complained of unseemly and undignified electioneering methods, of political machines and bosses, of cheaper politicians driving out finer in a kind of political Gresham's Law. But very few discerning people thought that the rule of the few in politics and society was any longer possible. For better or for worse the rule of the many had come to stay.

Intellectuals were inclined to worry about this, perhaps, more than to hail it. In his essay on *Democracy,* first published in 1861, and reissued in 1879, Matthew Arnold wrote, "Our society is probably destined to become much more democratic; who or what will give a high tone to the nation then? That is the grave question." A society is of real value not because large numbers of people are free and active, nor because of the creation of wealth; it is valuable insofar as it produces things that are noble and of good repute. When Arnold lectured in the United States of America on the need to "elevate" society, he seems utterly to have failed to make contact with the minds of Chicagoans. But America's sage, Walt Whitman, addressed similar warnings to his country's people in his old age.

Democracy in itself, considered simply as the principle of mass or numbers, is no ideal, can easily become moral anarchy or mammonism; the old criticism made by Plato was repeated often in the later nineteenth century. Nineteenth-century European thought is filled with outcries against certain aspects or consequences of "democracy." "The crowd is the lie," wrote Kierkegaard. Democracy is "a form of decadence," declared the well-known French writer Emile Faguet, who had been influenced by Nietzsche. "If I am a democrat, it is without enthusiasm," observed the great French political leader Clemenceau, who had once led the popular party in 1908. A notably hostile Victorian witness was Henry Maine (*Popular Government,* 1886). Nietzsche, treated later in this chapter, expressed hostility to democracy in aspects of his thought. The rule of inferiors, the herd spirit, the debasement of culture to the mass level, were to him among the chief diseases of modern civilization, to be cured only by the most drastic elevation of supermen-heroes to the helm of state, men strong and ruthless enough to whip and drive the masses toward some worthy goals. Like Dr. Stockmann in Ibsen's play "An Enemy of the People," Nietzsche believed that "the minority is always right." The leveling of the human personality into the conforming mass-man appalled him, and he thought democracy was responsible for this.

"It is a question," Edmund Scherer cried, "of knowing whether in traversing this crisis humanity will not lose everything of genius, beauty, grandeur; it is a question of knowing whether, in this tragedy of mediocrity, in this sullen and terrible adventure of the peoples, there is one which will not disappear from history." This esthetic antidemocracy, or at least antimass, permeated the *fin de siècle* with its damned poets, its decadent esthetes, its hatred of the vulgar crowd.

A further discovery of this era was that, paradoxically, the effort to implement democracy only leads to a new kind of elite rule. "Everywhere, whether within or outside democracies, politics is made *by the few,*" Max Weber put it. His friend, Robert Michels, discovered the "iron law of oligarchy" in accordance with which democratic institutions, especially the mass political party, fall into the hands of a small group of insiders. An "invisible government" of political bosses controlled the parties, which were the instrument of allegedly democratic government, in the United States. In the last analysis, all societies are governed by elites, and a so-called democracy is really only one way of selecting this ruling class—and not necessarily the best way. Those who make their way to the top in a democratic society may be those who, as U.S. President Theodore Roosevelt said, have a gift for office-mongering as others have a knack for picking pockets. They may be demagogues, or manipulators, or bureaucrats. Practical experience with mass democratic politics from 1870 on resulted in much disenchantment with the high hopes of democratic idealists. The best-known theories of elitism came from the

Italians, Vilfredo Pareto and Gaetano Mosca, perhaps because the *delusione* with soaring *Risorgimento* expectations was so severe in Italy from about 1880 on.

IRRATIONALISM: THE CASE OF FRIEDRICH NIETZSCHE

In part because of mass society, precipitate change, and technological revolutions, the thought of this end-of-the-century era was marked by a growing "irrationalism." The names of Nietzsche, Freud, Weber, Bergson, Sorel are enough to suggest it. Objective social reality and subjective cultural consciousness split apart. The "intellectuals" made their appearance as a group whose sensitivity involved them in an intolerable conflict with "bourgeois" society. The "masses" were losing their traditional folk culture in an urban environment which gradually eroded forms of community long basic to human living. Capitalism, urbanization (into megalopolis and beyond, which Lewis Mumford was to name necropolis), deracination, atomization, anomie, contract replacing status (Henry Maine's terms),[3] cash-nexus instead of human, an overly rationalized set of norms, *Gesellschaft* (society) rather than *Gemeinschaft* (community) in the famous words of Friedrich Tönnies—a bevy of social theorists gave different names to what at bottom was much the same thing. One might describe it as basically a conflict of the emancipated individual ego with mass, industrial society.

On the level of ideas, irrationalist strains gradually penetrated the European consciousness. Late in his life (1837) the philosopher Schlegel startled his listeners by suggesting that the truest thought is not rational-conceptual at all but intuitive-mythic—not so far removed, after all, from some romantic strains. The most famous exponent of irrationalism, however, was another and less reputable German philosopher. "Almost without exception, philosophers have placed the essence of mind in thought and consciousness; this ancient and universal radical error must be set aside. Consciousness is the mere surface of our minds, which, as of the surface of the earth, we do not know the inside but only the crust. Under the conscious intellect is the conscious or unconscious will, a striving, persistent, vital force, a spontaneous activity, a will of imperious desire." Thus wrote the eccentric essayist and philosopher Arthur Schopenhauer, an offshoot of the romantic and idealist German philosophers (see Chapter 1). Schopenhauer's distinction between Will and Reason, the former being fundamental, could be seen also in Darwin's scheme of nature in which the intellect is only a tool

---

[3]In 1875, Maine pointed out, the law of masters and servants was replaced by the law of employers and employees as the basis of British economic society.

of survival, a part of the whole organism that struggles to adapt to its environment. Schopenhauer, the pessimist, thought the world spirit tricks people into making the struggle; the enlightened philosopher outwits the world spirit by suppressing desire, renouncing the game of life. He had been influenced not a little by the Hindu Upanishads, which became known to the West near the end of the eighteenth century and attracted some of the romantic and idealist philosophers.

The Oriental pessimism of Schopenhauer did not make much of an impression, but the belief that the will is a deeper force than the conceptualizing reason left its stamp on the European mind. One whose mind was awakened by reading Schopenhauer was the brilliant German, Friedrich Nietzsche. Confronted with what seemed to him a decadent civilization, Nietzsche thought that he had found one cause of its enfeeblement in an excessive development of the rational faculty at the cost of a creativeness that comes only with the spontaneity of instinct or will. The brilliant young philologist and classicist, whose first book was a study of Greek drama (*The Birth of Tragedy*), traced this disease far back into Western civilization. It had begun with Socrates and Plato, the triumph of logic over literature, reason over will. Another antirationalist of this era, the Frenchman Georges Sorel, independently made this same discovery that Socrates had been the root of all evil rather than of all good as conventionally taught. Excessive development of the rational faculty enfeebles; the habit of conceptual thought paralyzes the will. Europe had intellectualized too long; the result was the weary mediocrity Nietzsche thought he saw about him in this age of bourgeois materialism. In perhaps his greatest work, Nietzsche has Zarathustra say, "I saw a great sadness come over men. The best were weary of their work. . . . All is empty, all is indifferent, all was." Western humanity had lost the capacity for believing in anything, intellectualizing had led to skepticism. The only solution lay in a new primitivism that would lead back to heroism.

The Birth of Tragedy (1871) revealed both his deep insights into Greek civilization and his almost frightening originality. Among other things, Nietzsche saw the genius of Hellas as stemming not primarily from joyous optimism (as so often suggested by the romantics) but from tragic suffering and consisting not in scientific and philosophical rationalism so much as in primitive emotionalism tempered by reason. Dionysus, whose cult engaged in ecstatic and orgiastic ritual dances, became for Nietzsche a symbol of this primitive force, without which men cannot be truly creative. The Greeks had been great because they had Dionysus as well as Apollo. They had not been rationalists, but were infused with the will to live. Their greatest age was the time of the early philosophers and dramatists, of Heraclitus and Aeschylus. Plato and Euripides already mark their decadence, which Western civilization unfortunately inherited more than their grandeur.

This electrifying reversal of previous perspectives was typical of Nietzsche's sharply iconoclastic thought, his "transvaluation" of values. A lyrical poet as well as a philosopher and deeply learned man, Nietzsche's challenging, radical books were to wake up intellectual Europe in the 1890s. He wrote most of these books in a frenzy of creativity in the 1880s against the threat of oncoming madness which was evidently the result of syphilis contracted in youth. Among his rejections were Christianity (a religion for slaves, denying life) and traditional morality ("morality is the most pernicious species of ignorance"). The supermen needed to rescue a decadent civilization must be beyond morality, for they must be "without pity for the degenerate." Democracy and nationalism, the vulgar superstitions of modern dwarf-men, also were targets for his sneers. More remarkable and celebrated was his atheism: "God is dead"; European man had killed him; one could no longer believe in any principle of cosmic order. Nietzsche did find something to believe in, escaping from his terrible skepticism to a "joyful wisdom" which to most others must seem scarcely less pessimistic: the love of life, as it is, in all its disorder, ugliness, cruelty, just because it is life (*amor fati:* love of fate). We are part of the cosmos, which is a blind incessant striving (it goes around in huge circles, coming back eventually to repeat itself), and we can affirm our own life force by living and striving. We can accept Dionysus and reject Christ. "You have understood me? Dionysus versus the Crucified"—these were the last words.

The universe is irrational, it simply *is*. One can reject it, choosing with Schopenhauer to renounce life by suppressing all desire like the Indian *fakir;* or one can accept it, fully realizing its irrationality, pain, and horror. Not easy to understand, and perhaps tending in his later works toward the madness that approached him, Nietzsche at his worst suggests a shocking hatred of civilization and a desire for barbarism; at his best, he reminds us that man can create values by his own nobility though the universe be hostile. The supermen he called for to reshape the human race should not be thought of as brutalized Hitlers, rather as enlightened poet-philosopher leaders. It must be said in his defense, and has been said by recent students concerned with rescuing him from wild misinterpretation, that he despised all nationalism and militarism, including German, and also was no racist or anti-Semite, though the Nazis later made use of him. His wilder ejaculations of rage against the human race can charitably be excused as products of the sufferings of a morbidly sensitive and physically sick man; of enduring value in Nietzsche is the hatred of falsehood and sham, of mediocrity and vulgarity, along with deep insights into human creativity and a fierce sincerity: one should live one's philosophy. His fantastic sensitivity to ideas makes Nietzsche a barometer registering virtually every variation of the modern mind.

Chief among these insights was an awareness of the role of the darker, submerged, unconscious, "Dionysian" elements in human nature, which by being "sublimated" enter into creativity. Nietzsche, like Schopenhauer, anticipated Freud. This force is partly sexual, and Nietzsche suggests that Christianity and conventional morality have grievously damaged Western civilization by surrounding sex with taboos. It is, more basically, just the joyous spontaneity of the animal. It is the dithyrambic dance of primitive man. Civilize it, smother it with morality and reason, and you destroy something necessary to humanity and to culture. The highest culture requires something of the intellectual element but too much of it means decadence.

Nietzsche combined and held in suspension an amazing number of modern attitudes. There is something in him of the alienated artist, saying with Baudelaire, "The world has taken on a thickness of vulgarity that raises a spiritual man's contempt to a violent passion." He is an important precursor of twentieth-century existentialism, in question here being his call for humanity to create its own values by sheer willpower, as well as his rejection of all merely theoretical philosophy. "I have written my works with my whole body and life," Nietzsche could say proudly. He is the gloomy prophet of the totalitarian state and modern mass-man. But most of all he is the philosopher of the will-to-power or life force—the irrationalist, prober of drives deeper than reason, anticipator of Freud and Jung, psychologist of the unconscious.

In all his moods and guises, Nietzsche is clearly something quite new and different, compared to Victorian orthodoxy. He has the flavor of the *fin de siècle*, over which indeed his influence was spread widely, André Gide, the French novelist, remarked that "The influence of Nietzsche preceded with us the appearance of his work; it fell on soil already prepared . . .; it did not surprise but confirm."[4] As so often happens, an idea's hour seemed to have arrived and a number of people felt it independently at about the same time. One of the ideas this period seemed destined to discover and probe was the unconscious irrational within the human psyche. Almost contemporary with the great writings of Nietzsche in the 1880s came the first work of the Viennese physician, Sigmund Freud. Nietzsche also greatly influenced Carl Jung.

It would be difficult to overstate the influence of Nietzsche. As a recent writer (Werner Pelz) has commented, "It is not a matter of agreeing or disagreeing with his philosophical conclusions, but of having passed through his corrosives of metaphysical, moral, and psychological doubts. They leave a man scarred and purified; certainly changed."

[4]In his article on "Nietzsche and John Davidson," *Journal of the History of Ideas,* June, 1957, John A. Lester, Jr., notes another case of one who "may have been a Nietzchean before he ever heard the name of Nietzsche," but whose native inclinations were stimulated by contact with the German. There were many such instances.

Through this fire the mind of modern Europe has passed. Nietzsche's influence spread widely over Europe, reaching England by 1904, after sweeping through France in the 1890s; the young Yeats felt the fire of Zarathustra as keenly in Ireland as Franz Kafka did in Prague, or Merezhkovsky in Russia. The influence was strongest on artistic and poetic temperaments, but affected all manner of people. Gustav Mahler and Richard Strauss set its spirit to music.

Nietzsche's political impact was in more than one direction, like Darwin's. Atheist, radical critic of conventional religion and morality, destroyer of all manner of orthodoxies, this most dramatic of thinkers held a natural appeal to the Left, and one finds many socialists and anarchists responding to his message, associating it with revolutionary activism. It seemed to suggest an apocalyptic ending to the whole Western past and the inauguration of a completely new age. He was the darling of the *avant-garde,* the bible of the defiantly alienated artist-intellectual. In his name one could throw off traditional religion, defy the conventional moral rules, scorn the bourgeoisie, and predict a day of doom. None were more revolutionary; and yet Nietzsche also scorned democracy and socialism, which he linked to the slave morality of the Judeo-Christian world view. He preached the inequality of man and could be used to sanction imperialism, despotism, and war. Benito Mussolini was deflected from left-wing socialism toward the new cult of fascism in good part by Nietzsche; Hitler and the Nazis subsequently glorified him, even if, as his defenders insist, they distorted him. During the war of 1914 to 1918, people in the Allied countries fighting Germany quite commonly linked Nietzsche to the ruthless war-making of the Hohenzollern legions, who were depicted advancing on their barbarous mission armed with Nietzschean admonitions to be brutal. If this was an hysterical caricature, the fact remains that German youth just before the war were strongly affected by the cult of adventure and heroism, derived in no small part from the aphorisms of *The Will to Power* (rather tendentiously edited by Nietzsche's reactionary sister) and other Nietzschean writings. "I am dynamite," the sage of Sils St. Maria had said; there was indeed an explosive quality in the rhetoric of this great writer. He could act as an energizing agent on all kinds of different people.

For Germans of this generation, Richard Wagner, the great musical composer and ideologist, sometime idol, later object of Nietzsche's anger—too Christian, too *Reichsdeutsch* also—functioned as a symbol of the new culture. Wagner's *Bayreuther Blätter* began in 1880 to proclaim the vital connections between religion and art, as one of the century's greatest geniuses turned from sublime music to dubious evangelism. In standing for totally committed art, Wagner played a role somewhat similar to Ruskin's in England or Charles Baudelaire (one of his early champions) in France, except that he became a national institution through his organizing abilities. Filled with a vague discontent at the whole of modern life, young poets and artists revered both Nietzsche and Wagner, overlooking their quarrel; a curiously significant work of 1890, Jules Langbehn's *Rembrandt as Educator,* the "Greening of Germany" of its day, preached a popularized mixture of the two giants.

HENRI BERGSON

A milder and more respectable figure than Nietzsche, the French[5] philosopher Henri Bergson contributed no less to the revolt against reason or against scientific positivism which characterized the *Zeitgeist* of the years from about 1885 to 1914, an "Age of Unreason." Bergson, whose first notable work appeared in 1889 when he was thirty, exerted so strong an influence that by the 1900s he was easily the most important force in French thought, being frequently compared to Descartes, Rousseau, and Comte among earlier sages of an epoch. His lectures at the University of Paris were likened to those of Abelard in the Middle Ages for the sensation they created, and his repute spread widely abroad too. His considerable role in twentieth-century thought is generally conceded. Bergson's gift of style assured him an audience. Like Nietzsche, he used metaphor and poetic imagery because he believed that conceptual thought does not best communicate the nature of reality. Also like the German, he appeared to his contemporaries as a liberator, opening up fresh horizons, calling for creativity, and expressing it in his richly gifted prose.

In a romantic manner, Bergson sharply distinguished between the rational, conceptualizing intellect and the intuitive understanding. The former, the scientific, analyzing function, is a practical tool, concerned with useful knowledge, but not truth-giving because reality may not be so divided up and conceptualized. (The student may here be reminded of Kant.) Reality is a continuum, to be grasped by the intuition. It flows through immediate experience as the "life force" that is in all things. Intuition (meaning instinct become self-conscious and reflective) takes us to "the very inwardness of life," while the intellect is not in this sense in touch with reality. Bergson said that he began his philosophical speculations by considering what is meant by *time* and found himself led to conclude that the clock time of everyday life or of the physicist is a convention very different from the real time of experience. The intelligence that analyzes and divides things has given us the former conception which is useful but not true to experience. When we grasp immediate experience by intuitive means, what we find there is an indivisi-

---

[5]Bergson was actually Jewish, the son of a Polish father and an English mother, educated in Switzerland as a boy. But, receiving his university education in Paris, Bergson went on to teach at the Sorbonne and was an ardently patriotic French citizen.

ble continuum, a "duration" that we can scarcely describe save in poetic imagery; this represents a fundamental reality. So it is in other things. Science tells us that the sound of a bell is a series of vibrations, but we experience it as a whole. A melody is not a series of notes; it cannot be described; we intuit it. Science, as Wordsworth had written, "murders to dissect." Reality is indivisible and hence unanalyzable; insofar as we do analyze it, as for convenience's sake we must do, we falsify it.

This is no attack on science within its limits, but it *is* rather sharp deflation of the pretensions of science to provide complete knowledge, pretensions which at that time existed. "Science consists only of conventions, and to this circumstance solely does it owe its apparent certitude; the facts of science and, *a fortiori*, its laws are the artificial work of the scientist; science therefore can teach us nothing of the truth; it can serve only as a rule of action."[6] (Nietzsche also had viewed scientific systems as basically myths.) Critics of pragmatist and Bergsonian indictments of the "conceptualizing" process, as conventional only, were not lacking, as might be expected, and often pointed out that these philosophers themselves could not escape the use of conceptual or intellectual language. To do without it would be to abolish thought. To follow Bergson all the way in his intuitionism would be to destroy all analysis and lapse into chaos. It was generally agreed that concepts and reality are not the same thing, also that conceptual knowledge does not exhaust reality or constitute the only mode of dealing with it; but the implication that the two realms are completely divorced, that science tells nothing at all about reality but only about its own arbitrary signs and symbols was frequently rejected. Still, the persuasively conducted Bergsonian offensive against science made its impact felt; the chief result was to vindicate and rehabilitate forms of "immediate experience" such as literature, religion, and various mystic or nonrational experiences.

Bergson proposed a vitalistic evolutionary theory, arguing against Darwinian mechanism that life has within it some purposive forces, without which evolution cannot be explained (*Creative Evolution*, 1908). Doctrines of "emergent evolution" received the support of a number of philosophers at this time, the most prominent advocate after Bergson being the British philosopher Samuel Alexander. Reality creates itself gradually, rather than existing from all eternity; life evolves ever new and unpredictable forms. We participate in a universe that is not finished and help in the making of it. A striking idea, and as Bergson noted, a radically new one in the Western tradition, "creative evolution" turned the rather somber mechanistic atheism of the Darwinists into a feeling for the wondrous freedom of a world in growth.

In general, Bergson's persuasively presented philosophy urged the

[6] R. B. Perry, *Present Philosophical Tendencies*, 1912, pp. 230-231.

importance of spontaneity, of intuition, and of immediate experience, as over against those "tentacles of cold, prying thought" (Nietzsche) which gives us useful knowledge at the cost of cutting us off from reality. Getting away from cold science and bathing in the refreshing waters of intuition clearly seems to have value for Bergson. To him as to the American pragmatists, the world properly seen is rich, inexhaustible, vital. Though his stress on spontaneity and immediate experience influenced the existentialists, Bergson was on the whole not a tragic philosopher but a joyous one. The antiintellectualism or antirationalism of which he may be accused was rather gentle, and to tie this deeply religious man to the subsequent movements of fascism or Nazism appears perverse. Few philosophers have attached such basic importance to liberty. Among his leading disciples in prewar France was the editor and writer Charles Péguy, who so far as he can be classified might best be described as a Christian democrat and socialist. He was, in fact, quite an individualist. Bergson, like the pragmatists, encouraged freedom unbounded by dogma and tended not to set up any "school." One French critic detected in the disciples of Bergson a sort of lyrical insanity, celebrating the chaos of things in "orgies of subjectivism"; he cited Albert Bazailles and Alphonse Chide. The same could be said of Péguy in some of his moods.

So the subjectivism which Kant and romanticism had begun was deepening; people became ever more aware that (1) truth is created by the free human mind, not found, as something objectively existing just as it is taken into the mind; and (2) myth, intuition, is the best means to this creation, rather than reason, conceptual thought. Bergson more than Freud or anyone else gave novelists the idea of presenting an unedited "stream of consciousness." His "life force" philosophy may be found prominently in that avid consumer and popularizer of ideas, George Bernard Shaw, who also introduced Marx and Nietzsche to a somewhat amazed British public. Colin Wilson has observed that Shaw's plays "are all about the same theme: the obscure creative drive of the 'Life Force' and the way it makes people do things they find difficult to understand in terms of everyday logic." "Our intellect—what a very small thing on the surface of ourselves!" Maurice Barrès, the important French writer and politician of this era, exclaimed. It was the theme of the hour.

The pragmatists and Bergson broadly agreed in their attack on intellectual or conceptual knowledge. Immediate experience is deeper and forms the matrix within which intellectual knowledge takes place. As John Dewey put it, there is an "experience in which knowledge-and-its-object is sustained, and whose schematized, or structural, portion it is." We encounter "reality" only in immediate, intuitive experience, as distinct from intellectual ratiocination. We must reject, as Nietzsche cleverly put it, the dogma of immaculate perception. If we want to know the music, we do not analyze it into notes or vibrations, we simply hear it. We can perform, and usefully perform, the latter function, but we should recognize it for what it is, a secondary and derivative one. In this respect Bergson and the pragmatists coincided with the aims of Edmund Husserl, today considered the founder of phenomenology, who was also philosophizing at about the turn of the century, though at that time much more obscure than Bergson. Husserl used the term "phenomenology" in 1900 to mean the systematic study of how things and concepts are given to the mind directly, at the deeper, more "real" level, exactly as it happens and not as it is formalized in conceptual thought.

The Englishman F. C. S. Schiller and the Italians Papini and Prezzolini represented pragmatism in Europe, where it was much less important than in the United States. The vigorous American William James was a man of international reputation who knew Bergson as well as Schiller and Papini. Pragmatism had affinities with the message of revolt and liberation; it denied the existence of final, abstract truth, asserting that we make the truth as we act. Life is an open experiment in which we constantly test our hypotheses against reality and use our intellects as tools. Pragmatism was popular for a time in Italy about 1900 but dissolved because of a certain vagueness; it stood for "freedom, creativeness, and originality" and appealed mostly to poetic writers. Papini subsequently became a fascist, indicative perhaps of pragmatism's tendency to take on the color of its surroundings and embrace any active creed that seemed to have vitality—something also alleged of Bergsonism.

In other ways, too, Bergsonism reflected broader currents of the day which may be seen mirrored in other minds. The stress on the value of religious experience, *qua* experience, found in William James's famous lectures on *Varieties of Religious Experience,* could be found also in the serious interest in supernormal psychical phenomena (to which C. D. Broad, Cambridge philosophy professor, among others, lent his name); in George Santayana's interest in the "splendid error" of the Catholic faith, a great myth: While religions are not of course literally true, it is a shallow person who thinks them disposed of when this is pointed out. It could be found in the Catholic Revival among men and women of letters, not only in France but in England and in many other places. There was unquestionably some weakness in treating religion as not true but useful, or nice to believe. Simone Weil later complained that Bergson presented religious faith "like a pink pill of a superior kind, which imparts a prodigious amount of vitality." But the turning to religion in a self-conscious way, treating it as poetry or a pleasing myth, was very typical of the *fin de siècle* vanguard. Carl Jung came to regard religion as good psychotherapy.

In Germany people spoke of the revival of metaphysics, citing Hartmann, Lotze, Eucken; Max Scheler is a good counterpart of Bergson or Santayana—a sensitive, esthetic, introspective, nondogmatic philosopher. In Britain Hegelian idealism was modified in the direction of a greater personalism, and an awareness of the multistructured nature of reality (Bradley, McTaggart). If Bergson contributed to the revival of both religion and metaphysics and to a nondoctrinaire subjectivism which stressed experience for its own sake—participating in the great stream of life—his most notable influence was on literature. He was very much a philosopher for poets and novelists. He directly inspired the imagist poets as well as the "stream of consciousness" novelists and had a good deal to do with others of the many literary movements that proliferated—symbolism, expressionism. For Bergson encouraged the artistic imagination to plumb its deepest levels, cutting loose from rational thought in search of spontaneous experience—finding there, he supposed, the utmost reality.

The Bergsonian message, like that of Nietzsche and William James, must be set against the background of science's virtual monopoly of knowledge; he broke through the ban on religious or metaphysical speculations decreed by the positivist regimen. "For the first time since Comte and Kant metaphysics had waged war against scientific determinism on its own ground and won it," Etienne Gilson has written in his recollections of what Bergson meant to his generation. Charles de Gaulle spoke of Bergson as one who "renewed French spirituality." Later events revealed some of the limitations of this cheerfully affirmative philosophy; it could lead to approval of almost anything that was active and dynamic, like war and fascism.

But Bergson lived on to add to his reputation with the book some think is his greatest, *The Two Sources of Morality and Religion,* published in 1932, a work of rich texture, interwoven with insights, whose general theme conforms to his guiding vision of humanity as needing to surmount its practical scientific reason with the creative insights of religion and poetry. Standing somewhere between Freud and Nietzsche, Bergson like them was essentially a gifted student of the human interior mind, the subjective dimension, the undiscovered self.

FREUD AND JUNG

It was an "age of the spirit," reacting against an excess of positivism. "The important thing was to 'have soul,'" Jean Guehenno remarks of this ambience from 1890 to 1914. "I have always considered myself a voice of what I believe to be a greater renaissance," wrote the great Irish poet W. B. Yeats in 1892, "the revolt of the soul against the intellect—now beginning in the world." Symbolist poets (discussed later in this chapter) experimented with a kind of expression that would convey inexpressible emotional moods—saying the unsayable. Many saw art as the only way of bridging the gulf between consciousness and society.[7]

Nevertheless science was far from dead. This revolt was a movement of a small minority of disaffected rebels, whose great significance is now seen but who were then far from the mainstream. As it continued to parent a host of technological marvels—this was the age of electricity, the first automobiles, radio, X-rays—science never stood higher in popular esteem. And among the acknowledged intellectual giants of this period, the Viennese physician Sigmund Freud was not a poet or prophet, but —apparently—a hardheaded empirical scientist. Perhaps, since most medical doctors rejected his thought as too fantastical, one had better say that he together with his coworker (until 1912) Carl Jung of Zurich represented a position halfway between scientific positivism and poetic mythology.

The Austrian doctor brought strange knowledge from the underworld of the human psyche but summed it up in perfectly rational concepts and offered a systematic clinical approach to it. Freud is one of the seminal minds of the modern age, by almost universal consent; he ranks with Newton and Darwin as one of those scientists who altered the fundamental conditions of thought and changed Western civilization's view of itself in basic ways. He ranks also with Marx and Darwin, it is frequently said, among the big three of the nineteenth century. This is despite the fact that, like those other two giants, his theories may prove to have been wrong in many details. Freud himself was convinced he had made epochal discoveries: "I have the distinct feeling that I have touched on one of the great secrets of nature," he wrote, and on occasion compared himself to Copernicus and Darwin. Freud was hardly an arrogant man, though inclined to be somewhat dogmatic, and in pointing to the importance of his ideas he was stating only a generally acknowledged truth. The greatest impact of Freudianism came in the 1920s and 1930s; today his place in modern thought seems secure, though there is increasingly a tendency to doubt that Freud founded an exact science or that his imposing structure of thought will prove any more lasting than other speculative ideas. The verdict on Freud may come to resemble that on Marx, in that he will be viewed less as a scientist than as a pioneer who opened up new horizons for others to explore. His name has become a

---

[7]In 1911, George Lukacs, the Hungarian critic and philosopher, published his first significant work *The Soul and Its Forms (Die Seele und die Formen)*, the beginning of his discovery of a "reified" world of human relations which has escaped human control to appear as an external, alien force. At this time Lukacs saw art as the only means of bridging the gulf between an ideal life and the actual one of triviality, confusion, bureaucracy. Marcel Proust, Franz Kafka, D. H. Lawrence, Robert Musil, and many other writers made the same discovery at this time.

household word, and his influence extends to education, literature, the arts, religion and philosophy, morals, popular culture.

It may be that like other household words Freud is really not accurately understood by most people. But the story of the path to his theory of the role of repression in neurosis is fairly familiar. As a physician engaged in treating mental illness, Freud found that patients under hypnosis related events in their lives and that this narration had a therapeutic effect. It was not hypnosis but the narration, it seemed, that was effective. Freud developed the free-association technique and confirmed beyond much doubt the often startling relief from various neurotic disorders that comes from talking things out. (It was a truth, perhaps, that confessors in the priesthood had always known in less precise ways, possibly bartenders too!) On this rather slender underpinning, Freud erected some ingenious, exciting, controversial theories.

Freud, who received his M.D. degree in 1881 at the age of twenty-five and explored these areas of psychiatry during the next decade in Vienna and Paris, presented his views about the cathartic effect of recall of a painful memory in 1893. The next year he added the assertion that these painful, repressed incidents were invariably associated with sexual matters. Thus began his celebrated exploration of sex, including childhood sex experience, with a new frankness. The child's erotic fixation on the parent of the opposite sex, also childhood toilet training (anal and oral types of character) as keys to adult personality, and homosexuality as related to early absence of the father were some of the shocking Freudian revelations or claims that empirical observation appeared partly to confirm, though some seemed beyond demonstration.

Freud soon presented the concept of the unconscious as the place into which shameful material gets pushed. The unconscious was already a familiar idea, having been suggested by Schopenhauer and the philosopher Eduard von Hartmann, among others.[8] Freud did not invent this term or discover the existence of the unconscious mind. But he thrust it into great prominence by making it a central part of his theory. Some things, particularly shameful things, get pushed down into the unconscious part of the mind and, festering there, cause mental trouble; bringing them up into the light of consciousness cures the illness. Later Freud drew a picture of the conflict in the mind between the *id,* the primitive unconscious where dwell all kinds of lustful drives and desires, and the *superego* at the other extreme, representing the inhibitions which society and conscience impose. The *ego,* in between, is a battle ground

[8]R. K. Gupta, "Schopenhauer and Freud," *Journal of the History of Ideas,* October-December, 1975, documents the philosopher's anticipations of Freud, including the significance of sex, repression, the importance of childhood sexual experience, and Freud's acknowledgment of this debt. Von Hartmann was a Schopenhauerian.

between these conflicting forces, a place of uneasy compromise between the id and the superego, the antisocial and the social.

Some of the implications of Freud were even more shocking than Darwin's. The natural impulses of sex are suppressed because society brands them as shameful; the sexual drive, or *libido,* Freud thought to be the strongest human impulse and the key to life. We have learned to be civilized at the cost of making neurotics and perhaps emotional cripples. Freud saw a tragic conflict between the demands of the individual and of society (especially in a later work, *Civilization and Its Discontents,* 1930). Sexual drives may be "sublimated" into great achievements. But suppression of antisocial wishes usually leads to varying degrees of unhappiness and neurosis. Freud more than anyone else has been responsible for a tendency in recent times to remove from sex some of the inhibitions and taboos. But it may be worth noting that on his own mature view, this will hardly solve the problem. The id, he believed, holds violent and antisocial impulses which society, and ultimately the ego itself, cannot tolerate. Freud appeared to think that rape, murder, sadism, all kinds of foul and nasty desires, lurk in the unconscious mind; and so any ordered society must in part sit on the lid of this disorderly basement of the human psyche. The superego is also a part of the mind, and its function is to discipline its uncouth relative downstairs. In presenting this image Freud only gave new terms for a very old vision of the duality of human nature—Plato's two horses pulling the soul in opposite directions comes to mind, and in the eighteenth century Diderot and Rousseau had written of the war in the human breast between natural and civilized desires. Nietzsche had invoked Dionysus and Apollo.

But his energy and imagination, combined with some of the trappings of empirical science, assured Freud's great reputation. It did not come quickly. Apart from the reactions of scandalized moralists, orthodox medical practitioners rejected and to a degree ostracized Freud as far too speculative. He started his own movement and gathered about him a few disciples, who gradually grew in numbers. In the 1900s, Freud was only just beginning to be known. It is said that *The Interpretation of Dreams* (1900) took eight years to sell its initial printing of six hundred copies in English. Finding an able and congenial partner in the brilliant Carl Jung, he founded the International Psychoanalytical Association in 1910. The Freud-Jung partnership, destined to break up three years later, was then in full swing; the two founders of psychoanalysis sensed that "the ferment is at work," though at times Freud feared that they were trying to move too fast. They lectured in the United States during 1909 and 1910, a landmark in the dissemination of their doctrine.

The Freudian movement may be seen as part of a larger evolution of European consciousness. He was not the only one working toward the frank discussion of previously taboo sexual matters. The pioneer sexologist, the Englishman Havelock Ellis, can be mentioned in this context. In 1910, Lou Salome—whom Nietzsche had courted, who knew Freud, and who became the mistress of the poet Rilke—wrote a book on eroticism (*Die Erotik*). D. H. Lawrence was beginning his literary explorations of eroticism, as was James Joyce. In the 1900s, Edwardian England said goodbye to Victorian "prudery" with the amorous adventures of King Edward, the plays of Shaw, and novels of H. G. Wells such as *Ann Veronica* (1911), in which a liberated woman practices free love. More popularly, a typical piece of Edwardian fiction was Elinor Glyn's *Three Weeks*, portraying sophisticated adultery. In all sorts of ways a freer, more "emancipated" attitude toward sexual morality, a greater openness in discussing physical sex, was beginning to spread, though largely confined to literary elites such as England's Bloomsbury set; it would continue into the 1920s. In bringing into the open what had long lain under restraints, Freud shared in the spirit of his age among the intelligentsia.

Freud lived on to become world famous in the 1920s and 1930s and will be discussed further in later portions of this book; no one did more to shape the mind of the twentieth century. His later works were more speculative and philosophical. Though claiming to be a scientist, professing atheism, hard-bitten and a little cynical, Freud was more a person of literature or philosophy, perhaps, than a scientist.

He was a man of wide interests and broad culture, "deeply versed in classical literature as well as the noblest examples of European literature," as his biographer Ernest Jones tells, and the close friend of such writers as Thomas Mann, Stefan Zweig, Romain Rolland—a man of genius who belonged to the great European intellectual tradition. Yet there was a certain acrid dogmatism about Freud, as about Marx, and this helped lead to the schisms which beset his "movement."

About 1912, Freud came to a rather painful break with the greatest of those who had followed, or accompanied, him in the pioneer explorations of the unconscious, the Swiss psychologist C. G. Jung. Jung, who lived until 1961, broke with Freud partly because of his belief that psychic energy is not exclusively sexual; Freud would tolerate no questioning of his gospel of the primacy of sex.

There were more basic reasons. Jung was less a sceintific rationalist than Freud. Some have wished to deny to Freudianism the title of "science," on the grounds that it erects mountains of speculation on very slender foundations of fact; but there can be no doubt that Freud approached his task of analyzing the human mind in a brisk, rationalistic spirit. Freud had no use for religion, which he believed to be a neurotic manifestation derived from the Oedipus complex. His tendency to "explain away" religious and other ideologies, or modes of expression, as the product of a more "basic" and quite naturalistic condition, links

Freud with Marx, Feuerbach, Durkheim, and others of this sort. If to Marx religion is a means of enslaving the proletariat, to Freud it is a means of compensating for a neurotic mind—to the former the excrescence of an unsound social order, to the latter the excrescence of an unsound psyche. This puts Freud in the camp of those who are "rationalists" in the sense of being foes of "religion," who believe that the healthy intellect should rest content with a wholly naturalistic view of the universe. This position is itself, however, an ideology or unprovable assertion of certain values—evidence of a type of mind or temperament, perhaps the type that William James called "tough-minded." (It is also an argument *ad hominem* that can be turned upon its user. If Freud tells me I am religious because of my mental history, I can retort that he is irreligious because of his.)

Jung, on the other hand, incurred the contempt of the scientific psychologists but the admiration of others by wandering into the fields of religion, art, literature, and history. Shocked by what he termed Freud's "materialistic prejudice" and "shallow positivism," Jung might have agreed with D. H. Lawrence who scolded Freud for creating a "technology of the heart." Those American disciples who took Freudian psychoanalysis to be a useful mechanical means of keeping one's psyche in good order represent what Jung and Lawrence were forced to reject. Jung moved toward a theory of the "collective unconscious," which he thought he observed to exist in remarkable ways, and he sought clues to the "archetypes," or patterns of imagery, which are basic to it. These appear in mythological motifs, in fairy tales, in art and poetry, as well as in dreams and in conscious behavior. They are found in all the great religions and in literature. A fabulous scholar and polyhistor himself, Jung cast his net widely over civilizations past and present in his search for the archetypes of the collective unconscious. His disciples have tended more toward comparative mythology and toward the analysis of art and poetry than perhaps anything else. He manifested some deeply mystical and religious tendencies.

To Jung, religion and art were essential to the healthy human psyche. The great "myths," expressing as they do the language of the mind at its deepest level, with roots in the collective life of humanity, satisfy fundamental instincts. Without them, human nature shrivels. Here Jung touches Nietzsche's conviction that the modern individual is overly rationalized and needs to regain contact with some healthy primitivisms. While Jung, too, always claimed to be an empirical investigator, his critics think that he often lost himself in fanciful speculations. But no other pioneer of what Jung called "the undiscovered self" except Freud himself has so drawn attention to this strange, fascinating realm that lies within each person, or so contributed to its elucidation.

Probably Jung's best-known contribution to psychology was his classification of personality types, into "extraverts" and "introverts" with subdivisions. He invented other striking concepts, such as "persona" and "shadow," which roughly correspond to Freud's superego and id. The *shadow* is a figure of the unconscious containing evil, antisocial impulses but also other nonconscious elements. The *persona* is our social role, the part society expects us to play, a mask of artificial personality. This seems to bear some relationship to what the existentialists later called the "unauthentic" or "other-directed" self. The fully mature or "individuated" personality must dissolve the persona and integrate the unconscious into the self. This is close to Freud's "sublimation" or to Nietzsche's fusion of "Dionysian" and "Apollonian" elements. The basic idea is that elements of the unconscious mind must be used in the interest of a higher creativity.

"The dynamism and imagery of the instincts together form an *a priori* which no man can overlook without the gravest risk to himself," Jung wrote in *The Undiscovered Self.* Overlooking them, he believed, could be held responsible not only for individual mental illness but also for such social horrors as German Nazism; for the forces latent in the unconscious will break forth in wildly irrational ways if they are not understood and administered to properly. Modern man still lives, he thought, in a make-believe world made up of rational concepts, ignoring the underlying emotional determinants. "The psychiatrist is one of those who know most about the conditions of the soul's welfare, upon which so infinitely much depends in the social sum." The popularity of psychiatry today, growing from nothing to the status of a great profession in this century, offers some evidence that what Jung wrote is true, though we still stand at the mere threshold of real understanding of the self. The popularity of mysticism, eastern religions, meditation and other such fads in recent years also shows that Jung was right in seeing the problem as less a scientific than a spiritual one. Rejected largely by the professional psychoanalysts, who much preferred the more rational and systematic Freud, Jung made a comeback in recent years among the bewildered youngsters in an overly technological society.

A younger man than Freud, Jung saved most of his creative life for the years after 1914 and so may be considered again later. The son of a Lutheran pastor who lost his faith, Jung discovered Schopenhauer and Nietzsche at Basel in his native Switzerland, found an idol in Sigmund Freud, then broke with this father figure rather as Nietzsche broke with Richard Wagner and Marx parted company with Hegel: The structure of genius often shows this using and then discarding of a giant predecessor who serves both as model and rival. The war moved Jung deeply and pushed him further toward a mysticism always congenial to his temperament. He shared with Freud a belief that "the great gains made by the evolution of civilized society . . . are made at the price of enormous losses."

Where Freud saw the cost as chiefly due to sexual repression, Jung stressed loss of contact with the realm of myth and symbol. He strongly believed that objective reason, the intellectual mode of our rationalized society, is a far poorer way of thinking than what he called "analogical" thinking: "archaic, unconscious, not put into words and hardly formulable in words." It is somewhat surprising, in view of this, that Jung wrote so much. But his writing does often have a strangely compelling power to arouse interest in myths, symbols, and mystic experiences. In this respect he has been a child of the twentieth century.

THE CRISIS IN SCIENCE

The popular prestige of science stood of course very high in this period when almost every year brought some fresh technical miracle, whether electric light, phonograph, or automobile. For the more thoughtful, science offered its exciting theories, of which Darwin's natural selection was but the most sensational. The periodic table of the elements, worked out by the Russian Mendeleyeff; the atomic structure of matter, developed by Dalton and others; the law of the conservation of energy, associated with Helmholtz and Kelvin, a striking tribute to the regularity and constancy of natural phenomena; and other great discoveries aroused awe, but not dismay, since they testified to the orderliness of nature and the ability of science to disclose cosmic principles. "The men of science had become the prophets of progressive minds," to an extent that may be measured by a statement in the British *Annual Register* for 1884 that few other subjects except scientific ones received any attention from the intellectual world. Lonely prophets and offbeat poets, despite the attention properly given them, did not at this time seriously compete with the scientists either in the popular or the intellectual world.

The widespread confidence in science rested on the belief that it was unfolding an accurate picture of reality, that it was solidly based and could not err, that other modes of knowledge such as metaphysics and religion were obsolete. This popular and slightly vulgar scientific materialism was purveyed in the works of such pundits as T. H. Huxley, John Tyndall, the Germans Emil Du Bois-Reymond and Ernst Haeckel (*The Riddle of the Universe*). But at the turn of the century science was about to lose its confident common sense air and to confront shattering paradoxes at the frontiers of physics.

The popular, common sense view of science included opinions such as that reality consists of material bodies, the atoms being thought of as little billiard balls; that these material objects act in a spatial field and temporal world of the sort familiar to human experience, with an objectively existing space and time; that all bodies obey the same scientific "laws," like Newton's laws of motion and the law of the conservation of energy. The universe was pictured as a large machine, consisting of physical bodies in dynamic relationships. Before long, an astounded public was forced to hear from the mouths of the scientists themselves the refutation of all this. Matter, it seemed, consisted of invisible and perhaps merely hypothetical units called "electrons," which within the atom refused to obey Newton's laws, an example of insubordination without precedent.

Even more surprisingly, time and space as they appear to human experience had to be abandoned, since these are relative to some arbitrary standard and no objective standard exists for the universe as a whole. Newton's law of gravitation, foundation of physical science for two hundred years, was evidently not accurate. It became impossible to picture the behavior of "matter" as corresponding to anything within the realm of human sensory experience, either at the subatomic or the cosmic level. The universe was not like a machine, nor was there anything in it that one could readily call "matter"; it was even possible for scientists to hold that reality fades into an idea when traced as far as possible. Matter, remarked Bertrand Russell, became a formula for describing what happens where it is not. Space, time, and matter all turned out to be fictions of the human mind, perhaps not so far from the convenient but unreal abstractions of scientific knowledge according to Bergson.

A starting point for these complex developments was the Michelson-Morley experiment, performed in 1887 by two Americans wholly unaware that they were about to stumble onto a new era in science. They were trying to measure the speed of the earth by measuring the time it takes light to travel with, as compared to against, the direction of the earth's motion. The extraordinary result, after repeated experiments, was to disclose the remarkable fact that no "ether" or other substance exists for earth and other bodies to move through. There is, in effect, no surrounding atmosphere. All through the nineteenth century, scientists had posited such an "ether" substance because of the discovery that light and electricity acted like waves, hence needed a medium through which to pass; this in addition to its uses as a measuring rod for space and time. The ether had become something of a scandal; necessary as a postulate if the behavior of all sorts of "waves" was to be visualized, it was something no one had ever seen or otherwise established directly as existent. The Michelson-Morley results brought matters to a head. It forced abandonment of the ether or any conception of a "something" space.

If there is no space, as a backdrop to the universe, there is no absolute standard of motion. All speed is relative to something else. The speed on the earth is measured by reference to the earth itself, postulating that it is stable; but of course the earth is in motion around the sun, the planetary system is in motion, too, relative to other systems and galaxies, and so on until the limits of the universe are reached. Then what can be found to measure by? The speed of light, as the Michelson experiment revealed, being the ultimate speed of things in the universe, is a constant that does not vary relative to other motion and cannot be used to measure them by. If there is nothing in the universe that constitutes an ultimate yardstick of measurement, there can be no absolute speed. The same thing is true for distance as for speed. Space and time viewed from a universal and not an earth bound angle must disappear as absolutes. From this, many odd conclusions emerged, for instance, that at the same moment it is a different time to observers in motion in different parts of the cosmos. If right now you are on one star and I on another, it is not the same time for us. If I journeyed to visit you on your planet and then returned to mine in a spaceship, I would find that a different interval of time had elapsed than that shown by my perfectly accurate clock. And so on.

Euclid's solid axioms of geometry were seen to be true only so long as kept to the boundaries of the earth; for outer space, there are other geometries, based on different physical postulates, which turn out to be equally rigorous logical systems. Thus, it seemed, the quality of objective certainty that had always attached to pure mathematics vanished in relativity too.

In regard to Newtonian gravity, the difficulty of conceiving a "force" of some sort acting at a distance had bothered Newton himself a little and had bothered others since. In the eighteenth century Berkeley and Leibniz had explored this weakness in a speculative manner. According to the great scientist Albert Einstein, whose first or special theory of relativity was presented in 1905, gravity is not a "force." One should not think of a pull exerted by objects on each other. Space having vanished in the sense of anything positive like "ether," this adjustment became necessary. Einstein's first theory asked a stunned public to believe that bodies move through the curvatures of space-time which, not being independent of each other, become merged in a single continuum. Others held that the physical principles of the universe cannot be visualized in terms of human imagery at all, they can only be indicated in mathematical formulae.

Whatever else this was, it was not common sense; the scientists were becoming more wildly paradoxical than the artists and poets. At the subatomic level, where in 1897, J. J. Thomson arrived at the concept of the electron or unit of negative electricity as the least unit of "matter," the belief that the atoms could be thought of as miniature planetary systems, with the nucleus as the sun and the electrons circling around it, soon had to be abandoned. Niels Bohr, the Danish physicist who lived until 1962 and became one of the leading theoretical pioneers of the age of nuclear energy, explained that the laws of motion holding for the solar systems do not apply at all within atoms. Thus the laws of Newton, always heretofore assumed to be universal, broke down on both the smallest and largest fields and remained valid only within a zone of fairly gross sense experience. They were crude approximations that worked well enough only when the demand for precision was not too great.

The world within the atom soon became most puzzling, the behavior of electrons breaking all sorts of laws heretofore regarded as sacrosanct. At the turn of the century, Max Planck's quantum theory asserted that energy is emitted discretely and not continuously, in little packages, as it were, and not in a continuous stream. Heat causes electrons to make sudden jumps from one energy level to another. Planck found a "constant," a number which represents the relationship between energy and frequency of radiation, a number which turned up again in wave mechanics in connection with the behavior of electrons. Like Kepler's laws, it is a discoverable regularity, the meaning of which lay hidden for the time being.

The electrons did not, then, behave as particles of matter would be expected to behave; they did not act at all the way "ordinary" objects do in the everyday world. Further research by Einstein, Heisenberg, and Broglie disclosed that electrons have properties of *both* particles and waves, being sometimes one and sometimes the other, or being something capable of behaving on occasion like both.

Since electrons must be used to observe electrons and exert a disturbing influence, one can never directly observe electrons but can only infer their nature. This, to some, was a disturbing reminder that science has limits beyond which human knowledge can never penetrate. Likewise, the behavior of the subatomic particles can be predicted only within limits of probability, thus striking at that certainty and complete determinacy heretofore claimed and thought necessary for physical science. For example, we cannot know both the position and the velocity of a subatomic particle in the way that we can know them of larger objects. If an airplane is bound for Boston from Chicago, naturally we can find both its exact position and its speed at any given moment. This cannot be done for an electron bound from one place to another. We *can* get general statistical trends, adequate for most predictive purposes, but the individual electron eludes determinacy and predictability. Heisenberg's "indeterminacy" principle, subsequently announced, indicated the unsatisfactory situation at the frontiers of physics. In his book *Physics and Philosophy* (1942), Sir James Jeans summed up the consequences of quanta theory in six propositions: (1) the uniformity of nature disappears, (2) precise knowledge of the outer world becomes impossible, (3) the processes of nature cannot be adequately represented within a framework of space and time, (4) sharp division between subject and object has ceased to be possible, (5) causality has lost its meaning, and (6) if there is a fundamental causal law, this lies beyond the phenomenal world and so beyond our access.

All this represented brilliant advances in the field of physics. Having for two centuries surveyed the land that Newton discovered, scientists now pressed on to a new world, and if at first this world seemed strange, that was only to be expected. Nevertheless, this experience forced basic changes in thinking almost as sweepingly as had the seventeenth-century scientific revolution, though the exact directions of change were not clear. Possibly Einstein was playing the role of Copernicus, with the Newton of the new age yet to appear. Breakdown seemed evident in the lack of any one set of rules or laws that applied to all matter and in the "uncertainty" invading such scientific bulwarks as continuity and causality, not to speak of time and space. The ultimate limits of investigation seemed to have been reached in the effort to track down reality to its smallest ultimate unit, and some philosopher-scientists were prepared to say that this vindicated the idealist position, overthrowing materialism. In the last analysis not even the scientist can get rid of the subjective factor, because as investigator the scientist in part creates the truth; and such concepts, moreover, as atom and electron, space and time, turn out to be mental constructs not necessarily corresponding to objective reality. The interference factor, which makes it impossible to observe the tiniest units directly, cannot presumably be overcome; indeterminacy of electronic behavior also apparently is an ultimate fact, not a deficiency in knowledge that further investigation may remedy.

So, far from making science useless, the new ideas yielded knowledge that led to such things as television, nuclear energy, radioactivity, X-rays, space satellites. The Einsteinian formula was brilliantly vindicated by a spectacular observation in May 1919, the most famous of all those that offered support to Einstein's gravitational theory, correcting Newton's. Of course, the most startling revelation that the strange world of Dr. Einstein was really true came in August 1945; the mushroom cloud was the final upshot of that innocent experiment in Cleveland in 1887. That $E = Mc^2$ was a deduction from all this theoretical physics which proved out in an awesome way. The absorbing quest of modern physics went on in the 1920s, which was in many ways its "heroic age," and into the 1930s. But the foundations were laid in the pre-1914 period, as were so many other foundations of the modern mind.

What were the implications? Of the theory of relativity, the Spanish philosopher Ortega y Gasset said that it is "the most important intellectual fact that the present time can show." There is general agreement on this, but less agreement, perhaps, on just why. The destruction of the long-familiar Newtonian picture of the world ("very little of the nineteenth-century picture of the world remains today," the editor of a recent survey of twentieth-century scientific thought observes) could hardly be otherwise than a gigantic intellectual revolution, affecting all of culture. It induced a degree of humility and allowed for that revival of metaphysics and that interest in the irrational which were other hallmarks of the times. Science ceased to be simple, perhaps ceased to lean on materialism and mechanism, revealed a "mysterious universe" destined always to remain, in part, mysterious and bumped up against puzzles it could not solve at the very heart of reality. Scientists themselves became a little more humble and talked of the mysterious universe rather than the march toward perfect knowledge. Lay people might still bow before the might of science, but they lost their ability to comprehend it. The "world view" of European civilization since Newton had been dominated by a certain picture of the cosmos as a mechanical model, familiar to human experience. It now became difficult to use any such model.

No one with a knowledge of Western philosophy, from Hume and Kant to Nietzsche and Bergson, could be much surprised by the conclusion that scientific knowledge must be in part subjective and also incomplete because phenomenal only. The limitation lies within the human sensory apparatus, which can hardly be adequate to full comprehension of the whole of cosmic reality. Why should we suppose that our senses or even our brains, fitted for living in a particular environment, should be capable of grasping and visualizing all this? Reason, employing mathematical abstractions and other tools, can take soundings of nature sufficient for practical advantages; but if by "understanding" we mean an adequate model or picture of everything, this must probably always elude us. In Kantian terms the "thing-in-itself" is not accessible to the categories of the understanding, while the intuition or imagination can only contact it fleetingly and imperfectly. This is the fate of humanity, which though marvelously endowed is not God. Ultimately, perhaps, this conclusion was the greatest consequence of the new science. It left civilization even at the peak of its grandeur, amid the greatest of its triumphs, shorn of its overconfident "titanism" and aware that after the best that science can do, vast mystery must always remain and there is abundant place for a religious attitude toward the universe.

THE CRISIS IN RELIGION

Religion too was in crisis. Nietzsche had announced that "God is dead"; Freud was an atheist; Darwinism had dealt blows to orthodoxy. The most severe blow to traditional Christianity probably came, however, not from any of these but from the "higher criticism." (In his careful study of *The Victorian Church*, Owen Chadwick finds the higher criticism and comparative religious perspectives far more a cause of

Christian crisis than Darwinism.) J. Wellhausen's *History of Israel,* first published in 1878, was a landmark of scholarship. For a number of years before this there had been uneasiness. In 1860 a turmoil in the Anglican Church over the book *Essays and Reviews,* in which some liberal clerics expressed the view that the Scriptures should be examined like any other book, led to a trial for heresy. Ernest Renan's *Life of Jesus,* and David Strauss's somewhat similar book in Germany, raised eyebrows all over Europe in the 1860s. They were followed by J. R. Seeley's *Ecce Homo* in 1865, not an irreverent book but one which did seek the human, historical Christ. The trend of romantic and Hegelian theology had been to play down literal Biblicalism.

Wellhausen offered persuasive support to a theory already advanced, that a substantial portion of the earlier books of the Bible (the Pentateuch) was not written until much later than the events they describe and, indeed, not put in its final form until about 400 B. C. (the time of Ezra), nearly a millennium after Moses. Wellhausen carried the day among the scholars, especially the younger ones. The second edition of his *History* appeared in 1883 and was translated into English in 1885, giving rise to a considerable controversy. A French scholar wrote in 1894 that "whoever is not totally prejudiced, whoever has not decided in advance that any kind of criticism is false, must accept the idea that the Priestly Code was not formed until after the Babylonian exile."

To some of the pious, this was a shocking conclusion, for it seemed to cast doubt on the Bible as revealed truth, infallible because divinely inspired. The arguments of liberal theologians, that the history of Israel and Judea in the broader sense justified the claim of a unique religious mission vouchsafed to the Jewish nation, carried little conviction to those brought up to believe (as did, for example, William E. Gladstone, the famous British statesman) that the literal truth of every line of Scripture was the impregnable rock upon which Christianity stood.

In 1872, George Smith called attention to a Babylonian version of the story of the Flood—a significant and shattering discovery. The leading feature of the "higher" as distinct from the "lower" criticism was its awareness of an immense literary tradition among the other peoples of the ancient world, which bore on the Bible at many points. No longer was the Bible seen in isolation, as a totally unique and marvelous book. The Old Testament fitted into an historical context that began to be recovered and understood; thus seen, it perhaps lost none of its wonder nor even its veracity, but it did inevitably become different—a part of human history, not simply the record of a continuous divine miracle. A good deal of the Old Testament has close parallels in the sacred and wisdom literature of the Babylonians and other ancient peoples with whom the Jewish people were in close contact. The uniqueness of the Hebraic outlook—monotheistic, ethical, messianic—remained, but in innumerable details the Biblical story lost its ability to pass as something quite outside the experience of the rest of the ancient world. The Jews could never again be quite the "peculiar people" in the old sense. (This was not displeasing to Hegelian philosophers, who declared the entire "world spirit" of an age to be more significant than single nations or individuals.)

Into this same pattern fitted that immense growth in knowledge about other peoples which was the fruit of anthropological research. Popularized in such books as James Frazer's widely read end-of-the-century success, *The Golden Bough,* this data compelled the conclusion that even primitive religions make use of archetypal beliefs similar to those of Christianity and Judaism. Awareness of Indic thought—a whole world of higher religions—advanced steadily in the nineteenth century. All this worked further toward eroding the uniqueness of Christianity. Comparative religion disclosed that the god who comes down to earth, is killed, rises again, redeems humanity, is found in many traditions other than the Christian one—these are virtually Jungian archetypes. Myths of the martyr, the victim, the miracle-worker, the Man of the People, the Wanderer, and others found in the Christ saga belong to the storehouse of stories told by every people.

By the end of the nineteenth century, also, critical research into the New Testament had arrived at conclusions concerning the Gospels, which included the view that the authors of Matthew and Luke leaned chiefly on the Gospel of Mark as a source, and even the latter contains theological interpolations not taken from Jesus himself. Again, the net result of intensive historical analysis was, roughly, to cast some doubt on the accuracy of the Gospels as accounts of the life of Jesus and on certain sayings and ideas attributed by them to Jesus. Opening up the problem of the historical Jesus by no means meant destroying Christianity, but simple folk among the pious might understandably think so. A quarrel between "modernists" and "fundamentalists" soon divided most Christian churches. Popularizers of the higher criticism, with an antitheological ax to grind, sometimes exaggerated it and declared that, for example, Jesus never existed and the Bible was a tissue of fables.[9] Scandalized Christians reacted by denouncing the whole critical movement, and it took some time before balanced judgment was restored. In the Roman Catholic Church, "modernism" received a cautious green light from Pope Leo XIII, but Pius X, his successor in 1903, checked this move toward liberalism as he did others, as for example, the Catholic democratic movement.

In 1864, Pius IX, embittered by the Italian liberal-nationalist

[9]Bertrand Russell, the eminent philosopher, held that "historically, it is quite doubtful whether Christ ever existed at all, or, if he did, we do not know anything about him." Russell's *A Free Man's Worship,* 1910, was a skeptic's manifesto.

movement which assailed the papacy's temporal power, had issued his celebrated Syllabus of Errors and in so doing placed the Roman Church in a state of war with much of the nineteenth century. Liberalism and democracy, as well as modern science, were declared to be irreconcilable with Christianity and the Church. In 1870, Pius IX had summoned the great Ecumenical Council, first since the Council of Trent in 1563, chiefly to solemnize the doctrine of papal infallibility. The goal was not achieved without a severe struggle, in which many of the German, French, and English bishops opposed the papal party, and after the decrees some liberal Catholics left the Church. Leo XIII, the great Pope who succeeded Pius IX, did not really retreat much from Pio Nono's position. Though anxious to encourage learning and a friend of the Catholic social movement, he continued to assert that the modern state, based on secular individualism, is fundamentally anti-Christian. In Italy, Catholics continued to boycott national politics on papal orders, though in France there was finally an adjustment to the Republic. In the 1900s, Catholics who embraced liberal and democratic principles were rebuked. They were reminded that political society must be based on Christian principles, not on liberal skepticism and indifference; in regard to democracy, they were told that the Church cannot attach primary importance to the form of government; it can get along with democracy but also with other forms, and what matters is that society be Christian, not that it adopt any particular political ideology. Marc Sangnier and the great Charles Péguy were perhaps the leading French Catholic Democrats who finally (1910) received this rebuke.

By that time, the Dreyfus affair had caused a sharp conflict between conservative and liberal France with the clergy ranged for the most part on the former side. The victorious partisans of Captain Dreyfus took their revenge by passing legislation to separate church from state in 1901, the occasion of further bitter exchanges between anti-clericals and churchmen. All in all, the Church found itself at war with basic trends in the modern world at this time and subject to some divisive conflicts. As in the case of the Roman Catholic Church, the same thing might be said in lesser degree of major Protestant denominations. There were liberals who sought to turn the church's major interest to social reform, abandoning traditional theology and accepting the higher criticism; there were conservatives who feared the extinction of Christianity if it thus merged itself into secular liberalism.

NEW SPIRITUAL CURRENTS

Strong winds blew in the direction of religion in this era. The trouble was that they tended to be diverted to nonorthodox, even non-Christian varieties of faith. The reaction against scientism, especially powerful in France, led to that interest in moral and interior experience already seen in the philosophies of Nietzsche, Bergson, and William James. There was indeed something of a Catholic revival, aided by the conversion of important men and women of literature. But this religion-seeking spirit more often ignored dogmatic orthodoxy. William James developed the viewpoint in his famous Gifford lectures on "The Varieties of Religious Experience" that the various myths or conceptualizations in which religions are objectively embodied are not fundamental; they are the mere husks of religion. What is basic is the instinct to believe, the need for the human spirit to express itself. One could, presumably, just as well believe in any myth. One might, like the great Irish poet W. B. Yeats, invent a private mythology; one might, like Annie Besant or Mme. Blavatsky, embrace esoteric Oriental religions. The former's "theosophy" became a fashionable creed. The "truth" of a religion became somewhat irrelevant; one could never know that anyway. What mattered was the fact of belief itself.

The point was driven home by a later remark of Emmanuel Mounier, who declared that a century ago almost everyone was either a Christian or else a rationalist opposed to all religion, whereas today there are not too many of either sort. One had faith, but not necessarily a Christian faith, or if so only very loosely.

The greatest prophet of the pre-World War I era was doubtless Leo Tolstoy. The Russian novelist was a personality of such gigantic proportions that he captured the world's imagination and became a living legend to whose estate at Yassnaya Polyana visitors came from all over the Western world to do homage. The brilliant novels *War and Peace* and *Anna Karenina* made him famous; but more striking was the spiritual odyssey of the later Tolstoy. Experiencing a deep crisis in which he saw life as absurd and meaningless, this man of passionate "commitment" (to use a modern phrase) was driven to reconsider the most fundamental questions of existence, and after finding neither the abstractions of the philosophers nor the facts and theories of the scientists to be of any help, he ended in a sort of primitive Christianity. There is much in the Russian's agony and redemption to suggest the later movements of existentialism and crisis theology. He found that Christ's true meaning had been falsified by formal religion and by rationalistic conceptualizing. Tolstoy found in the simple message of Christ deep truths which no mere formula could express. His religious writings (for example, *The Kingdom of God Is within You*) have tremendous force. He felt, also, the influence of the Oriental religions and tried to find the elemental truths that underlie all the great religions.

Tolstoy advocated and in some measure practiced a return to primitive Christian communism. Powerful denunciations of war and of all forms of coercion made him a hero of the pacifist movement and in political principles an anarchist. The principle of nonresistance to evil, which Tolstoy could not always obey himself, was the cornerstone of his religious belief. In suggesting a return to a simple life pared of all artificialities, he was reminiscent of Rousseau or of the American sage Henry Thoreau. Tolstoy, a member of the Russian upper class, ferociously denounced the corruption of this class and its European counterpart. Believing passionately in art and literature, he condemned the decadence of European literature and insisted that only the peasant masses were culturally sound, however ignorant of books. In later years he wrote the simplest of parables for the people, though it is unfortunately doubtful that the Russian peasant responded. But a variety of others all over the world did respond, and Tolstoy became a figure almost unique in Western intellectual history. The Russian government, most despotic in the world, dared not touch him though he advocated anarchism, pacifism, and noncooperation with government. The affair of the Dukhobors was perhaps the most astonishing example of Tolstoy's power. He set out to save this sect of Christian communalists from brutal persecution by the tsarist government, and succeeded in gaining his end and in raising a worldwide fund for the transportation of the Dukhobors *en masse* to Canada.

Tolstoy gave away the money from his literary works and eventually before his death renounced all his wealth. A modern saint, he was formally excommunicated from the Orthodox Church in 1891, which only added to his popularity within and outside of Russia. The influence of Tolstoy was enormous, though difficult to evaluate. It would be impossible to say how much he contributed to that undermining of the Russian political system which prepared the way for the Revolution of 1917—certainly something though this process was far bigger than even his outsized figure. He was a hero of the vigorous antiwar movement of this period; for example, one sees William Jennings Bryan from the American prairies making his pilgrimage to Yassnaya Polyana. His most prominent disciple in the realm of practical affairs was to be the great Mahatma Gandhi, leader of the Indian independence movement, legendary saint and father of the modern Indian nation. Tolstoy cried out against materialism, capitalism, the corruptions of bourgeois society, and demanded a spiritual rebirth. He did not explicitly become an antirationalist, was certainly no mystic, yet his wholehearted feeling of a need to find positive meaning in life through religious commitment was a more potent blast against merely cerebral philosophy or religion than anything else in his era, probably.

How unorthodox Tolstoy was may be judged from his reply to the edict of excommunication. He denied the Trinity, original sin, the divinity of Christ, and all the church sacraments, which he called "coarse, degrading sorcery." He accused the clergy of ignorance and deceptiveness.

Tolstoy's equally great countryman, Fyodor Dostoyevsky, shared with Nietzsche a preoccupation with the idea of God's extinction and what follows from this. In his striking parable of the Grand Inquisitor (in *The Brothers Karamazov*), Christ returns to earth to be arrested and condemned by the wise old Inquisitor, who sees that Christian freedom is impossible for humanity, enslaved as it is and must be by superstitions. Existing organized religion is a fraud, but perhaps a necessary fraud. We could not endure pure spiritual Christianity; it is possible for only a few, now. Into this parable, so often reprinted, is packed much of our modern religious agony and tension. Modern civilization is depraved, we need but cannot find God, orthodox old-fashioned Christianity is bankrupt, the truly religious today may be the atheist or anti-Christ. Dostoyevsky adopted a belief in the potential mission of the Slavic peoples to redeem decadent Europe because still capable of religion—a kind of spiritual Pan-Slavism. Nietzsche himself learned from this Russian genius, who spent some terrible years in Siberian prison camps for the crime of talking against the tsar's government then came to reject the revolutionary movement as spiritually shallow. No more significant figure exists for contemporary civilization.

Nicolas Berdyaev has mentioned Tolstoy and Dostoyevsky among those he called the "forerunners of the era of the spirit," the predecessors of the post-1914 Christian revival. Others in this generation referred to by the Russian existentialist were Solovyëv and Cieszkowski (a Pole) from the Slavic world and two Frenchmen, Leon Bloy and Charles Péguy. The latter, initially a Dreyfusard and a democrat, a moderate socialist, and a fine literary craftsman, edited prewar France's most important intellectual journal, the *Cahiers de la Quinzaine*, opening its pages to all kinds of expression. Though a Catholic, Péguy was essentially a free spirit, on whom the influence of Bergson could be seen prominently. Like Tolstoy, Péguy was in revolt against all that was false in a timid and shoddy civilization and sought to affirm the value of the human soul by preaching integrity, devotion to the spiritual and intellectual life, social justice, dedication to art.

So religion was abroad, but the winds of doctrine were various and confusing. The British scholar J. N. Figgis, writing just before 1914 of *Civilization at the Crossroads*, expressed his dismay at the babel of voices: Nietzsche, Bergson, James, Tolstoy, and Bertrand Russell—atheism, skepticism, intuitionism, the life force, the will to believe, the will-to-power. Had the European tradition dissolved into a thousand fragments? Did civilization evolve from unity to multiplicity, from the Virgin to the Dynamo, as the American writer Henry Adams suggested? Some of the manifestations of diversity in the 1900s were wild indeed. In Russia, where the composer Scriabin upheld the artist's role as messiah and announced himself the chosen one, while the poet Ivanov preached the mystical union of Christ and Dionysus in "ecstasy for ecstasy's sake," there was a mood in which "every kind of new religion and superstition proliferated" (Martin Cooper). At the other end of Europe, James Joyce in Dublin encountered the Hermetic Society and the Theosophical Society, where Madame Blavatsky, Annie Besant (who had passed through Fabianism en route to Theosophy), and other modern mystics and would-be prophets were read. Another magician was the Greek Gurdiyev, who offered occult spiritual forces taken from prerational cultures and associated with artistic creation. In Italy, D'Annunzio was a fabulous personality, tremendously popular, expressing much of the *malaise* of the times.

The serious interest in abnormal psychical phenomena (spirit messages, telepathy, clairvoyance, poltergeists, and so forth) might be added. As during the fourteenth century when papal control weakened and Europe was swept by witchcraft and magic, so now in the aftermath of Christianity's decline something similar happened. The comparison, at least, may be suggested.

ESTHETES AND LITERARY REBELS

One of the great adventures of the last half of the nineteenth century lay in the realm of pure literature. It is impossible to avoid the conclusion that, with the decline of the traditional Church and of any agreed-upon orthodoxy in either religion or philosophy, the great imaginative writers have supplied many of the values of the modern world. Further, it is equally true that art became something of a religion for many in this generation. While criticism from Voltaire and Darwin had eroded Christianity's power to compel unquestioned adherence, there was also disillusionment in this period with scientific rationalism, as has been seen. The philosophers of the era, among whom Nietzsche, Bergson, and William James stand out, tended toward intuitionism or naturalism, rather than rationalism in the sense of formal, conceptual thought, and expressed their views more in poetic metaphor than logical analysis. Perhaps the greatest single advance in knowledge of the era was being made by Freud, who charted the mysterious, nonrational side of the human psyche. Nietzsche's insights, too, haunted all the writers of this era. Thus most of the major currents of the age combined to focus attention on the poetic, myth-making capacities of humanity.

This was a time when Europe discovered, for better or worse, the depths of the mind that lie beneath rational thought, where myth and symbol reign and strange, formidable powers lurk in hiding. Neither philosopher nor scientist can guide one here, but the poet or novelist perhaps can. In addition to probing the unconscious, these writers gave voice to much of the social criticism that filled the age, criticism of one or another feature of a bourgeois, industrial, democratic society repellent to sensitive souls. But their alienation pushed them toward pure art and toward purely subjective "private worlds" of imagination, for they were disgusted with the public world. Estheticism, art for art's sake, the poet's elevation to preeminence, these attitudes naturally accompanied rejection of the social and moral order by which a hated civilization lived.

The beginnings of this literature of revolt may be found at mid-century or even earlier, when reaction against the older romanticism and disillusionment with a commercial and bourgeois civilization appeared together, a rock flung at Victorian orthodoxy, the esthetic counterpart of revolutionary socialism. The "art for art's sake" writers, offspring of Gautier and Baudelaire, were from the beginning a rebellious, less respectable lot, whose works sometimes had a *succès de scandale* as well as a genuine success of art. In 1857 both Baudelaire and Flaubert faced criminal prosecution, the former for his *Flowers of Evil* and the latter for the celebrated novel *Madame Bovary*. In England the Pre-Raphaelites were criticized as immoral, but this was nothing compared to the storm stirred up by the deliberately provocative poet Algernon Swinburne in the 1860s. These writers, as their slogan implied, tended to make of art and beauty a religion, often with results that shocked the moralists. They were aggressively hostile to Christianity and conventional morality. In Swinburne's unpublished novel *Lesbia Brandon* is the theme of homosexual love (handled also by Gautier in his seminal novel *Mademoiselle de Maupin*) accompanying an estheticism in which people cultivate their senses and live saturated in beauty. Baudelaire's "satanism," which seemed to ask the poet to seek out morbid and abnormal themes, was as famous as his theory that poetry should strive for a purity corresponding to color and music. Swinburne, John Morley wrote indignantly in 1866, was "the libidinous laureate of a pack of satyrs."

"Every twenty years theories change," a Zola character observes; the modern era in literature and the arts has indeed been marked by a restless generation revolt every few years. In the 1870s the new word was naturalism, and the French writer Emile Zola was its leading representative. Naturalism was an extension of the "realism" of the Flaubert era, realism of a more brutal sort. The naturalists made a career of literary slumming, going into "the living, swarming streets" (Huysmans) to discover criminals, prostitutes, gin-soaked wretches (but Zola did not forget the country where in *La Terre* he found brutality and depravity too). The purpose here was obviously in part to "disturb the bourgeoisie" by revealing the horrors of society as well as presenting shocking material. Naturalism drew intellectually on Darwinism and other scientific ideas,

A Manet painting of the picnic nude that shocked the public. (Caisse Nationale des monuments historiques francais, Paris.)

fashionable at this hour, of course. Zola's huge multivolume chronicle, generously peopled with the vicious and the depraved, was designed both as a kind of social history of contemporary France—the novel become documentary, factual—and as a demonstration that people are the determinate products of their heredity and their environment.

Grim pessimism, people the helpless victims of blind chance or a malignant deity ("The President of the Immortals had finished his sport with Tess," Hardy remarks at the end of a famous novel), may be found also in Zola's contemporary and fellow novelist, Thomas Hardy. These were the themes of pessimistic Darwinism, and alienated writers made the most of them. In principle naturalism upheld no ideals and found no values, it only exhibited the harsh realities of a world where chance and accident rule. In practice it was likely to stir sympathy for the poor wretches it described; but Zola's novel of industrial strife, *Germinal,* does not really condemn the mine owners for the misery and the tragedy that comes of it, because everyone is trapped on the wheel of fate.

No serious writers were more popular than the naturalists Zola, Hardy, George Moore, and, in the United States a little later, figures such as Jack London, Stephen Crane, Frank Norris, Theodore Dreiser.

They exposed the nastiness of industrial society while luxuriating in the fashionable atheism. Naturalism's vogue lasted a good while with some, but for the *avant-garde* it soon lost its ability to provide the necessary thrills (*frissons*). New literary and artistic movements arose; they were soon to arise in profusion. In sharp reaction against the rather heavy-handed social realism of the Zola school, the 1880s brought symbolism and the decadents. The latter attained notoriety chiefly through the famous novel by Huysmans, *A Rebours (Against the Grain)*, whose hero, Des Esseintes, was the prototype of all dandies, those "super-esthetical young men" whom Oscar Wilde and the *Yellow Book* were soon to introduce to an amazed Victorian public. Emaciated, depraved, and sophisticated, the decadent or dandy behaved as the last pale but exquisite flower of a fading civilization, and found amusement in art, vice, and crime. A carefully cultivated exoticism, an extreme artificiality marked this mode of writing. Picking up a copy of the notorious *A Rebours*, Oscar Wilde's hero in *The Portrait of Dorian Gray* felt that "the heavy odor of incense seemed to cling about its pages and to trouble the brain." "The first duty of life is to be as artificial as possible," Wilde wrote, adding that "what the second duty is no one has yet discovered." Cold, cruel, green-eyed *femmes fatales* filled decadent poetry and novels. Homosexual perhaps like Wilde, the dandy might shade into more sinister types representing what Mario Praz has written about as "the romantic agony." An exciting suspicion of nameless sins hung over this literary assault on respectability, around which grouped those who were weary of Victorian primness.

Less obviously designed to shock the bourgeoisie, symbolism, born about 1886, represented the ultimate in Baudelairean estheticism and produced some great poetry; its goal was to express the inexpressible by an experimental verse that followed the logic of the interior mind, revealing the reality behind the appearances of things by the use of archetypal images or symbols. Much of modern poetry lies under its influence. Verlaine and Mallarmé, later the brilliant young poets La Forgue and Valéry, were its prophets.

This sounds like a more sophisticated version of romanticism, and this is not far from the truth, insofar as the idealist and poet-as-seer elements are concerned. For the poet was indeed a seer, *a voyant*, to the symbolists. But the mood of symbolism was deeply tinged with the related currents of estheticism and decadence. Turning their backs on a disgusting social and material world, many of the symbolists were distinctly otherworldly. Their most celebrated literary character, the hero of Villiers de l'Isle Adam's *Axel's Castle* (which is the title Edmond Wilson gave to his classical study of this movement), lived alone in a Wagnerian castle studying occult philosophy; when he and a girl who had come to murder him fell immediately and sublimely in love, they decided on

Caricature of Oscar Wilde. (Ashmolean Museum, Oxford. Caricature by Max Beerbohm.)

suicide because reality could not possibly measure up to the perfection of their love as they felt and experienced it at that moment. Living, Count Axel and Sara thought, is too vulgar; "our servants can do that for us." In the same spirit, Oscar Wilde once said that "any fool can make history, but it takes a genius to write it"! Art is superior to life. The earlier, "classic" romanticists had not so distinguished and separated art from life.

About the turn of the century, the more alert young writers of Europe were all smitten with the symbolist message. The young James Joyce, his brother tells us, liked poems that "sought to capture moods and impressions, often tenuous moods and elusive impressions, by means of a verbal witchery that magnetizes the mind like a spell, and imparts a wonder and grace. . . ." Poetry must not be rhymed prose; if it is, there is little point in writing it as verse. Poetry is *sui generis,* its purpose being to convey, not ideas, not conceptual knowledge, but "moods and impressions," the subtle inner world of the mind with its emotional states. This is an appeal to immediate experience—the *données* of consciousness, as the philosopher Bergson called it—which lay very close to the heart of the matter in this period. The French poet Rimbaud, who believed that the poet's vision has power to penetrate a deeper reality and show how to live (a romantic idea), also believed that the poet can bypass conceptual thought to express reality, somehow, in an immediate, symbolic sense—a conception that may bear comparison to traditional religious mysticism but was here presented by a man whose life was that of an alienated rebel. This strange genius has been made the object of a veritable religious cult by some moderns. Like Paul Gauguin the painter, Rimbaud fled Europe, to be followed by many others; "Europe bores me," André Gide exclaimed. A premodern, *sauvage* world was more attractive.

The French symbolists' antisocial extremisms may perhaps be excused on the grounds of their intense indignation against a social order that was destructive of all beauty and integrity—the rule of plutocracy, of capitalism, of the bourgeoisie, "a hideous society," as Des Esseintes exclaims. The achievements of the symbolist school are beyond question; they set the tone for modern poetry, especially in France but with a heavy influence abroad, too. T. S. Eliot brought symbolism's manner and mood into English poetry a few years later. Just prior to 1914 the American Ezra Pound, along with T. E. Hulme and others, founded the "imagist" movement in England, influenced by Bergson and related to French symbolism, with some debts also to Japanese poetry.[10] The object was to get at reality in a moment of flashing insight embodied in a single image:

> The apparition of these faces in the crowd;
> Petals on a wet, black bough.

Symbolism came to Russia too—always an eager importer of European fashions in ideas and expression; Russian symbolism was more mystical and more activist than its western counterparts, on the whole. Seer and prophet, the artist penetrates arcane mysteries not available to the scientific reason; then, according to the "mystical anarchism" of symbolist poet Vyacheslav Ivanov, this wisdom should be used to transform life and build a new world.

The impulse to create a "pure" poetry, purged of the traditional narrative or argument, was found earlier in Baudelaire and Verlaine and the French school known as "Parnassian" in the 1860s; it is one important ingredient in the modern movement. Its goal was to distin-

---

[10]A minor chapter in intellectual history in this period relates to the discovery of Japan, so recently and dramatically drawn into communication with the West, by European writers and American ones (Lafcadio Hearn) too—discovery especially of the estheticism that runs through Japanese life. Impressionist painting also owed something to Japanese art.

guish poetry from prose by its content as well as its form, a revolt against all previous literary doctrine and against the highly popular Victorian narrative or descriptive poem, such as Tennyson and Browning wrote. Poetry should not be an alternate mode of discourse. In the making of modern poetry the Parnassian strain joins the irrationalist (the mysticism of the Word, Rimbaud's "reasoned disordering of the senses") and the symbolist (allusion, indirect statement, subtle symbolisms) as the leading operative features.

Into this artistic *mélange,* of course, went ingredients from the philosophers who stressed art as the foremost kind of communication and chief avenue to truth—Schopenhauer, Nietzsche, Wagner, known all over Europe. A *Revue Wagnérienne* was founded in Paris in 1885, the sage of Bayreuth became a French rage—not merely his music but his philosophy of total art. Wagner and Nietzsche, with their doctrines of art and individual integrity, also influenced the Scandinavians Ibsen and Strindberg, the former possibly the most stimulating and controversial writer of the epoch. Upon the performance of Ibsen's *Ghosts* in London in 1891, a shocked respectability called it filthy, disgusting, and immoral, demanding its prohibition. George Bernard Shaw was impelled to write a book, *The Quintessence of Ibsenism,* in defence of the Norwegian, a book which stands as one of the major critical works of the era as well as a tribute to the vitality of Shaw and of his age. For once, England vibrated to a theatrical controversy as France had often done; *Ghosts* was the modern *Hernani.* In his book on Ibsen, Shaw asked how it was that some hailed the Norwegian as the greatest living dramatist, the modern Shakespeare, a genius beyond compare, while others requested his suppression in the name of common decency and public order. (This occurred all over Europe, not just in England, the alleged home of Victorian prudery.) The answer to the latter question lay in Ibsen's shattering attacks on conventional morality. By later standards Ibsen was hardly daring, but in the 1880s and 1890s his brilliant plays were a brand of defiance hurled in the face of the dominant European bourgeoisie. In *Ghosts* (1881), an apparently model wife and mother is shown to be living amid lies, unfaithfulness, and corruption, much as Nora Helmer is in the famous *Doll's House* (1879). In *The Enemy of the People* (1882), respectable society persecutes the honest person who would interfere with its material prosperity by telling the truth about the evil source of that prosperity. Hating *Pillars of Society* (the name of one of his plays), Ibsen had no use either for romantic, idealistic reformers. His *Peer Gynt* is a modern Don Quixote who makes himself ridiculous by blindly living as if dreams were reality. With all his symbols, Ibsen was a naturalist too, exploring with Zola the seamier sides of modern life, if a little more subtle in his definitions of the sordid.

Shaw's own plays reflect a considerable Ibsenian influence, with a

George Bernard Shaw (Washington, D.C., Library of Congress.)

special flair for the drama of ideas and a flashing, Voltairean wit lacking in the Norwegian. A peculiar sensitivity to ideas marked this versatile Irishman, along with the ability to present these ideas in dramatic form. Some of his plays expose social evil or hypocrisy, in the Fabian spirit; others reflect his fascination with Nietzschean and vitalist ideas then so much in the air. Most of them slightly shocked the public but amused them so much that they tolerated the unconventional element. Shaw like Voltaire became a licensed iconoclast, privileged to criticize the idols of respectability because he did it in such a scintillating manner. Bold, free spirits stride through Shaw's plays, knocking down the proprieties and teaching people to assert their individuality. Following a suggestion of Nietzsche's, Shaw had his Don Juan find that the really best people are in hell, not heaven. The common rules are always reversed: Women drink brandy and smoke cigars, while men are cringing and cowardly; honorable professions are dishonorable and *vice versa*, Mrs. Warren's profession (the oldest) is really no worse than any other. Shaw's Caesar is a Nietzschean superman, action controlled by reason, beyond good and evil. *Back to Methuselah* popularized the theory of creative or emergent evolution, and indeed the "life force" became a persistent Shavian theme. Shaw lived on to a ripe and creative old age in the postwar years, another trait he shared with Voltaire being an amazingly long literary career. His noonday was between 1900 and 1917, his mission to force novel ideas on bourgeois England.

One of the more notable denunciations of the new literature appeared in Max Nordau's book *Degeneration* (1895). Nordau, a rationalistic socialist, saw nothing but "degeneration" in the new literature and philosophy. Nietzsche, Walt Whitman, Wagner, Tolstoy,[11] Ibsen, as well as the French decadents, symbolists, and realists, all he declared to be so many morbid diseases. They were mad, they were antisocial, they were sex-obsessed (sexual overstimulation ruins civilization, Nordau believed). Nordau, one suspects, was almost prepared with Plato to banish the artist from society altogether in the interest of social stability, though he did declare his respect for the "healthy art" of Dante, Shakespeare, and Goethe. Few of the moderns—Hauptmann's *Weavers* was an exception—passed his critical inspection. He rejoiced that the average person remained immune to these siren calls, continuing to prefer music-hall melodies to Wagner, farces to Ibsen.

Nordau's outburst was characteristic more of popular reaction than of *avant-garde* thought, though he himself was a highly literate person. Nevertheless quite a few scholars and critics reared in the older literature bridled at the new mode of expression, and the mob persecuted it. Oscar Wilde, the chief prophet of the new literature in England in the 1890s, brilliant playwright and epigrammist, ended a broken man after being arrested and jailed for homosexuality. His illness neglected by the prison authorities, Wilde died at forty-six, a martyr to the popular dislike of the estheticism he flaunted.

The next decade, the years from 1900 on to the war, brought even more startling literary and especially artistic novelties which might have shocked Oscar. The "modernist" revolution in painting spawned a whole series of new schools and spilled over into architecture and music. A compilation of esthetic "manifestos" printed in Europe from 1890 to 1910 turned up no fewer than 730 of them.[12] This era's "fanaticism for art," Stefan Zweig recalled in his memoirs, was such as could hardly be imagined or reconstructed. There were Fauvists, acmeists, cubists, supremacists, vorticists, expressionists, futurists—the last two movements stood out from the rest and to some extent were terms subsuming most

[11]Who, in *What Is Art?* (1897), condemned the new literature and art as elitist, antisocial, and incomprehensible.

[12]D. Bänsch and E. Ruprecht, ed., *Literarische Manifeste der Jahrhundertwende, 1890-1910* (Stuttgart, 1970).

of the others. "Little magazines," experimental reviews, secessionist salons were a feature of this artistic revolution, which stemmed from a crowd of young rebels breathing defiance of the established forms. "Burn down the museums!" was a futurist battle cry. The artistic revolutionaries broke drastically with tradition. The total breach between the culture of the bourgeoisie and that of the intellectual *avant-garde* occurs at this time.

Faced with the startling novelties of cubists, postimpressionists, expressionists, the general public responded with cries of outrage. A riot greeted the performance of Igor Stravinsky's *Rites of Spring* in Paris in 1913, more famous than a similar one in Vienna accorded the musical offerings of Arnold Schoenberg and Alban Berg. The young British novelists, D. H. Lawrence and James Joyce, could not find printers for their epoch-making novels at this time. Journals called *The Storm, Blast, Action, The Torch,* painters dubbing themselves Wild Beasts and Blue Riders made known by their very names the revolutionary intent of this painting, poetry, music, and sculpture, which was found everywhere in Europe, from Ireland to Russia.

The expressionist credo characteristic of this generation of art rejected realism in the vulgar sense to experiment in abstract forms or inner visions, a parallel to the subjectivism of literature and philosophy. "There is an inherent truth which must be disengaged from the outward appearance of the object," Henri Matisse explained. "Exactitude is not truth." Cubism used formalized geometric patterns to try to get at this "inherent reality." "Objects hinder my meaning," declared another great painter, Kandinsky, whose first abstract painting belongs to the year 1910. "Away from the Thing, away from Matter, back to Spirit" was the motto. This intense antirealism was a feature of the new art that contributed to its unpopularity, of course; the man in the street could not "recognize" anything in the painting or sculpture. He suspected these artists of poking fun at him, in which there was a grain of truth. Behind expressionist retreat from the "real world" lay an abhorrence of that world, the social world of bourgeois mediocrity, mechanization, bureaucratization, triviality. At the same time there was a genuine metaphysical quest for deeper truths, dredged up from the subconscious mind or found, perhaps, in the designs of geometry. Certainly this era produced a superb abundance of genius, today acknowledged as such, in painters such as Kandinsky, Paul Klee, Pablo Picasso, Matisse, Mondrian, and many others. These were the pioneer "modernists." They broke through the older confines of visual art to create a brilliant feast of colors and shapes for the eye.

If all these new art forms represented anything more than a protest and a probing for novelty, that something was the intuition of Bergson or the unconscious mind of Freud. Beneath and beyond merely conceptual or intellectual thought, art as pure expression might get in touch with a reality denied to logic. Its symbols might be the language of the human soul at a level deeper than formal thought. These exciting and disturbing paintings, poems, and musical compositions did certainly bespeak an atmosphere of revolt and novelty. They were created largely by "bohemian" artists, Picasso and his friends being denizens of the Paris slums at this time.

THE RISE OF SOCIOLOGICAL THOUGHT

It was "the time of human consciousness," Anatole France said (in his tribute to Zola and Tolstoy). A new self-consciousness about human relations in society appeared not only among the psychologists and the artists but in the development of the new science of sociology. The years from about 1890 to 1914 marked the brilliant coming-of-age of sociology. It was the generation that followed the trailblazing during which Comte, Marx, and Spencer had hewed a rough trail. Now came people such as Emile Durkheim, Max Weber and a host of only slightly lesser lights to refine the crude generalizations of the pioneers, while retaining much of their scope and dramatic power. Durkheim carried on Comte, Weber largely began where Marx left off; though British sociology failed to keep up with French and German, the evolutionary hypotheses of Spencer and the social Darwinists formed a significant backdrop to all social theory.

The leading social stimulus to the development of sociology was the rapid alteration of environment from rural to urban, traditional to modern society. It should be observed that in the hands of a Weber or Durkheim or Robert Michels (who indeed referred to "political sociology") the boundary between sociological and political studies was not sharp. "Sociology," as the "scientific" study of social phenomena, can be applied to all manner of things; the sociologists of this period were much inclined to apply it to politics. Weber studied the forms of political authority and the origins of the Western economic order; Michels examined the structure of political parties. And the interest Durkheim showed in the relationship between individuals and the community had behind it an urgent feeling about the problems of contemporary European society as it proceeded rapidly into an urban industrial setting. Graham Wallas's *Human Nature in Politics* (1908), a landmark in the history of British political thought, declared that political science had heretofore dealt with abstractions rather than considered real people in the real world. When one turns to this reality, Wallas thought, one sees the fallacy of assuming that people act rationally. "Most of the political opinions of most men are the result, not of reasoning tested by experience, but of unconscious or half-conscious inference tested by habit."

There had been an actual decline of rationality, Wallas suggested, owing to the "de-localizing" of people, uprooted from the village to be thrust into the mass anonymity of the huge city. In such passages the British Fabian socialist repeated some of the characteristic interests of this generation of sociologists and political scientists.

If one wonders why something called sociology rose to importance at this time, having not existed before (at least under this name), the best answer is that it was precipitated by the disintegration of traditional society, with the emergence of urbanism and what Maurice Barrès, the French novelist, called *uprootedness*. When society is stable the questions which lead one to study it do not arise, it is simply taken for granted. The prominence of sociology in Germany was due to the unusually sudden industrialization of that country in the later nineteenth century, passing from traditional society, marked by the village community, quite rapidly into advanced modern technology with large cities, factories, and the alienation of the individual from society. The leading pioneer of German sociology in the 1880s, Friedrich Tönnies, was preoccupied with the distinction between what he called community and society (*Gemeinschaft* and *Gesellschaft*)—the tightly integrated community, small and cohesive, such as people had generally lived in since primitive times, and the "great society" of the modern state, vast and complex, in which the individual might feel freer yet lost. George Simmel, too, one of the early German sociologists, tried to examine the impact of the city, this new environment, on human lives: "The deepest problems of modern life derive from the claim of the individual to preserve the autonomy and individuality of his existence in the face of overwhelming social forces. . . ." The urban situation was one of more freedom, greater stimulation, more opportunity for expansion of the mind, but also one of rootlessness, loss of social ties, and consequent disorientation.

The great French sociologist, Emile Durkheim, also made this his theme. He was preoccupied with the loss of social solidarity, as he called it, and thought of sociology as a study that could help modern humanity find its way to some higher form of it, having lost its primitive type. The term associated with Durkheim, and surely one of the most significant terms of modern times, is *anomie*, which was his name for the uneasiness which afflicts the individual when there is no accepted social authority to use as a guide. The individual, Durkheim argued, needs such an authority; without it, limits cannot be imposed on the ego and happiness cannot be achieved. The individual who feels bewildered and alone in a huge, impersonal world, who has lost the guidance of tradition and religion (which Durkheim felt were very closely connected) and can find no source of values outside of self, who has lost contact with the community—such a person is surely all too typical of modern urbanized and industrialized society, and the pioneer sociologists directed their attention to this problem. Their own personal lives often pointed directly to this interest. They came from the village to the city and experienced cultural shock. The Jewishness of Durkheim and Simmel added to the sense of being outsiders, perhaps. The brilliant Durkheim felt isolated as a student at the Sorbonne, to which he later returned as professor. These men would seem to have experienced the crisis of the individual thrown into the vastness and confusion of modern urban life.

The greatest in this golden age of sociology was undoubtedly Max Weber. A scholar whose tremendous range and productivity is reminiscent of Freud and Jung, Weber, a professor at Heidelberg, suffered intermittently from illness and died in 1920 at the age of fifty-six. A good part of Weber's inspiration stemmed from Marx, whose crudities he wished to refine, but whose central conception of a scientific approach to social, economic, and political phenomena he shared. Perhaps best described as a liberal, Weber longed to play an active part in public affairs but, in Imperial Germany, of which he was often a keen critic, found this path largely blocked. (He did perform some public functions in World War I, which he supported as a patriotic German, though he sharply criticized German policies.) He was a friend of the Social Democrat, Robert Michels, and when the latter was refused a university post because of his left-wing politics Weber bitterly denounced the vaunted German academic freedom as a fraud. All in all, Weber's combination of brilliance, erudition, and courageous political activism stamped him as an intellectual and moral leader of his generation in Germany; and his fame has endured through such of his writings as the stimulating *The Protestant Ethic and the Spirit of Capitalism,* his lectures in *General Economic History,* and his unfinished *Economy and Society.*

As a social scientist, Weber was aware of the irrational side of politics and made this one of his chief fields. He was fascinated by the forms of political leadership and by the path of historical development in society and state. One of Weber's leading interests was the principle of rationalization. He meant by this in general the tendency of things to get organized and subjected to rules and orderly processes. What Michels saw happening to the German Social Democrats, in their path towards bureaucracy, Weber saw as a universal principle in human history. Beginning in romance or magic, institutions or forms settle down into a stable routine. Music, for example, becomes a science. Government becomes bureaucracy. In this process spontaneity is lost, there is "disenchantment," the pedantic expert takes over from the free spirit; Weber sometimes with Nietzsche accuses the modern world of having lost its greatness of soul, producing petty time-servers rather than champions. At the same time efficiency gains. There is, however, Weber adds, a limitation to the institutionalized or bureaucratic form of authority; it cannot cope with emergencies, being attuned only to times of stability. In times of crisis there is still a reversion to the type of leadership Weber called "charismatic." The great individual arises, commanding allegiance by the peculiar force of personality or genius. Napoleon in the nineteenth century revealed charisma as much as Caesar two thousand years earlier, while on a lesser scale religious leaders and leaders of other sorts continued to appear. (Certainly there was no lack of prophetic figures in the late nineteenth century, from Tolstoy and Stefan George to Mary Baker Eddy and Mme. Blavatsky, exercising leadership in mysterious ways.) Charismatic creations are then institutionalized and reduced to routine, in tradition or bureaucracy. What is done or believed today from custom or because it is enshrined in the routine of law was yesterday the inspiration of some charismatic personality.

Weber shared with his friend Robert Michels, and with Pareto and also Georges Sorel, this interest in the forms and modes of authority—legal, traditional, charismatic, and combinations of these. A historical sociologist, his chief interest was in understanding just how this Western society, with its capitalism, its economic rationality, its powerful political state, came to be. Unlike Marx, he saw it not as one inevitable phase of all societies but as a unique thing, created through the centuries, owing something to ancient Judaism. What one may call the sociology of religion fascinated Weber as much as it did Marx and Nietzsche. In *The Protestant Ethic and the Spirit of Capitalism* he presented the famous thesis (often misunderstood) that religious ideas interact with worldly activities to produce a characteristic "style of life," and that Protestantism and capitalism had something to do with each other. The analysis of modern capitalism also interested Werner Sombart, who more clearly exposed his dislike of its bureaucratic and depersonalizing features.

It is here that Weber turns into a kind of foe of the Marxists, at least the simpler kind. For against the socialists he argued that collective ownership does nothing to liberate humanity; it "would only mark a further stage on the road to bureaucratization." The industrial society is essentially the same whether "capitalist" or "socialist." Division of labor, professionalization, bureaucracy, "rationalization," discipline, efficiency—the essential features and the essential problems of a modernized society relate to aspects of social organization not touched by the question of whether ownership is vested in the state or a large business corporation. Durkheim's location of the trouble in a loss of social solidarity, Tönnies's diagnosis of the disease of urban uprootedness—the other great sociologists joined Weber here in finding that *any* sort of advanced technological society will experience much the same difficulties. It remained for the future to demonstrate the essential rightness of this view, as opposed to any kind of utopian expectations.

Fritz Ringer has recently seen sociology as based on an attitude of pessimistic resignation in the face of modernization—"a heroic ideal of rational clarification in the face of tragedy." The Italian Vilfredo Pareto, brilliant and versatile thinker, said of his *Trattato di Sociologica Generale* (1915) that if he thought it would have many readers he would not have written it! In criticism of Marx, whom he accused of utopianism, Pareto saw a constant struggle for power between groups and classes, but one that never ends. If Marx's "proletariat" did win, it would become a new ruling class against which others would soon rebel—a quite accurate prediction of what did happen in Communist Russia and other Communist states. In his disabused or cynical reduction of all ideals to selfish power struggles Pareto reminds us of Hobbes, or his famous Italian forebear Machiavelli. Liberty, he would say, is best served when we are aware of the delusions lurking in ideals, aware of the realities of power and thus able to establish realistic checks on it as far as possible. We should aim at a circulating elite, one which draws the potential revolutionaries into the circle of power. But in general Pareto did not prescribe, he only described, and he was not optimistic about the chances of the existing European ruling class. An interesting feature of his sociology was the attempt to classify the basic emotional determinants of ideas, the "residues," in his terminology, which underlie intellectual systems.[13] Few more ruthless exposers of ideals and ideologies have ever written. This was the essential irrationalism of this brilliant generation of psychologists and sociologists: They were in revolt against formalism, they discovered the deeper, more obscure processes of the mind in which rational thought is embedded and of which it is sometimes a kind of protective screen.

Though enormously learned and often possessed by a disinterested quest for knowledge, these sociologists were far from uninvolved or value-free. They all tended to see a crisis. Raymond Aron says that Durkheim "spoke of sociology with the moral fervor of a prophet" and thought it could save the modern individual by explaining how to achieve solidarity and avoid anomie. Weber, at times hauntingly eloquent, is a kind of ancestor of existentialism: Karl Jaspers was his student. Pareto, apparently the most objective, was the most embittered, and it is plain that what forced him into detachment was his disenchantment. If you have really given up all belief in fairies, to endure life you must stand off and laugh at it all, adopting an Olympian stance. To many sociologists, their science is patently a strategy for rejecting or

---

[13]Pareto named six residues," but practically these seem to boil down to two main ones: the "instinct for combinations" and "persistence of aggregates." By these Pareto appears to mean something close to the modernized and the integral, organic society, or *Gesellschaft* and *Gemeinschaft*. The foxes who like combinations are capitalists and wily politicians; the aggregative lions are feudal, heroic, perhaps in Weber's sense charismatic. One can have fun comparing the vocabularies of the great sociological and psychological system-makers, to see how far they mean the same thing.

satirizing their society. The device of pretending to be a stranger, in order to say, "See what odd customs these queer people have! And what absurd things they do!" was an old stratagem of satire, used by Swift and Montesquieu. Certain sociologists do something similar. Someone defined sociology as the village atheist studying the village idiot; one recognizes the genre. The point is that sociology itself may be subject to sociological interpretation; it too was a philosophy, a set of ideas arising at a certain time and related to the social conditions of its time as well as to its intellectual antecedents. The main incentive, to repeat, was the dissolving of ancestral customs and institutions during the "modernization" of Western civilization from about 1800 on, the effects of which were keenly felt after about 1870.

New Social Theories

Weber, Durkheim, Pareto, Simmel were *universitaires,* a group for whom such vigorous amateurs and lay prophets of social thought as Gustave LeBon and Georges Sorel entertained much disdain. A varied array of intellectual and political journals testified to the liveliness of European thought in these years. The organized socialist movement carried on its controversies, often reaching a large audience. Serious social thought was by no means a monopoly of the professors.

While orthodox Marxists continued to preach the word as they understood it from the master, there was novelty in the 1900s and an increasingly strident, extremist, often irrationalist note. A few of the leading examples may be singled out. The two most notable French voices were the proto-fascist ones of Charles Maurras and Georges Sorel.

The intrepid monarchist Maurras, founder of the *Action Française,* was in the tradition of French classicism and rationalism, of Voltaire and Comte. He admired order and stressed the French national tradition, which he saw as classical and rational. He inherited Comte's dislike of modern society as too anarchic and scorned democracy as lacking a principle of order. A prominent theme of Maurras's thought was the need for leadership by an intelligent minority. "The mob always follows determined minorities." The *Action Française* organized the *Camelots du Roi* to engage in agitation and street fighting, an idea subsequently adopted by Fascists and Nazis. Among other ideas it bequeathed to the postwar Fascist movement was that of the "corporate state," a favorite idea of Maurras's that came to him from the Catholic Social Movement in France. Though hardly any threat to the state, the *Action* exercised a considerable influence on French university students just before the war. Violently hostile to the Republic in the 1900s, it tended to rally to its support after 1912 with war clouds on the horizon, for it was militantly patriotic and fiercely anti-German. It put out a well-known newspaper, and from Maurras's tireless pen flowed a stream of books and pamphlets. Nationalist, traditionalist, antidemocratic and anti-Semite, Maurras carried on a war against the liberal, parliamentary state, and he looms ominously as forerunner of the "revoluntionary conservatism" of the postwar period.

Georges Sorel ranks with Charles Maurras among the outstanding French political theorists in the years before 1914. A Marxian socialist originally, Sorel adopted the irrationalism of the hour and married a Nietzschean and Bergsonian spirit to his revolutionary radicalism. He charged the orthodox socialists with having become bureaucratized and respectable. Their rationalism and materialism, Sorel felt, were quite inappropriate for revolutionaries. Doubtless he was right in recognizing that Marxism is really an apocalyptical religion. He was quite willing to accept it frankly as such. Do not all persons live by "myths"? Socialism he compared to the church, the modern strikers being the equivalent of Christian saints and martyrs. He spoke of the social "myth of the revolution," or of the general strike. Sorel, a brilliant political theorist, had lost faith in reason and in society; in combining the twin spirits of Nietzsche and Marx, he suggested something like what later appeared in Mussolini's fascism or Lenin's bolshevism, for both of whom he expressed admiration. Essentially an anarchist, a hater of the state and coercion, Sorel disapproved of the element of statism and nationalism in Italian fascism, as he would have rejected Lenin's ruthless state dictatorship. But he did father the idea of a revolutionary elite violently sweeping aside bourgeois civilization in the name of a new myth or religion, that of proletarian socialism. In this "myth" the working class appears as clean, unspoiled, heroic, but brutal enough to dash to pieces the old corrupt order. Without difficulty one can recognize Nietzsche's "blond beasts" clothed in overalls. A civilization must believe in something; modern European civilization under bourgeois leadership had lost the life-giving capacity for such belief. Only the unspoiled proletarians had it: They at least believed in revolution.

At first placing his faith in the trade unions (*syndicats*) to become the agencies of proletarian revolution, Sorel by about 1910 grew disillusioned with them—they were much too materialistic and bourgeois—and turned to a flirtation with nationalism as the revitalizing myth, drawing close to Maurras. This was an ominous precursor of the postwar Fascist mixture of revolutionary *élan* and nationalist solidarity; and in fact Benito Mussolini owed a great deal to *Sorelismo*. Thus Sorel drifted even farther away from democracy, in which course he unquestionably went with a significant stream of thought in France from about 1905 to 1914.

On the far left as well as the far right, the theory of leadership by an elite appeared. Lenin, destined during the war of 1914 to 1918 to become a successful revolutionary leader "conceived a proletarian revolution as the product of great minds, who, conscious of inexorable trends, would create order and progress out of chaotic elements by organizing the raw material of history in a rational fashion" (Adolf G. Meyer). In this he differed from Marx, who had favored widening the franchise and other democratic political reforms, believing that these would facilitate the triumph of the proletariat. Engels, living on into the 1890s, definitely stated that the time of "revolutions carried through by small conscious minorities at the head of unconscious masses" had passed. The socialists of western Europe placed their faith in democratic processes which made it possible to gain power by legal means. If Marx was right, the laws of social development were working relentlessly to destroy capitalism; the number of proletarians along with their class consciousness was supposedly growing so that soon they would be in the great majority. Revolutionary conspiracies were out of date in western Europe, precisely because Marx had revealed the inevitability of the transformation to socialism. But in Russia, where revolutionary conspiracy seemed the only possible recourse against a reactionary absolutism, Lenin sought to reconcile it with Marxism.

He agreed with Sorel that trade unionism had turned out to be nothing more than "the capitalism of the proletariat" and that the working class, by itself, is capable of nothing more than a trade-union consciousness. Ridiculing the "requiem socialism" of the Second International, the man born as Vladimir Ulyanov, well-educated son of a district school supervisor, had been nourished in his youth on the full-blooded revolutionary writings of the populist movement, especially Nikolai Chernyshevsky's *What Is To be Done?* (1863). Embittered by the execution of his brother as a revolutionary by the tsar's despotic government, young Ulyanov would adopt the name of Nikolai Lenin and later write his own *What Is To Be Done?* He became a Marxist in the 1890s, when this was fashionable in Russian intellectual circles, but his imperious temperament was restive under its passive interpretation, and his restless intellect sought a justification for quick revolution. Granted that Russia must go through capitalism before it reached socialism, might not a revolutionary elite seize power and steer a more rapid course—doing the work of the bourgeoisie *for* them, hastening, telescoping the course of history? To a quick mind and a powerful will, Lenin added an utter dedication to the revolutionary cause which he had derived from Chernyshevsky, and a ruthlessness which occasionally amazed his best friends. (Lenin has no pity for the masses, Maxim Gorki said, they are to him "what minerals are to the mineralogist.")

To Lenin the proletariat represented the will of history, but only potentially so; it must be organized and shaped by the "vanguard" of trained Marxists. The laws of social development exist, but they must be understood and exploited by this alert leadership. History does not make itself; it is made by individuals. When the decisive moment has arrived, one must strike in a sudden act of revolution. The organized vanguard of the proletariat, disciplined, ruthless, and intelligent, must lead this revolution and install the socialist epoch. A Marxist, Lenin dissociated himself from mere revolutionary adventurism or terrorism but was equally scornful of the passive, legalistic social democrats of western Europe. They had been corrupted by bourgeois democracy, in his view. Not by parliamentary means, but by well-planned and prepared-for revolution would the proletariat succeed in its great mission, and this task called for the leadership of the vanguard elite.

At the Second Congress of the Russian Socialists in 1903 the party split on the issue of democracy; Lenin boldly opted for a tightly organized, highly disciplined elite party prepared to seize power and hold it by violent means. He had written *What Is To Be Done?* in 1902, with its thesis that not the working class but the "revolutionary socialist intelligentsia" is equipped to lead and guide the revolution—a position that seemed almost totally un-Marxist. Lenin spent most of the years between 1900 and 1917 in exile abroad, mainly in Switzerland; returning for a time during the revolution of 1905, he was encouraged in his belief that history's course might be speeded up. But most of the time Lenin was in a distinct minority within the Russian Social Democratic party. The 1914 war and the subsequent collapse of Russia gave him his chance to rise from obscurity to a grand place on the stage of history.

THE THEME OF ALIENATION

For the most part the story of this most exciting and formative period of European thought, just preceding the enormous explosion of 1914, has seemed a study in irrationalism. "Human reason was tired," Romain Rolland's hero Jean-Christophe reflects, in the last book of this pre-1914 epic novel, a sensation in the year 1913. "It had just accomplished a mighty effort. It surrendered to sleep ... Even philosphy wavered.... Even science manifested signs of this fatigue of reason." One may object that a violent excitability, rather than weariness, characterized the era's thought, which was immensely creative. But none of its students can miss the note of unreason. Just as obvious is the gulf that opened between *les intellectuels* and the mainstream of society.

Most of the serious thinkers and writers did not travel with the crowd. Indeed, their hallmark is very nearly a rejection of the crowd, of mass civilization, of the breakdown of values, the enthronement of mediocrity. They will use the word *bourgeois* as an epithet; likewise, often, the word *mass* or *popular*. By no means true of all, this is true of those who are the most striking and original: of Nietzsche, the symbolists and decadents, and the major political theorists. They did not find the nationalistic and democratic society of their time satisfactory, and they reacted against it as rebels, "outsiders," deniers and defiers of its conventions.

This is a remarkable feature of modern European thought, whatever one may think about it. The "alienation" of the artist and intellectual from society, these people retreating to a private world, inventing esoteric symbols, or even joining some nihilistic revolutionary movement in their hatred of the everyday world, mechanized, philistine, and commercial as it is, is a peculiarly modern theme. This is not to say that giants of thought were ever particularly popular with the majority. It is rather to say that the majority previously did not enter into intellectual society to any marked degree, while now they did. That which constituted the cultural community had been a restricted circle of the upper class, whether clergy, universities, or *salons*. Now this community was immeasurably broadened, and inevitably at first coarsened. At the same time the texture of thought and expression available to the educated or unusual person became more complex; individual sensitivity was sharpened and refined. So—one may hope temporarily—the gulf between writer and general public widened to a chasm, across which each looked at the other balefully and with bewilderment.

It does not appear to be correct to regard the divorce between popular and good literature as peculiarly modern. In her *Fiction and the Reading Public* (reprinted 1966), Q. D. Leavis suggested that in the earlier period—until the mid- or later-nineteenth century—nearly everyone who could read read the same literature, which was good literature— Smollett, Fielding, Dickens, Thackeray, and so forth. But others have since established beyond doubt that as long as there was a literate public there was a trash literature. In other words, the average person in the eighteenth century was not reading Fielding and Smollett any more than the average nineteenth-century reader was absorbed in Eliot and Hardy; they were reading very much the equivalent of James Bond and Zane Grey.

Nevertheless in its intensity estrangement was a new phenomenon. Of the early Victorian writers, Walter Allen remarks in his *English Novel* that they "were at one with their public. . . . They accepted the society in which they lived. . . . The assumptions of their age they fully shared." They might and did criticize, but they did so as those who operate within the family, not as alienated outsiders; they strove to improve the common culture, not throw bricks at it from a distance. Granted that the romantics in some measure began the myth of the alienated, lonely, superior artist, the Victorian age resembled the eighteenth-century society more than it differed from it in its integration, and the Victorian sage was no bohemian. But when arriving at Thomas Hardy near the end of the century, another world is entered; a threshold is crossed about the 1880s, whether looking at poetry, painting, drama, philosophy, or the novel. There is a real bitterness at the world's blind amorality, its utter lack of plan and purpose, its cruelty and its essential barbarity: Hardy's *Tess* does not live in the same moral world as the heroines of Trollope, Thackeray, Dickens, or even George Eliot. Something has happened. In part it was Darwinism, in part capitalism, in part mass culture, in part no doubt other things; the result is clear.

6

The West in Trouble: World War I and Its Aftermath

*The best lack all conviction, while the worst
Are full of passionate intensity.*

WILLIAM BUTLER YEATS

Men will wish Nothing rather than not wish at all.

FRIEDRICH NIETZSCHE

*My house is a decayed house....
I am an old man. A dull head among windy spaces.*

T. S. ELIOT

INTELLECTUAL ORIGINS OF THE WAR

Few need to be reminded that a good part of the twentieth century was to be dominated by the breakdown of international order in 1914, leading to four horrible years of mass slaughter, out of which came red revolution in Russia, black revolution in Italy, and subsequently nazism in Germany—the forms of modern "totalitarian" dictatorship. The war proved scarcely less demoralizing to the victor states than to the defeated. It hurled much of Europe toward bankruptcy and internal collapse. During the war, propaganda took over and truth suffered as

243

never before, and out of the war there emerged a new kind of cynicism, a loss of faith in humanity and values, such as Europe had perhaps never before experienced in modern history.

It is tempting to find some parallels between this crisis of the political order and the crisis of thought and culture that seemed to exist as of 1914. Historians customarily describe the origins of the World War in terms of diplomatic and political history, and quite properly so: the clash of national interests, the alliances, the military plans, the conferences and confrontations. The rise of nationalism was an obvious cause of the war. Now and again politicians could be heard observing, in a Darwinian spirit, that struggle, competition, and force are the laws of life. Democracy forced officials to take account of a public opinion that was often belligerent and narrow-minded, as well as fiercely nationalist. Diplomacy does not function in a vacuum; politicians are people of their age sharing its prevalent ideas. Historians need to "reconstruct the unspoken assumptions of the men they are studying" and "recreate the climate of opinion in which political leaders operated," James Joll has argued in a thoughtful lecture on *1914: The Unspoken Assumptions.*

These unspoken assumptions of 1914 included a distinct eagerness for war, which the writers and intellectuals shared—something a later generation finds hard to understand, but very much a part of the spirit of the "August Days" at the beginning of the war. The war was extremely popular in all countries at the start. Resisting the war spirit in Britain, Ramsay MacDonald was aware that he was pitted against "the most popular war in British history," a fact to which the incredible rush of voluntary enlistments bears witness. And in the van of these volunteers were the young poets, artists, university students, intellectuals. The story was not different in France, in Germany, in Russia (Hans Rogger has noted the spontaneous enthusiasm for war which swept through Russia in 1914), and soon in Italy. It is difficult to find important leaders of the intellectual community who held out against this martial spirit, and most of them were serving as its cheerleaders. Romain Rolland, one of the few who did try to fight it, cried that "there is not one among the leaders of thought in each country who does not proclaim with conviction that the cause of his people is the cause of God, the cause of liberty and of human progress," and felt himself wholly isolated. The list of "leaders of thought" who did indeed bless the war almost as a holy cause is a lengthy one and includes most of the great individuals discussed in the last chapter, those who were alive in 1914. Bergson, Charles Péguy, Freud (who "gave all his libido to Austria-Hungary"), poets and novelists such as Stefan George, Thomas Mann, were as prominent as historians, sociologists (Durkheim, Max Weber on different sides) and even socialists, who forgot their theoretical antiwar principles and rallied to the cause of their country. This was true of such revolutionaries as Kropotkin, Plekhanov, even some of the Russian Bolsheviks, Lenin being a rare exception; and of the German Social Democrats, the French Socialists, the British Labourites, with only a few exceptions. In England the idol of the hour was the young poet Rupert Brooke, who marched off proudly to die in the war along with so many others who gave their lives as a willing sacrifice to the Moloch of war. To be sure, Rolland exaggerated when he said "not one," for a small minority tried to resist the contagion. But they were all but swamped in 1914 by the rush to jump on the war wagon. As the war wore on and lost its glamor, the situation changed. But it is impossible to escape the conclusion that in the beginning the overwhelming majority of the spiritual leaders of Europe heartily approved of the war.

The reasons for this extraordinary belligerence lead back into some pre-1914 themes. Among the more obvious ingredients in it were: (1) a desire for excitement, adventure, and romance, which was associated with the protest against a drab, materialistic, bourgeois civilization; (2) a feeling that the war provided the opportunity for a spiritual renewal through its break with the past and its outpouring of unselfish idealism; (3) an exultation at the healing of a divided society, bridging the gap between classes and between individuals in an organic kind of national unity; and (4) a sort of apocalyptic, Nietzschean mood which saw in this catastrophe both an awful judgment on a doomed civilization and the necessary prelude to a complete rebirth.

Clearly all these attitudes involved prewar intellectual themes. In regard to the protest against bourgeois dullness, the connection is obvious. More interesting is the thrill that people of thought secured from what Karl Vossler (writing to Benedetto Croce) called "the magnificent drama of the exaltation of a nation of 70 million people, all without exception one . . . each one living for all, for the Fatherland. . . ." Sophisticated minds such as Max Scheler had come to have as their chief concern "a quest for unity and community in a pluralistic society" and saw in the war a return to the "organic roots of human existence." Barrès's concern about "deracination," the "integral nationalism" of Maurras, and the sociological quest for social solidarity may all be recalled in this connection. A surprising number saw the war as a remedy for modern anomie.[1] The men in the trenches developed feelings of close solidarity in this war, an experience which many soldiers held in high value and hoped to carry into the national life after the war.

Anyone who has studied the mood of 1914 with much care knows that a *mystique* was decidedly present, above all in the young people and those of poetic temperament, the idealists and the restless ones. War, still seen romantically, came as a welcome relief from years of pettiness and greed, triviality and bickering. People turned to it, as Brooke wrote, "as

---

[1]Sociologists have established that war is indeed a remedy for anomie. Suicide rates fall in wartime.

swimmers into cleanness leaping, glad from a world grown old and cold and weary." This mood had been growing in the years just before the war. In France, the period from 1905 on witnessed a sharp revival of what Eugene Weber, who has studied it carefully, sums up as "Discipline, Heroism, Renaissance, *Génie National.*" The conversion of Charles Péguy from socialism to nationalism in 1905 was a landmark; thereafter the former Dreyfusard wrote as a militant patriot, an antipacifist, a fervent prophet of the coming war against Germany. A well-known inquiry into the mood of French university youth in 1913 found that Péguy was the leading influence, along with Barrès and others of the same breed.One of them was Paul Claudel, whose plays and poems radiated heroism and religion and French tradition. In Germany, the years just before the war gave birth to a youth movement whose fierce idealism subsequently was channeled into the war. The *Wandervoegel* of the *Jugendbewegung* were in revolt against their elders, filled with lofty visions of reforming the world, and inclined to a Nietzschean spirit of drastic spiritual renewal accompanied by apocalyptical violence. Poets like Stefan George indulged in visions of a purifying war. That the war would bring "the moral regeneration of Europe" was held by so relatively mild a philosopher as Henri Bergson.

This frenetic preparation for conflict in the mind of the pre-1914 decade and the eager way war was welcomed when it came seemed incongruous later and was therefore somewhat forgotten; it is not well understood today. People soon grew bitterly disillusioned with the war; by 1917 a new mood had set in, which carried through into the despairing postwar years. Yet the spirit of 1914 had existed and had something to do with the coming of the war. Not that the poets and intellectuals deliberately contrived the war, which seemed to come out of the blue, totally unexpected by the vast majority. But when it came they welcomed it almost as a divine omen and gladly marched off to fight in it, thinking that they were redeeming their own lives and rescuing civilization. "Happy are they who die in a just war," Péguy sang before he went off to be killed on the Marne in the early days of the war.

The young Bosnians who killed the Archduke Franz Ferdinand and thus provided the spark that set off the flames were themselves aflame with the restless ideas of pre-1914 Europe. Their idols included Gorki, Andreyev, Whitman, Wilde, and Ibsen. They had learned tyrannicide from 1848 romanticism (Mazzini, "William Tell") and revolution from Ibsen; they lived in an atmosphere of youthful literary romanticism, fed by the exciting writers of the hour, with considerable symbolist and decadent influences. They were in touch with the international anarchist movement.[2]

[2]See among other sources Vladimir Dedijer's article, "Sarajevo Fifty Years After," *Foreign Affairs,* July, 1964, and his book, *The Road to Sarajevo* (1966).

That the war was a just one was, of course, the almost universal assumption, each side firmly believing itself to have been attacked by the other. The socialists rationalized their support of the war by arguing that if they did not fight, their country would be destroyed and with it their movement. The Germans further held that a victory for Russia would be a victory for the most reactionary of European powers. The French similarly believed that a German conquest would be reactionary, wiping out many social gains already made in France. The working class everywhere tended to be strongly patriotic, and the intellectual socialists were not in fact prepared for the kind of situation that occurred. The Second International had often rhetorically declared that the workers of the world would never fight against each other in a war forced on the people by their wicked rulers; but this war did not happen like that. The great majority knew only that their country was being attacked and must be defended. A small minority of the Socialists in Great Britain, Germany, and Russia thought otherwise but abided by party discipline. Within a fairly short time Karl Liebknecht in Germany, and Lenin, among the exiled Russian Bolsheviks, went into opposition to the war while Ramsay MacDonald resigned the Labour party leadership in England; but these were voices crying in the wilderness for several years. It was dangerous to oppose the war: In England Bertrand Russel was imprisoned, Shaw was snubbed and boycotted, D. H. Lawrence suffered from a feeling of isolation because he could not participate in the *mystique* of the war.

Intellectuals participated in the war to a striking degree. They went off and fought in it, of course, eagerly volunteering in the first rush of battle rapture. They wrote poems to it, hailed it as a regenerating process, celebrated its *mystique*. Many of those who did not serve in the trenches lent their talents to the propaganda side of the war. Arnold Bennett, one of England's leading literary figures, became a director of British propaganda; distinguished historians fashioned handbooks proving the eternal wickedness of the foe (this happened in the United States, too, after the U.S. joined the war in 1917), and authenticating stories of barbarous atrocities. And of course many died in the war. A sampling of those sacrificed to the war could include the British poets Rupert Brooke, Wilfred Owen, Isaac Rosenberg, Charles Sorley, Edward Thomas; Ivor Gurney went mad. The brilliant Austrian painters Franz Marc and Egon Schiele; August Macke, Raymond Duchamp-Villon, Umberto Boccioni were other slain artists; the poet George Trakl and the sculptor Wilhelm Lehmbruck committed suicide. Of 161 students of the famous *Ecole Normale Superieure* in France from the classes of 1911, 1912, and 1913, 81 died in the war and another 64 were wounded. A French anthology of writers killed in the war contains five hundred names, among them Péguy, Alain-Fournier, Apollinaire, Psichari. Such a list might go on and on. The heaviest casualties in the murderous war were among the junior officers, where typically one found educated youth. One is led to wonder what potential earth-shaking achievements were buried with the tens of thousands of brilliant youth killed, what *Ulysses* or Relativity Theory or *Wasteland* was *not* created by some even more talented Joyce or Einstein or Eliot who happened to fall in battle.

Disenchantment soon set in. The reality of war was anything but romantic. "One week in the trenches was sufficient to strip war of its lingering traces of romance," Herbert Read recalled. As the war dragged on and the sickening slaughter mounted, protest against it inevitably arose. In the end, most of those who survived were likely to be ashamed of having been taken in by a romantic view of war. Yet it is well to remember that this was not so in 1914, when a generation of rebels found their great crusade in the war. "We were all flame and fire," Isadora Duncan remembered. Young people lived in fear that the war would be over before they could get into it (it was widely believed that it would be a short one), and of these the educated, university, thinking youth were the foremost. It was the hour of Rupert Brooke ("Come and die, it will be such fun"). In the strange story of 1914 the story of the intellectuals is one of the strangest. The student of intellectual history will find much to connect this state of mind with the ferment of ideas in the preceding generation; for the revolutionary message of Nietzsche, Bergson, Jung, Sorel, Baudelaire, Wagner, and all the rest was just making its major impact on the mind of Europe as the war broke out.

The comradeship of the trenches, alas, is apt to remind one of Adolf Hitler, who carried back into peacetime favorable memories of the war's *Gemeinschaft*. The Storm Troopers were a carryover from the war. Still, others than the Nazis entertained a nostalgia for this aspect of the war and hoped that after it was over a more democratic, less class-ridden society might emerge from it. Yet the most obvious results of the war were fascism, followed by nazism; and the communism which had gained control of Russia during the almost total breakdown of the Russian state that occurred in 1917 as a result of the war's intolerable demands. Benito Mussolini, brilliant left-wing Italian Socialist, broke away from the majority of the party on the issue of Italy's entrance into the war in 1915, which he supported. Free to launch ideological ventures of his own after this, he fell increasingly under the influence of Nietzschean and Sorelian ideas and emerged in the troubled days after the war as *duce* of the new movement known as fascism. As for Lenin, few are unaware that he came back to Russia from exile in 1917 following the February Revolution to take charge of Bolshevik strategy and seize power in October, to begin the long dictatorship of the Communist party in Russia.

The prewar socialists were badly split by the war. Though initially the party supported it, a fraction of the German Social Democrats voted against the war in the party caucus, later brought their opposition into the open, and by 1917 created a major split in the party by voting against the war credits. Though Social Democrats took the lead in establishing the new republic which emerged from defeat in 1919, they had to employ armed force against left-wing socialist uprisings and thus threw themselves into the arms of the Right.

POSTWAR PESSIMISM

If the war was initially popular and blessed by the writers, it eventually gave rise to bitter disillusionment. "War is hell, and those who institute it are criminals," Siegfried Sassoon wrote from the trenches. This was the final verdict. The progress of disillusion may be followed in the war poetry—of which this war produced a great deal of high quality. (It remained a writers' war all the way and even in its disappointment produced splendid literature; no other war can compare.) The initial "visions of glory" faded to sorrow and pity and ended in bitterness. The wretchedness, the terror, the nerves tortured by waiting for death, the gassed soldiers, the obscene wounds, even the lice were what the men in the trenches wrote about:

> In winter trenches, cowed and glum,
> With crumps and lice and lack of rum.

Soon they began to scorn the people at home who could have no notion of what the war was really like, and whose knitting of socks or singing of songs seemed a mockery and a sacrilege. A comradeship of suffering and death drew the soldiers close together and sometimes drew them closer to their fellow victims of war in the opposite trenches than to the smug ones at home—or to their own officers. As bitterness developed against the top leadership in this frustrating war which no one could win, soldier-poets wrote of the scarlet majors at the base who "speed glum heroes up the line to death" and would themselves toddle safely home to die in bed. Those who did not die in the first battles but, like Wilfred Owen, lived through almost the whole war (he was killed within hours of the Armistice) could feel nothing but the horror, the pity, and the futility of war. This attitude endured; the romance had gone from war forever and abhorrence of the very thought of war colored the entire postwar era; aiding, ironically, the coming of the next one since a pacifist-minded opinion in the victor countries permitted a revenge-bent Germany to overturn the peace settlement and the balance of power.

The collapse of prewar socialism was not the least of the many interrupted and shattered traditions; discredited by their acceptance of the war, the great majority of its leadership lost control of their own movement from 1917 to 1919. Lenin's Bolshevik faction seized power in Russia and proscribed the Menshevik's along with all other political parties as enemies of the Revolution. In Italy, the ambivalence of social democracy helped pave the way for Mussolini's Fascist dictatorship. The Italian Socialists could not decide whether to be revolutionaries or to defend the democratic constitutional order and ended by doing neither. When the smoke had cleared, Communists looking to Lenin's Russia had greatly increased their following at the expense of the moderate socialists almost everywhere in Europe, though nowhere except in Russia had they been able to seize the state. Their embittered violence frightened the conservative classes into backing extremist regimes in Italy and, within a few years, Germany. In Great Britain, the war wrecked the old Liberal party forever and caused a great increase in the Labour party, which though not Communist had a hyperradical wing and pacifist leadership.

The war years produced a large crop of plans for peace in order to prevent a recurrence of 1914. This was true in all countries. There were League of Nations Societies and Associations, Committees for a Durable Peace, Unions of Democratic Control of foreign policy. These plans were not only at variance with each other but wore an odd air of unreality in most cases; intellectuals struggled in an element alien to them and tended toward utopianism. Most of them were disillusioned with the real League of Nations that struggled to an imperfect birth in the atmosphere of power and hate at the Paris Peace Conference of 1919. The hundreds of tracts and pamphlets written during the war ended as less a contribution to human progress than a curiosity for the historian, a fact which contributed no little to the postwar despair.

Most of the liberals who had so earnestly drawn up blueprints for the postwar world felt that the treaties negotiated at Paris in 1919, along with the League of Nations as adopted, was a betrayal of their ideals and perpetuated old-fashioned "power politics." The postwar years brought a complete revision in ideas about the war's origins. In France, Great Britain, and the United States, nearly everyone assumed it was the Germans who were the criminal unleashers of war; a few combated this notion even during the war, and immediately afterward a momentous investigation into the causes of the war began—with results that were likely to be "revisionist." If scholars did not seek to show that Russia and France were more guilty of the war than Austria and Germany, they at least concluded, typically, that all had been trapped in a circle of fear where one could not well speak of "war guilt." No nation had been entirely innocent, none criminally guilty; the guilt might be said to lie with a system, or a civilization, or in the nature of humanity itself. This historical controversy gave rise to a vast and interesting literature, which proved only that no historical event is simple enough to grasp scientifically, but which suggested to millions that their leaders had deceived them in charging all blame on the enemy. At the same time the atrocity stories were radically "de-bunked," as propaganda ministers ruefully confessed they had manufactured most of these.

Sickened by not only the physical slaughter of millions of Europe's youth but by the moral carnage of a world convulsed by hatred and lies, the postwar generation was the "lost generation." Lost were faith and hope, belief in progress, confidence in the civilization of the West. By way of introducing what was after all a marvelously creative generation too, one may catalog some of these cries of despair that filled the years destined to follow one Armageddon and precede another.

It is difficult to think of any of the great writers of this era—D. H. Lawrence, André Gide, Ernest Hemingway, James Joyce, T. S. Eliot—who did not reject the civilization in which they lived, though it is no less true that this rejection usually antedated the war. They were marked wanderers; the American "expatriates," who joined Gertrude Stein in Paris or Spain, had a counterpart in such as Lawrence, who hated his native England and lived at various times in New Mexico, Mexico, and Italy; or Joyce, a refugee from Ireland who lived in Trieste, Paris, and Zurich. There were, of course, Russian refugees from communism, Italian from fascism, and subsequently German from nazism. Physical flight from the homeland went along with imaginative flight from Western civilization, expressed in Lawrence's admiration for the Etruscans or the Aztecs, in Ezra Pound's importing of Chinese, or what he imagined to be

T. S. Eliot: A Caricature by David Low. (Low Trustees, London Evening Standard. Historical Pictures, Inc., Chicago.)

Chinese, literature. "An old bitch, gone in the teeth"—such was Pound's verdict on European civilization, while the usually optimistic, still liberal-socialist H. G. Wells (who coined the phrase "war to end wars" during the war) thought that "this civilization in which we are living is tumbling down, and I think tumbling down very fast." It would be a work of supererogation to reproduce all such comments.

This straying "after strange gods" included a desertion of intellectuals to communism or, less commonly, to fascism. Pound and Wyndham Lewis might be placed in the latter camp, but the major movement was toward faith in Soviet Russia as a place where a brand-new and hopeful civilization was being shaped, however roughly. This attitude on the part of Western writers and intellectuals was quite obviously a projection of their own cultural despair onto Russia as wishful thinking, and after a few years as Communists or fellow-travelers the harsh realities of Soviet tyranny freshly disillusioned all but the blindest. This was "the God that failed" for a significant segment of serious people, especially in the 1930s, and this "pink decade" will need to be discussed again. Those who briefly believed in the charisma of Mussolini or Hitler as creative forces were also speedily disillusioned, of course. In the 1920s one mostly believed in art or in sex, if one believed in anything; in the 1930s, poets tried to be proletarians, and novelists went off to fight in the Spanish Civil War. But the latter gesture turned out to be almost as despairing and futile for most as the former.

If there was whoring after strange gods, there was also an effort to return to ancestral ones. The neo-Anglicanism of T. S. Eliot, American-born mogul of English letters (another odd case of literary expatriation), had counterparts in the neo-Thomism of a significant group led by Jacques Maritain in France and the neo-Calvinism and neo-Lutheranism of Karl Barth and Emil Brünner. The return to religion resulted from the collapse of liberal beliefs in secular progress. These theologies in some ways were not orthodox, for they usually "de-mythologized" the Bible, perhaps drew on Jungian conceptions, and regarded Christianity as existentially rather than literally true. But they found in original sin and Christian humility an antidote to the shallow complacency of those prewar liberals and socialists who had believed in rationality and progress. Perhaps old-fashioned Christianity could be a cure for the diseases of a civilization whose sins had been denying its own birthright, succumbing to pride, forgetting the meaning of Christ. Christ was seen less as a preacher of humane ethical precepts than as the apocalyptic or "eschatological" prophet who announced the end of the world and asked people to choose between God and the world. This was especially the bent of Continental neo-orthodoxy, which in the form of the "crisis" theology of Barth came near to Christian existentialism. "It is essential not to have faith in human nature," historian Herbert Butterfield has written. "Such faith is a recent heresy and a very disastrous one." At bottom, the tragic view of life is the true one, asserted many a chastened optimist of the postwar years.

Karl Barth's 1919 *Epistle to the Romans* commentary marked a sharp break with the prevailing liberal and idealist German theology, which had seen the course of history as in large part a fulfillment of God's plan, hence good, a view which could almost blend with the secular idea of progress. The Hegelian influence may readily be seen: God's Reason is immanent in the record of human development, his purposes are realized through Humanity. Regarded quite widely as the greatest theologian of his times, Barth denied as fiercely as possible (in his initial manifestos) that God's kingdom is of this world. There is no synthesis uniting God and Humanity; the two are almost utterly estranged, humanity is incomplete, needing God for fulfillment but unable to find him except in the one tenuous revelation contained in Scripture—the Word. The apparently quite reactionary features of the new theology (variously called "Crisis," "Dialectical," "Kerygmatic")—back to original sin and Luther's hapless human creatures in need of rescuing by divine grace— actually made it seem revolutionary. One rejected a corrupt world and refused to accept a flat, vapid, institutionalized Christianity, demanding life-meaning and relevance in one's faith.

The same general features could be found in Martin Buber's Jewish theology and in N. Berdyaev's voice from the world of Russian Orthodox religion (Berdyaev, initially a Communist, fled from Lenin's police state to Berlin and then Paris in the 1920s). These were exciting voices, some of them far less "orthodox" than Barth. Barth's close associate, Rudolf Bultmann, mediated the message for more modernist minds by his "de-mythologizing" idea, which meant that the language with which the Word is expressed in the Bible is a mere husk containing the kernel of essential, true-to-life statements. The neo-orthodox were normally not "fundamentalist" but "modernist" in their view of the Biblical text, but they rendered this old debate irrelevant by their insistence that the real message is embedded in the myth.

Whatever the variations in their contours, these postwar theologies were alike in rejecting the old belief in Progress. In a book on the subject in 1920, Dean William Inge, the "gloomy dean," saw the idea of progress as "the working faith of the West for about a hundred and fifty years" and found it a fraud. With hope in social progress shattered, the dream of perpetual onward-and-upward laid in ruins by the hideous facts of the mass slaughter just ended and the moral and political confusion that followed it, the world broken and lost, a personal religion became a tower of retreat in the 1920s. Pessimism was not confined to the religious. Oswald Spengler's *Decline of the West* came out of a Germany shattered by defeat, but its message of Western civilization's senility went all over the world and was repeated in varying accents by many others. It was at this time that Arnold J. Toynbee began his even vaster historical study of the rise and fall of civilizations, the first three volumes of which came from the press in 1934. Toynbee has told how, spared from military service by an illness and watching so many of his classmates mowed down in the war, he felt a special duty to devote his life to an inquiry on the causes of such cataclysmic collapses of civilizations. In the same way, the tragedy energized others who had been spared that fate. (Harold Laski, for example, tells a similar story.) Toynbee was led to nothing less than a gigantic comparative analysis of the life cycles of all the civilizations he could find in world history and finished his monumental opus only after another world war made the topic even more timely. But his initial inspiration came during World War I.

The book of the hour right after the war was Spengler's, more hastily written than Toynbee's—though in fact Spengler had begun it before the war—but based on the same premise that civilizations, like people, have life cycles. Needless to say Spengler found many signs of decay in the contemporary West, whose zenith he thought had come in the later Middle Ages.

The Spaniard Ortega y Gasset's brilliant essay, *The Revolt of the Masses,* conveyed a somewhat similar theme of European decadence from lack of creative leadership. Paul Valéry's famous essay on the European crisis and T. S. Eliot's even more famous poem, *The Waste Land,* might be mentioned in this context. Proust's mammoth novel chronicled the decay of French society. Of course, Communists, Fascists, and Nazis all proclaimed the decadence and imminent death of the old society; that they did so helped eventually to rally some support for traditional European civilization, since these rebels against it so obviously purveyed something far worse. But the 1920s echoed with dirges for the passing of the European age. Eliot's poem said it all: It began with a quotation from Petronius, "we yearn to die." "April is the cruellest month," it no longer brings forth new life, the European world has lost its creativity. Using all the devices of symbolist technique, Eliot, an American-born migrant to England, found images to express the futility of religion, love (it is now known he was registering an acute personal crisis more than he was recording the downfall of the West, but his readers accepted the latter meaning all too readily):

Here is no water but only rock.

The energizing springs that had fertilized culture in the past had dried up, leaving fear and timidity. "I show you fear in a handful of dust." The great tradition ends not with a bang but a whimper.

A revulsion against popular culture aided this alienation of the intellectuals as the age of the mass media dawned. During the 1920s the "people" seemed more interested in sports events, airplane flights, detective novels, mah-jongg, crossword puzzles, movies stars, and Mickey Mouse than serious ideas or good literature and art. The common man was a sad joke, cultural democracy the last absurdity of an expiring civilization. The mass newspaper and journal with their low intellectual content pervaded society, it seemed. The "shop-girl mentality" and the common man as "boob" (H. L. Mencken) were familiar sneers. Mencken's own United States was a favorite scapegoat: a land without art or culture, home of philistines, prototype of the mindless "ant-world"—*America the menace,* as the subtitle of a French book of the era declared. Europeans eagerly embraced American literature, oddly, for the first time; but it was likely to be Sinclair Lewis's assaults on his own society of Babbitts and Gantrys that they relished. Visiting the United States in the 1920s, Bertrand Russell, repeating Tocqueville's point of a century earlier, found it a land without freedom: "It is obvious that, in such a community, freedom can exist only *sub rosa.*" The land of pious peasants was now leavened by a commercial plutocracy. In castigating American civilization, European intellectuals were joined, of course, by young American rebels of the sort who wrote the savagely critical *Civilization in the United States* (1922) and thereafter fled to Paris. Nor did these Europeans like their own cultures much better; America was only an extreme example of the menace that sooner or later threatened everyone.

Contributing to the gray mood of the 1920s were things other than the war and the mess it had left behind, though doubtless the latter contributed the most. What Walter Lippmann once called "the acids of modernity" had corroded belief, leaving behind a cloud of skepticism. These years felt the full force of those deeply subversive ideas developed just before 1914. Freud, for example, now became widely known. Doubtless one can interpret Freudianism optimistically, as many did, particularly in America, regarding it as a new technology supplying medicine for all that ails the mind. But Freud himself was a deeply pessimistic person, especially in his later years, and his books of the '20s, such as *Civilization and Its Discontents,* express a conviction that the battle between the individual and society can never be ended. Ordered society demands that the Id suppress its impulses; "the price of civilization is neurosis." Of course, it is hard not to see Freud as chipping away at the boundaries of the rational mind, pointing to "the cobra-filled jungle of the unconscious" (Chad Walsh) which is the real determinant of human conduct. Freudianism contributed to the iconoclastic mood of the 1920s, to the sexual revolution and the hatred of bourgeois prudery. At times the Freudian message coincided with the return to religion. In an essay on Freud, Reinhold Niebuhr related him to the pessimism of the Barthians;

for though Freud was an atheist he agreed with them in seeing the human being as a tragic figure, torn apart by conflicts. Certainly the great psychologist, turned social philosopher increasingly in this latter period of his life, believed that humans are naturally aggressive creatures who will exploit, rob, even torture and kill their fellows if not forcibly restrained. "Who has the courage to dispute it in the face of all the evidence in his own life and in history?" he wrote to Einstein.

His onetime colleague and now rival within the psychoanalytical movement, Carl Jung, also extended his reputation. More than Freud, Jung pointed to the psychic need for religion and indeed for a restoration of the holistic, nonintellectual modes of thought of premodern humanity. Nothing more effectively undercut the pretensions of modern civilization with its science to have mastered nature and led the way to "progress." Civilization had only destroyed its psychic balance to become an emotional cripple. The use of myth in the literature of the 1920s was at least partly due to the influence of Jung—to whom James Joyce sent his daughter for treatment and who was consulted by many of Europe's cultural elite. T. S. Eliot used myth in his *Waste Land,* Joyce filled his *Ulysses* with it. Eliot saw it as a weapon against chaos, against the fragmentation and confusion of modern life, "a way of controlling, or ordering, of giving a shape and a significance to the immense panorama of futility and anarchy which is contemporary history" (1923).

The new scientific revolution also worked as a dissolvent of certainties in the 1920s, when the new physics became front-page news. A chapter in Joseph Wood Krutch's *The Modern Temper* (1929), the theme of which was that "skepticism has entered too deeply into our souls ever to be replaced by faith," deals with the downfall of "the last certitude," science. Einstein, Planck, and Heisenberg might have been brilliantly uncovering new truths, but popularly they appeared as destroyers of what had seemed the one solid body of unassailable truth. The circle of skepticism seemed complete when even Science, god of the late Victorians, found the universe mysterious and incomprehensible. The Uncertainty Principle was the discovery of the decade. The day of the signing of the Treaty of Versailles in 1919 brought news of an observation confirming Einstein's law of relativity, and throughout the 1920s the doings of the scientists made big if somewhat mystifying news. Einstein became a household word though the "man in the street" professed to find him as incomprehensible as Gertrude Stein or the surrealists. In the 1920s, through the work of Heisenberg and Broglie, the startling implications of quantum theory became evident in the dual manifestations of the electrons: They behave sometimes as particles and sometimes as waves, breaking through barriers heretofore assumed to be absolute. It became necessary to resort to something like the "as if" philosophy of Vaihinger (1911) and say that all scientific terminology represents "useful fictions."

Albert Einstein. (Yerkes Observatory Photograph, University of Chicago, Williams Bay, Wisconsin.)

Observations are real, but these observations can be extended to form such generalizations as electricity, energy, atoms, matter, only as hypothetical mental constructs. It became known, also, that the subatomic particles are subject only to probability and that the observer inevitably interferes with them, preventing perfect observation; the limits of science had been reached because no one can step outside the universe, humanity being a part of it.

One might make what one chose of all this, but clearly many old certainties were gone and the new Einsteinian universe was less tidy: Bertrand Russell said it was more individualist, even anarchist, with no central government! Among the popular expounders of the new physics, Arthur Eddington adopted an idealist position, pointing out that the scientist creates truth, the answers depending on what questions are asked. James Jeans spoke of the mysterious universe and found more room for God than Laplace or Darwin had left. Science was the new mysticism. Alfred North Whitehead explored the implications of the new science for Western metaphysics, showing that the mechanistic framework dominant since Newton no longer sufficed: he and others proposed a "pan-psychism" which saw the universe as composed of organisms; thus electrons and atoms became in a sense endowed with spirit, a return full circle to the Greek-medieval outlook on nature.

The disillusionment of the 1920s appeared fashionably and brilliantly in the novels of Aldous Huxley, which were really fictionalized tracts or sermons. One sees in *Antic Hay* (1923), a succession of object lessons in the failure of values. Gumbril, the hero, listens to the clergyman, and then the schoolmaster, and finds both of them useless; the artist fails him, and so does the scientist. Romantic love is a sham, but the amoralist who tries to find satisfaction in perverse or diabolical behavior is equally absurd. The mordant criticism of all attitudes that try to give life meaning continued in *Those Barren Leaves* (1925) and *Point Counter Point* (1928); these clever, sophisticated studies in pale melancholy hit the decade just right and made Huxley a household word. That he was the grandson of the famous Victorian scientist and believer in progress made his gloom about the human race the more piquant. A search for values always goes on in the astringent Huxleyan way, and in *Point Counter Point* the memorable character gallery of failures—scientists, artists, politicians—turned up one slightly hopeful face in a somewhat Lorenzian philosopher (Huxley was a good friend of D. H. Lawrence). Perhaps by a return to healthy instincts one might make one's way out of the desert. *Brave New World* (1932) carried on Huxley's war with modern civilization. In the 1930s he began to find consolation in withdrawal and mysticism. Not a great novelist, Huxley was a subtle prober of values and a sensitive barometer of the moods of his day among sophisticated Europeans who felt themselves in a dying culture and searched almost in vain for a firm intellectual anchorage for their lives. The same spirit may be found in many another novel, poem, or play of the twenties and thirties. Set in a Swiss tuberculosis sanitarium, Thomas Mann's *Magic Mountain* (1924) also contains figures representing types of the modern mind: a scientific rationalist, a Dostoyevskyan irrationalist, a pagan sensualist, and others. And the hope of salvation seems to resemble Huxley's: Hans Castorp almost dies in a snowstorm but rouses himself by a great effort of the will.

It might be noted that the mood was not, really, tragic in the deepest sense. There is a sunset charm about the dying culture; talk is brilliant, personality and ideas both richly abundant, there are always marvelous books to read. What literate person could really be unhappy in a decade that produced Joyce, Lawrence, Proust, Kafka, Mann, and a parade of other stunning commentators on the sickness of civilization? A funeral that attracted so many notable pallbearers had at least its compensations. It remained for World War II to confront Europe with stark tragedy; for the time being, ruminating among the ruins was far from unpleasant. The civilized upper class to which Huxley belonged still existed, if it had gone slightly to seed. If this was not "la belle époque" of pre-1914, neither was it yet the nightmare world of nazism, communism, depression, and war. The thirties and forties brought these things.

Nevertheless the disgust which their civilization inspired in many European writers was both real and ominous. It could lead them to disaster. One example from many: Louis-Ferdinand Céline, in 1932, wrote *Le Voyage au bout de la nuit,* a shocking book, both in style and content, misanthropic much beyond Huxley, scatological beyond Lawrence, a terrible satire on the human race—a book which had a considerable vogue. This talented writer ended an anti-Semite, a pro-Nazi, a collaborator with the German conquerors of France during the war—out of sheer hatred of his native culture, one surmises. He was truly one of those of whom Lawrence wrote in *Kangaroo,* a person driven to defiant estrangement from his fellows. A disgust with the absolute corruption of the world may be found in the brilliantly witty novels of Evelyn Waugh, who converted to Roman Catholicism; and in the subtle psychological probings of French novelist François Mauriac, among others of the great literary names.

THE RENAISSANCE OF THE '20S

Tinged as it was by despair, the writing and art of the postwar years had a brilliance seldom matched, for it marked the stylistic maturity of the whole modernist movement—shocking, perhaps, but dazzlingly creative. The literary revolution, whose roots lay in the prewar period, burst upon the general public in the 1920s. Graham Hough has placed "between 1910 and the Second World War" a "revolution in the literature of the English language as momentous as the Romantic one of a century before." Perhaps it came earlier in France. But so far as concerned the English-speaking world, such names as Joyce, Pound, Eliot, and Lawrence came to the fore after the war though they had begun their careers just before it. Wyndham Lewis called Ezra Pound, T. S. Eliot, James Joyce, and himself "the men of 1914": This quartet who led the revolution in English literature emerged exactly as the war began. D. H. Lawrence's first major novel, *Sons and Lovers,* was completed in 1913; he wrote *The Rainbow* and *Women in Love* during the war. Joyce had *Ulysses* ready to launch on the world at the end of the war years. Elsewhere, too, buds of the prewar years burst into bloom. Paul Valéry and Marcel Proust in France may be instanced. The latter's great symphony of novels, *Remembrance of Things Past,* appeared between 1913 and 1927, though Proust died in 1922 at the age of fifty-one. The German master Thomas Mann reached the peak of his reputation in the 1920s as did the Frenchman André Gide and the Irish poet W. B. Yeats.

Moreover the new art and music, associated with the names of Picasso and Stravinsky, predated the war in its origins but moved into the limelight once the guns were silenced. The year 1913 had seen those famous riots in Paris that accompanied the first performance of

Stravinsky's *Rites of Spring* and also the public tumult aroused by an exhibition of the new nonrepresentational art in the United States. A young American emigré named Gertrude Stein was already buying the paintings of her friend Picasso in Paris—for a song. Picasso was at that time living in poverty among a gloriously bohemian set in the attics of Montmartre. Cubism was born from 1908 to 1910, but the paintings produced by this and other *avant-garde* movements were as yet little more than the obscure eccentricities of certain social outcasts. But after the war, conditions became favorable for the reception of anything new, startling, revolutionary. An embittered "lost generation" of rebels against the purposeless wartime slaughter had no interest in defending the values of their fathers, whether artistic, moral, or philosophical.

In Paris in 1919 writers and artists launched their protest against everything; they named it dada (a nonsense word). Everything seemed nonsense—literature, morality, civilization. Action is vain; art is vain; life is vain. All is absurd. Dada was a combination of literary and intellectual sophistication—all has been said, all ways have been used—with the despair of the years from 1917 to 1919, years of slaughter and stupidity. Dada's activities were expression of its bitter derision; it held public meetings, well advertised by post-futurist posters, at which people made nonsensical speeches. Tzara, a Hungarian-Swiss who was one of its chief founders, wrote poems by clipping words from a newspaper article, putting them in a sack, shaking them up, and then taking them out one by one. If most dadaist poems did not go quite so far, they specialized in incongruity:

> The aeroplane weaves telegraph wires
> and the fountain sings the same song.
> At the rendez-vous of the coachmen the aperitif is orange
> but the locomotive mechanics have blue eyes.
> The lady has lost her smile in the woods.

Which is not without charm though definitely without meaning.

Needless to say dadaism was a thing of the moment, but its young literary leaders were to be found in the vanguard of other movements of the 1920s. Of these the most important was surrealism. Something of dada's wish to deliberately derange meaning appeared in surrealism, and also some of its violently disruptive political protest, both however made a bit more constructive and coherent. Surrealism borrowed from Freud and Jung the idea that in dreams and semiconscious states the mind is freed from the tyranny of the rational and can produce fresh, authentic symbols. "Psychic automatism" was its method of writing poetry (suspend thought and let the words come). It may indeed be regarded as a continuation of prewar symbolism with Freudian additions.

Underneath such extravagances there was a romantic faith in the autonomy of the realm of art, which the poetic vision might contact beyond the realm of merely rational concepts. It was a kind of mysticism of art, philosophically an idealism. Surrealism long continued to be the dominant force in French poetry. In addition, the surrealists proclaimed themselves political activists and enemies of "bourgeois" society, which they held responsible for the unhappy divorce of art from life. At first they tended to join the Communists, who were the most vigorous foes of the "bourgeoisie," but later they grew disillusioned, along with others, with Communist tyranny and intolerance. Their sociology, like their politics, tended to be slapdash in the extreme, though occasionally inspired. It was in painting that surrealism, cubism, and related modernist modes had their greatest success. Gertrude Stein's attempt to duplicate in surrealist prose the success in painting of her friend Pablo Picasso did not really come off, though her personality made her one of the most celebrated women of the 1920s. Her mystifying style ("A rose is a rose is a rose"; "How do you do I forgive you everything and there is nothing to forgive") was perhaps not intended to be understood. ("Nobody knows what I am trying to do but I do and I know when I succeed," Gertrude declared.)

The greater writers of a great age of literature were not always incomprehensible. Of the trinity of major novelists, Joyce, Lawrence, and Proust, only the first departed from reasonably straightforward statement, and he only to any marked degree in his last work, *Finnegan's Wake*. The novels nevertheless included daring, experimental, and controversial elements. Joyce's *Ulysses* was banned before publication and stirred up one of the chief literary rows of the decade, matched only by Lawrence's *Lady Chatterley's Lover*. The difficulty lay in the frank approach to sex and the use of words hertofore not permitted in polite discourse. To Lawrence, return to a healthy primitive sexuality was important, not in itself but because he thought people who know how to live know how to love. Sex to him was the key to creativity: taproot of all energies, it is the source of beauty, religion, everything wonderful and vital. So far from being a mere hedonism, this resembled romanticism's doorway of the senses to a transcendent realm of truth and beauty; a great deal bolder and buttressed by modern psychology, to be sure. Lawrence castigated the effete intellectualism as well as the timid bourgeois conventionality of the modern world, feeling acutely the need for something more sincere, more intense, more real. This neoprimitivism sent him back to the Etruscans and the Indians, or, if he had to live in the modern world, to Mediterranean peasants. It sent Arthur Koestler and other Communist converts to the strong, silent workers.

The integrity and "committedness" of Lawrence, as well as his tremendous creative vitality, made him one of the chief of the modern age's seers. Joyce's *Ulysses,* which then so shocked people, has since received wide recognition as one of the greatest literary achievements of modern times. Its "message," if any, was less clear. A vast allegory on the condition of humanity, a commentary on the futility of human existence, a great symphony in words, an affirmation like Nietzsche and Lawrence of the chaotic abundance of life? It was all of these. Like Eliot's poetry, it made use of startlingly modern techniques to recall modern humanity to its civilized heritage. Whatever else it meant, it was a triumph of art and meant that the artist shapes and gives reality to the world—a message similar to Proust's. These works were testimonies to the autonomy of art and pointed to a withdrawal of the artist—a withdrawal Joyce and Proust made quite explicit—from society, to go it alone.

The excitement of the new literature owed much to its ability to probe the inner world in all its irrational complexities, its occasional nastiness, its vibrant realities. A Lawrence novel takes us immediately into its characters and makes us *be* them as they struggle with their lives and problems; we are engaged with them. In a famous essay Virginia Woolf accused the older novelists, such as Arnold Bennett, of depicting only the external aspects of people; in wanting to see them from within, as their minds actually work almost minute to minute, Woolf was squarely in the center of the new novel.

So there was excitement and creativity in literature, yet also a great sadness, for there is an explicit rejection of the public life. Virginia Woolf's Mrs. Dalloway cannot endure her life as the wife of a leading politician, the whole thing bores her and kills the life of the spirit, found in the cultivation of sensibilities in purely private ways. When Sir Charles Snow, more recently, charged all the literary set with an irresponsible attitude toward politics he had in mind this profound revulsion from the public life that one found in virtually all the great writers of the modernist phase. In the last analysis these artists echoed the decadent view, that in the dying days of a civilization the only consolation lies in art. "I hate politics and the belief in politics, because it makes men arrogant, doctrinaire, obstinate, and inhuman," Thomas Mann wrote in his *Considerations of an Unpolitical Man.* "I have to recognize that I don't care a farthing for political principles," Aldous Huxley exclaimed. Ludwig Marcuse was characteristic, in the 1920s era of political mediocrity, in recalling later that "I don't remember if I voted in those years— certainly not for whom." It was the age of Calvin Coolidge, Stanley Baldwin, and a parade of short-lived nonentities in France and Germany. The Common Man was a sad joke, democracy a farce, politics was the enemy of culture to the Lost Generation's troubled intellectuals.

The interwar years also brought a new architecture and a new music. Le Corbusier (Charles Edouard Jeanneret) led a whole school of

architecture that denounced nineteenth-century eclecticism and demanded buildings for the machine age—"functional" and not traditional. Proclaiming that "the past must be destroyed," this architecture
had affinities with futurist art and literature. Walter Gropius headed a
similar movement in Germany, where the ill-fated Weimar Republic,
destined to succumb to Adolf Hitler's Nazis in 1933, experienced a brief
renaissance in the mid-twenties. Munich rivaled Paris as a center of
modern art and the Bauhaus architectural and art school, located at
Weimar and then Dessau, brought together artists of the caliber of Walter Gropius, Mies van der Rohe, Paul Klee, Vassily Kandinsky. At once a
community, a school, and a place for creative design, the Bauhaus aimed
at creating a style suitable for twentieth-century civilization—urban, industrial, technologically modern, yet beautiful. When the advent of Hitler in 1933 forced him out of Germany, Gropius together with Mies van
der Rohe brought the new architecture to Britain and then the United
States.

Both Le Corbusier and Gropius, as well as the American genius
Frank Lloyd Wright, had started their work just before 1914 but reached
their creative period after the war. These dates correspond closely with
those of the pioneer modernists in painting, music, and literature, and
indeed Le Corbusier, who was also a painter, was deeply influenced by
cubism and futurism. But almost no one had heard of Le Corbusier,
Gropius, the Bauhaus, and "functionalism" before the 1920s, and then
they were forced to do battle against outraged traditionalists. One of the
larger engagements in this war took place in connection with the League
of Nations building at Geneva, supposedly a great symbol of the postwar
era, and it is significant that Le Corbusier's modernistic design lost out,
even in his native Switzerland, to the sedate neoclassical edifice that still
stands there in Geneva. Still, the new style was much discussed and won
some triumphs. Dubbed "functionalist," it was in actuality never considered simply as utilitarian by its founders, but was intended to be a
modern esthetic. Under cubist influence it tended to be severely
abstract-geometrical at first but came to include considerable poetic feeling.

In music, abandonment of tonality was the counterpart of abandonment of perspective in painting and the daring innovations of
functionalist architecture. The twelve semitone scale, abandoning the
conventional keys, or whole-note scales, represented only one type of
musical innovation, reflecting an urgent desire to escape the bondage of
the Beethoven century and do something different. Wagner and Dé-
bussy had already tampered with the traditional diatonic system;
Stravinsky just before World War I caused riots with his violent rhythms
and dissonant chords. Arnold Schoenberg's "serialism" invented a new

conception of musical structure. There now began a tendency to dispense with thematic development or musical continuity, searching for a "pure" music in a way similar to some of the modernist poets.

There were infinite riches for the eye and ear in these immensely creative years, the years of Picasso, Kandinsky, Gropius, Le Corbusier, and all the others. Though traditionalists might suspect sheer anarchy in their art forms, actually the authentically modern mode in the arts was at work, transforming the way one looks at things and hears them, just as it was at work in Einsteinian physics. It is small wonder that this was a revolutionary epoch in other ways too.

THE TOTALITARIAN TEMPTATIONS: FASCISM

With Mussolini proclaiming the "lie of universal suffrage" in Italy and Lenin the decadence of bourgeois democracy in Russia, democracy was under attack in the 1920s. It found few defenders among the Western intelligentsia. To Ortega, the Revolt of the Masses was a menace to historic Europe; to Spengler, the Decline of the West began with liberalism and ended with democracy, a soil on which Caesarism, he thought, flourished. Like Georges Sorel, George Bernard Shaw, to whom democracy substituted the rule of the incompetent many for that of the corrupt few, admired both Lenin and Mussolini—any enemy of democracy was his friend. In Spengler's scheme of decline, democracy is the detritus left behind by the decay of organic civilization, a view reminiscent of Plato. Weimar Germany produced whole schools of neoconservatives who lamented *The Rule of the Inferiors,* the title of a 1927 book by the Lutheran romantic reactionary Edgar Jung (later killed by Hitler); Jung was close to the Austrian Catholic advocate of a return to the Middle Ages, Othmar Spann. Many Italian intellectuals were half implicated in fascism, since like the philosopher Benedetto Croce they believed in the rule of superiors. "It is a myth that the Nazi movement represented only the mob," George Lichtheim observed. "It had conquered the universities before it triumphed over society." If this judgment goes too far, reigning intellectual fashions in the 1920s did come measurably close to fascism or nazism and often displayed an initial sympathy towards them.

The poet-turned-nationalist and adventurer, Gabriele D'Annunzio, may well be given credit for inventing the *mystique* of Italian fascism, as the German poet Stefan George provided elitist ideas and symbols to Hitler's movement. The cases of Martin Heidegger, Carl Jung, and Croce, among great leaders of thought, who apparently felt some initial attraction to fascism or nazism, have been much discussed. But antidemocratic ideas were by no means confined to Germany and Italy. H. G. Wells called for a "samurai" class of governing experts, as did the American, Walter Lippmann, in such books as *Public Opinion* (1922) and *The Phantom Public* (1925). The powerfully committed literature and thought of D. H. Lawrence was antidemocratic: "I don't believe in democratic control. . . . The thing must culminate in one real head, as every organic thing must." Though Lawrence never accepted Mussolini as meeting his standards in Caesarism, Ezra Pound did. Evelyn Waugh approved Mussolini and later Franco's right-wing dictatorship in Spain. Robert Brasillach, Drieu la Rochelle joined the older figures Charles Maurras and Maurice Barrès, still active in the 1920s, among French intellectuals who were Fascist or semi-Fascist. Fascism was, in fact, an international movement, found almost everywhere in varying degrees. Only in Italy, however, did it manage to lay hold of national power in the 1920s. (Adolf Hitler's German National Socialist movement was then an obscure one.)

A result of the demoralization following the war and a disappointing peace, as well as of frustrated national pride, Italian fascism was hardly a consistent doctrine, but rather a fusion of discontents, successful because of the near collapse of society. It owed something to the fierce strife between socialist trade unions and the industrial capitalists, and to the Socialist's paralysis of will in a divided mind, as well as to the continued failure of parliamentary democracy to function well. A mass movement, it appealed to various inchoate emotions. In part it was the nightmare of Ortega, of Spengler, of Lawrence, and of Huxley come true: a revolt of the dehumanized masses, who were then to be enslaved by the totalitarian state. But fascism had its intellectual aspects, and made use of some interesting ideas. Its leader, Benito Mussolini, a man of humble birth, had been a left-wing socialist, and was a journalist with an inquisitive and somewhat intellectual turn of mind. He had absorbed at least superficially the advanced political ideas of the pre-1914 generation—from Nietzsche, Sorel,[3] Bergson, and Pareto. He got from them the need for a complete revolution of values, to replace the decadent ones of bourgeois civilization, but also a contempt for materialistic socialism; a belief in elites rather than democracy; in the superiority of intuition over intellect.

Of the Fascist and Communist revolutions, much the same thing may be said as was said of the French Revolution earlier: Ideas did not cause them, but they did guide and shape them. Discontents and the breakdown of order existed, the result of war and postwar problems (economic troubles, demobilization of soldiers). There was a host of other accumulated grievances. Italy had suffered from frustration ever since the rebirth of the nation in 1861, an event which was supposed to lead on to the glory befitting descendants of the Romans but instead

---

[3]Sorel's influence was especially strong in Italy; see Jack J. Roth, "The Roots of Italian Fascism: Sorel and Sorelismo," *Journal of Modern History,* March, 1967.

brought only a series of humiliations. All this would in any case have brought on trouble, perhaps violence; but ideology helped shape this into a coherent, or more or less coherent, pattern of revolution.

The swashbuckling novelist and adventurer, Gabriel D'Annunzio, actually played a more creative part than Mussolini in setting the pattern. A man of ideas as well as of action, D'Annunzio put himself at the head of some exsoldiers and marched into the disputed city of Fiume in 1919, accompanying his seizure of it with flamboyant gestures of the sort soon copied by Mussolini—the uniformed private army, parades and mass meetings, the leader addressing crowds from the balcony as they roared slogans back at him. Admirer of Wagner and Baudelaire, author of decadent novels, D'Annunzio had been a literary prodigy in the 1890s, after which he turned to the preaching of political adventures. "For Italy's younger generation," writes Ernst Nolte, "he was Nietzsche and Barrès rolled into one." He was a poet who became a national hero. Then he plunged into the world war, became an aviator, lost an eye, was decorated for bravery. No one better symbolized the "Leonardist" and "futurist" spirit which was Italy's version of the Nietzschean will-to-power, the Bergsonian *élan vital*. A Dionysian and a powerful leader of the masses on his own view, he impressed others as an egotist and a charlatan. He was certainly a fertile source of slogans, one of them being the idea that Italy was a proletarian nation which should wage class war—as a united people—against the rich, plutocratic states. The spirit of fascism was very much this spirit of the romantic gesture, action for action's sake, and the mobilization of mass psychology. One may read here the whole mystique of the *avant-garde* movement of the day: the Nietzschean incitement to embrace life and "live dangerously," the rebellion against bourgeois legality, the alienated artist's hatred of respectable society, the socialist and anarchist call to revolt.

Despite the somewhat disreputable character of Mussolini, there were some ways in which fascism was smartly up-to-date—more up-to-date than Lenin's Marxism, for it had absorbed the lessons of irrationalism and psychology. It stressed "charismatic" leadership and "superman" activism. The Fascists managed to project an image of dynamic leadership aimed at reviving the Italian nation, sorely distressed and apparently unable to do anything about its troubles. Their weakness was the weakness of the new irrationalism: no system or program, just action for the sake of action, belief in belief itself, creation of "myths," whatever they might be.

To supply the element of nationalism lacking in Nietzsche and Sorel, Mussolini invoked Hegelian strains, popular in Italy for some time. He confided the construction of Fascist philosophy to the distinguished neo-Hegelian philosopher, Giovanni Gentile. The state represents the ethical ideal, and is superior to the individual, Gentile held.

Both the individualism of bourgeois liberalism and the divisive class struggle of Marxian socialism are antisocial. Materialism was rejected as ignoble, and an organic conception of society approved. Claiming at first to stand for the individual against the state, Mussolini moved steadily toward more and more statism, a movement of the mind obviously not unaffected by the fact that fascism had seized the state and increasingly subordinated the individual to the community.

In addition to the above idea, fascism seemed to revert to Jacobin conceptions of the general will, of which Il Duce, with his Grand Council of Fascism, was said to be the embodiment. Fascism represented itself as an answer to the degenerate liberalism of the parliamentary system. Also, the idea of the corporate state, developed in Catholic social thought and carried forward by Charles Maurras, became a part of Mussolini's system. Fascism thus appears, on its ideological side, as a pastiche of a number of ideas, with a heavy stress on statism, elitism, and irrationalism. Perhaps its marriage of statism (from Rousseau and Hegel) to the dynamic revolutionary romanticism of Nietzsche and Sorel may be regarded as its most striking achievement. (But the antiromantic conservative thought of Maurras was also somewhat in evidence.) One may argue with some plausibility that fascism simply grabbed at various bits and pieces of ideas to justify its seizure of power. But it does not seem possible to dismiss its ideological aspects, for these were potent factors. It may be that this was why fascism and nazism had such startling success: Their leaders were aware of the power of ideas, whereas the anemic liberalism of the time was not. Debased as it was, they offered a religion or faith to live by to modern humanity, which had need of it. For a few years Italy's most distinguished philosopher, Benedetto Croce, approved of fascism because it had overcome traditional Italian indifference to politics and the state, revived national morale, and seemingly justified itself by its results. An impressive number of notable Italian writers, artists, musicians, including Papini, Pareto, Pirandello, Puccini, Toscanini, praised the new Italian regime at first. Almost all became severely disillusioned within a few years after 1922.

Mussolini strove to destroy the "lie of universal suffrage" and parliamentary democracy by substituting a strong, heroic elite; he only succeeded in putting Italy under the heel of a corrupt oligarchy. He broke the power of the trade unions, but his "corporate state" scarcely provided any creative principle of economic cooperation. Fascism as a new religion was stamped on the mind of youth through control of the educational system and the organization of youth movements, but it soon ceased to interest anyone of intellectual quality. Mosca, the old proponent of elites, publicly regretted that he had ever criticized democracy, for the rule of the Fascists was worse yet. In brief, whatever promise there had been of a genuine new creed or spirit in fascism soon vanished with only the old face of state tyranny in evidence, this time backed by the resources of modern technology. It is true that Mussolini for a while put on a reasonably convincing performance of the hero-leader, with some "charismatic" appeal. In many ways he was a genuinely talented man. But he wilted under the demands of the superman role and became rather ridiculous. Quite a few of Italy's better minds fled into exile. Others, like the great writer Ignazio Silone, were turned into Communists who fought the Fascist tyranny as best they could underground.

Fascism, as defined by historian Robert O. Paxton, was "a mass anti-liberal, anti-communist movement, radical in its willingness to employ force and in its contempt for the upper-class values of the time, sharply distinct not only from its enemies on the left but also from its rivals on the right, traditional conservatives." Its leaders, such as the autodidact Adolf Hitler, as well as its support tended to come from well down on the social scale, from "little men" with a pattern of frustrated ambition, often self-taught, "outsider" intellectuals. At the first meeting of the German Workers party that Hitler attended on September 12, 1919, the forty-five members included a doctor, a chemist, a painter, two engineers, a writer, five students, the daughter of a judge, along with artisans, businesspeople, soldiers, white-collar workers—quite a cross-section of society, bound together mostly by a susceptibility to seizure by simple ideas and a profound malaise of spirit, as well as frustrated ambitions. Konrad Heiden called the Nazis "the armed intellectuals." Thomas Mann dubbed them "truants from school." Among the would-be intellectuals in the early Nazi party were amateur economists (Gottfried Feder), Wagnerian poets and folklorists (Dietrich Eckhart), founders of pagan religions (Alfred Rosenberg)—a weird lot, laughed at initially by the respectable educated. Hitler, with his hillbilly accent and lowbrow anti-Semitism, was nevertheless in his way a man of ideas, fanatically so; ideas which he had accumulated in intensely indiscriminate reading during his down-and-out years after failing to gain admission to the Vienna Academy of Fine Arts in 1907 and 1908 (the academic bureaucrat who turned him down must surely bear a heavy burden of twentieth-century guilt!). From them he shaped his *Weltanschauung,* and no one was more aware of the power of ideas.

Hitler borrowed from Mussolini, whom he admired, but went much beyond the relatively civilized Italian *duce* in the ruthlessness of his methods, where he found Lenin more to his liking. Like Mussolini, Hitler and his group hated democracy, preached a "national" socialism in place of the Marxist sort which they regarded as poisonous, and were fanatically nationalistic and statist. Nazism, too, thrived on defeat, national humiliation, and the disorders of the postwar era, which were very severe in Germany for several years after 1919. It owed a special debt to Richard Wagner and featured anti-Semitism, not conspicuous in Italian fascism. It also opportunistically made appeal to all sorts of emotions. It denounced capitalism, communism, the Jews, the traitors who had allegedly caused the defeat of Germany, the pacifists and liberals who continued to weaken that nation; it demanded a strongly led government capable of voicing the entire national will and leading Germany back to its place in the sun. Its brown-shirted gangs specialized in brutal violence. The Party, with its leadership principle, borrowed heavily from Lenin's Russian Communist party in its organization. There were echoes of pre-1914 Pan-Germanism in Hitler's program of German expansion; there was also the "crude Darwinism" which caused Hitler to act consistently on the principle that life is a ruthless struggle in which the weak, the wounded, and the allegedly "biologically inferior" have to perish. Racism came from Wagner and a few other nineteenth-century writers, such as the Frenchman Gobineau, owing something, too, to the fashion for genetics, which sometimes took the form of belief in racial improvement by selective breeding. From Nietzsche (selectively) the Nazis took slogans about supermen, heroic leadership, and the need to purge the old order ruthlessly. Sadly though he may have misunderstood that great tragic seer, Hitler was to make Nietzsche—who hated anti-Semites and despised German nationalism—into the Third Reich's official philosopher.

In the crude thought of the demagogue Hitler, the Jew appears as a scapegoat, blamed for everything: among other things, for capitalism, democracy, socialism, decadent estheticism, modern art and literature, modern skepticism and unbelief. Hitler's taste was severely classical; he shared with Stalin's Communists at least this one trait, a hatred of all modernistic art. In the slightly more sophisticated theorizing of the Nazi "philosopher" A. Rosenberg, the Jew is identified with intellectualism, which is related to internationalism, both to be set off against the sound instincts of a cultural people. Christianity has been corrupted by both Judaic and Mediterranean elements, but there is a sound "Aryan Christianity" which should be encouraged. The decadent phenomena, blamed primarily on Jewish influence, are the internationalist, intellectualist, uprooted, atomistic ones; the sound things are rooted in the soil, national tradition, close group integration, intuition, and custom rather than abstract reason. It is easy to see in this sort of thinking many echoes of German and European thought, from early nineteenth-century conservatism and romanticism, from Wagner and Nietzsche and German sociologists like Frederick Tönnies. They were not all disreputable ideas; perhaps they ought not to be blamed because they fell into the hands of the Nazis. The specifically Nazi contribution was the mysticism of race, which is generally considered to have been complete nonsense. This went so far as to assert that there was an Aryan science and to reject Einstein's theories as Jewish-decadent! In flight from the modernized society, nazism was a desperate attempt to turn the clock back and re-create primitive social solidarity at the level of the nation state. To do so, it invented the myth of racial purity.

Talk about the "Nordic race" and its superiority was quite common and respectable in the later nineteenth and twentieth centuries, as may be seen, for example, in England's Cecil Rhodes, whose Anglo-American scholarships, still awarded annually and considered a high honor in the United States, were established for the purpose of knitting together "the Nordic race"; or in such Americans as Josiah Strong and John W. Burgess, a popular clergyman and a leading professor of political science. The United States rang with laments about the "mongrelization" of the native stock through immigration from "inferior" Slavs and Latins as well as Jews. Anti-Semitism was familiar in Great Britain: A recent writer has observed that "fifty years ago anti-Semitism was a political force in England that respectable people supported and with which honourable people sympathized" (Henry D'Avigdor-Goldsmid, *History Today,* April 1964). The Dreyfus case in France in the 1890s brought forth the first major appearance of modern anti-Semitism. Hitler learned his in Austria. There, the Germans as a minority in a sea of Slavs, Hungarians, and Jews developed an often hysterical Pan-Germanism as well as "master race" ideologies. Rosenberg was a Baltic German, again revealing the psychology of the colonist or resident alien. All this is to record the unhappy fact that racial prejudice and belief in racial or cultural superiority was hardly confined to Germany, or typical of it. German National Socialism was destined to write the most odious and detestable chapters of this disease in all history; the ideas were far from exclusively German. Anti-Semitism had been far more virulent in Russia and eastern Europe, where vicious mistreatment of the Jew was common practice; in Germany the Jews had apparently become assimilated and there was no "Jewish problem" until the Nazis invented one.

The Nazi mysticism of race contained an echo of Jung's unconscious archetypes, alleged however to be a phenomena of *race:* Each race has its soul, its symbols, its myths, which are carried in the blood.

Also, Hitler appropriated ideas from the German conservative writers, a group that included Oswald Spengler, Ernst Jünger, and Moeller van den Bruck, though they did not much approve of him, and after seizing power he persecuted this group as relentlessly as others. These thinkers responded to the defeat and humiliation of Germany in World War I by proposing a Spartan recovery program. Spengler and Moeller wrote of the need for strength of will, national resurgence, and a leader capable of embodying the people's will. All weakening forces, such as democracy (alien to the "Prussian style"), liberalism, and class conflict must be eliminated. These ideologies stemming from the French Revolution were the virus poisoning Germany, which must return to conservative principles to regain unity and strength. Moeller and Spengler were the "conservative revolutionaries" who would use revolutionary means to bring about a conservative, that is, nationalistic, goal. But they were not racists and Hitler to them was a disreputable rabble-rouser. There are some striking affinities between these writers and nazism, but not complete identity.

Ernst Jünger was a spokesman of Germany's restless youth, who just before the war had created a youth movement expressing the urge to get back to nature and renew contact with elemental forces, a protest against the urbanized rationalism of modern life. Something similar existed in France and other countries. After the war, the "fatherless generation" or the embittered exsoldiers were revolutionary in spirit. This youth movement was intensely idealistic, yearning for something much better, earnestly if fuzzily convinced that the existing order—capitalist, mechanical, bourgeois, soulless—was bankrupt. The youth movement with its *Bünde* was separate from the National Socialists but often merged into it. Hitler took advantage of it; in the long run he did not represent its idealism, and it is clear that many young Germans who initially hailed Hitler soon became severely disillusioned with the new slavery his regime introduced. (By that time it was too late.) Radical, revolutionary as it was, young Germany was searching for something to believe in, something exalted and pure. The tragedy was that the figure it thought represented such revolutionary idealism turned out to believe in nothing except himself.

The Nazi and Fascist movements were profoundly anti-intellectual. "When I hear the word 'culture' I reach for my gun," said Joseph Goebbels, Hitler's lieutenant. These movements came to be led by the brutal, the ignorant, and the criminal. They were extremely clever at exploiting the irrationality of the masses, for whom they often expressed great contempt. Keen students of propaganda, the Fascists and Nazis borrowed liberally from all the great mass movements of the past. They employed the language of religious conversion, freely using such words as faith, deliverance, miracle, rebirth, sacrifice. Nineteenth-century nationalism did so too, as one may recall. They took much from the Communists, as well as from ritualistic orders such as Jesuits or Freemasons, and from the army; it has been suggested that they also learned a good deal from American advertising. They played on symbols from the national past. Hitler and the Nazis "looked back into the stream of earlier German thinking and selected that which they found of value to them" (Otto Klineberg). There was a deliberate use of "myth," a disparagement of objective truth, a frank acceptance of the need to lead the masses by techniques directed at the irrational mind. All these ideas had been brought forth by such important prewar thinkers as LeBon, Sorel, Wallas. The war itself had exhibited the possibilities of nationalistic propaganda and helped undermine respect for truth, as governments resorted to what amounted to systematic lying. Thus in many ways the Fascist and Nazi movements dredged up all the worst in prewar and war culture. They were the evil spirits of Western civilization, but they did not create the evil so much as exploit it. They were intellectual parasites, borrowing the ideas of others to use as tools of power.

It should be stressed that fascism was a Europe-wide phenomenon. If it emerged first in Italy, with strongly French intellectual antecedents (Sorel, Maurras) under the leadership of an ex-Marxist who held no brief for Italian national traditions, it sooner or later appeared in all parts of Europe (and America). There were Belgian Rexists, and an Austrian Fascist movement, the *Heimwehr* led by Prince Stahremberg (which predated the Nazis and was destroyed by them after Hitler took over Austria). In Rumania the Iron Guard, preaching return to ancestral customs, rejection of modernism, hatred of the Jew as symbol of capitalism and modernism, combined this sort of deep conservatism with a radical, populist program of land redistribution. There were such manifestations everywhere. In Britain, the man regarded as the most brilliant young Labour party leader, Oswald Mosley, imitated Mussolini and tried to create a British Fascist party. If fascism failed to capture power in other countries as it did in Italy and Germany, the reasons were chiefly accidental ones of time and circumstance.

Certainly in France the Fascist movement could not be described as insignificant. In February 1934, two hundred thousand demonstrators attempted to storm the Chamber of Deputies in Paris and fought police in an all-night battle during which thousands of both police and demonstrators were wounded and a number killed—a melee hard to match even in the long and bloody annals of Parisian street uprisings. These protestors were right-wing followers of the Fascist leagues, seeking to bring down a left-of-center government. The largest of the French Fascist leagues, the *Croix de Feu,* claimed seven hundred fifty thousand members and may have been the largest of all voluntarily recruited Fascist groups. Fascism never won in France, partly because there were too many different Fascist groups—the old *Action Française* now being joined by several other similar factions.

One of France's leading Fascists was a renegade Communist, Jacques Doriot. What, in the last analysis, *was* this post–world war phenomenon that so oddly combined extremes of Right and Left? That it *did* so combine things, formerly thought to be unmixable opposites, is indisputable. It appealed to the young and the outcast, demanded drastic change, practiced violent methods. It sought an image of dynamism as well as youth: Mussolini and Hitler made a point of dashing about on motorcycles or in fast cars and otherwise displaying qualities of energy and *élan*. Fascism's specific programs were normally anticapitalist, appealing to the "little people" against the monopolists; and it called itself Socialist, though rejecting the materialistic and class-struggle socialism of the Marxists. Its leaders tended to be one-time Marxists—true at least of Mussolini, Doriot, Oswald Mosley, and others. In all these respects it was radical. But in other ways it was deeply conservative. The demand for national unity, cultural integration, what the Germans called *völkisch* qualities was close to the heart of fascism/nazism. Their hatred of Jews and Marxists came to the Fascists from their dislike of things that disrupted organic culture unity and divided the national community. Their extreme intolerance, their contemptuous rejection of democracy and liberalism, their almost insane attempts to create a national ideology— *German* religion, *German* science—along with their racialist fantasies, all this flowed from the impulse to beat back the tides of pluralistic modernism and recreate a truly organic community. The Fascist ideology glorified the country against the city, tried to inculcate blindly obedient patriotism, stressed the family, traditional values, old customs.

This radicalism of the Right was, of course, deeply infused with the irrationalism of the prewar thinkers. An old-fashioned rationalist like Bertrand Russell stood aghast at all this sound and fury, and could only say, "The world between the wars was attracted to madness. Of this attraction nazism was the most emphatic expression." Watching Hitler's parades and mass meetings, listening to his hysterical speeches to roaring, chanting crowds, many others too could only assume that a kind of madness had seized hold of Germany. (In actuality, it would appear, not many Germans paid much attention to the ideology, privately laughing at it; they approved of Hitler because he got things done, restoring Germany to economic health and international success.) But still others pointed out that people, not being rational animals, have need of ritual and romance, a need neglected in modern times, rationalized, bureaucratized, and mechanized as its life had become. Fascism reminded them that modern Western humanity is in search of a religion, to replace a lost Christianity, and found here a substitute. It turned out to be a disastrous one.

7

The Pink Decade

Marxism is an all-inclusive whole reflecting our age.

JEAN-PAUL SARTRE

Marxism is . . . an opiate for the people.

SIMONE WEIL

Who live under the shadow of a war
What can I do that matters?

STEPHEN SPENDER

COMMUNISM AND THE INTELLECTUALS

In the 1930s, reaction against nazism provided a rallying point for the shattered morale of European intellectuals. At this time they were precipitated in large numbers into the camp of communism. The "red decade," or at least the "pink" one, had begun.

Quite early, the new Communist government of the Soviet Union received significant support from Western intellectuals. "In this muddy age its ten years shine," wrote the American liberal magazine, *The Nation,* on the tenth birthday of the Russian Revolution in 1927, voicing orthodox liberal-left doctrine. In 1932 the venerable Fabian socialists, Mr. and Mrs. Webb, who had always stood for political democracy and personal liberty, heaped praise on "Soviet Civilization" in a substantial study; they praised it among other things for "liquidating the landlord and the capitalist." At just that time Stalin's ruthless war on the kulaks was driving peasants to starvation in a way one can hardly imagine the Webbs approving. What became almost a stampede of writers and intellectuals to the Communist bandwagon later appeared inexplicable, even to the people who joined it. There were, however, some reasons for it.

Bolsheviks and left socialists profited, first of all, by having none of the blood of the world war on their hands. Lenin and a few others, for example Ramsay MacDonald in Great Britain, had rejected the conflict from the beginning. As soon as the Bolsheviks fell heir to collapsing Russia in November 1917, they issued an appeal to the workers of the world to lay down their arms. They continued to denounce the whole European state system as an iniquitous capitalist scheme and to cloak themselves in the garb of pacifism. Lenin provided a Marxist explanation of the great war—caused by imperialistic capitalism—and socialists alleged that universal peace would follow the extinction of the capitalist system. The unpopularity of the war, and the hatred of all war, that pervaded these years redounded to the credit of the Communists. A good deal of sympathy for the Russian bolshevist government, also, was aroused by the shocked horror with which respectable circles regarded it; by their efforts to destroy it through military intervention in 1919–1920 (though these were feeble and halfhearted), and by their treatment of it as a pariah for some time after 1920.

Perhaps it is not quite possible to explain the pro-Soviet mood in a rational way. It became a symbol for all those who hated the "establishment." The disillusioned and the naturally rebellious, the unhappy young men and women of the "lost generation," saw here a successful revolution, led by a leader of genius and vision, which had overthrown a vicious and reactionary government in Russia. But whatever sympathy the Soviet "experiment" aroused before 1930, it was the impact of the great depression that caused the rush to Marxism. The Webbs, in the study mentioned above, praised especially the Russian "abandonment of the incentive of profit-making, its extinction of unemployment, its planned production for community consumption."[1] The Western de-

---

[1] Fabian socialism was in considerable confusion because its solutions had seemingly not worked. In her diary, Mrs. Webb observed that "we went seriously wrong . . . in suggesting that we knew how to prevent unemployment. We did not." By 1931 there had been two Labour governments in Britain, yet the expected miracles had not come about. "I am beginning to doubt the inevitability of gradualness," Beatrice Webb sighed.

The Webbs visited Russia for only about three weeks, used materials supplied them by the Soviet government, and allowed Stalin's government to read and correct the manuscript.

mocracies struggled almost hopelessly in the mire of economic depression in the 1930s, while in Russia things seemed to go forward with vigor and drive. The first of the great "five-year plans" for the industrialization of Russia was launched in 1928. "There is no unemployment in Russia": The explanation might be that there was economic slavery there, but in the grim atmosphere of the jobless thirties even that seemed better than unemployment. As a matter of fact, uncritical books by friends of the Soviet Union poured from the press, indicating that something like a paradise for the worker was being created, with all the old vices missing—vices such as greed, selfishness, prostitution, crime, ignorance. "Planned production for community consumption" had replaced the anarchy of capitalism.

The existence of fascism and then nazism polarized political attitudes and diminished the middle position. Mussolini and Hitler excoriated bolshevism, as did all right-wing, conservative people; therefore if you attacked it you could be accused of being a Fascist, or as good as one. (Marxist logic featured a method of reasoning by which "objectively" one could be a Fascist without even knowing it.) Some very intelligent people admitted that they backed Soviet Russia because it was attacked by those they disliked; they loved it for the enemies it made (*vide* André Gide). Communists did fight fascism and nazism; they led the way in the famous Spanish Civil War which pitted the two elements against each other. They showed outstanding courage in fighting as best they could the Fascist and Nazi dictatorships in Italy and Germany.

Much aiding this detente with the Communists was the popular front strategy adopted by the latter after 1934. Prior to that the Communist line had been to denounce the moderate Socialists and Social Democrats as "social fascists" and refuse cooperation with them. Some of the fiercest polemics of the '20s were exchanged between the old Socialists and the new Communists, who had split off from the Second International to establish the Moscow-directed Third International. Recognizing after Hitler's triumph that they had gravely underestimated fascism (in their blindness, the German Communists actually helped Hitler bring down the Weimar Republic, believing, as their dogma taught, that the collapse of "capitalism" must inevitably lead to socialism and communism), the party line shifted and from Moscow came orders to make friends with all shades of left and liberal opinion and form a united front against fascism. It was one of a number of abrupt and sometimes bewildering shifts which earned the Communists the mistrust of others; but at least it meant, in 1935, that the Communists welcomed the friendship of other left-wing elements, no longer denouncing these as "traitors to the working class" because they refused to join the Communist party. Soon there was a Popular Front government in France, headed by the venerable and prestigious Socialist Leon Blum, a Jaurès

disciple. It had its troubles keeping so various an amalgamation of doctrinaires together, but for a short time about 1936 and 37 the Popular
Front seemed a success.

An additional attraction that may be suggested in explanation (if
not extenuation) of the intellectuals' defection to communism was Soviet
literature and art. The arts in Russia had not yet been placed in an
official strait jacket, destroying their creativity and interest. They were
still reasonably free, progressive, and graced by such names as Maxim
Gorki, one of the greatest of living novelists in the 1930s (a holdover
from the prewar era, but an enthusiastic convert to the Soviet regime);
Eisenstein, the genius of the silent cinema; Prokofiev and Shostakovich,
the composers. Culturally, today, the world of communism has virtually
nothing to attract the educated Westerner; this was not so true in the
1920s and early 1930s. Stalinization of all artistic and intellectual activity
was not completed until about 1935. After World War II it reached
fantastic extremes during the reign of Zhdanov as cultural minister,
when even music could be denounced as "ideologically incorrect" and
scientists were persecuted for not paying sufficient heed to dialectical
materialism. In fact, tension between artists-writers and the Party developed in Russia fairly early in the revolution. Lenin denounced as
"hooligan Communists" some of the high-spirited poetic types who welcomed the revolution. Mayakovsky, most talented of Russian poets,
wrote an ode to Lenin but was soon satirizing the new breed of bureaucrats; he killed himself before the decade was out. Many Russian artists
and intellectuals joined Sergei Rachmaninoff, Igor Stravinsky, Nicholas
Berdyaev, and others in a massive migration to Paris and other Western
cities. Nevertheless the Soviet Union maintained its reputation as excitingly creative in the arts, in the main, until the 1930s.

So about 1930 writers grew interested in communism. They had
grown weary of the skepticism of the 1920s. Their mood changed sharply with the coming of the great economic depression and the rise of
fascism. They wrote off the esthetes of the 1920s as irresponsibles. "But
quite suddenly, in the years of 1930-1935, something happens. The
literary climate changes. A new group of writers . . . has made its appearance, and though technically these writers owe something to their predecessors, their 'tendency' is entirely different. Suddenly we have got out
of the twilight of the gods into a sort of Boy Scout atmosphere of bare
knees and community singing" (George Orwell). Writers became serious,
political, almost social-messianic in the spirit of 1848. Conversion from
gloom and alienation to hope and social purpose seemed a miracle at the
time; only later did Orwell, who went through it, see it as he so wryly
describes it above. Writers turned to social realism in the 1930s and
pinned their hopes on red revolution. "Drop those priggish ways
forever, stop behaving like a stone," the poet W. H. Auden admonished

his fellow writers. "Start at once to try to live." Come down from the ivory tower and join a picket line.

The intellectuals, it may be noted, had swung to extremes of commitment and withdrawal in alternate generations ever since the earlier nineteenth century. The exalted idealism of 1848 gave way to pessimism and consolation in art and science; then the intellectuals threw themselves into the great crusade of World War I only to fall back in dismay during the '20s. There now occurred another sudden swing of the cycle. The mood was not unlike 1914 in its structure, though almost diametrically opposite in its content. A final crisis seemed to confront civilization. One must choose:

> Singing I was at peace,
> Above the clouds, outside the ring. . . .
> None such shall be left alive:
> The innocent wing is soon shot down,
> And private stars fade in the blood-red dawn
> Where two worlds strive.
> The red advance of life
> Contracts pride, calls out the common blood,
> Beats song into a single blade,
> Makes a depth-charge of grief.
>   *C. Day Lewis*

The flight of the intellectuals to communism reflected in substantial measure their own spiritual predicament. Edward Upward wrote that "I came to it [communism] not so much through consciousness of the political and economic situation as through despair." Koestler commented on "the intellectual comfort and relief found in escaping from a tragic predicament into a 'closed system' of beliefs that left no room for hesitation and doubt." Though not proclaimed as such, but rather as an exact science, the Communist ideology clearly functioned as a substitute religion, too, especially appealing to intellectuals. ("The strongest appeal of the Communist party was that it demanded sacrifice," Louis MacNeice recalled. "You had to sink your ego.") Yet, as such, it proved to be—in the words of a famous symposium on the subject—the god that failed.

The artists and intellectuals who rushed into the arms of communism expected to find there greater freedom, greater creativity, a liberating force. Picasso said that he went to communism as to a spring of fresh water. The great irony is that by 1931, communism had become a system of slavery and an intellectual straitjacket, so that the intellectuals who entered it were condemned to frustration. The Communist party was being so organized as to destroy all intraparty democracy in the USSR and also so as to put the various other party units firmly under the control of Moscow. Communists in other countries were required to serve the Stalin-dictated party line blindly. In the name of socialist unity they had to agree that the homeland of socialism, the USSR, must be defended at all cost. They were led into the role of apologists for whatever might be done by Stalin, and in the middle thirties this included the astonishing reign of terror that "purged" almost all the old bolsheviks along with literally millions of others as Stalin systematically destroyed all resistance to his dictatorship.[2] In 1939 it included suddenly becoming the ally of Hitler. While a few agreed to submit their individuality entirely to the party and suspend all ethical considerations for the duration of the battle against capitalism, most found the conditions of intellectual servitude imposed on them intolerable and became disillusioned with the USSR. This was the more true when the party line on literature in the 1930s condemned, as "formalism" and "bourgeois decadence," all the modernisms that were most exciting to Western writers. Kafka, Joyce, Eliot, surrealism, everything that had happened since the turn of the century had to be rejected in favor of "socialist realism." Nor was even this realism supposed to be too realistic, by criticizing the Soviet Union or the Communist party.

Arthur Koestler noted that actual entrance into the Communist party on an active basis, which was his experience, choked off literary expression, but that mild contact with Marxism as "fellow travelers" stimulated any number of writers in the 1930s. John Dos Passos and John Steinbeck wrote memorable works of "social realism" in the United States; Barbusse, Romains, and Malraux in France; Brecht and Seghers in Germany. Some of this mock-proletarianism later seemed ridiculous. The esthetes of the 1920s tried to become democratic "hearties" if not Communist revolutionaries; from the Kremlin, the real thing undoubtedly laughed at them, while making use of them as best it could. Lenin is supposed to have taken one look at the British Communist party and immediately abandoned all hope of a revolution in England. But from the most intellectual circles of Cambridge University in the 1930s emerged Guy Burgess and Kim Philby to penetrate British foreign office and intelligence citadels as long-time spies for the Soviets, down to the 1950s. Well might Karl Radek (soon to be a victim of Stalin in the high ranks of Soviet leadership) boast that "in the heart of bourgeois England, in Oxford, where the sons of the bourgeoisie receive their final polish, we observe the crystallization of a group which sees salvation only with the proletariat." For a time in the mid-30s it was *de rigueur* for any young person who aspired to be intellectually alive to praise and even to serve the great Soviet Experiment and to admire extravagantly its mighty leader, Joseph Stalin. ("The man whose silhouette on the gigantic post-

[2]Careful research indicates that no fewer than twenty million people perished as victims of the Stalinist state in Russia between 1930 and 1950, far surpassing Hitler's more famous "holocaust" in numbers. See Robert Conquest, *The Great Terror* (1971).

ers appears superimposed on those of Karl Marx and of Lenin, is the man who looks after everything and everybody," Henri Barbusse wrote in his laudatory 1935 biography of Stalin.) Poets like W. H. Auden, former surrealists like Louis Aragon in France, announced their conversion to communism. Even Virginia Woolf could be found writing for the *Daily Worker.*

That spectacle of all his heroes abasing themselves before a great tyrant and mass-murderer, in Malcolm Muggeridge's words, caused many a person later to have doubts about the political wisdom of intellectuals. Their hatred of nazism and fascism was worthy of respect; their naivete in being taken in by Stalin's "guided tours" of the USSR was another matter. Few seemed to want to know much about the real Russia: "I never met any who had the slightest interest in any side of Russia which was not Stalinist propagandist presentation," Stephen Spender recalled of the intellectual Communists. But an exodus from the Party began in 1937, increased in 1939, was somewhat reversed during World War II only to resume during the post-1945 cold war years, when cries of "mea culpa" became a chorus of the Western 1930s generation. They might not abandon their revolutionary or Marxist views in leaving the party; they might claim (plausibly) that Stalin had betrayed the revolution and perverted Marx, as well as Lenin. But the exodus from the party that began about 1937 led most of the converts eventually away from the whole Marxist framework.

Whatever their future destinations, the Left writers departed for them from their Red rendezvous at the end of the 1930s and later treated it for the most part as a mistake. A great deal was written by the one-time Communists about their odyssey in and out of the Party. In his great novel *Darkness at Noon,* Arthur Koestler tried to depict the self-destroying psychology of the Communist who had given over his mind and soul to the Party. Koestler has described his own rather horrifying experience within the Party as a "spiritual discipline" that he would not wish to see expunged from his past, though he came to regard it as an intellectual error. (See *The Invisible Writing.*) A few, like Picasso and Bertolt Brecht, remained; the latter faced and accepted with unusual clarity the decision to lose one's individuality in the Party, to cease thinking and become nameless and faceless, "blank sheets on which the Revolution will write its orders," prepared to "sink into the mud" and "commit any vileness" in order that the cause might prosper. It was a decision any Communist had to make if staying in the Stalinist party. But it was a singular position for writers or artists to accept, and Brecht was one of the few great ones able to do so. (Brecht's experience suggests the difficulties of the creative writer under communism; for his plays, written in a "modern," *avant-garde* manner, were not performed in Communist countries though he became their most distinguished literary property.

In actuality Brecht was never comfortable in the Soviet Union, from which at one time he had fled.)

Leon Trotsky, Lenin's chief lieutenant in the Revolution, who was driven into exile and ultimately assassinated by Stalinists, provided a rallying point for some who wished to remain revolutionary Marxists while repudiating Soviet communism under Stalin. Trotskyites regarded Stalinism as having perverted socialism by the errors of bureaucratization and the cult of personality. They were prone to criticize the lack of intraparty democracy and even the lack of personal freedom in the USSR, yet they remained attached to revolutionary Leninism including the rule of the party as "vanguard" or proletarian elite. On the whole, this group faded out too, after playing some part for a time as the resting place for those disillusioned with events in Russia but not prepared to abandon revolutionary socialism. It would revive a generation later.

An examination of the multitudinous self-analyses of ex-Communists of the '30s and '40s leads one to conclude that the chief reasons for disenchantment were the following: the discovery that Marxist ideology is an illusion blinding one to reality; concern about destruction of moral integrity from having to subordinate truth and standards of decency to the Party cause; the Party's ruthless subordination of the individual to its demands; failure to find artistic fulfillment in communism, indeed the opposite, a stultifying effect; and eye-opening discoveries about conditions in Russia, especially the tyrannical treatment of people. Inherently undisciplined, freedom-loving artists were usually quite miserable if they actually entered the Party and were required to submit to its iron discipline. Harold Laski, distinguished left-wing theoretician of the British Labour party who was pro-Communist in the 1930s, reacted at length against "deception, ruthlessness, contempt for fair play, willingness to use lying and treachery ... dishonesty in the presentation of facts." Changes in the party line required embarrassing shifts: A. MacIntyre cites the case of a British Party faithful who first lauded Yugoslavia's Tito, then slandered him, then suppressed the latter book when Tito was restored to favor again. What one believed depended on the latest word from Moscow. Stalinism gradually destroyed whatever artistic creativity and freedom of thought there had been in Russia and erected a monstrous tyranny which killed and imprisoned millions. This became increasingly obvious to even the most ideology-blinded partisan.

During World War II, wartime friendship between the Soviet Union and the Western democracies brought a temporary resurgence of communism within the latter, but the strained relations between Russia and the West after 1945 had the opposite result. Dogmatic Marxism suffered a precipitate decline in Great Britain and the United States. It declined to a lesser degree in Italy and France, perhaps because of a curious affinity between its dogmatic and apocalyptic mood and that of Roman Catholic Christianity. Especially on the Continent, a revival of Marxism lay ahead, but it was another kind of Marx people now discovered—not the Stalinist deformation, the obsolete dogmas, but the ethical protest against capitalism, the denunciation of the workers' alienation from work and from society, which they regarded as the essence of Marx. Of this, more later.

OTHER SOCIAL MOVEMENTS

There were other "progressive" social movements in the decade of depression that were not Marxist but which assailed the existing order of capitalism. The great economic depression caused a searching reappraisal of existing, "classical" economic theory. Among the revisers of economic orthodoxy the Englishman John Maynard Keynes stood out as an acute, penetrating, and incisive mind with a gift of literary expression. Keynes, who had challenged conventional public finance methods in the 1920s, came in the 1930s to put his views in the form of a general theory (1936). Pared down to its essentials, the Keynesian view was that contrary to the old theory there is no automatic tendency toward full employment in the free economy (Say's law); rather, there can be stagnation with unused human resources. This is because, among other things, the community's total savings are not necessarily invested in capital equipment. The interest rate, which is supposed to provide the automatic mechanism for insuring the investment of savings (the rate falling as savings rise), may not function effectively because liquidity preference (desire to keep funds in cash form easily obtainable) causes savers to accept a lower return on their money than they could get. Keynes stressed the propensity to over-save and under-invest in a mature capitalist economy; the result can be economic stagnation. The economy cannot be counted upon to right itself, as the older economics taught. It may have to be righted by the intervention of the government. Formerly the approved policy for dealing with depression was for the government to pare its expenditures and balance its budget, and governments did this during the early stage of the 1930s depression, with apparently ineffective results. The new economics called for an unbalanced budget, the government throwing its overspending into the economic stream to break the logjam.

Thus the new economics, as advocated by Keynes and his followers along with some others (the Swedish school was prominent), encouraged statism though not socialism (public ownership). The private economy can work effectively but it requires regulating with the great fiscal resources of the government used as a balance wheel. Interest rates can be manipulated by government action, the expenditures of the government can be varied, taxes raised or lowered according to the needs of the economy at any given time. The Keynesian view, roughly, prevailed, in that orthodox economic theory soon accepted a modicum of the new economics while governments, even conservative ones, accepted their responsibility to "maintain full employment" by use of a variety of powers such as those mentioned. This was an economic revolution and perhaps by implication a political and social one. It cast the "public sector" of the economy in a new and much more active role. It provided, as some saw it, a democratic alternative to Communist totalitarianism in the area of national economic planning. To others, the "Keynesian revolution" and the "welfare state" were steps on the "road to serfdom" (F. A. Hayek) only slightly less alarming than red bolshevism; they too reflected the coloration of the Pink Decade.

The infatuation of creative writers with social issues in the 1930s left behind remarkable literary deposits, now somewhat out of style but bound to remain as landmarks for the historian to contemplate, some of them awe-inspiring in their sheer magnitude. For example, Jules Romains, the French socialist novelist, wrote ten thousand pages in his mammoth multivolume novel of social realism, *Men of Good Will,* outdoing Marcel Proust in length if not in quality, and intended to rival Balzac's great *Human Comedy* of a century earlier as a picture of the social world. Politicians, capitalists, industrialists, as well as intellectuals seeking to set the world right, fill these pages. The criticism made of Romains and other novels of this sort (the Englishman Robert Briffault and the American Upton Sinclair were among others addicted to it) is, for one thing, that they really had no firsthand knowledge of capitalists and politicians (or workers!), but invented stereotypes of what Marxist or left-liberal theory required them to believe of such individuals. Social realism was often wildly unrealistic. And it was frequently unutterably dreary: sermons flavored with melodrama. It was often enough the fruit of a blind ideological faith. Romains's huge opus is nevertheless a tribute to the moral earnestness of the writers of the thirties and their desire to bring life back into the scope of art and intellect.

While simple and drastic positions such as Stalinist communism tended to prevail in the anxious '30s, during which the Western world suffered the ravages of economic depression and watched the drift toward another war, there were subtler variations on the theme of Marxism. The Frankfurt Institute for Social Research to which belonged such German intellectuals as Max Horkheimer, Herbert Marcuse, and Theodor Adorno, specialized in a nondogmatic, more humanistic Marxism. Thrown out of Germany by Hitler in the early thirties, the Institute ended in New York City as part of that great cultural migration of German scholars, scientists, and intellectuals that so altered American intellectual life. The moment for this critical Marxism, more concerned with the quality of culture than with revolutionary violence, came much later: Marcuse as an old man was to become the sage of the youth movement of the 1960s, in one of the many odd twists of intellectual history. In the interwar period these sophisticated social theorists discovered Marx's unknown early writings, rejected both Stalinism and Social Democracy as simplistic perversions of Marx, experimented in Freudian, existential, or phenomenological graftings onto Marxism. They were an esoteric elite at this time but were later to be seen as pioneers. There were other such left-wing groups in Germany during the Weimar years, all of course destroyed by the Nazi revolution, which did not pause to distinguish between shadings of Marxism, the more so since these circles tended to be heavily Jewish (this was true of the Frankfurt school).

Throughout everything, whatever their other disagreements, writers, intellectuals, political leftists, clergy, and almost everybody else joined in one fervent sentiment: *nie wieder Krieg,* no more war. The war dominated literature. Romains's epic, just mentioned, paused for a whole volume at the battle of Verdun; Ernest Hemingway immortalized Caporetto; the most famous and poignant of all, Erich Maria Remarque's *All Quiet on the Western Front (Im Westen Nichts Neues),* cemented the postwar reconciliation of Germans and French and English on the common sentiment of shuddering abhorrence of the whole grisly event. But a few outstanding examples cannot begin to suggest the extent to which the war provided themes for the novel, memoirs, and likewise serious thought. The huge historical *post mortem* into the causes of the war extended to the popular level. The fashionable radicalism attributed war to the dynamics of the capitalist system or, more naively, to the conspiracies of munitions makers. Such analyses often partook of fantasy more than fact: The widely read book of a British aristocrat turned Communist, John Strachey, *The Coming Struggle for Power* (1932), predicted a war between the United States and Great Britain as the climax of world capitalism's imminent collapse (and also predicted Communist rather than Nazi victory in Germany). But they suited the spirit of the times. Young people took the Oxford Oath, in England, vowing never again to fight for king and country. A typical extremism of the intellectuals led them to disavow *all* war, without exceptions, without distinction. They repudiated this vow, under the threat of nazism, in the later 1930s. This feeling was in good part responsible for the weakness of the Western democracies in the face of Hitler's post-1935 Nazi challenge; a generation fed on antiwar literature could not admit the thought of war even against the worst of evils. The final tragic irony of this generation was that it had to go back to war, which it hated, in order to destroy fascism and nazism, themselves products of the first war's brutalization of humanity.

Despite its startling modishness, the left-wing socialist or Communist position by no means monopolized the 1930s. Apart from the few who followed fascism, a rather distinguished traditional rightism struggled to stem the leftward tide. The Christian revival associated with Karl Barth, Jacques Maritain (neo-Thomism), and Reinhold Niebuhr continued without much interruption. It might sometimes interact with the eschatological visions of the far Left, but in the 1930s, T. S. Eliot announced himself a royalist and a High Anglican and as editor of *Criterion* sought to rally religious humanists to a defense of traditional values against both fascism and communism—which he saw as debased rival religions, successful only if Christian culture failed to assert its message. In France there were many right-wing journals of the intellectuals; Georges Bernanos and Emmanuel Mounier are examples of deeply committed, rather unorthodox, but in some ways highly reactionary leaders of thought. Evelyn Waugh and C. S. Lewis made their way back to "mere Christianity," while Arnold J. Toynbee's impressive multi-volume inquiry into the causes and possible cures of civilization's decline (*A Study of History*, 1934–1939) looked to a religious revival as the only way to recovery.

REVOLUTIONS IN PHILOSOPHY: LOGICAL POSITIVISM

A. J. Ayer, the British philosopher identified with "logical positivism" in the 1930s, recalled that "there was a moment when Philip Toynbee almost, but not quite, persuaded me to join the Communist Party. I have to confess that my reason for refusing was not so much that I disbelieved in dialectical materialism as that I recoiled from the idea of party discipline." There was undoubtedly some connection between the mood of this "revolution in philosophy" (self-styled) and the decade of political radicalism.[3] Logical positivism began life as an iconoclastic doctrine, whatever it may later have become; "the old men were outraged," as Ayer recalls with glee. But its origins went back some years, and led, curiously, to Vienna as well as to the British universities, especially Cambridge.

Logical positivism originated with a group of philosophers and mathematicians active at the University of Vienna from about 1920 until nazism and war dispersed them in the 1930s, whereupon many of them went to Great Britain and the United States and exerted a considerable influence while blending with certain native traditions in these countries.

---

[3]The Vienna Circle tended to be leftish: Otto Neurath had been a member of the brief Spartacist revolutionary regime in Munich in 1919. The Circle was broken up when the Nazis seized Austria in 1938, its surviving members fleeing to England or the United States.

These included Schlick, Carnap, Neurath, and Wittgenstein, the latter going to Cambridge University early. They owed something to the pre-war teaching at Vienna of Ernst Mach's "empirio-criticism," a careful analysis of the immediate data of experience based on the neo-Kantian view that only sense data exist and one cannot know the thing-in-itself.[4] In Britain, the influence of Ludwig Wittgenstein (*Tractatus-Logico-Philosophicus*, 1921) blended with a somewhat related movement stemming from G. E. Moore and Bertrand Russell, Cambridge philosophers who broke with the dominant school of idealism beginning about 1900. Their roots were plainly in British empiricism; this was the spirit of Bacon, Locke, and Hume, marked by a tendency to avoid all metaphysical flights, concentrate on careful analysis of actual experience, break problems down into their smallest components, watch out for the loose use of terms, and construct no "systems." The early Wittgenstein joined forces with Russell's "logical atomism"; the later Wittgenstein's keen interest in the logical structure of language reenforced Moore's influence to open up marvelous horizons of subtle inquiry to a generation of "linguistic analysts" and "semanticists."

The basic postulate was that philosophical method must be "scientific." Science is not only clear, logical, rational, analytical, but also "verifiable by sense experience." The application of these criteria suggested that for philosophy there is no specific end or content; its function must be to help the sciences—which alone can provide knowledge, since empirical investigation is the only sort of knowledge. "The business of philosophy is not to establish a set of philosophical propositions but to make other propositions clear." To clarify the meaning of words and statements might seem a modest goal but it can be most useful. If science experiments and verifies, philosophy defines and clarifies. Many meaningless problems and much nonsense may be removed by the rigorous analysis of words. Indeed the method might be extended to other fields, such as politics or ethics, to clear up confusions by defining terms, thus locating the problems. The early Wittgenstein held that one may by analysis reduce reality to simple, atomic facts (the Viennese had learned from Russell's "logical atomism") and then frame statements which correspond to these facts.

Perhaps this revolution in philosophy may be best characterized by saying that philosophy ceased to be a "search for wisdom" or a quest for absolute answers and became instead just the logic of science or the

---

[4]Lenin, reading Mach, wrote a furious rebuttal defending Marxist materialism, which he felt to be threatened by this disguised idealism, arguing for a direct-copy realism in which objective reality simply prints itself on the mind without the latter contributing anything substantial (*Materialism and Empiriocriticism*). Philosophers generally found this naive. Lenin accused the phenomenalists or "empirio-critics" of opening the way for reactionary mysticism.

clarifier of scientific methods and concepts. To those who protested that philosophy was abdicating its chief function and leaving modern humanity, which never so needed help with its values, high and dry, the answer given by philosophers of the new dispensation was that unfortunately this cannot be the philosopher's function. These philosophers were "positivists," that is, they carried on the tradition, with a greater rigor and clarity, of regarding metaphysics (absolute being and value, transcendental reality) as not a true object of knowledge. One cannot really say anything rational about that. If some, the poets or the seers, want to speak to this question, let them; this is not the realm of clear logical thought which is the philosopher's. Reproducing an argument among the nineteenth-century positivists, some of the new positivists said that statements beyond the realm of verifiable sense experience are merely beyond the competence of the philosopher, while others denied the right to talk about them at all.[5]

The most extreme statement of the new school came from the English philosopher A. J. Ayer in the 1930s. No problems exist, Ayer suggested, except the factual ones of science. All the others can be shown by linguistic analysis to be nonexistent, pseudo-problems. Most of the things philosophers and theologians and moralists had been worrying about through the centuries—God, freedom, spirit, purpose, morals, and so forth—were complete wastes of time. They can be shown to be either wrong statements of the problem or else purely personal or "emotive" projections of the feelings of the individual concerned, about which there can be no fruitful argument. Some of them can be reduced to empirical, testable statements, and these in principle can be solved by the scientist (empirical investigator). The rest must be dismissed as so much empty wind.

The shock effect of this position is evident. As someone has remarked, theologians who were accustomed to being told they were wrong found themselves speechless at being told they were not saying anything at all! Applied to morality, logical positivism might be extremely subversive. Statements of value not being empirically verifiable, they become mere expressions of preference. "I think adultery is wrong" is the same sort of statement as "I hate spinach" or "I dislike abstract art." (Though Hume had said something similar in the eighteenth century, he had been willing to fall back on custom and the consensus of humanity;

[5]Neo-Kantianism strongly revived in Germany in the later nineteenth century, influencing such social philosophers as Wilhelm Dilthey and Max Weber. Their distinction between the natural and human sciences (*Geisteswissenschaften*), which unlike the natural ones do not seek lawlike generalizations but the understanding of subjective meanings, owed something to this philosophic school, as did also Weber's conviction that empirical science cannot find values, which are the province of religion, leading to his advocacy of a "value-free" social science.

twentieth-century skeptics had scant respect for either.) It will be recalled that some of the bolder Enlightenment writers had equated right with pleasure and wrong with pain, the only categorical moral imperative being to satisfy one's urges. Sober academic philosophers now indirectly endorsed their hedonism. Strictly speaking, they only pointed out that logical thought can supply no sanctions for behavior; we must look elsewhere for values of this sort. It is open to us to find them in religion or in social utility. At the same time, the frank equation of moral tastes with other kinds of personal taste might be construed as issuing an invitation to moral libertinism. Presumably I should choose my conduct in the same sort of way I choose my neckties—all a matter of personal taste. And if I try to defend one sort of conduct against another by any sort of rational argument, I am talking nonsense.

Language was always a preoccupation of the logical positivist school. To avoid the dread beast Metaphysics, one must be careful to use only words such as relate to empirically verifiable facts. Meaningless words, like God, the Idea, the Absolute, have been responsible for metaphysical nonsense. Rudolf Carnap tried to create a logical language, whereby we would use symbols rather than words in the interest of greater clarity. Since languages as they are tend to be untrustworthy guides, disguising and distorting thought, we must purify or clarify them or invent an entirely new, logically sound one. The astringent critique of terminology could lead to such statements as "all philosophy is a critique of language" or "most of the propositions and questions of philosophers arise from our failure to understand the logic of our language." Accused of trivializing the great questions of life by turning them into quibbles about words, philosophers of the linguistic analysis school were convinced that misuse of language is the prime source of confusions in thinking. But in his later years Ludwig Wittgenstein, Austrian-born Oxford professor who was the most colorful and incisive philosopher of his age, changed rather dramatically. Well known only after his death in the 1950s, Wittgenstein's later thinking was marked by skepticism rather than certainty, for we do not, he thought, have any way of knowing whether our language fits external reality or not; we are its total prisoner. All we can do is play by consistent rules of the language game or games that enclose our thought.

An arid verbalism and a cloistered timidity marked the linguistic school, critics claimed; existentialists and analysts stared at each other uncomprehendingly at philosophic conferences, in one of the many little wars of knowledge characteristic of recent times. But "the absence of any dogma or jargon, any universal method, any claim to finality" together with the keenness and closeness of its thought impressed other observers of English philosophy. In the 1920s and 1930s, logical positivism's astringency, skepticism, and almost nihilistic tendencies recommended it.

It was in part a kind of nose-thumbing at all the old pomposities; it was a paring back, a getting down to brass tacks preparatory to rebuilding the world of knowledge from the ground up. And in this respect it bore some resemblance to such other phenomena as the prose of Ernest Hemingway. One has only to read the first sentence of Ayer's "manifesto," *Language, Truth and Logic* (1935), to sense this mood: "The traditional disputes of philosophers are, for the most part, as unwarranted as they are unfruitful."

The astringent and analytical spirit appeared also in English literary criticism. The magazine *Scrutiny*, edited by Oxford professor F. R. Leavis, founded in the 1930s and published until 1953, encouraged what its title suggested, a meticulous line-by-line examination of poetry, in reaction against both the chatty sort of armchair talk about literature that had passed for criticism in Victorian times and against lack of clear literary standards. For somehow it was expected that close scrutiny would clarify standards. The scrutinizers thought of themselves as cutting away large husks of sentimentality with a keen razor of critical analysis, in order to get down to the solid core of real literary value. Like the analytic philosophers, they were to be accused of aridity and pedantry; in 1945 a fairly strong reaction against them set in. But they succeeded in introducing what seemed like a scientific expertness in the examination of the arts. Somehow this was bracing.

For science commanded great respect. Progress went on in numerous areas of science, though sometimes it seemed rather gloomy progress. It was at this time that genetics became a fashionable study. Psychology, in the universities, lay more under the influence of J. B. Watson, the behaviorist, and the Russian, Pavlov, than of the more speculative theories of Freud and Jung. Eschewing any attempt to analyze interior states of mind as unsuitable for the scientific method, the behaviorists stuck to measurable observations of external behavior. This was an American school but for a time found considerable international favor. In its more dogmatic moods it was inclined to insist that human nature is determined by its environment in a mechanical sort of way, that life is made up of a series of conditioned reflexes, and that mind, as such, does not exist, there being only a pattern of electric reactions in brain tissue. Very positivist, even eighteenth-century.

"Scientific humanism" was a term much in use; what it meant, roughly, was the possibility of raising humanity to new heights by the use of science alone, with heavy overtones of hostility to traditional religion. But to many the march of science threatened dehumanization. In his *Brave New World Revisited* (1959), written twenty-seven years after his famous depiction of what might be the fate of humanity in a few centuries when it had been totally organized in accordance with scientific techniques, Aldous Huxley noted the use of Pavlovian theories in the

Sigmund Freud. (London,
BBC Hulton Picture Library.)

brainwashing techniques practiced by the Chinese Communists. His
Brave New World, he felt, had all but come true in a mere quarter of a
century. Freedom and individuality would be sacrificed to the demands
of the machine, large-scale organization, and technological progress. In
the years since 1920 there has always gone on a lively controversy between those who hail science and technology as the liberator and savior
of humanity and those who fear it is being enslaved and spiritually
destroyed by these terrible servants. With the spectacular advances in
science and technology of these years, the issue became an urgent one.
To raise it at the most urgent of all levels, nuclear fission was achieved in
1938 (following the work of Mme. Curie and M. Joliot in 1934 in induc-
ing radioactivity by bombarding certain atoms with neutrons) and would
be developed into the atomic bomb during the war that lay just ahead.

EXISTENTIALISM

The triumph of severely analytical, rational, scientific modes of
philosophizing in England, Austria, the Scandinavian countries, soon in
the United States (carried there directly by Rudolf Carnap and other
Austrian refugees after 1938 as well as by British influences and

offshoots of native pragmatism) was, strangely enough, completely reversed in much of the rest of continental Europe, where a highly nonrational sort of philosophy came into prominence in the 1930s.

In the epoch of the world wars European intellectuals lived in a state of shock, in a nightmare world, such as one finds metaphorically projected in the fantasies of Franz Kafka (*The Trial, The Castle*). If unlucky enough, one might have watched the mass slaughter at Verdun, seen the bolshevik terror in Russia, observed the black-shirted and brown-shirted hysteria in Italy and Germany, the riots of starving workers during the Great Depression, fought in the Spanish Civil War, noted the appalling drift to world war again in the 1930s, and perhaps ended in a Nazi concentration camp, after having destroyed whole German or Japanese cities from the air. It was seemingly a world of terror and inhumanity, marked by the almost total breakdown of civilized processes and political rationality. On the other hand, one could have observed extraordinary wonders, too, not only scientific and technological but literary, philosophical, scholarly, suggesting a fund of creative energy in Western civilization that might yet save it. Evidently the chief problem was one of values: something in which to believe that sophisticated modern humanity *could* believe in, something to serve as a directing principle for the aimless power of scientific technology, something to teach to the hundreds of millions of democratic citizens who, now "free," were slaves in their freedom for want of such values.

The serious concern for humanity, which must find values amid the general wreckage of traditional ones and act upon them in a nightmare world, is a theme that leads to the group known roughly as existentialists. Born between the wars chiefly in the writings of the German or German-Swiss academic philosophers Martin Heidegger and Karl Jaspers, "existentialism" (Heidegger talked of his *Existenzphilosophie* while Jaspers used the term *Existentialismus*) did not become well known until just after World War II, when it leaped into international prominence largely owing to the brilliance of one of the outstanding writers and thinkers of modern times, Jean-Paul Sartre. Sartre, once a student of Heidegger's, has been novelist, playwright, editor, essayist, and political activist as well as philosopher (author of the long and difficult *Being and Nothingness*)—a combination of talents that, given the quantity and range of his writings and his role as moral and intellectual leader of a generation, makes him something of a modern Voltaire. Sartre helped the French Resistance movement of World War II; postwar existentialism received the flavor of the bitter and lonely experiences people went through in this war, whether in the *maquis* or the concentration camps. His fellow Frenchman, the Algerian-born essayist and novelist Albert Camus, killed in an accident in 1960, joined Sartre in leadership of the "second lost generation" after 1945. With all gods really dead now, nothing to believe in, the existentialists quite remarkably turned to humanity itself to find new values.

Though the experiences of the war are often regarded as decisive in the shaping of existentialism, the fact is that Sartre's mind was formed in the '20s and '30s, and his bitter alienation as well as his ambivalent attachment to Marxism came out of that epoch. He studied philosophy in Germany under Heidegger[6] and mastered a good deal of the existence philosophy, learning also from the pioneer phenomenologist, Edmund Husserl. Husserl, who died in 1938 at an advanced age, was writing as early as 1900 in the phenomenological vein. What he then proposed to do was pare away all the specific content of consciousness to get at its pure state—what is in the mind before anything is in it, one might say, what is the nature of its pure subjectivity before objects are present. Husserl, an extraordinarily inventive philosopher, later decided this task was impossible but still tried to study basic acts of consciousness in their intentionality or meaning. Martin Heidegger was Husserl's student, as Sartre was Heidegger's (though both teachers repudiated their students!).

Sartre's was no merely academic personality, and he participated in the cultural atmosphere of the between-the-wars epoch. His first novel, published in 1938, set the tone for everything that followed: *Nausea*. It was Sartre's special contribution to take Heidegger and Husserl off the academic shelf and give them sharp relevance to contemporary life: a metaphysics that bore directly on the most immediate life situations of living people. In Sartre's hands it became bitterly pessimistic yet tinged with just a dash of desperate, disabused hope.

Existentialism drew on earlier ideas and indeed one of its attractive features was its absorption of much of the gropings of European thought and expression since 1800, or perhaps even earlier, into one structure; there is something here of a *philosophia perennia*. In one sense it is the ultimate Nietzscheanism. Sartre once wrote that "existentialism is . . . an attempt to draw all the consequences from a consistent atheist position." "Dostoyevsky has written that if God did not exist, all would be permitted. That is Existentialism's starting point." If we really grasp the meaning of modern godless man's plight, we are at first reduced to nausea and despair. We must pass through the awful sense of depression that accompanies a real insight into man's condition. He is alone, for he cannot really communicate with others. He finds himself in a world to

---

[6]Heidegger, who succeeded Husserl at Freiburg University in 1928 just after publishing his epochal *Sein und Zeit (Being and Time)* in 1927, impaired his standing in the eyes of many German intellectuals by joining the Nazi Party and heiling Hitler during 1933 and 1934. A profound hatred of the modern technological society, which he regarded as dehumanizing, may have led Heidegger to this unfortunate initial sympathy with nazism. Sartre, his philosophical disciple, was of course far to the Left politically.

which he is utterly alien and which has no purpose or meaning. Society, too, is at work trying to depersonalize him, make him into a cog in the machine, make him play a role that crushes his individuality. But on the far side of this abyss (existentialism is a "philosophy of the abyss," Emmanuel Mounier said) there is one message of salvation, one ground of hope: man, the human consciousness, is after all left. He is somehow here, able to react; even in feeling despair, he shows the possibility of bestowing value on the meaningless world. As Camus noted, the world is absurd; but then it could not be absurd unless men judged it to be so; this feeling of the absurd itself is the start of philosophy. One is reminded of Pascal's "thinking reed."

Man is unique in the world; his own peculiar kind of being is radically different from all others. Heidegger, who called himself an ontologist, was preoccuppied with the nature of Being—of what it means, in general, for anything to exist, and in particular what human existence is. For man, "existence is prior to essence," Kierkegaard had already asserted. This striking idea found reenforcement in the naturalistic outlook of Darwin, as well as in the psychology of Freud. Reason does not precede and determine man, but vice versa; man exists, and his will to exist leads him to invent "rational" systems, which are thus not ultimate but are a product of his drives, instincts, fears, hopes. It is of the nature of the human being to be unique, a concrete particular not to be understood by membership in a class or group, like other objects. True, insofar as a man is flesh he is the usual kind of being; moreover society is always at work trying to make him into a stereotyped object. But the human personality *ought* to be unique and free, not directed from outside or resembling an object. Heidegger's distinction between "authentic" personal existence and "being-in-the-world" became in Sartre's hands a distinction between being *en-soi* and *pour-soi*—in-itself and for-itself.

Being-in-itself is the mode of being for all things except humanity—for physical objects, anything that has objective identity. My own past, insofar as I look at it as something vanished and dead, is being of this sort, which is the normal kind of being. It is subject to essences, to generalizing; it is, we might say, the data of science; it is like Bergson's realm of the scientific intellect; it can be conceptualized. But human consciousness, as it exists in our minds every moment, *now,* is a radically different kind of thing—*pour-soi*, in Sartre's terminology. It is actually not being at all, but a kind of "hole in being"—a nothingness, in a sense. This striking analysis of human consciousness owed a great deal not only to Husserl but to Hegel's *The Phenomenology of Mind.* Thus there is an undercurrent of thought here reaching back to the earlier nineteenth century, as in the case of Freud.

Critics of Sartre (by no means lacking) have reproached him

among other things for calling "nothing" what is patently something; but Sartre's general meaning seems reasonably clear. Our consciousness requires objects to respond to, we cannot have consciousness of consciousness. And our immediate conscious experience is not like anything we can think of; it is just conscious experience. If Sartre's analysis of this elusive substance is sometimes a bit fuzzy, it is a remarkably stimulating effort to examine what seldom has been examined. It provided him with the basis for both his pessimism and his optimism. There can be no God, for our consciousness-being submits to no generalization, there can be no being-in-general. And there cannot really be any happy relationships between people. The other person is an object to me, and I to the other person. We try to reject the other person's reducing us to an object. The realm of interpersonal relationships is to Sartre condemned to frustration, at best. "Hell is other people," as one of the most famous of his plays points out. The individual could only be happy if able to structure the entire universe to fit the ego, and this of course is impossible.

Yet the nature of this protean nothingness, the *pour-soi* or human consciousness, is to be free, and to create itself. Defined only by our acts, we are free to assign values, to give our lives meaning. Sartre and the existentialists do not undertake to tell us what to believe in, how to act, for each of us must decide that individually; to be other-directed is to be inauthentic, to be guilty of "bad faith." Like the positivists, so different from them in many ways, the existentialists refuse to provide creeds and dogmas. Their function is to point out the importance of making choices and the need to make them with utter integrity. One must win the way to authentic personal existence by refusing to be absorbed "in the world" or made an object. Man is an ambiguous creature; condemned to freedom, he has to act, but there is really no creed to tell him how to act (if he believes so, he is guilty of bad faith), and so he is anxious and forlorn. When he surmounts the crisis of feeling the absurdity of his situation, he acts in full understanding of this autonomy as free creator of his own values.

Perhaps the elaborate and, to some people, somewhat mystifying Sartrean ontology is not so important as the ethical message, though it does provide an impressive foundation. The essential existentialism is the message to be authentic, to avoid bad faith, to refuse to be depersonalized. "Existentialism is the struggle to discover the human person in a depersonalized age," William Barrett has written. How can we be authentic individuals? Existentialists give a few hints. We should reject intellectualism, or merely speculative knowledge; this does not speak to the human condition. We must presumably pass through the crisis wherein we see that there is no God, no meaning in the universe as such, nothing or no one to help us. Then we realize the uniqueness and wonder of man the creator of values. "This world is without importance, and whoever recognizes this fact wins his freedom," one of Camus's characters observes. When we realize that with each choice and act we not only make ourselves but give the whole universe what value it has, we have discovered the dignity of being human. Then we must be "committed," we must believe nothing that is merely idle opinion—what we believe must be for life. Like Nietzsche we must grasp it with our whole heart and soul, not merely with the "cold prying tentacles" of conceptual thought.

Perhaps existentialism may be understood by comparing its subjectivism to that of Kant. The Kantian revolution placed the focus of attention on the subject, the mind, rather than the object of knowledge, thus beginning something basic to modern philosophy. But Kant's subjectivism confined itself to the realm of logic, supposedly built into the human mind; it remained rational, merely transferring rationalism from outside to inside, as it were. Existentialism and phenomenology go still further, behind rational thought, which is seen as the product of deeper experience, to a strange world of myth and symbol hardly yet explored. Kant's was a rational subjectivism, theirs an irrational, better infrarational. The rational is *not* the real, as Hegel taught. Existence is not rational, but even absurd; it simply is, and we cannot possibly reason about it—being it ourselves. Only some superhuman being could do that. Existence is a brute fact. We come to realize that people have invented reason to hide their fears or rationalize their desires. Baffled by this knowledge, we must nevertheless choose and act. As Yeats wrote, "We cannot know the truth but we can live it."

Religious Existentialism

Existentialism will be returned to, for it persisted and indeed came into its own after 1945 as a major theme of contemporary thought. But at this point the companion and variant forms of Sartre's atheistic existentialism, whose parents were Nietzsche and Heidegger will be introduced. This religious form went back chiefly to the obscure nineteenth-century Danish Lutheran, Kierkegaard, a major rediscovery of the twentieth century (translated into German, 1909, Italian 1910, French 1929, English 1938). "The Kierkegaard renaissance is one of the strangest phenomena of our times," F. Heinemann remarks. But the time had at last become ripe for the "lonely thinker" who lived between 1813 and 1855 and died at age forty-two, a poor unknown.

Soren Kierkegaard left little mark on his own time (outside his native Copenhagen) and was to remain largely unknown until he became a discovery of the existentialists. He was a savage critic of Hegel's deterministic system, as he construed it. (In this he owed something to the views of F. W. Schelling in his last years.) Such objective thinking—reasoning—destroys individuals making them a part of the collective.

Kierkegaard resisted this with all his being. In proclaiming that "existence is prior to essence," he asserted the primacy of the individual person over any abstraction. He complained that Hegel's system was not "for life" and demanded a faith that was. (Careful students of Hegel complain quite properly that this is unfair, for at times Hegel himself could be quite "existential." Still, the contours of his main system as widely understood doubtless conform to Kierkegaard's indictment.) This was the same thirst for absolute commitment, for a creed related to one's life situation, that one finds in Nietzsche, who never read or heard of the obscure Danish parson. But Kierkegaard, unlike Nietzsche, was deeply religious, though his intense personalism caused him to attack the Church as a menace to real faith. Through anxiety and despair, individuals must make their own way to God. The Dane's intense suspicion of conformism, the crowd, institutions, phony external substitutes for inward experience, are somewhat reminiscent of certain of the esthetes, and it may be significant that he was a contemporary of Baudelaire (who in the end turned to religion himself).[7] But Kierkegaard, a pastor of the Lutheran Church, also pointed back to the great founder of his church, who demanded a faith based on personal experience and denounced sacramentalism along with the moralism of salvation via good works.

This intense stress on the inner life of the spirit, with its fierce assault on both intellectualized, philosophical Christianity *and* on liberal, moralistic Christianity, was scarcely suitable to nineteenth-century religion, which was going in exactly these latter directions. The "return to orthodoxy" in Continental theology after World War I, previously discussed, owed something to Kierkegaard. Nicholas Berdyaev, a Russian of the Orthodox Church; Martin Buber, a Jew; Jacques Maritain, French Catholic; and the Protestants, Lutheran and Calvinist respectively, Karl Barth and Emil Brunner were influenced by Kierkegaard though they might disagree with him in particulars (see Martin Buber's well-known essay on Kierkegaard in which, from the viewpoint of Jewish Hasidic communalism, he reproached the Dane for being too antisocial, while testifying to the importance of *Fear and Trembling* in his own development).

Buber's *I and Thou* appeared in 1923; Berdyaev, who had known exile under the tsar and had drifted close to Marxism before the war, hailed the Revolution of 1917 but found himself arrested and exiled by Lenin's dictatorship in 1920, after which he taught, lectured, and wrote in Berlin and Paris. Buber was born in 1878, Berdyaev in 1874, Maritain in 1882; all these men grew to intellectual maturity before World War I

---

[7]According to Kierkegaard, spiritual development leads one through the esthetic stage to the moral and finally to the religious. Only in immaturity is one content with mere literary form. But one infers that Kierkegaard had passed through such a phase.

but then had their lives sharply altered by that event. They became the greatest of modern theologians.

Christian existentialism touches closely on these imposing figures who attempted to revive a somnolent religion in refutation of Nietzsche's and Sartre's claim that "God is dead." Maritain tried to reconcile his neo-Thomism with existentialism. The "crisis theology" of Barth comes close to it, as does the I-Thou experience described by Buber (a distinction between a person's relation to other persons and to things, with God as the "eternal Thou" to be encountered in a dialogue). Paul Tillich and Gabriel Marcel, from the Protestant and Catholic camps respectively, were more explicitly existentialists.[8] The trend was decidedly away from a rationalized religion, a polite and moral one, an easy and conventional one. In dread and anxiety the soul realizes its dire predicament and then makes the "leap" to faith. The individual chooses and wins his existence by reaching out to a transcendent Being who is not "understood" but is encountered, addressed.

Certainly not all modern theologians accepted existential ideas, but it is significant that an earnest revival of theology centered on such doctrines as Original Sin, the nature of Christ, and atonement. Relegated at one time virtually to the scrapheap of vanished dogmas, these issues once again became important in an era when human pride leading to self-destruction appeared as historic fact. Christian or Judaic thinkers pointed out that one does not need to desert our basic Western traditions and embrace an anarchy of strange beliefs; it is possible to come to terms with the modern experience through the medium of an enlarged but basically traditional religious outlook. The Bible, in the words of Rudolf Bultmann, has been "de-mythologized"; the assaults of the higher criticism have become irrelevant, for it is not the literal truth but the existential truth of this spiritual record that matters. Without God, or some transcendent source of value, humanity is condemned to destroy itself. One can sit in the wasteland and wait for the end or can go forth to seek through the mists the God that is lost.

Modern Christian thinkers have tended to see in the totalitarian regimes and world wars of the unhappy twentieth century a consequence of the despiritualization of humanity through deChristianization. Liberalism, capitalism, and materialistic socialism, reducing men and women to mere factors of production and atomizing them, prepared the way for the terrible explosions of nazism and communism, which these thinkers see not as products of the peculiar evil or misfortune of individual nations but as general cultural phenomena of

---

[8]Practically all those who use the existentialist approach wish to deny that they are "existential*ists*." Tillich has said that while "the existential element has a definite place" in his thought, "I would not call myself existentialist."

modern Western civilization. ("Germany is not the sin of Europe, but of the entire modern world, the sin of a world so profoundly corrupted that peoples corrupt each other; and the last service rendered by the German people to the old civilization it formerly honored is to show to each nation, as in a monstrous mirror, the image of that which it perhaps is today without knowing it, and which it will surely be tomorrow," wrote Georges Bernanos shortly after World War II.) Liberty and civilization depend on religious belief. The heroism of members of the Christian churches, Protestant and Catholic alike, in suffering martyrdom at the hands of Hitler's pagan totalitarianism advanced the prestige of religion in Europe; and subsequently the confrontation between the West and Soviet communism encouraged a definition of the former's position as historically Christian.

Existentialism has been introduced at this point because it was definitely born between the wars, when Martin Heidegger and Karl Jaspers were at work, and Heidegger's student Sartre began his literary career; when the revival of religion with overtones of an existentialist nature took place, through Buber, Maritain, Barth, Niebuhr, Berdyaev. But during that feverish decade of political alarums and excursions, the 1930s, which began with the economic hammer blows of the Great Depression, moved on to Hitler's Nazi conquest of Germany, then to the war brought on by Nazi hatreds and aggressiveness, with Stalin's Five-Year Plans and purge trials a part of the picture, little else gained much attention except these economic and political questions. Then came a war more dreadful than the last one, and more inhumane: the terror bombing of European cities by the Allies, the murder of the Jews by the Nazis, incredible and untold suffering, great and sometimes unrecorded heroism. This traumatic experience helped make relevant the insights of the existentialists, and after the war this "philosophy" achieved large popularity.

Politically, existentialism was somewhat ambiguous. It stressed action and commitment and was defiantly hostile to the kind of society that existed in the West. In its Sartrean form it was bitter, alienated, filled with scorn for the whole quality of contemporary life, inclined to consort with only a small minority of outcasts and rebels. Thus it could blend easily with revolutions of the Left—or with revolutions of the Right. Its founder, the celebrated philosopher Martin Heidegger, hailed Hitler. Sartre, though, was for many years a Communist sympathizer. Even the religious existentialists were, as Reinhold Niebuhr has written of Paul Tillich, "affected by Marxist catastrophism," and in World War II some of them fought cheek by jowl with Communists in the anti-Nazi underground, giving rise to a certain sympathy that endured in the postwar years. On the other hand, existentialism in its very nature was hostile to the dogmatic scientific materialism of the Marxists, to their determinism and their system-making. To adopt such a dogma is a form of bad faith to existentialists, whose extreme individualism rendered them utterly unfit in any case for the discipline of the Party. Sartre's struggles with communism, which he alternately defended and assailed, constitute a large chapter in the story of his intellectual career. After 1945, Albert Camus and Maurice Merleau-Ponty emphatically rejected communism, quarreling with Sartre, and existentialism became connected with the political quietism and personalism of that decade. The answer does not lie in political nostrums but in personal development. Existentialism has a conservative side. Believing as it does only in integrity, in behaving according to one's real nature, it is necessarily protean, supporting no one creed or position. All that the existentialist ethic really tells— perhaps not so new an admonition—is to be sincere, true to one's own selves, and not afraid to act on one's convictions.

By its own standards there cannot really be an "existential*ism*," the whole idea is to escape *isms*. Each person's truth will presumably be different. In fact, the major figures of the school have disagreed with each other on various questions. Christian existentialists are of course in basic disagreement with the atheistic ones. To Gabriel Marcel, Sartre is "a degenerate disciple of Heidegger," and he disapproved of Heidegger! Sartre has expressed much of himself in plays, Camus in novels; perhaps existentialists have made their most striking contribution in the examination of various concrete life problems. Sartre on the nature of love and why the individual is condemned to frustrate himself, a "useless passion"; Simone de Beauvoir on what it means to be a woman; Camus on the man as rebel: These and other products of French existentialism are classics of this time. Such plays as Sartre's *No Exit* seem clearly destined to be classed among the serious literary statements of its age. And possibly the most fruitful application of existentialism appeared in the realm of psychiatry, where such people as Binswanger, Boss, and Laing brilliantly developed its possibilities and threatened, in more recent years, to supersede Freudian and Jungian techniques.[9]

Seen in this light, existentialism is an aspect of the modern movement in literature and psychology, going back to Baudelaire and to James and Freud, with their keen interest in the inner world of humanity. Existentialism has been defined as "an attempt at philosophizing from the standpoint of the actor instead of, as has been customary, from that of the spectator" (E. L. Allen). It is a dimension of what Jung called "the undiscovered self." Subjectivism is a theme of the contemporary West. And this is why the intellectuals of the 1930s, who tried to be Communists, could not do so.

[9]Further on existentialism and phenomenology, see Chapter 8.

8

Contemporary Ideas in the West: Trends in Thought since 1945

There are many reasons for thinking that European man is raising his tents from off that modern soil where he has camped for three hundred years and is beginning a new exodus toward another historical ambit, another way of life.

JOSÉ ORTEGA Y GASSET

Man's existence is now nearing an absolute decision.

ROMANO GUARDINI

We live in a moment of history where change is so speeded up that we begin to see the present only when it is already disappearing.

R. D. LAING

EUROPE AFTER THE WAR

As Europeans awoke from the nightmare of World War II to stand amid the ruins that assured them that the horrors had really happened, they were understandably tempted to reject all the old and start anew. If World War I damaged the respect felt for ancestral tradition, the second such cataclysm twenty years later seemed likely to destroy it. Gabriel Marcel, to quote but one example, has written of "the more than physical horror and anxiety I experienced in walking among the ruins of inner Vienna in 1946, or more recently in Caen, Rouen or Würzburg." Almost any European city between the Channel and the Dnieper could have qualified, though German cities suffered most, as a result of the incessant allied aerial bombings. He went on to note that for many the corollary was a total rejection of the European heritage (*The Decline of Wisdom,* 1954). These physical ruins were manifestations of the moral ruins displayed in Hitler's ghastly extermination of the Jews; the gas chambers of Auschwitz and Dachau brooded over a European atmosphere heavy with the smell of death.

Apart from the sheer physical and moral damages of the war, there had occurred what one historian phrased in the title of a book, *The Passing of the European Age,* or as the distinguished German, Alfred Weber, brother of Max, titled a little book of 1946, *Abschied von der Bisherigen Geschichte,* translated as *Farewell to European History.* In 1946, H. G. Wells, who had preached progress toward utopia for half a century, wrote *Mind at the End of Its Tether,* in which he decided that the end of civilization, of humanity, and perhaps of life on earth was rapidly approaching. A shattered and exhausted Europe was occupied by American and Soviet soldiers, both of whom most Europeans looked upon as barbarians from outside. Before long it became evident that the Russians, at least, intended no liberation but a new enslavement to communism. The Americans were to be looked upon as allies against the menace of Soviet power, and many Europeans were glad to clasp hands with the democratic land of the New World. The fact remains that quite a few bearers of the European culture continued to regard "Russia and America as the same," basically; as Martin Heidegger put it, "the same dreary technological frenzy, the same unrestricted organization of the average man" (*An Introduction to Metaphysics,* 1959).

For those who had expected brighter days with the Allied victory over Hitlerism, the coming of peace and the establishment of the United Nations, the years just after 1945 were deeply disappointing. As economic ruin engulfed Europe, a quarrel between the Soviet Union and the Western powers threatened a renewal of war—another war in the apparently self-perpetuating cycle of "wars in chain reaction," as a French writer (Raymond Aron) titled a book. The war had ended with the ghastly explosion of the atomic bomb over Hiroshima, wiping out an entire city; by 1954 far more destructive nuclear weapons carried by intercontinental missiles were available to guarantee that the seemingly inevitable next war would put a finish to much of the world. Pending this last apocalypse, the world was far from at peace, for there was war in Korea (1950–1953), in Indochina, in Palestine, and elsewhere.

Whoever controlled Europe, Europe and the West no longer held the same monopoly of world power, prestige, and influence as formerly. The world had shrunk and yet enlarged, as Weber noted: Smaller because of modern transportation and communications, it was filled with all kinds of peoples formerly almost beyond the fringes of Europe's consciousness. For the peoples of Asia and Africa, too, in addition to the powerful United States of America, had arrived on the scene. They had gained or were about to gain their independence, they were "out of control" and demanding a place in the sun, and though as yet not powerful states they could no longer be ignored. Loosely united in attitudes shaped by their former vassalage to the West, they were a "third force" in world politics, of vast significance. Suddenly Europe became aware that it was after all a fairly diminutive peninsula on the huge land mass of Eurasia, and that what happened in Iran or the Indies, or in the Congo and Algeria, was of some consequence. This was a revolution in geopolitical perspectives that announced a new epoch of world history, perhaps the first one since the fall of the ancient Oriental empires.

The other radically new perspective was a technological-scientific one, signaled by the explosion over Hiroshima. What the atomic age meant no one could foresee—whether the passing of the human race or its ascent to incomparably higher levels of material civilization. For the time being, it meant assuredly that military power rested overwhelmingly with those who held the capacity to make and deliver nuclear weapons, which included only the Americans and, soon, the Soviets. Apart from this confirmation of weakness and dependency, atomic energy drastically transformed basic thought processes about the material world, driving home to all some of the implications of the new physics heretofore appreciated by only a few, such as the disappearance of matter in a sea of waves and electrical energy, the different laws of motion inside the atom, and so forth. After Hiroshima, no one could regard these things as just interesting theories.

On the other hand, there were countervailing tendencies working against the picture of bleak despair. The terrible war had at least purged Europe of much: of nazism, anti-Semitism, and even, to a degree, of nationalism. The need to rehabilitate a culture drew people together. Survivors of the terrible experiences of the war, whether living under the nightly threat of terror and death from the skies, or in the hell of a Nazi concentration camp, or as fighters in the "underground," often testified to the strange kind of value in such experiences. Life was given more value by being precarious; simple objects acquired value. Such situations were at least a cure for empty complacency, a reminder of the tragic and serious nature of life, a precipitant of elemental human values. To come up against and face the absolute worst is a kind of purgative; this is the message that emerges from much of the postwar European writing.

It is clear that in many ways the shock of adversity was good for Europe; from the enormous evil of World War II much good was to come—an example, no doubt, of that law of compensation in human

Something of the post-1945 spirit seems reflected in the depiction of a mythical family solidarity by the great British sculptor, Henry Moore, in this "Family Group." (Henry Moore, *Family Group*, 1948–49, Bronze cast 1950, 59¼ x 46½", at base 45 x 29⅞". Collection, The Museum of Modern Art, New York, A. Conger Goodyear Fund.)

affairs which many thinkers have noticed—*ex malo bonum.* To take the case of France, its defeat and occupation by the Germans, bitterest humiliation in French history, provided a stimulus and an opportunity for economic modernization. The war visited physical destruction so that railroads and plants could be rebuilt and modernized, but it also shattered old political alignments, brought former enemies together, raised up new leaders, altered attitudes. A new unity and a new vision of France, "competing in growth, vigor, and material power with her neighbors," as Robert Paxton writes in his history of the Occupation, emerged from the trauma of the war. Karl Marx's remark that war is the midwife of revolution was exemplified in a veritable revolution of opinion leading to France's economic modernization and, in its social policy, a creative combination of free enterprise *with* "planification." For Germany, too, the war even more drastically was a challenge to rebuild on sounder foundations, wipe out the stain of Hitlerism, show the world that German culture was capable of creative democracy.

Standing together against the Soviet threat and then building a new Europe from the ashes, a Europe that might at last have learned to unify itself in a federation—these were goals that gave the common life some meaning. Europe began to make a spectacular economic recovery which swept on through much of the 1950s and brought to birth a unified European economy, the Common Market, that resulted from the Rome Treaty of 1957 and was expected to lead on by stages to full political federation. Hope returned with the development of the NATO alliance between North America and the states of Western Europe, and with the avoidance of major war. Though life as always was filled with problems, many Europeans saw the light breaking through in the second decade after the war, with prospects even of Europe again assuming its place in world affairs—no "passing of the European age," despite the power of Russia and of America, and the arrival of the non-European peoples. The change between 1945 and 1963 was summed up by Raymond Aron: "In 1945, western Europe was a mass of ruins; today it is one of the most prosperous regions of the world."

Just ahead lay worse times; the later 1960s brought student riots all over Europe, a new malaise, and the beginning of a sharply reduced rate of economic growth. The conservative '50s gave way to the radical '60s. It was by no means clear whether the rally of the postwar years, which had brought spectacular recovery from the ashes of destruction, was a momentary flicker of the flame before final extinction or an almost epochal surmounting of the long crisis that had begun in 1914, continued during the Great Depression, and climaxed with the horrors of World War II. One thing was certain: There was a crescendo of books, ideas, consciousness. Intellectually at least, it was with a bang and not a whimper that the world was ending, if it was ending. This explosion of thought accompanied an educational revolution, enlarging Europe's charmed circle of the higher literacy at least tenfold. It is a difficult task to take stock of the human condition today as reflected in philosophy, literature, and religious, social, and political ideas, for never were there so many. Trends become harder to establish; the river of history has perhaps ended "in a sea where all waters mingle confusedly together."[1] Nevertheless, a sharp general change can be noted between the 1950s and the 1960s.

THE END OF IDEOLOGY

Unquestionably the postwar climate of opinion was overshadowed by the sense of catastrophe and disaster, because of war, power, and the bomb. J. M. Cohen, in the concluding statements to his book *Poetry of This Age*, remarked that "events have dwarfed all possible comment" on public affairs and driven the poet to purely personal statement. "All that he can hope to rescue from an ever-imminent disaster will be a moment of love or insight or a clear conception of truth, which, having once been, can never be destroyed." It is possible to wonder whether this contingency of life is really so new. Every person's life is contingent every

---

[1]Roland N. Stromberg, *After Everything: Western Intellectual History since 1945* (New York, 1975), p. 105.

moment and always has been. Apart from that, earlier generations lived under the threat of starvation, disease, and other afflictions from which many moderns are by comparison almost free. In terms of the totality of human life, the modern world with its massive and longer-lived populations would be far ahead of any previous age even if it experienced a thermonuclear war. (The greatest world problem, today, according to many, is *over*population.) Nevertheless, the reminder of one's contingent being, one's constant confrontation with death, the possibility of centuries of progress being extinguished in a few moments (which might even be the result of an accident)—all this undoubtedly further undermined nineteenth-century beliefs in a secular utopia or the progress of humanity toward perfection. The "boundary situations" about which existentialists talk seem all too real in the world as it exists today.

Thus the turn to "personal statement," to an insight of the moment and away from the ideologies or total faiths. The retreat from ideologies was a prominent theme after World War II. The political activism characteristic of the 1930s fell to low ebb in the 1950s. "Outside the Communists," a French writer observed in 1952, "French youth is almost totally disinterested in politics today." The same could be said for British youth, German youth, Italian youth. Strong at the war's end in France, communism weakened badly during the Cold War years, when the behavior of Stalin destroyed it in Germany. There was a profound reaction against Soviet Russia under the Stalinist dictatorship, a regime which sent millions of people to prison and labor camps without fair trial, showed itself willing to employ every sort of iniquity in the crudest "means justified by the end" credo, and threw international relations into chaos, while also destroying creative Russian thought and literature by a straitjacket of political control. In the sight of Western intellectuals, who had once seen it through a veil of illusions, the last of these was torn from the ugly face of Soviet communism by the enslavement through military force of the peoples of eastern Europe. And many held that this moral bankruptcy was implicit in revolutionary Marxism, because of its deification of the historical process, its fanatical faith in a future utopia held to justify any amount of death and crime now.

To some extent, too, the "end of ideology" has been facilitated by the failure of ideology in the Soviet Union itself. In Stalin's era the high priests of the Communist party, charged with the zeal and dogmatism of the Marxist faith, made decisions. In the Khrushchev era (1953–1964) and afterward this power tended to gravitate towards bureaucracy, a process summed up by one authority as a "transition from charismatics to mathematics." In general, the element of breathless, apocalyptic exaltation in the Soviet Union, that was a legacy of the great Revolution and was perpetuated in the Party, tended steadily to wane as rationalization and normality took over. Not even the charisma of Lenin is safe from the corrosions of time and life. If Stalinization debased it, the post-Stalin era completely destroyed it; the New Jerusalem of Marx and Lenin became just another managerial and bureaucratic society.

For some, the moment of final disenchantment was 1948, when the suicide of Jan Masaryk marked the end of Czechoslovak independence; for others, it was 1956, when, even after the death of Stalin and the disclosure of some of the enormities committed during his reign by the new bolshevik leaders themselves, Russian tanks poured into Budapest to put down a Hungarian uprising against Soviet rule. The blood shed in the streets of Prague in 1968 was only a dismal postscript to the story of Soviet oppression in all the countries of eastern Europe, most especially in those countries for whose liberation from Nazi power the war had originally been fought—Poland and Czechoslovakia. Meanwhile in Russia itself those who had predicted a humanizing and liberalizing trend following the demise of the terrible Georgian were proved wrong by the subsequent treatment of critics of the Soviet regime. A brilliant and courageous group of young writers who claimed a right to do something else than parrot the official government line was imprisoned or sent to mental institutions. The story of the trial of Daniel and Sinyavsky and the proscribed writings of Solzhenitsyn and Pasternak, became known in the West. At the same time exhaustive research by Western scholars, exemplified in Robert Conquest's *The Great Terror,* stripped the last veils of illusion from the picture of a benevolent Soviet Union, revealing an inhumanity that surpassed even Hitler's. The fiftieth anniversary of the Revolution, in 1967, provided an opportunity for reappraisal, and it is significant that even those from the Left were overwhelmingly unfavorable. A bureaucratic society with a bourgeois culture and a reactionary foreign policy, not altogether converted from its nasty habit of killing off anyone who dissented in the slightest from a mindless orthodoxy—the Soviet Union was Orwell's nightmare of *1984* come true.

Influenced by Max Weber, social theory now strongly reiterated the point that a modern industrial society has essential features of bureaucratic, rationalized organization whether it is "socialist" or "capitalist." Whether the managers work for the state or a large corporation, whether the machine-tenders receive their paychecks from the government or the private company makes relatively little difference. Alienation is a function of the process, not the technicality of ownership. If anything, socialism is likely to be even more bureaucratic and alienating than capitalism, since the administrative units are larger. The European socialist tradition had based its indictment of the capitalist socioeconomic order on its alleged inefficiency; socialism promised more machines, more production, more and larger cities—all the things for which there was now a revulsion. Salvation, if any, would have to come from a different direction.

When in the 1960s a more radical political mood returned, it found world communism divided as never before; one might choose to follow the Chinese brand, more highly emotional and aggressively ideological, or the Cuban brand, none of them in agreement with the others. Communist parties in the West were released from rigidity and freer to develop in different directions. But this meant an end to the onetime god, now fragmented in a host of minor deities, and in fact the new leftists of the '60s were gloriously anarchic, quite undisciplined, wholly unlike the old Communists, though some of them might pay passing respects to Castro or Mao or Ho Chi Minh simply because they were enemies of the West. It was a highly existentialized, extremely unorthodox Marxism that inspired these younger rebels, grown up since the '30s and no longer knowing its idols.

Let that story be postponed for a moment. The '50s was by and large a conservative decade and even its despair was quiet. If Marxism was generally rejected, any other fervent sort of political mystique was equally suspect. There was little enthusiasm for democracy—two cheers for it, as E. M. Forster wrote, but not three; it is the worst of all forms of government except for all the others, as Winston Churchill had put it; one accepted it as the elimination of ideologies, not as an ideology. In France, the Fourth Republic set up immediately after the liberation of 1944 to 1945 was more democratic than the Third had been, but gave way in 1958 to the considerably less democratic (or at least less parliamentary) Fifth, headed by national leader Charles de Gaulle, hero of the war. The Gaullist state was in some ways progressive, for it aimed at modernizing France technologically. But it proposed to do this chiefly by a Saint-Simonian expertise of government administrators, bypassing the old game of party politics and operating beyond the old ideologies. De Gaulle hoped to restore a national community in a semifascist way, though without the harsh and tyrannical methods of the Nazis. The great writer André Malraux was foremost among the intellectuals who, in their disillusionment with the failed god, Stalin, found in the war hero an authentically great historic personality, offering a fresh vision of France and of Europe reborn to greatness. But in the end, despite impressive achievements in modernizing France, extricating it from imperialism, and restoring national morale, de Gaulle offered little that was new. He was himself rather characteristic of the low-key '50s in his disabused realism, his skeptical antiutopianism. "I am like Hemingway's Old Man of the Sea, I have brought back a skeleton," he sighed in the end.

Something similar happened in Britain in that the Labour party, elected to office in 1945 on a tide of socialist idealism, was voted out in 1951 in an atmosphere of considerable disenchantment with its policies. It tended thereafter to become much less ideological. The Conservative party held office from 1951 to 1964. In place of total solutions, political theorists suggested piecemeal solutions (Karl Popper). "Rationalism in politics" is a snare (M. Oakeshott); the art of politics is an adjustment of differences in pragmatic ways. After experiencing all those "cruel or fierce political ideologies [which] have played havoc with human welfare," wrote famed British historian L. B. Namier, the mature political community learns to do without them altogether. Namier gave his approval to the condition described with some degree of alarm by philosopher Stuart Hampshire: "There is a tired lull in English politics, and argument on general principles has largely died.... Both political parties are now in this sense conservative, tied to day-to-day expedients." While a modernized Conservative party accepted the welfare state, Keynesian economics, and the managed economy, the Labour leader of the '50s and early '60s, Hugh Gaitskell, asked his party to stop being dogmatically socialist and appeal to a wider public than the doctrinaires. Someone coined the word "Butskellism," joining the liberal Tory R. A. Butler to the moderate Socialist Gaitskell—there was not much difference between the parties, "consensus" was the word. The model of the successful economy, a mixture of free enterprise and government direction, was almost the same for a majority of both political parties. Labour theorist W. Arthur Lewis opted for a more vigorous kind of entrepreneurial capitalism.

Political writing took the form of close analysis of actual political behavior (such as voting), which often left few romantic illusions about the rationality and responsibility of "the people," or ordinary citizens. Analyses in any wider sense were apt to bypass ideology, too. Bertrand de Jouvenel, writing *On Power (Du Pouvoir)*, found the most significant aspect of political evolution to lie not in the forms of government, aristocratic or democratic, but in the steady growth of the apparatus of coercion, regardless of forms—the growth of power.

Similarly in economic thought, argument and analysis were likely to transcend the old issues between capitalism and socialism. For example the discussion of economic growth, carried on in such books as those of W. Arthur Lewis, Colin Clark *(The Conditions of Economic Progess)*, and W. W. Rostow, who subtitled his *Stages of Economic Growth* "a noncommunist manifesto," noted among other things that ownership of property is not as such a vital factor. Neither David Ricardo nor Karl Marx is very relevant to twentieth-century economic problems, whether they are those of the "affluent societies" of the Western democracies or the youthful near-primitive economics of new African and Asian nations trying to find a shortcut to affluence. Even in the Soviet Union, realism began to prevail over Marxist dogma. Economic reforms of the sort associated with Evsei Liberman in the USSR and Ota Sik in Czechoslovakia, brought forward as a remedy for a decidedly unsatisfactory economic performance under the rigidly centralized Stalinist system, asked for a greater role for individual enterprises in the planning process, and for profit incentives in a quasi-market economy. Khrushchev encouraged such new ideas, which the Chinese Communists called "a restoration of capitalism"! Those who talked about the "convergence" of the two systems, capitalism and socialism, thought that each would approach a middle ground from opposite directions—the mixed economy of public and private sectors together, the only workable one for a modern industrial society.

The study of power was an outstanding feature of postwar political and social thought. "We have all become intensely aware of power as the major phenomenon in all societies," Raymond Aron wrote. In addition to Jouvenel's brilliant book, the works of the Heidelberg sociologist A. Rüstow, writing in the shadow of Max Weber, may be instanced among the general theoretical studies. The theme comes through in any number of more specific studies of foreign policy and international relations.[2] George Orwell's *1984* gave expression to the frightening possibilities of power in the modern state to enslave its citizenry. This popular fantasy-satire described a condition in which the government disseminates all knowledge. Technology enables the state to control everything, even to read thoughts; "Big Brother" is everywhere. Thought control has become accomplished so thoroughly that people have ceased to think, they have been brainwashed into automatons by their government. This fear for liberty under the conditions of modern life ran counter to prewar progressivism in that the latter, whether Marxist or Keynesian, tended to be statist. The new political thought, whether of Left or Right, showed greater mistrust of the power of the state, whoever may be in charge of the state. It returned to Lord Acton's motto that all power tends to corrupt and absolute power corrupts absolutely.

"The mighty invasion of government into economic life," it has been often noted, constitutes "one of the most fundamental contrasts between the twentieth century and the nineteenth." The depression of the 1930s frightened people into accepting large measures of government regulation, a trend aided by the new economic theories of Keynes, while World War II brought total war and with it, of necessity, total organization under government control. It is obvious that modern industrial society is too complex and specialized to be run by the laissez-faire rules of the nineteenth century. Since 1945, a continuing vast military defense program and a "space" program of gigantic dimensions

---

[2]See also the studies of "power elites" within nations by such sociologists as Theodore Geiger and C. Wright Mills, or such historians as Sir Lewis Namier and his disciples (a very important school in England) or, in France, Jean Lhomme (*La grande bourgeoisie au pouvoir*); also political scientists who dwelt on "pluralism" and a competition of elites in a "polyarchical" order of power.

have meant an expanding role of government in most countries. This increasing statism, while ardently defended by a variety of collectivists, including neoliberals as well as socialists, aroused protests against it in the name of the sovereign individual, of spiritual autonomy, and of esthetic and moral values opposed to the reign of bureaucracy and the rule of the machine. Orwell's *1984* may be regarded as representative of such protests. (See also Huxley's *Brave New World Revisited.*)[3] And, indeed, students of "dystopias" such as Chad Walsh and Judith Shklar noted the appearance in recent times of a whole category of such literature, contrasting with the utopias of the nineteenth century. (One of the first, which influenced Orwell, came from a disillusioned Russian Communist as early as 1920—see Yevgeny Zamyatin's *We.*) Utopia has turned into nightmare.

THE POPULARITY OF EXISTENTIALISM

Utopianism, based on optimistic views of human nature, became most unfashionable. A quotation from the distinguished American theologian Reinhold Niebuhr may suffice: "No cumulation of contradictory evidence seems to disturb modern man's good opinion of himself. He considers himself the victim of corrupting institutions, which he is about to destroy or reconstruct, or of the confusion and ignorance which an adequate education is about to overcome. Yet he continues to regard himself as essentially harmless and virtuous." Against this Enlightenment outlook Niebuhr and other contemporaries reacted with ferocity. "It is necessary not to believe in human nature." Carried on by such internationally famous men as Paul Tillich and Rudolf Bultmann, the German neo-Protestant message that originated with Barth and Brunner continued to attract attention. Existentialists of all varieties told individuals that they are responsible for their own being, cannot put blame for their actions on society or anyone else, and cannot find salvation in social utopias.

Many in the modern world continue to fear more than anything else the eclipse of liberty and of the free personality under the exorbitant encroachment of statism and mass society. They may differ in their terms, or in the exact identification of the enemy: Is it the state, or the democratic mass-man, or machine technology, or all of these? But there is broad agreement about the nature of the problem. "Personality is losing all along the line against power," J. B. Priestley wrote in 1955 ("The

[3]In his acute book *The Liberal Mind* (1963), Kenneth Minogue pointed out that liberalism suffers from, among other things, the contradiction of wishing both to enlarge the individual's freedom by diminishing state action and to promote welfare by increasing state action. Basically individualist, the liberal seeks to harness the state to serve individual purposes, yet sanctions an evergrowing network of statist restrictions on personal liberty.

Gentle Anarchists"); the popular British author added that the younger generation "takes regimentation for granted," having become accustomed to the loss of liberties which everyone enjoyed until a few decades ago.

This deep concern about authentic individuals in an age that seems to conspire to destroy them has been a leading cause of the existentialist vogue, which continued strongly in the postwar years. The formidable Sartre, philosopher, Resistance fighter, and popular playwright and novelist, edited the most influential journal of ideas, *Les Temps Modernes*, and, flanked by Simone de Beauvoir, presided over a circle that included the glamorous Algerian, Albert Camus. Paris was still the leading center of world ideas. A popular existentialism emanated from its cafés. To a rather bewildered American newspaper observing it in 1947, it was something invented by a Nazi (Heidegger) and was, like nazism, a philosophy of "nihilism." But Sartre and Camus had fought the Nazis, and Sartre supported the Communists at least until 1956. And what of the others, like Gabriel Marcel and Paul Tillich, who were deeply religious? The Kierkegaard renaissance continued. There was also a Nietzsche renaissance: Previously viewed in England and America as somehow connected with German militarism and with nazism, the German poet-philosopher now appeared as a mighty prophet of the modern predicament and a perceptive diagnostician of humanity' s fate when all gods are dead. To realize fully that the world has no meaning; to know loneliness and dread; to reject conventional morality and religion; and then, "on the far side of despair," to affirm one's freedom to act and thus to create values—this existentialist recipe soon became known to every undergraduate.

The popularity of existentialism is to be explained less by the talents of its promulgators than by the appeal it made to post-1945 humanity. People hardly needed to be convinced of tragedy and absurdity in the world, not after Auschwitz and Hiroshima. They were disabused of ideals and wary of ideologies. They had seen the apocalypse happen, not once but twice—and life went on. There was nothing left to believe in—except, as the existentialists declared, life itself, in its concrete particulars. Nazi nihilism and Communist cynicism disgusted them, and they wanted to affirm the dignity and value of the human person. But the old religion was dead, for any thoroughly "modern" mind; nor did science and rational philosophy (analytical) offer anything more than the dry bread of skepticism. Belief in belief itself, the recipe of James and Sorel, entered somewhat into the existentialist recipe for nihilism; it added an imposing body of speculative thought about the individual consciousness, more up-to-date than Freud.

Writers of the hour, such as the attractive George Orwell, who was hardly philosophical enough to have embraced anything so pretentious as existentialist ontology, reflected its basic mood: Down with systems, down with generalities, stick to the individual existent person. Orwell told how a Belgian who had called for the death of all Germans saw one real German corpse and changed his whole outlook. The false imagination, as someone said, can hate whole races, nations, and classes; the true imagination cannot hate a real human being. Orwell used his touchstone of human values to reject and assail the Communist pattern of dogma, lies, and hatred, but he also maintained a stance somewhere on the Left as a searching critic of false values in a materialistic and dehumanizing capitalist society.

Though it had its bitter side, and Sartre might be accused of seeing humanity as a "useless passion" condemned to eternal frustration, existentialism was not a wholly gloomy philosophy. Faced with absurdity, we do at first feel dread and anxiety, but then we rise above them to create values by squarely facing our situation and responsibilities. We choose, act, and win through to authentic existence, thus endowing the universe with value. Existentialism is an optimistic and activist creed, leading us back to life and not leaving us in a Buddhist rejection of it. It is an expression of the defiant energy of the West in the teeth of all adversity. It is easy to accuse it of intellectual confusion or even charlatanry, but not of passivity. It is not its fault that "God is dead"; that was the fault of modern science and rationalism. It tells us what we may do about this cruel death.

Christian socialism or Christian democracy emerged temporarily after the war as a promising substitute for the older political ideologies. It had the advantage of being nondogmatic and dedicated to the spiritual individual. Under strong leadership (in Italy, De Gasperi was the leading statesmen of the postwar decade), Christian Democrats showed concern for the welfare of worker and peasant and emerged as the strongest political party in France, Italy, and Germany soon after the war. They tended, however, to dissipate from vagueness of doctrine. While political parties bearing their name might continue to exist, these lacked any very specific ideological content. This was natural, for the Christian position is not positively political and may be turned in any number of different directions. Under existential influence, Christianity in the postwar world undeniably carried on its post-1919 revival; but often it meant only the imperative of commitment and involvement, a personalism that cared deeply for the individual and the inner life but did not stand for any very clear dogmatic position.

Like Christianity, existentialism could be turned in almost any political direction; it only demanded sincerity, authenticity, integrity. In a letter to a German friend who had embraced nazism, Camus wrote:

> I continue to believe that this world has no higher meaning. But I know that something within it has meaning, and this is man, because he is the

only being who demands it. This world has at least the truth of man, and our job is to prove his cause even against destiny itself.

A fair statement of the existentialist case; but why, on these terms, should Camus object to his German friend choosing National Socialism? Camus went on in this letter to appeal to "justice." On existential terms, can there be any such abstraction? Justice must be what one affirms. Issuing a timely call for integrity and individuality, existentialism actually left the rest fearfully vague and could be accused of an anarchic irrationalism which makes the criteria of truth just one's own fantasies, thus dangerously undermining all critical and realistic social thought.

In the 1950s, a largely conservative decade, existential thought on the whole supported an apolitical, antiideological, personalist mood. In the 1960s it blended violently with radical political ideologies. Sartre always claimed that Marxism was the only possible philosophy for modern humanity, though his Marxism was of a highly unorthodox kind by Kremlin standards. A new wave of radicalism would arrive in the 1960s, featuring an existentialized neo-Marxism (it is treated further in this chapter). In the 1950s, despite some absorption of Marxist elements into an existentialist ethic with the approval of Sartre, the leftism of the 1930s was no more, arousing only occasional echoes among the immature and the provincial intellectuals. "Vegetating in the utopias of the last century" as a French writer (Jean Duvignaud) put it, seemed futile; "new dreams must be invented for a new world." Raymond Aron wrote of "the end of the socialist myth."

OTHER PHILOSOPHICAL SCHOOLS

In academic philosophical circles, existentialism's more respectable cousin, phenomenology, made steady gains, especially on the Continent. What Sartre called "a great emptiness, a wind blowing toward objects," the phenomenologists thought they might get at: raw consciousness, prior to all ideas or concepts. These attempts constitute a considerable chapter in the story of recent philosophy. Husserl's last major work, *The Crisis of European Sciences and Transcendental Phenomenology,* made it clear that he disapproved of Heidegger and of existentialist irrationalism; phenomenology must be "a rigorous science of philosophy," even if Husserl's science, like Freud's, was rather different from the "positivistic" kind most scientists recognized. Persecuted by the Nazis, the Jewish philosopher died in 1938, leaving behind a vast corpus of manuscript writings which rather miraculously were rescued from destruction and smuggled into Belgium (the Husserl archives are still in Louvain). As a "hermeneutical" inquiry into unique, concrete human meanings, phenomenology in practice blended with existentialism, with *chosisme,* with the poetry of private states of mind, in brief with the introspective, personalist humanism so characteristic of the 1950s. System-making in the older philosophic way has no place in phenomenology. Its practitioners are engaged in a kind of super-Kantian exercise in discovering the non-rational categories of the mind, and these turn out to be numerous, ambiguous, not reducible to any order. Phenomenology bears some relationship to the recent school in literature which describes itself as *chosiste,* or thing-ist: dedicated to the full exploration of objects *qua* objects, the thing for its own sake, not seen as a symbol of anything or as part of any logical scheme. One remains content, in both *chosisme* and phenomenology, with concrete existents, experienced and described as they are, just because they are.

Even those philosophers who belonged to the very different tradition of logical positivism, which was described as dominant in England and Scandinavia, tended toward some of the same conclusions the existentialists reached, even if they arrived by a different route. The formidable Ludwig Wittgenstein, it will be recalled, was thought to be the high priest of the positivist school. His earlier work was regarded as rationalist, scientific, and antimetaphysical. Yet even the earlier Wittgenstein had been fascinated by language and aware of the problems it presents. The later Wittgenstein (chiefly in the posthumously published *Philosophical Investigations,* 1953) concluded that language is a screen almost completely cutting us off from reality. The world of facts outside this screen cannot be known except as language permits it. The point would seem to be quite similar to Hume's, that other scientific rationalist who reasoned his way to the most irrationalist conclusions back in the age of the *philosophes.* The inferences from this skepticism were similar: One falls back on the language of everyday life, for one. Many of the Oxford philosophizers of the analytical school did just that. At any rate they continued to feel that philosophy has no great messages to deliver, being a method and not a creed—its job, to help clarify thoughts. Under the influence of Wittgenstein II it tended in the '50s to become ever more absorbed in linguistic word games. It drew back in horror from any suggestion that philosophers might construct systems, or assert truths, or discover values. Like the phenomenologists, the analysts took things as they found them, preferring concrete particular problems, tending to deflate all abstractions and generalizations. The modesty, or perhaps false modesty, of this school was reflected in J. L. Austin's characterization of his work as "something about one way of possibly doing one part of philosophy"! "Doing" philosophy, the fashionable way of putting it, connoted the limited goals—no finding or making of great truths—as well as the brisk professionalism of an academic exercise. To those who occasionally complained that philosophers were supposed to offer more help than this to beleaguered modern humanity, these Anglo-Saxon professors answered, in effect, "Sorry, old boy, not our job." In which, of course, they differed much from the existentialists, and there were the famous uncomprehending confrontations of the two groups at international congresses in the '50s. But this mistrust broke down somewhat, and books began to appear pointing out that analytical and phenomenological philosophy had after all some points of contact.

Professional philosophy as well as other disciplines, cut off from the larger public to be immersed in the specialized subculture, with incentives to be original, invent a new thesis, be clever, proliferated all sorts of combinations during the '60s and '70s in the burgeoning universities. A glorious but confusing eclecticism set in. There were phenomenological sociologists (Schütz, Gadamer), linguistic psychoanalysts, and so forth. Based on linguistics, structuralism arose as an important new tendency, which will be discussed later. Sociologists complained that more than half a dozen different schools—functionalists, structuralists, phenomenologists, behavioralists, Marxists, existentialists, Symbolic Interactionists—disputed the mastery of their terrain in complicated methodological quarrels that left students bewildered before they could begin. Much the same thing was true in psychology. A 1975 assessment of philosophy[4] found such diversity—from Zen Buddhists to Logical Positivists, from revolutionary activists to austere purists—as to defy the judgment that this is a single subject. This, perhaps, was one cause of the student uprising of the later 1960s: Learning, the enraged students complained, had become irrelevant to life.

The New Radicalism

While the 1950s were politically quiet, they were hardly complacent. As the Cold War between the rival power blocs of Russia and the West threatened to erupt at any moment, in a decade punctuated by international crises (Korean War, Berlin crises, Suez/Hungarian joint crisis in 1956, Cuban missile crisis in 1962), the development of the nuclear hydrogen bomb and intercontinental missiles kept humanity cringing under the threat of annihilation. Among the most widely read serious books of the decade were Orwell's *1984* nightmare of total war between totalitarian slave states and Neville Shute's picture of the horrors of atomic war, *On the Beach,* to which one might add William Golding's parable of boys reduced to savagery, *Lord of the Flies.* Such highly esteemed novelists as François Mauriac, Graham Greene, Angus Wilson, Evelyn Waugh presented a gloomy view of human nature derived from

[4]Charles J. Bontemps and S. Jack Odell, ed., *The Owl of Minerva: Philosophers on Philosophy* (New York, 1975).

traditional Christianity, as did the older T. S. Eliot, whose brilliant modernist delineation of *The Waste Land* now gave place to the Christian humility of *Four Quartets*. The decade was not revolutionary, since it had ceased to believe in Marx's romantic epic of history and had seen his disciples end by establishing a new tyranny. In literature, the decade had turned away from socialist realism, whose tracts seemed unutterably dreary.

Signs of discontent began to appear toward the end of the decade. Curiously, the discrediting and then the splitting up of world communism opened the way to a freer development of the Left. After 1956 some of the Communist parties, for example the British, cut loose from Moscow's moorings altogether and sailed off on their own toward some kind of neo-communism. The Italian Communist party moved far away from the rigid dogmatism of Stalin's day to become almost an open-minded party of the Left, willing to discard old shibboleths and seek fresh formulations. In Italy and France a "dialogue between Catholicism and Communism" began, receiving encouragement from new currents in the Catholic Church, expressed in Pope John XXIII's extraordinary 1963 encyclical "Pacem in Terris," which issued a call to liberal thought and social action in the Church. With the fragmentation of the world Communist movement, which began in the late '50s and carried on into the '60s, Chinese Maoist and Cuban Castroist versions of the revolutionary faith became live options for leftists; there was a good deal more charisma and mystique in these than in the old, tired Moscow version, which still hopefully presented its lives of Lenin but was now run by bureaucrats in gray flannel suits. New revolutionary heroes such as Che Guevara appeared. Or, if one preferred milder brew, some of the east European satellites of the Soviet Union produced revisionist Marxism which tried to soften the harsh Leninist variety by administering doses of Kantian ethics or other humanizing ingredients. In France a *Union de la Gauche Socialiste*, created in 1957, experimented in a more eclectic socialism drawing on Proudhon, Jaurès, and the Christian socialism of Lamennais and Sangnier. It dreamed of defanaticizing the Communists and undogmatizing Marx, in order to fit them into this "Popular Front." In brief, the demise of historic Soviet communism as a world revolutionary faith allowed fresh breezes to blow through the dried-up landscape of the Left and inaugurated a period of confusion but considerably greater vitality there.

Another cause of the new radicalism was a new generation, as usual rebelling against the attitudes of its parents. The 1950s were still dominated intellectually by the generation that had matured between the wars, had known Hitler and Stalin and the Red Decade, had experienced the gigantic trauma of World War II, and had ended disillusioned with all ideologies, unable to believe in any utopias. A younger generation, to whom these events were but faint memories, began to find a voice, at first hesitantly, in the later '50s. In Britain, John Osborne's play *Look Back in Anger* (1956) has come to seem a curiously significant landmark. Other writers and critics asked for more commitment and social relevance; a debate about this, initially between critic Kenneth Tynan and veteran dramatist Eugene Ionesco, enlivened the later '50s. Few mature writers in the '50s dared to say a word for social realism, which raised memories of the dreary propagandist tracts of the '30s; Ionesco, existentialist and personalist, was almost as famous as Samuel Beckett, whose *Waiting for Godot* was the classic existentialist stage statement of the forlorn human condition. The Angry Young Men now demanded action. It was not altogether clear what they were angry at—at Britain's declining power, at the "caste system" of a still somewhat snobbish society, or just angry, with the natural rebelliousness of youth. By comparison with the rock-throwing militants of a decade later they were quite mild, and many of them, like Kingsley Amis and John Braine, later became conservative. But their somewhat incoherent protests together with their demand for a less quietly resigned voice in literature marked a certain turning point.

With France somnolent under de Gaulle and communism in disarray, the British writers commanded the center of the world stage for a time.[5] Activism coalesced momentarily in a strong pacifist campaign, influenced among others by the nonagenarian philosopher Bertrand Russell (always a maverick), which culminated in the Campaign for Nuclear Disarmament along with attacks on American foreign policy and demands to take Great Britain out of the North Atlantic alliance. The decade of the '60s began with the first of many protest marches, organized by the C.N.D. in behalf of its demand for Britain unilaterally to abandon her nuclear weaponry. In the *New Left Review,* those impatient with the Labour party's caution and pragmatism tried to discover new roads to socialism. The "establishment" came under attack from satirists. The new spirit was mocking, irreverent, and impatient.

If a few years from such uncertain beginnings it reached a stage of near delirium in violent student uprisings, the causes lay as usual partly in the realm of ideas and partly in social circumstances. Among the latter must be included the revolution in higher education which sent far more students into institutions of higher learning, many of them new. In England, for example, the virtual monopoly of university education and of intellectual life by the two ancient universities, Oxford and Cambridge, with a place made for the University of London in certain subjects, had never been challenged and ensured the supremacy of a small

---

[5] But in West Germany, where the student rebellion was to begin early and with extreme bitterness, "angries" quickly arose in imitation of the British. Let us be sand rather than oil in the world's machinery, one of them said.

intellectual elite steeped in the classical literary traditions of Western civilization. Now a considerable number of new universities served tens of thousands who would formerly never have gone to college. In 1970 there were some 450,000 university students in Great Britain, with talk of another doubling in the next decade. A hundred years earlier, the most advanced country in the world in this respect, Germany, had but 14,000, with considerably fewer than this in Britain. The number of French university students increased from 60,000 just before the war to around 600,000 by the late 1960s, a tenfold growth mostly since 1950. This educational explosion occurred all over Europe.

The new universities were taught by a kind of intellectual middle class, less prestigious than Oxbridge but more receptive to nontraditional studies: Sociology flourished there in England, experiencing a remarkable boom in a land which heretofore had almost neglected it. The students were less subtle and perhaps less able but often intensely interested. The immense expansion in numbers of university students clearly bore some relationship to student radicalism; students might complain of the mass effect, feeling unrecognized and "processed" rather than educated. In many universities, a critical situation due to dreadful overcrowding obviously existed. There may also have been an overproduction of degree recipients in such fields as sociology, leading to frustration.

But other factors entered also. A widespread *malaise* among the young at the sheer dullness of contemporary life lay behind their restless, often aimless protests. A spirit something like that of 1914 might be detected; not that the young wanted this time to march off to war, for their protests were likely to be directed *against* war. But they craved excitement, demanded romance, and took to violence in their marches and protests. Their bitter complaints, directed vaguely against "the system," "the establishment," or other whopping abstractions, more often reproached the quality of life in a society ever more technological, ever more specialized, ever more organized. It was Max Weber's "iron cage" of "rationalization" that closed in on them; they echoed Ruskin's complaint about people being fragmented by the division of labor, while art and adventure and spontaneity disappeared from life. They looked for some Great Adventure. They faced a long list of exhausted options: no more wars, no more revolutions, no great crusades, no more great movements in the arts, no more undiscovered lands or exotic places. Whether destined for the factory or the office, they found the prospects of work unexciting.

Whatever one's preferences in a list of the causes of the "youth rebellion"—and many would wish to include the factor of affluence, of enough wealth to permit the spoiled children of yesterday's bourgeoisie to indulge all their fantasies of a world without work—it is obvious that ideas entered in. There were special intellectual currents abroad in this period that shaped the contours of radical thought.

An article in 1973 in the Soviet Union, whose Communist orthodoxy criticized the "New Left" radicalism of the students and was in turn rejected by them, named all the following as "revisionist" misleaders of youth: Scheler, Husserl, Unamuno, Heidegger, Jaspers, Camus, Garaudy, Adorno, Horkheimer, Marcuse, Fromm. The well-informed student will recognize here most prominently the existentialists along with members of the Frankfurt school (critical Marxists). Well might the essay have added Chairman Mao Tse-tung and the Chinese Communists, much more popular with youth than Moscow's old-fashioned Reds; the student attempts to take over the universities were indeed modeled after Mao's Great Cultural Revolution in China. It should have mentioned Jean-Paul Sartre, who had transferred his existentialist *engagement* to the cause of total, violent revolution. This intoxicating ferment of ideas stemmed from neo-Marxism, nourished on the discovery of the master's long unpublished early writings and on wholesale reinterpretations of his thought, freeing Marx from bondage to boring Kremlin "diamat"; from existentialist and Freudian amalgamations with Marxism; from Third World champions of revolt in Cuba, Vietnam, Algeria; from the Maoist model; and from other sources as well. The sexual revolution was well underway. (A much-discussed event of the year 1960 which may prove to be a landmark of cultural history was the British court case which adjudged D. H. Lawrence's *Lady Chatterley's Lover* not obscene. The decision opened the gates to a flood of pornography.) The word was "liberation." The black flag of anarchism was as much in evidence as the red one in student demonstrations; and the new Marxism talked less about economic exploitation than about the alienation of the individual in a false society. Herbert Marcuse, in fact, accused capitalism of producing not too little but too much, thus corrupting the working class. Affluence, more than poverty, was the target of criticism; even more so was bureaucracy, the whole industrial society, the technological society—shades of Max Weber, as well as Marx and Bakunin.

The necessary revolution against a culturally impoverished, "one-dimensional" capitalism cannot be led by the workers, the New Left gospel taught, for they have become a part of the system, seduced by bourgeois values. But Lenin's vanguard party has also proved to be a terrible delusion, leading only to bloody tyranny without cultural progress. The revolution must be the work of those completely outside the system, such as students, dropouts, and the guerrilla bands in the colonial world. Seizing university buildings in campus uprisings, the revolutionary students hoped to set off further revolts throughout the society, which is linked together indissolubly in a single system. Total negation, rejecting the society *in toto*, was seen as the key to drastic social change, after which all would live freely in sexual and esthetic fulfillment. Both Marcuse and the Sartre of *Critique of Dialectical Reason* seemed to reject any kind of group organization on a permanent basis; all "structures of authority" must be abolished, the self-motivating individual left free to find self-realization. This *mélange* of fantasy, utopia, and negation, as can be seen, contained echoes of almost every strain of European social thought from the past two centuries—not only Marx and Freud and Nietzsche and Weber but the early socialists, the anarchists, Trotskyists, existentialists. It all came to a glorious explosion in the period of campus revolt during 1967 and 1968, climaxed by the great Paris Spring of May 1968, when for a moment it looked as if the students would indeed bring down the established order.

VARIETIES OF MARXISM

Some moments of revolutionary ecstasy in the late 1960s, corresponding perhaps to Sartre's "group in fusion" which manages to achieve solidarity without alienation, proved ephemeral, ecstasy being a perishable commodity. A public reaction against student disruptions was not a greater cause of New Left failure than its own vagueness, utopianism, and incurable divisions. And of course for most of the students this adventure had to be a rite of passage; most of the would-be campus Lenins, the Dutschkes and Cohn-Bendits and Tarif Alis, either dropped back into obscurity or found new interests after leaving school. A rage for occultisms and new religions in the "counterculture" soon supplanted guerilla warfare in the classrooms as the next trend.

Well might some detect a profound sickness of modern culture in this frenzied "neophilia," or incessant quest for novelty. A succession of bizarre fads in the visual arts was a case in point; even the directors of the great art museums surrendered to these yearly competitions of eccentricity, as leadership of the art world passed from Paris to New York. The generation effect kept speeding up, in step with the intensity of social interactions in the modern city. Once the tides of taste changed every century, then every thirty years; today they change almost annually.

Student militants frequently claimed to be rejecting all "ideology," all programs and positions. The editor of a compilation of revolutionary materials from this era comments that the movement "owes more to Marinetti, Dada, Surrealism, Artaud, the Marx Brothers, than to Lenin or Mao." Belief in action for action's sake and a mistrust of all intellectualizing led to charges that the New Left was "left-wing fascism"—charges indignantly denied, needless to say. In fact, youth had been deeply if confusedly moved by ideas. The *Thoughts of Chairman Mao* were in every student pocket, Regis Debray's book about Che Guevara sold a million copies as did Frantz Fanon's *Wretched of the Earth,* a plea for revolutionary violence. At the height of the Paris student revolt in 1968, Jean-Paul Sartre addressed ten thousand students; an almost equal number showed up for debates about the Marxist dialectic between Sartre, Louis Althusser, Roger Garaudy.

From the furor of the '60s the most significant theme to select for brief comment was this revival and transformation of Karl Marx. The discovery of a large body of previously unpublished and largely unknown Marx-Engels writings as a factor in this process has been mentioned; also the effect of emancipation from Stalinism in freeing the Marxist mind for new interpretations. In the 1960s several older revisionisms received full recognition, as if their time had come. Long at work seeking to rescue Marx from the dogmatists, the Frankfurt School, which had migrated to New York in the 1930s where its scholars worked in (and with!) considerable obscurity, gained fame with the popularity in his later years of Herbert Marcuse, who died in 1979, an idol of the student revolutionaries. Also belatedly acclaimed were the works of Italian Communist theoretician Antonio Gramsci, written in prison in the 1920s but published only after the war; likewise George Lukacs, Hungarian literary critic and philosopher, who like his friend Bertolt Brecht had clung with leech-like adherence to the Communist party while attempting to save it from Stalinism. Paris professors, concerned that Marxism was "dying of boredom," tried to revivify it by injections of Freudianism, phenomenology, and other stimulants. Most significant of all, Sartre turned his existentialism more pointedly towards Marx, announcing that as the essential and unavoidable doctrine of our time, Marxism must be rescued from the dead hand of "official" Kremlin dogma. He proposed to "recapture man in the heart of Marxism" with the aid of his 1960 *Critique of Dialectical Reason*. While this work remained unfinished—a sign of true devotion to Marx, perhaps, who seldom finished his great works—Sartre aroused great interest in the humanizing of Marx, to which east European philosophers such as the Pole Kolakowski also contributed, and which led to the "socialism with a human face" ideology of the 1968 Czech movement.

Far from the simple sloganizer once dismissed by heavy thinkers or serious scholars, Marx as fully revealed was a profound and subtle thinker, his new interpreters claimed. Though Marx had turned away from Hegel, the trend now was to re-Hegelianize him (Lenin himself had begun this during the period from 1914 to 1916), which meant less economic determinism, less historical necessity. "Who sees in ideologies the mechanical, passive product of . . . economic processes," Lukacs declared, "understands absolutely nothing of their nature and growth, and holds not Marxism but a caricature of it." The Chinese Communists added their voice to the charge that Russian "dialectical materialism" had distorted Marx and led to an elite dictatorship. Lukacs, Gramsci, and the Frankfurt School all broadly agreed that the true Marx was no system-maker who created an objective science of history or society. *Das Kapital,* Gramsci said, is a bourgeois book! (Hannah Arendt, too, stressed the "bourgeois" character of Marx's economic determinism, denying the autonomy and dignity of politics which she saw as regrettably degraded in modern industrial society.) Like most interpretations, this one took what it liked from Marx, excluding the rest; it preferred the early Marx. It startled older Marxists in talking less of economic impoverishment than cultural oppression. Indeed, the neo-Marxists tended to admit what was obvious, that "capitalism" was all too successful in material terms; it had bought off the workers (evidently all too willing to be seduced) with automobiles and television sets, but at the cost of cultural values.

The new Marxists were almost all critical of Soviet society as well as Soviet Marxism, which they saw as linked. A monstrous state bureaucracy, suppressing dissent and dehumanizing labor, was clearly not what the founding fathers of communism had intended. Stalinism had debased Marxism into a crude mechanical determinism which led to an elite ruling stratum, in effect a new ruling class. The Soviet Union's alleged Marxism-Leninism was a sad misunderstanding of both Marx and Lenin. From Lenin, the Lenin of *State and Revolution,* one might salvage something—a decentralized society run by the workers, not the bureaucrats.

Drawing heavily on modern psychology or phenomenology and criticizing Soviet Marxism for having no knowledge of human nature— "total loss of the sense of what man is," Sartre put it—Western critical Marxism was typically subjectivist and at times almost irrationalist. Some of the Frankfurt School writings assailed "science" as a product of bourgeois culture. Lukacs's "reification" of consciousness, allegedly a product of capitalism, is a result of too much of what Max Weber had called "rationalization." Influence from Weber and Heidegger crept in, though Marxists found much to reject in these thinkers whom they accused of fascistic tendencies. Walter Benjamin, in a well-known Frankfurt essay, shuddered at mass production of art objects, as Adorno deplored jazz and Marcuse despised "one-dimensional" popular culture—a strain of cultural elitism in these thinkers, which allowed the Kremlin to brand them "bourgeois decadents." But Moscow, condemning rock music, long hair, drugs, and sexual freedom, was very much out of it among college youth in the '60s, while Marcuse, rejoicing in "bodies unsoiled by plastic cleanliness," had their ear for a while.

Some stressed the democratic side of Marx, who had seldom sanctioned revolutionary conspiracies after 1848. Gramsci declared that before the working class makes a revolution it must first conquer in the cultural domain. "Politics is only the means, the end is culture," Lukacs agreed. When, in the 1968 Prague Spring, Alexander Dubcek declared that "it is not possible for a small minority to introduce and maintain socialism"—a heresy which quickly earned him armed intervention from Moscow—he reflected the influence of the new breed of humanist Marxists. And the Soviet suppression of the Czech movement, which sundered a world Communist movement already shaken by the quarrel between China and the USSR, was a watershed beyond which most Marxist waters ran steadily away from the long admiration for Russia as the land of the first great proletarian revolution. The Communist parties of the West, above all in Italy but also in France and Spain, now began to repudiate violent revolution and dictatorship, to talk of appealing to groups other than the "proletariat" and of reaching power by democratic means. They were reevaluating their whole heritage in the light of conditions both in the Soviet Union and in the West. Euro-Communism was now mature enough to stand on its own feet, no longer needing to lean on Moscow, said the leader of the Spanish Communist party. If some disgruntled *gauchistes* accused the party of selling out to the bourgeoisie, other people took heart at the absorption of an alienated minority into the body politic.

These were permanent changes, and in the long run even Soviet Marxism would feel the impact of liberalizing influences. Courageous reformers within Russia such as the Medvedev brothers paid for their efforts with imprisonment or deportation, but the thaw which Khrushchev had begun in 1956 with his "secret speech" denouncing Stalin went on, if with what seemed glacial slowness. The world watched the saga of the great Soviet dissidents, from Pasternak to Solzhenitsyn, noting that the new Soviet establishment did not shoot them without trial, as Stalin would have done, but repressed much more hesitantly. Theorists of "modernization" thought that sooner or later, both being modern urban-industrial societies, the capitalist and Communist regions would "converge" toward a similar social order.

The student uprising foundered on its inconsistencies, contradictions, and divisions, most basically perhaps the contradiction of complete outsiders claiming to lead a democratic, "power to the people" movement while at the same time eschewing elitist dictatorship and claiming the right of a tiny minority to totally revolutionize society. (If the existing society is as corrupt as they claim it is, how can a better one come from it?) As for existentialized Marxism, the laws of neophilia condemned it to come under attack soon from a fresh generation. Louis Althusser led a movement back to Marxist objectivism and scientism, back to *Das Kapital* and away from Hegel, away from "humanism," even if not a return to Stalinism. Academic Marxist disputes became so involved that few except the experts could follow them; Althusser was pronounced incomprehensible. (British Marxist scholar David McLellan complained of Althusser's *Reading "Capital"* that "large parts of the book are virtually unintelligible.") Marxism had become an arcane science mastered only by professional philosophers or social theorists, with almost every point in interminable dispute—light years away from the simple faith of those earlier Marxists now scornfully dismissed as "vulgar." Revolutionaries took to acts of terrorism, mindlessly, while intellectuals frequently confessed to despair at their inability to contribute anything helpful to practical politics. Whether or not Marx had been "embourgeoisfied," he had certainly been mystified.

STRUCTURALISM

Althusser's Marxism received influences from a new school of thought, rising to prominence in the late '50s and early '60s to reach a peak in the later '60s; whether a passing fancy of the neophiliac age or a permanent contribution to the intellectual landscape of Europe, it might be too early to judge. As a fashion in French ideas it was the successor to existentialism. Structuralism as expressed by anthropologist Claude Levi-Strauss issued an explicit challenge to Sartre. Its mood was cool, detached, objective; it was antihistorical and specialized in mathematical analysis—a new Cartesianism, in some ways, opposing the rather frenetic subjectivism and romanticism of the existentialists. The roots of structuralism were in linguistics; Levi-Strauss applied it to anthropology (myths, kinship systems); it soon became a tool in literary criticism, sociology, psychology, Marxism; a mode of thought, or a method, that could be used almost anywhere and, as such, able to transcend narrow specialization and exert a general intellectual appeal.

Unquestionably the brilliant Levi-Strauss, of a French Jewish family, was the person who put structuralism on the map. It is true that he borrowed the idea from the linguistic scholar Roman Jakobson, who had migrated from Moscow via Prague to the United States, bringing with him the insights of Russian "formalism." And a younger scholar, Noam Chomsky, influenced by Jakobson, made something of a sensation in 1957 with his book *Syntactic Structures*. Chomsky found a "deep structure" underlying the surface forms of sentences, a structure expressible in mathematical symbols: Some kind of built-in human capacity to understand basic grammatical principles and convert these—generating or transforming them—into language as it exists. It was a kind of linguistic Kantianism. Wilhelm Dilthey, Max Weber's teacher, had called his work a "critique of historical reason." Sartre had written his *Critique of Dialectical Reason*. Chomsky might have titled his book the critique of linguistic reason. The transcendental *ir*rational had been the object of Husserl's quest. Immanuel Kant lived on in all these modern projects; but the structuralists did away with the subject. People, they declared, do not count; the structures which determine language and, by extension, all culture, are determinants which use individuals, as Hegel's "cunning of reason" had done. Hegel's agent had been the World Spirit, working through human history. Structuralism's was a hidden harmony of things, generating languages, patterns of culture, ideologies, and institutions.

Structuralism was a rationalism: One does not discover the hidden harmonies or patterns by amassing empirical studies but by means of abstractions, mental constructs. A homely analogy might be taken from the daily newspaper: It is its "layout" that the structuralist is interested in and which is found to be arranged in a grammatical manner, like a sentence. The content would be less interesting; Levi-Strauss affected to be uninterested in the content of the hundreds of North American myths which he classified, tabulated, and found to be logically related according to their components.

It is easy to read into structuralism the last stages of a"decadent" weariness. All ideas have been expressed, all novels written, it only remains to play games with their elements. Levi-Struass was a passionate advocate of the "cool" world of the primitive, to which he had turned (going to Brazil to find the last ones unspoiled by contact with "civilization"). Roland Barthes, French structuralist critic, found only "untiring repetition" in literature; the same components used over and over. An ultrasophistication was evident in the structuralist manner, which tended to be excruciatingly difficult; the complaint about Althusser's forbidding prose applied also to Barthes, Jacques Lacan (who applied structuralism to Freudianism, as Althusser applied it to Marxism), and other high priests of the new arcana. They were extremely alienated. Lacan was described as "Freud crossed with structural linguistics and strained through some of the most harrowing French since Mallarmé." Their most scandalous aspect, the ultimate shocker of the good bourgeois, was their antihumanism. Humanity has been abolished; it was an invention now seen through. History is a process without a subject, its formations imposed on people by a "hidden mechanism," just as language forces one to think in certain ways. The author is irrelevant to the study of a work. *Escape from the Self*—the title of a book said it all.

Whence come these hidden mechanisms, these deep structures that underlie and determine? This is a mystery one can never resolve. Structuralists joined the later Wittgenstein, and perhaps even Heidegger in his later years, in seeing people as ultimately prisoners of language, which one cannot get outside of, no more than the physicists can find an observation point outside nature. Structuralism was however a fascinating new way of looking at everything human and cultural, with which clever people could play complex games. But in some ways it offered a new principle of certainty. It was an answer to historical relativism, since it gives us "a science of the permanent," as Levi-Strauss claimed. Overriding the boundaries of the various academic disciplines or departments of knowledge, a fragmentation which threatens the intellectual disease of tunnel vision, structuralism provided a unifying perspective, tying together not only all the social sciences but all the human studies, including literature, art (*The Hidden Order of Art* was a notable structuralist title), popular culture. Perhaps the ultimate mathematical order, indeed, is the same for all of nature. This logic printed into the human mind—all human minds—may be akin to that which the mathematical mystics, from Pythagoras on down, have viewed as the key to the riddle of the universe. "The penetration of mathematics, mathematical methods, and above all the mathematical way of thinking, into areas which previously appeared to be closed to it," Johannes Weissinger marked as one of the most extraordinary of recent intellectual trends.[6]

A yearning for wholeness has run through much of twentieth-century thought, a response to the disunity so obviously existing in the complex realm of ideas. Carl Jung said that his long quest for the principles of the psyche was a search for the whole self amid the "fragmentation, confusion, and perplexity" of our age. Humanity, he believed, is one, having the same psyche underneath all the epiphenomena of culture. Jung's feeling closely resembles that of many of the more recent structuralists, and indeed he may be classed as a forerunner. In one of his last books, devoted to the phenomenon of *Flying Saucers,* Jung suggested that numbers may be the great mediator between the human world and a higher world. Perhaps it is. But unification at this level of abstraction may not offer much consolation.

A common tension or controversy in all the human studies was that stated in the title of a book of readings in Psychology: *Without/Within.* Psychologists were polarized between the mechanists—the behavioralists, studying conditioned reflexes and looking upon the human being as a lower animal, subject to social engineering, as B. F. Skinner thought—and on the other hand depth psychologists—existentializing psychologists, "humanistic" ones (following A. Maslow), who were indignant at such reductionism. The most emotional dispute among historians was between the "quantifiers," with their computerized methods and their pages of statistics, and those more traditional historians, who sought the concrete experiences in all their uniqueness. Sociologists were divided into several schools among which a line was evident between

---

[6] In Thomas L. Saaty and F. Joachim Weyl, ed., *The Spirit and the Uses of the Mathematical Sciences* (1969); the same idea is frequently expressed throughout this volume. Structuralist approaches also entered from the side of "organismic" biology, "gestalt" psychology, and other "holistic" methods, which stress the need to look at the whole system first, rather than at the parts.

For a debunking of some of these fashions see David Berlinski, *On Systems Analysis: An Essay concerning the Limitations of Some Mathematical Models in the Social, Political, and Biological Sciences* (Boston, 1976).

phenomenologists and "symbolic interactionists" on the one side and objectivist, behavioralist schools on the other. It seemed impossible to capture both the richness and inwardness of specific reality and the universality of lawlike generalizations. The generalizers produced statistical tables and "laws" so abstract, or tautological, as to be meaningless. The particularizers described endless numbers of actual cases but lost track of the larger meanings. Within Marxism, the two strains have fought from the beginning, down to Sartre versus Althusser, and were present in Marx himself.

In this perennial antinomy, which Kant had indicated in his unresolvable dualism of phenomenal and noumenal realms, the structuralists seemed to come down heavily on the objectivist side. Alienated from the excessively "hot" twentieth century with its chaos of individual egos, they would wipe out the subject and abolish consciousness. Yet their own principle of organization was an inward one: Structures derive from that logic printed in each mind, the world has meaning because we endow it with such. In this they would seem to agree at bottom with their foes, the existentialists.

THE FRAGMENTATION OF THOUGHT

Despite yearnings for wholeness, themselves an indication of its loss, the trend of Western thought was toward ever less unity, ever more fragmentation of knowledge. The old dream of the *totum scibile,* the sum of the knowable, which might be mastered by a single mind, was doubtless always an unobtainable ideal, but it had existed as a goal.[7] Now it had to be given up, along with the quest for some absolute system of values. One might endow chaos with the less opprobrious name of "pluralism" and gradually learn to live with it. "This situation does not bother me," a recent writer on the theater remarks, the situation being one where "there exists in the West no set of artistic, cultural or social standards so sacrosanct that they are not constantly under attack nor any standards readily at hand to replace them."[8] The "de-structuralizer," Jacques Derrida, who trumped the structuralists' ace, took joy in a Nietzschean caprice of things, otherwise known as God's plenty. One can perhaps, in the late stages of a civilization, enjoy such romps in the overgrown gardens of culture, but in the end it may portend the death of culture.

Among the leading dilemmas of modern humanity is the factor of sheer size. It is not less a factor in the realm of ideas than it is in social life

[7]For a note on this ideal as a nineteenth-century scholar felt it, see John Sparrow, *Mark Pattison and the Idea of a University* (1967). In his last, unfinished novel, *Bouvard et Pecuchet,* Flaubert records the efforts of two retired office workers to make an inventory of all human knowledge.

[8]John Elsom, *Erotic Theatre* (New York, 1973), p. 193.

generally; in fact, it is above all a problem here. Consider the quantity of writing. It has been estimated that more books have been published since 1945 than in the entire preceding 490 or so years since the birth of printing. A hundred thousand or so books are published each year in western Europe and the United States, not to count the thousands of periodicals. Scholarship and criticism have proliferated with the multiplication of university posts; a vast number of people have been brought somewhere near the region of serious thought and expression as mass higher education spreads. This region was, as recently as the earlier part of this century, inhabited by a small intellectual elite, numbered probably in the low thousands for western Europe. That number has now swelled to millions. Never were so many books read by so many. Encouraging, no doubt; and yet bringing with it, as the inevitable price of quantity, fragmentation, loss of unity, and intense specialization. "Literature today is fragmented. . . . Scholarship is fragmented too; so is life." Thus was the recent (1968) lament of a distinguished British scholar.

Specialization, with technical competence in a high degree but compensating losses in range, depth, and linkage with other fields, is found wherever one looks. It has infected philosophy itself, no longer monarch of the intellect but largely content to be a specialized branch of experimental science. Economics, also, has fallen victim to specialization, as has sociology, in that the grand classical syntheses have been abandoned in favor of microanalysis, the examination of particular situations rather than the whole of society. It would be impossible to find a branch of learning not afflicted with this sort of crisis. There is far more knowledge; it is far less meaningful because less integrated. This dilemma has also appeared in other disciplines formerly more humanistic. Much literary criticism in recent times has spurned the historical, biographical, or moral aspects for close verbal or structural analysis of the work of literature itself—a sort of literary linguistic analysis. The branches of creative literature themselves have shown a similar pattern. A distinguished contemporary English literary critic (Graham Hough) has spoken of the enormous gains in "technical competence, sheer skill in handling the tools" since 1935 or so—of the conquering, among other things, of a whole new realm, the unconscious—and yet accompanying this a "loss of authority," a loss also of range and substance, a tendency to deal with the "ripples on the surface" of life.

Widely noted in the 1960s was the crisis in the arts, with the apparent playing out of the "modernist" movement in a paroxysm of fads. While thousands of "little magazines" flourished, and public poetry readings testified to an urgently felt need, the net effect was aimlessness and sterility. The modernists—in the age of symbolists and expressionists, of Eliot, Yeats, Joyce, the surrealists, all that dazzling exhibition of virtuosity and audacity that lay between Rimbaud and Pound—

had played with the fire of extreme subtlety and subjectivity—statements personal, elliptical, complex, multileveled. They were often aware that after them, almost nothing else could be except chaos. In the words of Stephen Spender, himself a great modern poet, "to go further would lead to a new and completer fragmentation, utter obscurity, form (or rather formlessness) without end." Nietzsche had foreseen the "dissolution of art" once it had cut loose completely from the discipline of the classical rules and bounds. Rimbaud, Verlaine, the surrealists, and the dadaists did it once; but one cannot add to them, one can only repeat them in ever more violent and therefore feebler ways. Writing of the contemporary *avant-garde*, Ken Baynes remarks that "the artist's brave cry of freedom has turned into the shout of a buffoon."

In the more institutionalized areas of knowledge, technique has brought precision, has eliminated much untidiness, and cleared up errors, but it would seem to have entailed a loss of vitality and to have fragmented thought and culture into unrelated pieces. Historical writing today takes the form of well-researched, technically accomplished studies, making use of archival material—the sacred emblem of the historian's guild—but lacking the literary skill, the grand manner, the sweep of older historians. (To the archives have now been added the statistics analyzed by computers.) Complaints about the "Ph.D. pestilence" which requires or encourages useless and graceless pedantry in the humanities as well as the social sciences, could be heard more frequently perhaps because of the institutional necessity of writing theses and dissertations, under conditions of contemporary mass education.

If the arts offered less scope for Western humanity's spirit, the same could perhaps be said for science. A considerable chapter in the history of recent thought can be written around the theme indicated in C. P. Snow's widely read and discussed book of 1959, *The Two Cultures.* Sir Charles, a novelist of note as well as a public administrator with a keen interest in science, charged the entire literary-humanist camp with a disregard for and ignorance of science, as well as with a general irresponsibility toward all public affairs. There was a good deal of merit in his charge, though he overstated it. Since the dawn of modernism the novelist and poet had cultivated a domain of private sensibilities, scorning the area of "normal" life where dwelt such hopelessly philistine souls as politicians and businesspeople. (If they turned to politics, they hoped to revolutionize it completely and were quite unrealistic.) It was a function of their profound alienation from modern society. Science, needless to say, was one of the West's grand intellectual traditions, if not *the* grand tradition, and the realm of Galileo and Newton remained central through the Enlightenment and into the age of Darwin and Pasteur. Educated, enlightened people normally expected it to lead the march of progress toward a better, more decent life for all. Even if, like the socialists, they rejected the way modern industrial society is organized, they expected a better organization to release the beneficial effects of scientific technology. Marxism, and the example of the Soviet Union, helped promote the myth of science and technology as brave, clean, helpful servants when brought under human control and given proper direction.

Now the myth of science appeared to fade as it was increasingly identified with the kind of society intellectuals hated. The technological society looked uncivilized as well as polluted. Science meant technology. Its crowning achievement of the '60s was a trip to the moon, much heralded and looked toward; but when it happened the thrill did not last. The real frontiers for contemporary humanity lie within the human heart and must be crossed with the help of studies quite other than the rational science for which Western civilization had long been famous. Such was the burden of many a book and essay. There were complaints that an excess of products and wastes upsets the balance of nature and corrupts air and water. Here was an ambivalence: Science went on, technology went on, not only because there was no way of stopping them but because many of the things they created could not be rejected. Not even intellectuals appeared to want to do without the comforts offered by modern technology. Yet there was a serious questioning of the values of "more and more," of material goods for their own sake, questions Carlyle and Ruskin had raised long before but which now spread widely throughout society. As a basis for intellectual synthesis, natural science no longer sufficed; the disarray produced by the Einstein and Planck new scientific revolution continued. The new physics was more bizarre than any science fiction.

The urge to unify knowledge in the teeth of vast undigested quantities of it created a dilemma. In the east of Europe, the great Soviet State has conducted since 1917 an experiment in the monist or monolithic society built on a single ideology. There are advantages in having one faith but also disadvantages. It is tidier, but it involves suppression, and in the long run one cannot achieve unity except at a terrible price in tyranny. This is the medieval experience all over again. In the modern world, it must in any case fail, as is indicated by the trend in the USSR since the death of Stalin. Those who reproach Western civilization for its chaotic lack of unity are undoubtedly right in part, but they may be forgetting that for the last several hundred years civilization—modern European civilization—has been committed to pluralism and freedom. "Monolithic social ends," as Karl Popper writes, "would mean the death of freedom: of the freedom of thought, of the free search for truth, and with it, of the rationality and dignity of man." The case for European liberalism rests on the value of the "open society" as well as on the hatefulness of persecution for conscience's sake. It rests on the belief that only through the free inquiry of many minds working in many ways can we hope to find solutions to our manifold human problems, still so numerous as almost to stagger the mind. The retreat to an island of dogmatism enforced by the sword is a shallow, superficial, erroneous answer—really an abdication.

The divergence between Soviet and Western thought may be illustrated by some exchanges to be found in the *History of Mankind* published under the auspices of UNESCO (United Nations Educational Scientific and Cultural Organization). In the first volume, *Prehistory and the Beginnings of Civilization,* written by two British historians (1963), Soviet historians dissented frequently, the general grounds of their dissent being that the Western historians present history as "no more than a kaleidoscopic change of whimsical patterns with no inner consistency and no principle in their development" (page 508), and more particularly that they fail to put the facts in the Marxist framework of concepts and stages. (All societies must involve "exploitation" by a bad ruling class, all history must exhibit an evolution from slavery to feudalism to capitalism, and so forth) The reply of Sir Leonard Woolley to Professor I. M. Diakonoff and his Russian colleagues was of course that to represent history as the latter desire would be to misrepresent it, since the facts exposed by empirical investigation reveal no such neat agreement with the Marxist categories. The frequent exchanges between Diakonoff and Woolley recorded in the notes for each chapter leave the impression of a doctrinaire *a priori* approach on the Russian side which Western historians could only regard as naive, but which the Soviets obviously consider to be the only way of rendering history intelligible at all. (Purely factual matters were often in question, but clearly the bias or presuppositions of the historians helped decide what they thought the facts were.) And it must be admitted that the Soviet historians could have written a better organized, more lucid account than is contained in the more than eight hundred large pages of this volume, replete with suspended or uncertain judgments and revealing as it does the enormous complexity of ancient history. Their history would have been clearer; but it could not have passed critical scrutiny by the eyes of knowledgeable experts in the West.

The pluralism and sophistication of the Western intellect create difficulties, though they are a source of strength. It now finds it difficult to believe in anything; it tries, but it is too self-conscious, it knows that its faith will be a myth. Modern achievement in every field is marked by great technical mastery. But the specialist has taken over at the expense of a general culture; and amid a wealth of specialized techniques for unearthing scientific, factual knowledge, modern humanity has the greatest difficulties finding values. These are among the leading dilemmas of modern persons, who struggle to integrate all the intellectual subcultures into something like a single culture, and to find something our logic will let them believe in. Contemporary culture lacks unity and lacks faith; yet in some degree people want and seek these things.

The postwar years witnessed some valiant attempts at integration of knowledge. Arnold J. Toynbee's vast tapestry of universal history with its sweeping claim to unearth the laws governing the rise and fall of civilization was not favorably received by most professional historians. Yet the literate public eagerly bought and read it, indicating a thirst for "philosophical" history, not assuaged by most historical writing today. With vast erudition and an appropriately grave and classical style, Toynbee set forth on the somewhat romantic quest of finding in history the secret of the sickness of Western civilization. He offered a study in comparative civilizations, identifying twenty-one different civilizations in human history and seeking to show the common pattern of their inception, growth, decline, and disintegration—some, in his view, having perished completely. A meditative if sometimes platitudinous style, a deeply spiritual outlook, an awareness of an amazing range of ideas as well as historic facts, lent to Toynbee's leisurely *Study of History* (altogether in twelve volumes, the substance of it abridged by D. S. Somervell in two volumes) a great appeal. His conclusions were not regarded by most of his competent critics as having much validity. "Laws" turn out to be truisms; there is doubt about the neat isolating of civilizations as separate units; comparisons mean little when stripped of Toynbeean rhetoric. A landmark of these times, Toynbee's massive work testified to the global perspective and to the technical resources of the modern historian—the historian of no previous generation could have assembled so much knowledge from all over the world—and to the perennial interest in the great question, whither mankind? But it scarcely provided an answer.

Toynbee protested against too much narrow specialization but fell afoul of specialists. Most historians seem content to plough well their own narrow furrow, each building his own separate tunnel to the past, as one historian has recently put it (J. H. Hexter). This is the tendency in all branches of knowledge. Martin Heidegger wrote in 1929, in one of his searching criticisms of modern civilization, that "the scientific fields are far apart. Their subjects are treated in fundamentally different ways. Today this hodgepodge of disciplines is held together only by the technical organization of the universities and faculties and preserves what meaning it has only through the practical aims of the different branches."

Overspecialization is a particular danger because it may cut off that cross-fertilization of the disciplines that has so often proved stimulating in the past. Students of intellectual history are especially aware of those cases in which Darwin received vital stimulation and critical ideas from Malthus, Kant from Rousseau, Kepler from Pythagorean mysticism, and so forth. If the disciplines—or even worse, small sections within each discipline, as seems to be the case today—are cut off from each other and from a matrix of general ideas common to all, we have a formula for scientific desiccation. Our sciences as well as our general culture will dry up, humanity itself will shrivel, the human personality lose itself in a wilderness of jargon and pettiness. This is the fear, and it seems well-grounded. Gabriel Marcel (*The Philosophy of Existence,* Chapter 1) has pointed out that the individual in modern specialized society loses the human personality to become "an agglomeration of functions." This destruction of a sense of whole being seems to be what the existentialist psychotherapists (such as the German Binswanger) have in mind as the basic cause of neurosis and psychosis in the individual. Marxists talk of "alienation" meaning ideas as well as institutions which escape human control, take on a separate existence of their own, and lose their original purpose of meeting some real human need.

It may be noted that this complexity and specialization defeats the dreams of the individual's mental power and thus ends a long epoch in modern history. The realm of knowledge becomes far too vast for any one mind to grasp, even in the most general terms, and one gives up the quest, resigning oneself to being at the most a cog in some incomprehensible machine. People of the Renaissance, Enlightenment, and romantic era thought it possible to understand everything. In the sixteenth century, Walter Ralegh observed casually that he bought *every* book that was published! In the eighteenth, a Voltaire, a Hume, a Jefferson kept a-breast of just about all branches of knowledge, also without impeding their numerous other activities. The last of those who still sought omniscience were the great nineteenth-century synthesizers, Hegel, Marx, and Spencer, but their schemes broke down. Synthesis is beyond the grasp of anyone today, evidently. Such virtuosi of erudition as Toynbee and Teilhard reach toward it, but even these are far from achieving it. This dream must be abandoned; and if so, the failure would seem to entail a fundamental alteration in Western humanity's outlook: a defeat for in-dividualism, for rationalism in the older sense. The assault on what David Knowles calls "a single reasoned and intelligible explanation of the universe on the natural level, and a single analysis of man and his powers . . . valid for all men and final within its sphere" came under attack as early as the fourteenth century with the skepticism of Ockham and was further eroded in the Reformation. And yet, as Knowles adds, this skep-ticism "was never wholly victorious, and never finally accepted": Euro-pean humanity clung to its dramatic belief in an ultimate knowledge accessible to the enlightened mind. Doubtless both Hegelianism and Darwinism in their different ways undermined it; doubtless no one had ever really been omniscient; and yet the great Victorians did continue to believe in the unity of knowledge and the individual's ability to grasp in a general way this unity. If we are driven to complete fragmentation, we are at the end of rational individualism. Perhaps we are at the end of personality as well as philosophy—condemned to be interchangeable with computers or to be intellectual drones who heap up useless knowledge. (French structuralists announce the death of human nature.)

Another consequence of overspecialization, or at least a related cultural phenomenon, is the gulf between the average person and the expert or adept. There is no audience, no common ground. The complexity and diversity of thought, breeding a situation in which a few experts in any area communicate only with each other, leaves a vacuum in the popular mind which must be filled largely by rubbish. While the popular market for fiction and nonfiction alike is mostly satisfied by low-quality journalism, serious thought and advanced expression go on among isolated and esoteric minorities. Cultural distance between popular and advanced thought has always existed and perhaps always will; but there have been cultures wherein a general consensus or forum was closer to a possibility than in the vast democratic nations of today. This is sometimes blamed on their being vast, or their being democratic; but the true culprit, in the main, would seem to be the intellectual fragmentation that has been discussed.

THE SEARCH FOR VALUES

A major dilemma of modern humanity obviously is its need for life-giving values, which can evidently come only from some sort of religious faith (religious in the widest sense), while its heritage of skepticism prevents any such belief. This dilemma is substantially that expressed by a Shavian character who cried that "we have outgrown our religion, outgrown our political system, outgrown our strength of mind and character. The fatal word NOT has been miraculously inscribed in all our creeds."[9] "I've been looking for something to believe in," says Alan Squier in Robert Sherwood's *Petrified Forest* (1936). "I've been hoping to find something that's worth living for—and dying for." Modern poets, novelists, dramatists, philosophers, preachers have now and again found things worth living and dying for. They found it in the 1930s and 1940s in the struggle against nazism and after that possibly in the fight against communism. These were negative crusades—against something evil that had appeared, something itself the result of modern spiritual illness— and it is not clear that they provided the basis for a positive structure of value. Plainly many people believe in and struggle for such things as social justice, racial equality, honest government, the elimination of extreme poverty, national self-government for peoples who do not have it, and so forth. The questions remain, freedom for what? (Georges Ber-

[9] *Too True To Be Good*, 1934.

nanos, *La liberté pour quoi faire?*, 1953). A higher standard of life to what end? Can liberty, equality, and democracy really be ends in themselves, or are they not rather the means through which humanity can achieve some goals and values of life? If so, does not achievement of the former without the latter lead only to an ignoble materialism, an affluent society with vulgar tastes, the spiritual deserts of suburbia so often seen today in the United States?

In this dilemma there were signs of a yearning to return to traditional creeds. The great Italian writer and former Communist, Ignazio Silone, has declared that "the rediscovery of a Christian heritage in the revolution of our time remains the most important gain that has been made in these last years for the conscience of our generation" (1946). Both world wars quickened interest in religion. Silone joined the late W. H. Auden, the late T. S. Eliot, Graham Greene, the late François Mauriac, and many another distinguished elder representatives of the literary world in embracing a Christian creed, sometimes after having followed strange gods earlier.[10] Others have been led to such exotic shores of faith as India and Japan in their search for a tenable religion for modern humanity; still others explore the possibility of a higher religious synthesis between East and West. Jung directed attention to the universal symbols or archetypes underlying all religious experience. Zaehner, Kerenyi, Eliade, and others engaged in a massive exploration of the domain of comparative religions. Never has there been greater interest in historical and theological studies of the Christian past. Outstanding in the Christian world in recent times has been the ecumenical movement, the quest for unity. Breaching the walls between sects and churches erected in Reformation times (or earlier, in the case of the Greek-Roman schism) has made some progress and given rise to searching reexamination of church history and doctrine. The exciting pontificate of John XXIII in the Roman Catholic Church was epochal for its turn in this direction. Many exciting world conferences have made what seem promising gains for ecumenicalism.

Yet though there is keen interest in religion, there is little assurance of what religion it is one is to hold. If Christianity, it must evidently be radically "de-mythologized" or revised. Some of the dilemmas confronting a Christianity that wishes to adjust to the modern age have been illustrated by recent "secular theology" which in its earnest desire to get back in the swing of things has virtually bracketed out any Christian content. The position popularized in England by the Bishop of Woolwich (*Honest to God*) and elsewhere by all kinds of swinging, protestlead-

---

[10]For a rather startling example, see Malcolm Muggeridge, *Jesus Rediscovered* (1969). The Oxford and Cambridge scholar C. S. Lewis, one of the most brilliant men of his generation, had earlier found his way to "Mere Christianity."

ing, guitar-playing and folk-singing clergy prided itself on being liberated from anything specifically Christian in the way of formal creed or liturgy. Leaning on "situation ethics," the Church could bypass conventional Christian morality; it could even talk of atheist or religionless Christianity. Critics of the "Honest to Godders" wonder whether such sweeping concessions to secularism will not soon liquidate historic Christianity altogether. Laudable in their desire to make the church and its teaching "relevant" to contemporary humanity, these Christians find that they must abolish Christianity in order to do so.

A series of books titled *Religious Perspectives,* issued by a leading American publisher, dedicated to "dealing with basic spiritual concerns in the hope of defining a doctrine of man," illustrated some of the uncertainties. It distinguished religion from theology, defining the former as "the feelings and aspirations of men . . . a sense of the sacred and the transcendent." *"Religious Perspectives* is an effort launched by informed and learned world leaders to guide us toward the spiritual serenity which is nowhere found amidst the mechanical triumphs of the rocket century," a distinguished scientist and historian wrote in the prospectus. Humanity hopes, somehow, for "spiritual serenity" (which reminds us of the Stoic's quest during the period of the decline of the Roman Empire in ancient times) or for "feelings and aspirations." Granted the need and the sincerity of those who express it, one wonders if this vague yearning can possibly bear fruit in real religion.

Sixty years of atheist rule in the USSR had not destroyed the Russian churches, and the great Solzhenitsyn in his crusade against Stalinist society reaffirmed the Orthodox creed. In the West, a host of cults ranging from scientology and astrology to the Unification Church and other sometimes bizarre sects eloquently registered the need for faith. All sorts of mixtures of eastern and western religions, neo-superstitions and pseudo-scientisms were available, especially if one lived in California. Harvey Cox, trendy-religious holder of a chair of Theology at Harvard University, testified in his 1978 *Turning East* that "within twenty blocks of the intersection of Massachusetts Avenue and Boylston Street, forty or fifty different neo-Oriental religious movements thrive" in Boston. But such extravagances were not merely American; the mass, urban culture is rapidly becoming a global phenomenon, with high-rise apartment complexes, supermarkets, bowling alleys, sports "palaces" about the same whether the setting is Turin, Toulouse, Liverpool, or Milwaukee. In Paris, a computer named Astroflash on the Champs d'Elysée gave a horoscope, while one of the most popular magazines was *Planete.* In London as much as in San Francisco there were visionaries like John Michell who received messages from beyond the earth portending the end of an age and the beginning of another marked by a new "expansion of consciousness"—code words in the anticities where dropouts from the conventional society explored alternative life-styles. (A famous one appeared inside Copenhagen, staid Danish capital that emerged astonishingly as the porn capital of Europe for a time in the early 1970s.) Here evidently was the counterpart of that religious ferment which had marked the declining days of the ancient world. Apocalyptic themes appeared everywhere, and even children's literature, according to a German report, changed from the traditional happy optimism to preoccupation with "psychic catastrophes, violence, injustice, unmerited destruction" (*Stimmen der Zeit,* November, 1976). The children of affluent French, Swiss, German, Italian parents could be found along with Americans roaming the roads of India in search of salvation in Hinduism or hashish. Meanwhile in West Germany another report indicated that 10 to 12 percent of all people would at some time or another in their lives seek psychiatric help, while the widespread use of tranquilizing drugs by respectable Americans accompanied a flourishing trade in books offering advice about how to "cope," to handle stress, and so forth.

All this is familiar; anxieties are as obvious as liberations, the "expansion of consciousness" as evident as the troubles it brings along with its pleasures. An increasing number of people find that, paradoxically, the most affluent of societies is the least endurable. Quite often a chiliastic hatred of the great Babylon of the world, accompanied by ecstatic visions of a future perfect state, resembled nothing so much as early Christianity. And perhaps the children living in communes as hippies are engaged in bringing forth a second Jerusalem. Certainly many of them see visions and believe in signs and portents. They predict the end of the world and cultivate witchcraft. Such a strange variety of spiritual phenomena has not been seen since the age of the Reformation.

As has previously been suggested, there is (it is alleged) a degree of moral nihilism about the dominant mode of academic philosophy in the Anglo-Saxon world. If existentialism urges us to believe in something, no matter what, just so we believe, logical positivism tells us that no sort of moral belief has any rational defense and so one belief is as good as another—or perhaps none at all is best. C. E. M. Joad, in his book *A Critique of Logical Positivism* (1950), made the point eloquently. No community can survive, he pointed out, without a vigorous belief that some things are wrong (killing, cruelty, lying, faithlessness), yet our philosophers tell us these cannot be shown to be wrong but are merely subjective expressions of emotional preference. Nor can any civilization be vigorous unless its members are energized to action by their conviction that to do something is important, whether this be painting pictures, building steel mills, or raising food; yet contemporary philosophy declares all values unverifiable and thus implies that they are hardly worth holding. "Communism and Fascism," Joad added, "are the natural byproducts of skepticism and nihilism. Most men need a creed and there is nothing in the empirical world upon which a creed can be based." If this indictment of our philosophers is overdrawn, as doubtless it is, it yet contains some truth.

Philosophy such as that of the analytical school would seem to be in danger of suffering the same fate as that which overlook the medieval philosophers. "Thought divorced from life must always wither, and the philosopher of the fourteenth century withdrew more and more into his own world, in which definitions and conclusions were no longer controlled by all other kinds of human experiences.... Thought preyed upon itself, and suffered fragmentation." David Knowles's comment on these people might be applied with equal force to the contemporary academics. If so, it is suggestive of decadence and the end of an age, despite the subtlety of contemporary philosophical analysis. The late Middle Ages had their subtle doctors, too, but they were swept aside in the revolution of Renaissance and Reformation.

Desperately needing a religion, modern humanity cannot really believe in any. Perhaps the last major article of belief was a belief in History itself, the natural process of human evolution, as having a plan and a goal, to which one might look for guidance. But, as was noted, empirical investigation reveals no such clear pattern, and can only be affirmed by a blind act of faith. The moral bankruptcy of a naturalistic ethic, which tries to endow with absolute value what is supposed to happen next, has been revealed as much by the dogmatic Marxists as by the social Darwinists. People still look to history for a clue to what they should believe. Thus the very intelligent Frenchman, Bertrand de Jouvenel: "If we look at the history of Man since the Stone Age, we find that men have always been altering their processes; this, then, pertains to our species; as a believer I must conclude that we were meant to do so and therefore that it is good." It may seem a doubtful argument; is one to imitate all that "pertains to our species," including war, torture, greed, corruption, exploitation? Any set of values ranged against these all-too-human traits must in the last analysis come from outside humanity itself, outside the bald record of what it has done. Where to find such values?

Amid desperate attempts to affirm a faith gratuitously, there are those who insist that scientific truth must be the touchstone of any faith. British empiricism as represented by Lord Russell and others remained unconvinced of the merits of anything not founded on experimental verification and the critical reason. "As soon as it is held that any belief ... is important for some other reason than that it is true, a whole host of evils is ready to spring up," Russell remarked. And it is more than doubtful that he would regard the truths of Jung, of the existentialists, and of the crisis theologians as demonstrable. Julian Huxley, for his part, spoke at various times of "scientific humanism," "evolutionary humanism," and just "humanism." The term suffered from considerable vagueness, but Huxley was clear enough about (1) his dislike of Christianity and others of the classic "religions," such as Buddhism, and (2) his conviction that Western humanity desperately needs some sort of substitute for religion, some kind of integrating and orienting idea-system, rooted in science yet able to supply values. This feeling bears some relationship to the Russian-American social theorist P. A. Sorokin's call for an "integral" philosophy, to combine the best of all of his alleged sociocultural modes, the idealist, sensate, and ideational—in other words to get the best of the religious, philosophical, and scientific worlds. So Huxley's humanism comes to look very much like Comte's religion of humanity, as he abjures one in effect to worship human nature. In the view of existentialist and religious critics, Sir Julian's man-worship leads to those very totalitarian systems he most abhors, to nazism and communism, which are the fruits of godlessness and "titanism." But this vigorous scientist, who later became the first director of UNESCO, would say that only through the scientific reason can one find the way to sanity in an age of irrationality.

If religious need is, as C. E. M. Joad has written, "a product of man's consciousness of his loneliness and helplessness in an alien and indifferent universe," then this need has never been greater than it is today; for with all its technological apparatus modern humanity must realize as never before how frightening are the cosmic forces it confronts. Hopefully launching our rockets at the moon, we cannot but be aware, if we reflect, what strange and terrifying adventures may await us if we probe into the incalculable vastness of the universe with its other possible worlds. At home, we suffer from the paralyzing fear of a nuclear war that would cause the most ghastly suffering in our history, while we continue to be plagued by political conflicts suggesting that we have hardly advanced much in this area since Thucydides and Plato tried to fathom the causes and cure of war and civil strife. Moreover, all our economic affluence has not given us happiness.

"The spirit of man in the present age has been under a gray pall of uncertainty, insecurity, skepticism," a well-known British philosophical writer, Lord Samuel, remarked a few years ago. In the present age, it has also exhibited unconquerable vitality, defying a hostile universe to assert new values, in a truly Promethean gesture. But there remains a deep schism in the soul of the West which it is hard to see being altogether cured, so long as it retains the knowledge and subtlety of which skepticism is the natural fruit. This dilemma has haunted the most sensitive and creative minds of the twentieth century. *The Castle,* Franz Kafka's symbolic novel, depicted modern humanity frantically and unsuccessfully searching for those who will tell it what to do and to be. This feeling lies behind the desperate evocation of the primitive (back to the Etruscans or the blond beasts) which some of the most profound moderns have so strangely attempted. Fascism, nazism, and communism may be seen as equally desperate reactions against the cultural crisis of a civilization built on skepticism, on freedom to do—what?[11] And this dilemma may explain why intelligent non-Westerners have been puzzled by the West's apparent lack of faith in itself. (Dr. Malik, the Arab philosopher, remarked a few years ago that "the Western mind . . . has been softened and undermined from within and without. The effect of this softening has been for this mind to lose faith in itself. . . .")

Despite signs of revival and of a toughness that defies disaster, one must surely concede extensive evidence of decadence in contemporary Europe. The European world shows signs of having exhausted its usable traditions. Paradoxically, in the midst of so rich an inheritance it finds no gesture that gives satisfaction, but compulsively repeats stale ones that have lost their magic. Or it may decide simply that life is absurd, and celebrate its absurdity. The "theater of the absurd" and the novel of the absurd are prominent features on the recent literary scene. *Avant-garde* musical composers give up all attempts to shape a work of art and simply record "environmental sounds and noises" or permit each instrument of the orchestra to play what it wishes (John Cage). Painting and sculpture, in total disarray, are subject to outlandish fads which change virtually every month.

The more serious of recent attitudes toward thought and culture deplore any effort to render it meaningful as a whole. This trend was noted in the case of phenomenology in philosophy and *chosisme* in the novel: concentration on the immediate and particular, the object or momentary mental state as such, with total rejection in something like horror of any attempt to build a system, formulate a total ideology, or even extract any larger significance from the object or experience itself. In a book about Ezra Pound (1964), the notable British poet and critic Donald Davie reproached the poets of Pound's generation for taking the whole of history and culture as their subject matter. One settles for utter pluralism and lets it go at that. Perhaps we shall learn to do so and live happily in a world of immediate sensations. But without unity—or continuity—can culture long survive? Do we return to the primitive from which we sprang? If so, the whole process would no doubt begin all over again. With a Vichian roll of thunder, the historical cycle is renewed; "the world's great age begins anew."

A study of André Malraux by William Righter finds the clue to that

---

[11]Erich Fromm, *Escape From Freedom* (1941): Freedom, so long striven for, turned to ashes in the mouth of modern man and brought a terrible loneliness, from which he flees, because of the absence of values. Lewis Mumford, *A Faith for Living* (1949): "Fascism . . . reveals certain obdurate truths about life itself which never entered the doctrines of those who believed in automatic progress." Robert S. Lynd, *Knowledge for What?* (1939): The source of fascism is "in the human soul, not in economics."

extraordinary Frenchman in a restless search for a cause. In turn revolutionary, novelist, art critic, and politician, this modern Chateaubriand, child of Nietzsche, Spengler, and Pascal, with a sense of modern humanity's tragic predicament has tried to escape it by finding a worthy goal to pursue. Though he has tried many, it is not clear that Malraux ever settled on one, and so rather like baroque man he has simply been a man in movement. It would be possible, with Heraclitus and Montaigne, to rest content with an ephemeral and illusory world, seeing change itself as the only value. But European humanity obviously is not happy with such a solution; it must find some absolute. Yet it seems unable to do so.

THE NEXT STAGE?

Having pointed out some notable areas of tension afflicting common civilization today—between technology and humanism, reason and faith—and some signs of decadence, it would be wrong not to add that every civilization confronts similar conflicts, along with others, and that Western civilization possesses terrific resources of vitality with which to encounter them. It is not amiss to include a tribute to Europe and the West. Coming home from a trip to the Orient in which he investigated aspects of Indian and Japanese thought, Arthur Koestler in his interesting book *The Lotus and the Robot* said "I started my journey in a sackcloth and ashes and came back rather proud of being a European." Western civilization has revealed powers of renewal and regeneration many times before. Its history is a history of renaissances, of which *the* Renaissance, the postmedieval renewal based on rediscovery of the ancient classics, was only one. Battered by the terrific crisis of the Reformation, Europe came up with the scientific and intellectual renaissance of the seventeenth century, a renewal based on the creative use of older materials. Shaken by the French Revolution and its wars, Europe integrated this revolution into its traditional culture in the nineteenth century. Mass democracy, specialization, and industrial technology today present a challenge that Western civilization may be able to meet.

The somewhat tentative and inconclusive quality of this final chapter testifies principally to the historian's inevitable uncertainty in the present. Tomorrow is necessary to understand today. That is the very reason for writing history: With the passage of time, the past falls into perspective—into various perspectives, indeed—and events or ideas which then seemed chaotic reveal their meaning. The historian is at a loss to predict the future. "Historicisms" of the past which claimed that they had found the key to all history, past, present, and future, stand forever discredited; we can no longer believe in this particular brand of theology disguised as science. Evolution creates ever fresh forms which are outgrowths of the past but could not have been predicted; lucky guesses are possible, but systematic prediction and control are not. If one knew only the seed one could hardly foretell the plant. In history, too, we are in the position of not knowing what the final result, if there is any, will be. We can see where we have been, and from this suggest some possibilities for the future, but possibilities only. Of all people, indeed, the historian is probably most aware of diversity and contingency in humanity's affairs.

One guess which seems very nearly a certainty is that the West must and inevitably will make fruitful contacts with non-Western peoples, including not only the richly developed Oriental civilizations but also peoples much closer to the primitive than ourselves. Asia and Africa have entered into history, and the world has taken on new dimensions for European humanity. A typical comment is this one by Mircea Eliade: "Western culture will be in danger of a decline into a sterilizing provincialism if it despises or neglects the dialogue with the other cultures. . . . The West will have to know and to understand the existential situations and the cultural universe of the non-Western peoples. . . . Furthermore, this confrontation with 'the others' helps Western man better to understand himself." The last point is an illustration of the familiar fact that we as individuals or as social units commonly define ourselves, in good part, through our relation to others and to a larger organism consisting of ourselves and these others.

Professor Eliade, a leading student of comparative religions, adds that some recent developments in Western thought have prepared us for this task. Depth psychology, including Jung's interest in the world of myth as related to the dynamism of the psyche, is one; and in general that discovery of the unconscious irrational which came to Europe in the age of Nietzsche and Freud, and of the symbolists in art. *Myths, Dreams and Mysteries: The Encounter Between Contemporary Faiths and Archaic Realities* is the title of Eliade's book from which the above quotation came. Cultural anthropologists have been at work, ever since the later nineteenth century, probing the psychology of the contemporary primitive and suggesting theories of the role of myth and religion. A good deal of what Christian Europe and rationalist Europe formerly dismissed as simply superstitious nonsense now has become of deep interest, because it reveals the primordial workings of the human mind, and insofar as it probes the religious element, it can be of more than clinical interest.

This "dialogue between East and West," or between civilized and primitive, need not submerge Western civilization in a syncretic world culture, though it might. It could result in more sharply defining and discovering the West's own being, as effective dialogue can do. It might wake that old civilization up and save it from its weary skepticism. It can remove misunderstandings between civilizations thus helping to reduce conflicts and wars. There is a great deal of mixing and mingling going on today, as everyone knows. Americans assist in the founding of African universities; people from all over the world come to American, British, French, and Russian universities; thousands of scholars annually exploit the lavish subsidization of international intellectual exchange.

The outcome of all this is most problematical; but no one would deny that it must eventually entail some sort of a revolution in the mental outlook of all humankind. What sort, it is impossible to predict. Wyndham Lewis spoke of "cosmic man," denationalized and made into a common mold; he thought the Americans represented this process, having no particular national culture but being products of the modern machine age, and that the rest of the world would sooner or later be "Americanized." It is a fate many European intellectuals would regard as worse than death, yet there may be something in it. Their own lands are in fact being to a degree "Americanized" by the penetration of modern technology and its by-products (business methods, and so forth) and of cultural democracy. (One of the most widely read serious books of recent years in France was *The American Challenge*, by the brilliant politician-journalist Jacques Servan-Schreiber.) Neither machine technology nor democracy was invented by the Americans, they only arrived at their full fruition earliest in the United States. Television and the cinema are "cosmic" cultural forces, along with the business and industry of a world increasingly knit together commercially. The "international style" in architecture may be as depressing as most motion pictures made on the French Riviera by American producers using Italian actresses; it may be equally depressing to some to watch Tokyo change from a Japanese city to a kind of exotic imitation of New York. Fads for Zen or for African art may seem the shallow pretensions of pseudointellectuals. But all this happened once before in history, at the time of the Alexandrian and then Roman Empire. And perhaps out of this vast process of syncretization will emerge new civilizations, as Western Europe emerged from the decay of the ancient world.

Within Europe there were some signs of "convergence" between the Communist and Western capitalist, pluralist segments. The thaw in the Soviet Union of the Stalinist ice-block of dogmatism and isolation might seem agonizingly slow, but it went on steadily. Defiantly refusing to accept in principle any equation of the two "industrial societies," and continuing to insist that socialism leading to communism must replace and supplant "capitalism" as the highest and last historic form of society, the aging leaders of the USSR in fact watched the dissolution of their utopian dreams. Their society was neither more efficient nor more enlightened nor more moral than the West, if anything less so, and was becoming steadily more open, more modernized, less distinctive. Students of Soviet intellectual life noted the convergence as often as did those who looked at the economic system or the popular culture: The attempt to mark off a Marxist science and philosophy and literature which differed from and was superior to that of the corrupt and decadent capitalists failed at point after point and was quietly abandoned, except in public rhetoric. In both societies, a range of problems was similar. While even the western Communists gave up their belief in "Soviet civilization" and young radicals looked elsewhere for their inspiration if they looked anywhere, the only excitement coming out of Russia concerned the courageous dissidents, the Solzhenitsyns and Medvedevs and Sakharovs, who dared to denounce the cancer wards of an ugly repression and to point to the moral bankruptcy of an order that revealed the horrors of Stalin's tyranny but did not dare repudiate it. The collapse of communism as a viable alternative to capitalism spread over the world, until revolutions in non-European countries directed against Western influence denounced *both* Moscow and Washington, seeing them as much alike. The Age of Lenin died in 1968, with the flagrant armed intervention to prevent Czechoslovakia from adopting a democratic socialism—at the same time as the student revolutions in the West signaled the bankruptcy of *its* order.

At any rate this dialogue and this mixing go on and must surely hold one of the keys to the future. The process underscores the radical change that is taking place in the world of ideas. It looks very much as though this is a critical stage in humanity's long journey and that what comes next, perhaps in the next century, must decide the question of its future on earth. A series of crises threatening all civilization deeply involves intellectual history: The "legitimation" crisis in politics, the crisis of social authority and discipline, have their roots in skepticism or liberation, a questioning of all values, an inability any longer to accept what are now seen to be "myths." It should be noted that this nihilism affects not only the established institutions and values but also their revolutionary challenges. Revolutions are based on acceptance of positive values, on "myths": The French Revolution, and later the Russian, had their powerfully optimistic and affirmative beliefs. No one now can believe in these, for history has exposed their inadequacy. And so revolution degenerates into meaningless acts of terrorism or into the sad charade of Fascist-like retreat found in the Iranian revolution, which rejects Soviet communism as much as American capitalism. Death threatens all values.

EPILOGUE

Redemption from such nihilism, if it is possible, must inevitably lead back to the sources of intellectual traditions. Quite a few European historians and intellectuals in the past century have evoked the picture of the traditional European culture, rooted in the classics and carried by a literate elite, being borne under by a tide of mass-humanity which has increasingly thinned and degraded the great traditions. It is a familiar picture, and from Kierkegaard and Nietzsche to Jaspers and Ortega y Gasset it has inspired poignant lament. Its implication that what has ruined modern society is democracy repels the socialist left; and insofar as it blames the decline on machinery and industrialization, it is obviously a vain lament. But the concern to preserve culture—conceived of broadly as a power of serious, sustained thinking within a context of accepted knowledge—against the modern barbarism of mass media and on the other hand overspecialization must be the enduring mission of those whom Henry Mencken liked to call the "civilized minority"—the clerks, the intellectuals, the teachers, writers, and readers. On the one hand lie the comic book, the tabloid newspapers, advertising, paperback sex, the average television program, opening up horizons of mental degeneracy never before known, not even by the primitive who had more dignity and content in myths than this. These things represent a negation of all the high ideals of life in favor of a kind of least common denominator of the consciousness; they reflect the condition of people cut off from contact with any accepted and orderly body of expression and learning.

On the other hand is a vision of mountain ranges, reaching back through the centuries, of the poets, philosophers, and great thinkers, ultimately back in the far distance to Plato, Aristotle, and Homer; nearer lie high peaks called Shakespeare, Milton, Montaigne, Rousseau, and an incredible number of other hills. It has now become too formidable a terrain to be entered for most people; perhaps it always was. But it constitutes the West's spiritual home. Today the citizens of this mighty realm live in mud huts on the plain nearby, fearing to enter the magic land that was their home. They seem to have lost the map. This "schism in the soul," to borrow Toynbee's term, has developed in the last two or three centuries—certainly since Shakespeare's time, when high culture and low were not thus sundered. It is our task to put them back together.

By way of brief epilogue to a book already overly long, though far too short for its subject, it may be noted simply that ideas do live on. Madame Sevigné, celebrated seventeenth-century wit, once remarked that Cartesianism, like coffee, would prove a temporary fashion. She was wrong (doubly!). There have been temporary fashions often enough in the world of ideas, now largely forgotten; but even the most obscure left some stamp on the human race, and Madame Sevigné's ghastly error reminds us that some leave a very heavy impress indeed. They shape our civilization, it is not too much to say. At least they shape the way we conceive and describe it, which comes to very nearly the same thing. We can hardly escape them.

Taking stock of Western civilization after World War II, Georges

Bernanos opined that its future would have to be Cartesian or Hegelian (perhaps, as E. Morot-Sir has rejoined, it must manage to combine the two). Others, like Sartre, declare that we cannot escape coming to terms with Marxism, the "unsurpassable" ideological statement for our age. Still others would suggest that it is the Enlightenment, especially as summed up by Rousseau, that must be digested or thoroughly regurgitated, the central problem of our civilization.

Without pausing to examine or explain such statements, we can surely see roughly what they mean and in what sense they are valid. Ideas sum up epochs, generalize whole realms of individual human experience. "Cartesianism" is shorthand for the challenge of technological power and a scientific culture; Hegelianism for nationalism and secular messianism; Marxism for the problem of creativity in an industrial age. Ideas, the ones that survive, have their roots in social reality and express urgent human needs. They enable us to think about these needs and so to begin to meet them. As an aid to such thinking, they need to be studied with the utmost care, and by more people; for as John Locke said, "in truth the ideas and images in men's minds are the invisible powers that constantly govern them."

This is the realm of what Father Teilhard de Chardin has named the "noösphere," the realm of the mind and all its products. Here, as Julian Huxley has written, man finds "floating in this noösphere . . . for his taking, the daring speculations and aspiring ideals of men long dead, the organized knowledge of science, the hoary wisdom of the ancients, the creative imaginings of all the world's poets and artists"—all this and much more too. The organization of the noösphere, as both these great modern biologists suggest, is the great task of the future and one which has scarcely yet begun. Huxley has noted how much of the vast amount of knowledge presently being accumulated, in the various special branches of learning, is "lying around unused" because "not integrated into fruitful concepts and principles, not brought into relevance to human life and its problems" (*The Humanist Frame,* 1961).

If the most urgent task confronting us is the organization of our ideas that they may be creatively used, and if these ideas indeed are "the invisible powers that govern men," then the systematic study of ideas, in relation to life, that is, the social and historical context, would seem to be not the least important of the many studies currently pursued. A great deal of work remains to be done.

Suggested Reading

Chapter 1

On the ideas of the French Revolution:
William F. Church, (ed.), *Influence of the Enlightenment on the French Revolution* (1964); J. L. Talmon, *Origins of Totalitarian Democracy* (1960); Renée Waldinger, *Voltaire and Reform in the Light of the French Revolution* (1959); Jacques Godechot *La Pensée revolutionaire en France et en Europe 1780–1799* (1964) and *Le Contrerevolution 1789–1804* (1961); Paul H. Beik, *The French Revolution Seen from the Right* (1956). Elizabeth Eisenstein, *The First Professional Revolutionary: Buonarroti* (1959) brings out the Revolution's socialist Left, on which the classic study was probably Jean Javrè's old *Histoire socialiste de la revolution* (1901–1904). Paul Beik also has an essay on "The Meaning of the Revolution" in Charles K. Warner

(ed.), *From the Ancien Regime to the Popular Front* (1969), on which theme see also Richard Cobb, *Reactions to the French Revolution* (1972). Gita May, *Madame Roland and the Age of Revolution* (1970) concerns a prominent revolutionary intellectual. Joan McDonald, *Rousseau and the French Revolution* (1965) explains how the revolutionaries used but distorted Jean-Jacques; a similar type of study is Raymond O. Rockwood, "The Legend of Voltaire and the Cult of Revolution," in *Ideas in History*, edited by Richard Herr and Harold T. Parker (1965). Alfred Cobban has an essay on "The Enlightenment and the French Revolution" in Earl R. Wasserman, *Aspects of the Eighteenth Century*, (1965); see also his *Social Interpretation of the French Revolution* (1965). *The Letters of Joseph Priestley in England and America, 1789–1802,* edited by Frank Beckwith and W. H. Chaloner (1970) contains fascinating material from one of the representative radicals of the revolutionary era, many of whose writings are still in print. A. Owen Aldridge's *Man of Reason* (1959) is an engaging biography of Tom Paine. Carl B. Cone, *The English Jacobins* (1968) is outstanding in treating British reformers of the revolutionary era; Colin Bonwick's *English Radicals and the American Revolution* (1977) reveals the impact of that event on British radical thought. See also John W. Osborne's studies of *William Cobbett* (1966) and *John Cartwright* (1972), as well as Ian Christie's *Wilkes, Wyvill, and Reform* (1963). Burke's *Reflections on the Revolution in France* and Tom Paine's *Rights of Man* are often reprinted; see also A. Cobban (ed.), *The Debate on the French Revolution* (1949). R. R. Fennessy has written about *Burke, Paine, and the Rights of Man: A Difference of Political Opinion* (1963). The large literature on Burke includes biographies by Philip Magnus, *Edmund Burke: A Life* (1939) and Carl B. Cone, *Burke and the Nature of Politics* (2 vols., 1957–1963); Charles Parkin, *The Moral Basis of Burke's Political Thought* (1956); Francis Canavan, *The Political Reason of Edmund Burke* (1959); other studies by Peter Stanlis and Ross J. S. Hoffman. Hoffman with Paul Levack edited *Burke's Politics* (1949). A useful introduction to Burke's political thought is Gerald W. Chapman, *Edmund Burke: The Practical Imagination* (1967). See also B. T. Wilkins, *The Problem of Burke's Political Philosophy* (1967). Burke's *Correspondence* in nine volumes has been edited and published at the University of Chicago under the direction of Thomas W. Copeland and others. The periodical *Studies in Burke and His Time* is essential for Burke specialists.

Another interesting book is Bernard N. Schilling, *Conservative England and the Case against Voltaire 1789–1800* (1959). Christopher Herold, (ed.), *The Mind of Napoleon* (1955) reveals the revolutionary emperor's often fascinating thought processes; a study of considerable interest is F. C. Healey, *Rousseau et Napoleon* (1957). Herold has also authored an engaging biography of Mme. de Staël, *Mistress to an Age* (1958). The best life of Mary Wollstonecraft is by Claire Tomalin. See also the old H. N. Brailsford classic, *Shelley, Godwin and Their Circle* (1913, often reprinted); John P. Clark, *The Philosophical Anarchism of William Godwin* (1977). John F. C. Harrison, *The Second Coming: Popular Millennarianism, 1780–1820* (1979) is a contribution to the cultural history of this turbulent era.

Kant's philosophy may be approached through Volume VI of Frederick Copleston's *History of Philosophy* (1960); Volume VII (1963) is from Fichte to Nietzsche. *The Critique of Pure Reason, The Critique of Practical Reason, Religion within the Limits of Reason Alone,* and others of Kant's writings are available in paperback reprints. Arnulf Zweig has edited *The Essential Kant* (1971), and Hans Reiss *Kant's Political Writings* (1970). Lewis W. Beck, *Commentary on Kant's Critique of Practical Reason* (1960) and Norman Kemp Smith, *Kant's Critique of Pure Reason* (2nd ed., 1962) are expert guides. Richard Kroner, *Kant's Weltanschauung* (1956) sees the philosopher in a broader framework; Leonard Krieger, *The German Idea of Freedom* (1957) finds the political influence of Kant less liberal than usually indicated. A symposium, *The Heritage of Kant,* edited by G. T. Whitney and D. F. Bowers (1962), can be recommended for the philosophically sophisticated. Among the numerous other books about the greatest of philosophers, H. J. Paton, *The Categorical Imperative: A Study in Kant's Moral Philosophy* (1967); Georges Vlachos, *La Pensée politique de Kant* (1962), extremely lucid; and another symposium, Robert Paul Wolff (ed.), *Kant: A Collection of Critical Essays* (1968). Jonathan Bennett, *Kant's Analytic* (1967) is philosophically sophisticated. See also Karl Jaspers, *Kant* (1962); Donald W. Crawford, *Kant's Aesthetic Theory* (1974); Gordon S. Brittan, *Kant's Theory of Science* (1978); William A. Galston, *Kant and the Problem of History* (1975).

Among other German worthies of the grand epoch, Herder found an outstanding American student in Robert T. Clark, *Herder, His Life and Thought* (1955) as well as F. M. Barnard, *Herder's Social and Political Thought* (1965). Barnard also edited *Herder on Society and Political Culture* (1969). René Wellek, *Kant in England* (1931) and John H. Muirhead, *Coleridge as Philosopher* (1938) reveal the effect of the German philosophy on the English; see also C. F. Harrold, *Carlyle and German Thought 1819–1834* (1963). George Boas, *French Philosophy of the Romantic Period* (1925), and Philip P. Hallie, *Maine de Biran: Reformer of Empiricism 1766–1824* (1959) are helpful on French philosophy.

F. L. Lucas, in *The Decline and Fall of the Romantic Ideal* (1948) counted 11, 396 books about Romanticism and this was before the knowledge explosion of recent decades. So one can only hope to cite a few of the more helpful general works. Jacques Barzun in *Romanticism and the Modern Ego* (1944) (also published as *Classic, Romantic, and Modern*) provided a broadly cultural and historical introduction. Northrop Frye (ed.), *Romanticism Reconsidered* (1963) contains essays in definition and reevaluation, as does Harold Bloom (ed.), *Romanticism and Consciousness: Essays in Criticism* (1970) and John B. Halsted (ed.), *Romanticism: Definition, Explanation, and Evaluation* (1965). René Wellek has several illuminating essays on Romanticism in his *Confrontations* (1965). Lovejoy's celebrated essay was reprinted in his *Essays in the History of Ideas* (1948); compare his treatment in *The Great Chain of Being* (1936, 1960), pp. 228–314. Meyer H. Abrams, *The Mirror and the Lamp* (1953) is a classic literary study, as are Herbert Read, *The True Voice of Feeling: Studies in English Romantic Poetry* (1947), and Frank Kermode, *The Romantic Image* (1957). Further on the poets, Graham Hough, *The Romantic Poets* (1953) and Shiv K. Kumar (ed.), *The British Romantic Poets; Recent Revaluations* (1966); Maurice Bowra, *The Romantic Imagination* (1961). Among other general treatments, Hugh Honour, *Romanticism* (1979); Anthony Thorlby, *The Romantic Movement* (1966); H. G. Schenk, *The Mind of the European Romantics* (1966); Malcolm Elwin, *The First Romantics* (reprinted 1967); Morse Peckham, *Romanticism: The Culture of the Nineteenth Century* (1965); Northrop Frye, *A Study of English Romanticism* (1968); and Walter J. Bate, *From Classic to Romantic* (1946) are worth inclusion on any list for the general reader. Morris Bishop, (ed.), *A Romantic Storybook* (1971) is a delightful collection. Montague Summers, *The Gothic Quest: A History of the Gothic Novel* was reprinted in 1964. Cf. Robert Kiely, *The Romantic Novel In England* (1972), and G. P. Thompson (ed.), *The Gothic Imagination: Essays in Dark Romanticism* (1974). Other special aspects: John Herman Randall, Jr., "Romantic Reinterpretation of Religion" reprinted in his *The Career of Philosophy,* vol. 2, *From the Enlightenment to the Age of Darwin* (1965); Crane Brinton, *Political Thought of the English Romantics* (1926), cf. to H. S. Reiss (ed.), *Political Thought of the German Romantics 1793–1815* (1956) and Gerald McNiece, *Shelley and the Revolutionary Idea* (1969); Walter Friedlaender, *David to Delacroix* (1952), on Romantic painting; S. S. Prawer (ed.), *The Romantic Period in Germany* (1970); E. Allison Peers, *A History of the Romantic Movement in Spain* (1940); Robert T.

Denommé, *Nineteenth-Century French Romantic Poets* (1969). Howard Hugo (ed.), *The Portable Romantic Reader* (1957) and Geoffrey Grigson (ed.), *The Romantics* (1962) allow the Romantic writers to speak for themselves; likewise Max Dufner (ed.), *Romantics: Kleist, Novalis, Tieck, Schlegel* (1964). Studies of individual figures are far too numerous to mention; samples only: Owen Barfield, *What Coleridge Thought* (1972), Walter J. Bate, *Coleridge* (1968), Carl R. Woodring, *Politics in the Poetry of Coleridge* (1961), J. D. Boulger, *Coleridge as Religious Thinker* (1965), and John Colmer, *Coleridge, Critic of Society* (1959) all deal with aspects of the most philosophical of English romantic poets, whom Kathleen Coburn, editor of his *Collected Works,* presents in briefer form in *The Inquiring Spirit* (1951). E. D. Hirsch, Jr., *Wordsworth And Schelling* (1960) also deal with philosophical issues. Donald Davie in *The Heyday of Walter Scott* (1961) discusses the romanticism of collective ties and ancestral feeling, so different from Byronic *Menschenhass*. André Maurois was the popular biographer of *Chateaubriand* (1958) as well as of George Sand and Alexander Dumas; cf. Richard Switzer (ed.), *Chateaubriand Today* (1970); Richard Holmes, *Shelley* (1974); Philippe Bertault, *Balzac and the Human Comedy* (1963), books which along with many others try to make the great Romantics more human.

Chapter 2

Studies of Burke and Coleridge, already cited, are applicable to the conservative ideology; general surveys, somewhat useful, are Russell Kirk, *The Conservative Mind: Burke to Santayana* (1953) and Réne Rémond, *The Right Wing in France from 1815 to de Gaulle* (English tr. 1965), as well as a compilation edited by Hans Rogger and Eugen Weber, *The European Right* (1965) and J. S. McClelland (ed.), *The French Right from De Maistre to Maurras* (1970). Bertier de Sauvigny, *Metternich and His Times* (1962) and Henry A. Kissinger, *A World Restored: Metternich, Castlereagh, and the Problems of Peace 1812–22* (1957) are concerned with the leading practical conservative creeds of the era of reaction. E. L. Woodward, *Three Studies in European Conservatism* (repr. 1963) and Douglas Johnson, *Guizot* (1963) look at other conservative statesmen. Jack Lively has selected from *The Works of Joseph De Maistre* (1965), supplying a long introduction. John Morley's essay in his *Biographical Studies* (1923) remains useful on "The Champion of Social Reaction." See also R. A. Lebrun, *Throne and Altar: The Political and Religious Thought of Joseph De Maistre* (1965). The best French treatment is that of Robert Triomphe (1968). On German conservative thought, see Klaus Epstein, *The Genesis of German Conservatism 1770–1806* (1966). Additionally on Coleridge, David P. Calleo, *Coleridge and the Idea of the Modern State* (1966).

John Stuart Mill's essay *On Bentham and Coleridge* has been reprinted with an introduction by F. R. Leavis (1950). On the former Leslie Stephen, *The English Utilitarians* (repr. 1950) still may be the best, though E. Halévy, *The Growth of Philosophical Radicalism* (repr. 1955) is more prolix, and there is a major work on Bentham by Mary P. Mack, the first volume of which, *Jeremy Bentham: An Odyssey of Ideas* (1962) carries the founder of the Utilitarian school down to 1792. Miss Mack also made a convenient selection of his writings in *A Bentham Reader* (1969) while Bhiku Parekh (ed.), *Bentham's Political Thought* (1973) is equally useful. Bentham's entire *Collected Works* have been published appropriately enough by the University of London's Athlone Press. D. J. Manning, *The Mind of Jeremy Bentham* (1968) is brief but incisive. J. R. Dinwiddy, "Bentham's Transition to Political Radicalism, 1809–1810," *Journal of the History of Ideas,* vol. 36 (1975) is an important essay, along with several by Gertrude Himmelfarb one of which is printed in her *Victorian Minds* (1970). D. H. Hodgson, *Consequences of*

Utilitarianism (1967) examines utilitarian ethics critically. David P. Crook, *American Democracy in English Politics 1815–1850* (1965) interestingly reveals how far the example of the United States affected utilitarian thinking. Graham Wallas's classic biography of *Francis Place* (1919) affords insight into Radicals in action. (Mary Thale has edited *The Autobiography of Francis Place,* 1973.) William Thomas, *The Philosophical Radicals* (1979) studies a number of this only partly Benthamite group, between 1817 and 1841. John L. Clive, *Scotch Reviewers: The Edinburgh Review 1802–1815* (1957) also provides a picture of the Radical intelligentsia, and incidentally carries on the study of "the Scottish inquiry." William C. Havard, *Henry Sidgwick and Later Utilitarian Philosophy* (1959) carries on the story of the Benthamite tradition in thought, while an interesting sidelight is Eric T. Stokes, *The English Utilitarians and India* (1959).

Harold Silver, *The Concept of Popular Education: A Study of Ideas and Social Movements in the Early Nineteenth Century* (1965) makes a contribution to a significant subject. Warren J. Samuels, *The Classical Theory of Economic Policy* (1966) is a useful study; further on the Political Economists, in addition to standard histories of economic thought, see Marc Blaug, *Ricardian Economics* (1958); Kenneth Smith, *The Malthusian Controversy* (1951); Lionel Robbins, *Robert Torrens and the Evolution of Classical Economics* (1958); and, in view of its modern importance, John Maynard Keynes's essay on Malthus (among other economists) in *Essays in Biography* (1951). Also Marian Bowley, *Nassau Senior and Classical Economics* (1968); D. P. O'Brien, *The Classical Economists* (1975); A. W. Coats (ed.), *The Classical Economists and Economic Policy* (1971), one of a series on "Debates in Economic History." Thomas Sowell, *Classical Economics Reconsidered* (1974) is a brief defense of a much-maligned body; another defender is the distinguished modern British economist Lionel Robbins, in *Political Economy Past and Present* (1976). Cf. H. B. Acton, *The Morals of Markets* (1971). R. K. Webb, *Harriet Martineau: A Radical Victorian* (1960) scrutinized the celebrated bluestocking who popularized the ideas of the Political Economists. The best study of *The Manchester School of Liberalism* is by William D. Grampp (1960), the author also of a two-volume survey of *Economic Liberalism.* Donald Read, *Cobden and Bright* (1968) is a well-researched appraisal of the twin stars in the Manchester constellation. In his readable *Victorian People,* Asa Briggs includes portraits of Bright as well as Robert Lowe and the celebrated Samuel Smiles. There is also a scholarly biography of John Bright by Herman Ausubel (1965). The advanced student of economics might explore the acute contemporary criticism of utilitarian assumptions offered by I. M. D. Little in *A Critique of Welfare Economics* (1956). The rejoinder of one who then rejected "the dismal science" is presented in W. F. Kennedy, *Humanist versus Economist: The Economic Thought of Samuel Taylor Coleridge* (1958).

On liberalism generally, see L. T. Hobhouse, *Liberalism* (1934); Harry K. Girvetz, *From Wealth to Welfare: The Evolution of Liberalism* (1950); G. de Ruggiero, *History of European Liberalism* (English transl. 1959); and Harold J. Laski, *The Rise of Liberalism* (1936), a Marxist interpretation. George L. Cherry, *Early English Liberalism* (1962) is useful as background. For a later era, Robert L. Kelley, *The Transatlantic Persuasion: The Liberal-Democratic Mind in the Age of Gladstone* (1969). Walter M. Simon edited a collection of documents on *French Liberalism* (1972). A reasonably representative selection of classic writings was made by David Sidorsky in *The Liberal Tradition in European Thought* (1970). Charles E. Timberlake, *Essays on Russian Liberalism* (1972) shows us a different environment than the West. Jack Lively, *The Social and Political Thought of Alexis de Tocqueville* (1962) authoritatively considers the ideas of one of the great nineteenth-century liberals. Among others who have been keen students of

Tocqueville in recent times are Edward T. Gargan, Marvin Zetterbaum, Seymour Drescher, and Irving M. Zeitlin. The French liberal *Prévost-Paradol* (1955) has been treated by Pierre Guiral. Richard H. Thomas, *Liberalism, Nationalism, and the German Intellectuals 1822–1847* (1951) is more restricted than the title suggests but offers revealing insights into some German circles. A fuller exposition, which argues that liberalism was a western European ideology borrowed and adapted by the Germans, is James J. Sheehan, *German Liberalism in the Nineteenth Century* (1978).

Vol. 1 of Leszek Kolakowski's *Main Currents of Marxism* deals with *The Founders* (1978) and may be compared with G. D. H. Cole's multivolume *History of Socialist Thought* which also began with a volume on *The Forerunners* (1953). Another comprehensive history is Carl Landauer, *European Socialism* (2 vols., 1960). Cf. George Lichtheim, *Origins of Socialism* (1969). The first three volumes of M. Leroy's monumental *Histoire des idées sociales en France* (Volume III was published in 1954, covering the 1848–1871 period) are a mine of information. Frank E. Manuel, *The New World of Henri Saint-Simon* (1956) is by an outstanding American intellectual historian; G. G. Iggers, *The Cult of Authority: Political Philosophy of the Saint-Simonians* (1958) ranks high among other studies of the great socialist pioneer; see also Emile Durkheim, *Socialism and Saint-Simon* (1958). Manuel's entertaining *Prophets of Paris* (1962) includes sketches of Fourier and Comte as well as Saint-Simon. There is less in English on Fourier, but N. Riasonovsky's *The Teaching of Charles Fourier* (1969) helps. Several recent editions of his writings, including the paperback *Harmonian Man*, (ed.) Mark Poster (1971), testify to interest in Fourier. Other books on the early socialists are Leo A. Loubère, *Louis Blanc* (1961), the life of a participant in politics as well as a framer of social ideas, one of the great nineteenth-century democratic socialists; and Henri Lubac, *The Un-Marxian Socialist: Proudhon* (1948), a more thorough study than the summary by J. Hampden Jackson in *Marx, Proudhon, and European Socialism* (1957). Also on the French anarchist, Alan Ritter, *The Political Thought of P.-J. Proudhon* (1969) and Robert L. Hoffman, *Revolutionary Justice: The Social and Political Theory of P.-J. Proudhon* (1972). Alan B. Spitzer, *The Revolutionary Theories of Blanqui* (1957), and Peter Stearns, *Lamennais: Priest and Revolutionary* (1968) deal with other French revolutionaries of the pre-1848 period; likewise Christopher H. Johnson, *Utopian Communism in France: Cabet and the Icarians, 1839–1851* (1974).

Biographers of Robert Owen include Frank Podmore and G. D. H. Cole, also Owen himself, whose 1857 *Life of Robert Owen, Written by Himself* has been reprinted. Sidney Pollard and John Salt, ed., *Robert Owen* (1971) was a collection of scholarly essays commemorating the British socialist's 200th birthday. The best book about the Owenite movement as a whole is J. F. C. Harrison, *Quest for the New Moral World: Robert Owen and the Owenites in Britain and America* (1969). Owen disapproved of the Chartists, the other most written-about movement in British socialism and labor history for this period. Chartist periodicals such as *The Red Republican, Democratic Review, Poor Man's Guardian* have been reprinted. Good examples of scholarship on the Chartists are A. R. Schoyen, *The Chartist Challenge: Portrait of George Julian Harney* (1958), along with *The Harney Papers*, edited by Frank G. and Renée M. Black (1969); Asa Briggs (ed.), *Chartist Studies* (1959); Dorothy Thompson (ed.), *The Early Chartists* (1974); J. T. Ward, *Chartism* (1973).

On Hegel, see Copleston's seventh volume (1963); J. N. Findlay, *Hegel: A Re-examination* (1957), which may be compared with the hostile Karl Popper, *The Open Society and Its Enemies: Hegel and Marx*, Vol. II (4th ed., 1962); Herbert Marcuse, *Reason and Revolution: Hegel and the Rise of Social Theory* (1941); Walter

A. Kaufmann, *Hegel: A Reinterpretation* (1965). Shlomo Avineri, *Hegel's Theory of the Modern State* (1973). Hegel's own writings are readily available in selections such as *Reason in History*, or Carl J. Friedrich (ed.), *The Philosophy of Hegel. Hegel's Political Writings* have been edited by Z. A. Pelczynski (1962). The Hegel renaissance of recent years has added many fresh interpretations; see for example Jean Hyppolite, *Studies on Marx and Hegel* (1969); A. MacIntyre (ed.), *Hegel: A Collection of Critical Essays* (1972); George D. O'Brien, *Hegel on Reason and History* (1975); Judith Shklar, *Freedom and Independence*, on Hegel's political thought (1976); Burleigh T. Wilkins, *Hegel's Philosophy of History;* Charles Taylor, *Hegel and Modern Society* (1979). An interesting context is provided by Nicholas Lobkowicz, *Theory and Practice: History of a Concept from Aristotle to Marx* (1967).

Chapter 3

On the Victorian era generally, Walter E. Houghton, *The Victorian Frame of Mind* (1957) rounds up a good deal of the age's thought while G. M. Young, *Victorian England: Portrait of an Age* (1936) is a classic. *Victorian People and Ideas* by Richard D. Altick (1973) is another stimulating overview. *Victorian Prose*, edited by Kenneth Allott, is Volume V of *The Pelican Book of English Prose* (1956). Gordon Haight has edited *The Portable Victorian Reader* (1972), an unusually good selection of readings. The crowded and brilliant Victorian intellectual scene can only partially be reflected in the following outstanding books: Mario Praz, *The Hero in Eclipse* (1956), a study of the Victorian novelists; Owen Chadwick, *The Mind of the Oxford Movement* (1960) and Geoffrey Faber, *The Oxford Apostles* (1936); Benjamin Lippincott, *Victorian Critics of Democracy* (repr. 1964); John Holloway, *The Victorian Sage* (1953); R. Robson, ed., *Ideas and Institutions of Victorian England* (1967); W. L. Burn, *The Age of Equipoise*, rich in content with much about ideas (1964); Gertrude Himmelfarb, *Victorian Minds* (1968) including essays on Acton, Disraeli, Mill, Leslie Stephen. Chadwick also has two volumes on *The Victorian Church* of which the first (1966) covers the years 1829–1860, and among many studies of Victorian religious life, David M. Thompson (ed.), *Nonconformity in the Nineteenth Century* (1972), in the "Birth of Modern Britain" series, presents vivid extracts from the Dissenters. Trygve Tholfsen, *Working Class Radicalism in Mid-Victorian England* (1977) and John Butt and I. F. Clarke (ed.), *The Victorians and Social Protest* (1973) focus on radical thought. H. J. Dyos and M. Wolf (ed.), *The Victorian City* (2 vols., 1973) is a stunning compilation of essays and pictures filled with vivid realizations of the intellectual and cultural life of London, while in the same series as Thompson, B. I. Coleman has edited an interesting selection of writings on *The Idea of the City in Nineteenth Century Britain* (1973). Among numerous individual figures, *Walter Bagehot* (1959) has been edited by Norman St. John Stevas and described by Alastair Buchan, *The Spare Chancellor* (1960); his *The English Constitution* (1867) is available. Lionel Trilling, *Matthew Arnold* (1949) is perhaps the outstanding book on another eminent Victorian; a useful selection of Arnold's poetry and prose has been edited by John Bryson for the Reynard Library (Rupert Hart-Davis, 1954), which also has a Macaulay edited by G. M. Young. Among Arnold studies of interest are books by William A. Madden and Fred S. Walcott. Edward Alexander has written about both *Matthew Arnold, John Ruskin, and the Modern Temper* (1973). On Ruskin, James Clarke Sherburne, *John Ruskin, the Ambiguities of Abundance* (1972); Kristine O. Garrigan, *Ruskin on Architecture: His Thought and Influence* (1973). Other Ruskin anthologizing reflects the tremendous interest in this formerly underrated Victorian; there are volumes selected by Joan Evans, *The Lamp of Beauty* (1959), John D. Rosenberg, *The Genius of John Ruskin: Selections from His Writings* (1963), and Kenneth Clark, *Ruskin Today* (1964). Rosenberg has written one of the best biographies of Ruskin, *The Darkening Glass* (1961). G. M. Trevelyan, the famous historian, edited a one-volume *Thomas Carlyle* (1954). Among a spate of Dickens books commemorating the centenary of the death of the century's most popular novelist, Angus Wilson's *World of Dickens* (1970) deserves priority. On another great mid-Victorian, see Bernard J. Paris, *Experiment in Life: George Eliot's Quest for Values* (1965), is especially interesting; among other perceptive students of this most interesting of Victorian women are Barbara Hardy (*Middlemarch*) and Barbara Smalley who has compared Eliot with her great French contemporary Gustave Flaubert; Hazel T. Martin, *Petticoat Rebels* (1968) discusses the novels of Eliot and Elizabeth Gaskell as social protest. Gordon Haight is her leading biographer. Among countless other biographies of eminent Victorian thinkers, W. H. Dunn's *James Anthony Froude* (2 vols., 1961–1964), presents a noted historian while George Feaver, *From Status to Contract* is a biography of Sir Henry Maine (1969).

One may keep up with the voluminous literature on Victorians through *The Pelican Guide to English Literature,* vol. 6 (*Dickens to Hardy*) and via the periodical *Victorian Studies.* A useful bibliographical handbook, *Victorian England 1837–1901,* was compiled by Josef L. Altholz (1970).

John Stuart Mill best introduces himself in the famous and oft-reprinted *Autobiography,* but a superb modern biography is that by Michael St. John Packe, *Life of John Stuart Mill* (1954). A rather controversial interpretation is Maurice Cowling, *Mill and Liberalism* (1963). Valuable studies are R. K. P. Pankhurst, *The Saint-Simonians: Mill and Carlyle* (1957), Iris W. Mueller, *John Stuart Mill and French Thought* (1956), John M. Robson, *The Improvement of Mankind: The Social and Political Thought of J. S. Mill* (1968); Joseph Hamburger, *Intellectuals in Politics: John Stuart Mill and the Philosophical Radicals* (1966); Dennis F. Thompson, *John Stuart Mill and Representative Government* (1976); David G. Ritchie, *The Limits of State Interference: Essays on Spencer, Mill, Green* (1962). Edward Alexander has studied *Matthew Arnold and John Stuart Mill* (1965). Shirley Letwin, in *The Pursuit of Certainty* (1965) deals with Bentham and Mill along with David Hume and Beatrice Webb in a lineage of British rationalists. Of much value on Mill the economist is the Pedro Schwarz book, *The New Political Economy of John Stuart Mill* (1973). A good selection from Mill's political writings was made by editor Bernard Wishy under the title *Preface to Liberty* (1959), and another by Gertrude Himmelfarb, *Essays on Politics and Culture by John Stuart Mill* (1962). The complete works have been edited and published at the University of Toronto.

Mill himself wrote on *August Comte and Positivism,* an essay reprinted in 1961. D. G. Charlton, *Positivist Thought in France 1852–1870* (1959) dealt with the second generation positivists in the heyday of the creed; Walter M. Simon, *European Positivism in the Nineteenth Century* (1963), a major work of scholarship, ranges far and deep in the positivist vein. Frank Manuel's *Prophets of Paris,* previously cited, has a chapter on Comte. So does Volume I of Raymond Aron's useful survey, *Main Currents in Sociological Thought* (1965). Gertrud Lenzer edited Comte's *Essential Writings* (1975). Christopher Kent, *Brains and Numbers: Elitism, Comteanism and Democracy in Mid-Victorian England* (1978) is among the studies of British positivism. On Renan, see R. M. Chadburne, *Ernest Renan as Essayist* (1957) and H. W. Wardman, *Ernest Renan: A Critical Biography* (1964). The ideas of the statesman who ruled over this era in France may be read in Brison D. Gooch (ed.), *The Napoleonic Ideas* (1969). *Schopenhauer* is introduced by Patrick Gardiner in the Penguin series on philosophers (1963); his own writings are available in several editions, but perhaps the most readable are the *Essays,* translated by T. B. Saunders (Barnes & Noble, 1957).

Basil Willey, *More Nineteenth Century Studies: A Group of Honest Doubters* (1957) detects the influence of Comte but it was much overshadowed in England by that of Darwin. On the latter there is of course a large literature, including the very scholarly *Forerunners of Darwin* (1959), edited by Bentley Glass; Milton Millhauser, *Just before Darwin: Robert Chambers and His "Vestiges"* (1959); G. G. Gillispie, *Genesis and Geology* (1951); Loren Eiseley, *Darwin's Century* (1958); Gertrude Himmelfarb, *Darwin and the Darwinian Revolution* (1959), an attractive summary of the impact on ideas; John C. Greene, *The Death of Adam* (1961); David Hull, *Darwin and His Critics* (1973); and W. Irvine, *Apes, Angels, and Victorians* (1955). Essential as background is Arthur O. Lovejoy's classic *Great Chain of Being* (1936). Alvar Ellegard carefully studied the reception of Darwin's theory in the British press 1859–1872 in his *Darwin and the General Reader* (1958). Other scholarly works on the controversy are Peter J. Vorzimmer, *Charles Darwin, the Years of Controversy, 1859–1862* (1971); Cynthia E. Russett, *Darwin in America* (1976); Michael Ruse, *The Darwinian Revolution: Science Red in Tooth and Claw* (1979). Eiseley uncovers another claimant to Darwin's mantle (Edward Blyth) in *Darwin and the Mysterious Mr. X* (1979); cf. H. Lewis McKinney, *Wallace and Natural Selection* (1972). Special aspects are treated by Neal C. Gillespie in *Charles Darwin and the Problem of Creation* (1979), and Lorna Duffin, "Women and Evolution," in Duffin and Sara Delamont (ed.), *The Nineteenth Century Woman* (1978). (The male chauvinism of nineteenth century science is the theme of an article by Flavia Aloya, "Victorian Science and the 'Genius' of Women," *Journal of the History of Ideas*, April–June, 1977.) R. C. Stauffer has edited the original, much longer Darwin manuscript on "Natural Selection" (1975). In addition to other editions of *The Origin of Species*, of great interest is Darwin's *Autobiography* which must be read in the 1958 edition, edited by Nora Barlow, the first complete one published. (See article by Maurice Mandelbaum, "Darwin's Religious Views," *Journal of the History of Ideas*, June, 1958.) *Darwin*, edited by Philip Appleman (1970) brings together a large amount of material spanning the whole Darwinian debate. For the influence of Darwin, see J. Herman Randall, Jr., "The Impact of Darwin on Philosophy," *Journal of the History of Ideas* (October, 1961); Walter J. Ong (ed.), *Darwin's Vision and Christian Perspectives* (1960); Basil Willey, *Darwin and Butler* (1960); L. J. Henkin, *Darwinism and the English Novel 1860– 1910* (reprinted 1963); M. T. Ghiselin, *The Triumph of the Darwinian Method* (1969); John Dewey, *The Influence of Darwin on Philosophy* (1960) and *Reconstruction in Philosophy* (1937).

Cyril Bibby, *T. H. Huxley: Scientist, Humanist, Educator* (1959), deals sympathetically with "Darwin's bulldog." Talcott Parsons (ed.), *Spencer's Study of Sociology* (1961) may be used as an entrance to the thought of this Victorian oracle. There is an illuminating essay by Robert L. Caneiro introducing his editing of *The Evolution of Society: Selections from Herbert Spencer's Principles of Sociology* (1967), and another by Irving Goldman on "Evolution and Anthropology" in *Victorian Studies*, Sept., 1959, an issue devoted entirely to Darwinism; likewise an essay on "Varieties of Social Darwinism" in Himmelfarb's *Victorian Minds*, and James A. Rogers, "Darwinism and Social Darwinism," *Journal of the History of Ideas*, April–June, 1972. Robert C. Bannister, *Social Darwinism: Science and Myth in Anglo-American Thought* (1979) finds Darwinism not an important rationalizer of competitive capitalism. J. D. Y. Peel has edited *Herbert Spencer on Social Evolution* and has also written a study of *Herbert Spencer: Evolution of a Sociologist* (1971). See also J. W. Burrow, *Evolution and Society: A Study in Victorian Social Theory* (1966). Bernard Semmel's *Imperialism and Social Reform* (1960, 1968) deals with some versions of social Darwinism. See also Frank M. Turner, *Between Science and Religion: The Reaction to Scientific Naturalism in Late Victorian England*

(1974). Murray J. Leaf has written a history of anthropology, *Man, Mind, and Science* (1979).

Chapter 4

A convenient selection of the source writings is Robert Tucker (ed.), *The Marx-Engels Reader* (1972); Penguin/Vintage has an 8-volume edition of Marx's works while the complete Marx-Engels *Werke* are being translated and published in English by International and Lawrence & Wishart, the Communist publishers, to reach some 50 volumes. David McLellan, *Karl Marx, His Life and Thought* (1973) is the most thorough and up-to-date biography. From the enormous body of writing about Marx and Marxism, the following is a selection based on up-to-dateness, an important consideration in view of the many recent discoveries of Marx material, as well as perceptiveness and balanced judgment: H. B. Acton, *The Illusion of the Epoch* (1954); S. Avineri, *Social and Political Thought of Karl Marx* (1969); Z. A. Jordan, *The Evolution of Dialectical Materialism* (1967); L. Kolakowski, *Main Currents of Marxism* (3 vols., 1978); R. N. Hunt, *The Political Ideas of Marx and Engels*, vol. 1 (1974), a second volume to follow; Tucker, *Philosophy and Myth in Karl Marx* (1961) and *The Marxian Revolutionary Idea* (1969); Irving Fetscher, *Marx and Marxism* (1971). William H. Shaw, *Marx's Theory of History* (1978) and Melvin Rader, *Marx's Interpretation of History* (1979) are the most recent contributions to an old inquiry which includes M. M. Bober, *Karl Marx's Interpretation of History* (2nd ed., 1965), Karl Federn, *The Materialist Conception of History, A Critical Analysis* (1971), and Helmut Fleischer, *Marxism and History* (1973); a still older classic was Benedetto Croce's *Historical Materialism and the Economics of Karl Marx* (repr. 1966). The Economics may be approached via F. M. Gottheil, *Marx's Economic Predictions* (1966), Ernest Mandel, *Formation of Marx's Economic Thought* (1971), Joan Robbins, *An Essay on Marxian Economics* (1966), Andrew Gamble and Paul Walton, *From Alienation to Surplus Value* (1972), M. C. Howard and J. E. King, *The Economics of Marx* (1976). Further biographical material is supplied by Oscar J. Hammen, *The Red '48-ers* (1968); Henry Collins and C. Abramsky, *Karl Marx and the British Labour Movement* (1965); C. Tsuzuki, *Life of Eleanor Marx* (1967). A fascinating aspect of Marx is fully documented in S. Prawer's *Karl Marx and World Literature* (1976); cf. Raymond Williams, *Marxism and Literature* (1977). Robert S. Wistrich, *Revolutionary Jews, from Marx to Trotsky* (1976) explores interesting if controversial psychological connections. Lucio Colletti, *Marxism and Hegel* (1973) contests the recently popular stress on Marx's Hegelianism. On the "young Hegelian" colleagues of Marx, see D. McLellan, *The Young Hegelians and Karl Marx* (1969); Z. Rosen, *Bruno Bauer and Karl Marx* (1978); William J. Brazill, *The Young Hegelians* (1970); L. Stepelevich, "The Revival of Max Stirner," *Jour. Hist. Ideas,* April–June, 1974; Julius Carlebach, "The Problem of Moses Hess' Influence on the Young Marx," *Leo Baeck Institute Yearbook,* 1973; Sidney Hook, *From Hegel to Marx* (1950). The best biography of Engels is by W. O. Henderson; see also Norman Levine, *The Tragic Deception: Marx contra Engels* (1975). Some other miscellaneous facets of the many-sided philosopher and revolutionary may be explored in E. Kamenka, *Ethical Foundations of Marxism* (1962); Bertold Ollman, *Alienation in Marx's Conception of Man in Capitalist Society* (1971); S. Avineri, (ed.), *Marx's Socialism,* a collection of essays (1973); Henri Lefebvre, *The Sociology of Marx* (1968); George Lichtheim, *From Marx to Hegel* (1971); Julius Braunthal, *History of the International* (1967); Anthony Giddens, *Capitalism and Modern Social Theory* (1971).

While some later versions of Marxism are discussed in portions of the next chapter, we may conveniently mention here books on some disciples and followers of Marx: Peter Gay, *The Dilemma of Democratic Socialism: Bernstein's Challenge to Marx* (1952) and Bernstein's own reprinted *Evolutionary Socialism* present the most important revisionist among the German socialists. J. P. Nettl, *Rosa Luxemburg* (1966) is an admirable study of the most important left-wing German Marxist. G. D. H. Cole's two volumes on *The Second International* in his *History of Socialist Thought* (1956) are good. David Footman has written a life of Ferdinand Lassalle, Marx's early rival within German socialism under the title *Ferdinand Lassalle, Romantic Revolutionary* (1947). Several scholarly studies detail the story of the great German Social Democratic Party: R. P. Morgan, *The German Social Democrats 1864–1872* (1965); Vernon Lidtke, *The Outlawed Party*, covering the years 1878–1890 (1966); and Carl Schorske, *German Social Democracy 1905–1917* (1955). An able synthesis is Leslie Derfler, *Socialism since Marx* (1973). As introductions to the Russian school, Samuel H. Baron, *Plekhanov: The Father of Russian Marxism* (1963); L. H. Haimson, *The Russian Marxists and the Origins of Bolshevism* (1955); Jonathan Frankel (ed.), *V. Akimov on the Dilemmas of Russian Marxism, 1895–1903* (1969); A. G. Meyer, *Leninism* (1957); Adam Ulam, *Lenin and the Bolsheviks* (1965); Donald W. Treadgold, *Lenin and His Rivals 1889–1905* (1955). Richard Pipes, *Social Democracy and the St. Petersburg Labor Movement 1885–1897* (1963), by one of the numerous able scholars working in Russian history, sheds light on the backgrounds of Lenin's thought. See also L. Blit, *The Origins of Polish Socialism* (1971). Among the best books on the French socialists are Harvey Goldberg's fine life of *Jean Jaurès* (1962) and George Lichtheim, *Marxism in Modern France* (1966). Several articles in the *Journal of the History of Ideas* help clarify the issues: Charles F. Elliott, "Problems of Marxist Revisionism," January–March, 1967; Edmund E. Jacobitti, "Labriola, Croce, and Italian Marxism," April–June, 1975; S. Avineri, "Marx and the Intellectuals," April–June, 1967. A chapter by F. F. Ridley in his *French Syndicalism* (1970), "The Socialist Tower of Babel," sketches the wider field of radical social doctrines and movements.

On the anarchist rivals of Marx, to the older works by George Woodcock, *Anarchism* (1962) and James Joll, *The Anarchists* (1964) may be added Leonard I. Krimerman (ed.), *Patterns of Anarchy* (1966); *Kropotkin: Selected Writings on Anarchy and Revolution*, edited by Martin A. Miller (1970); *Bakunin on Anarchy*, edited by Paul Avrich (1972), Avrich being the author also of an excellent work on *The Russian Anarchists* (1967). April Carter, *The Political Theory of Anarchism* (1971), and Robert Hoffman, *Anarchism* (1970) are general studies while David Stafford has written a significant study of Paul Brousse called *From Anarchism to Reformism* (1971). The master historian of French anarchism was Jean Maitron, *Histoire du mouvement anarchiste en France 1880–1914* (1951). Temma Kaplan, *Anarchists of Andalusia* (1976) sheds light on the important Spanish school in the latter half of the nineteenth century.

On other than Marxian socialism, A. M. MacBriar, *Fabian Socialism and English Politics 1884–1914* (1962) may be supplemented by the lively Norman and Jeanne MacKenzie, *The Fabians* (1977) for coverage of the most interesting British group; also Willard Wolfe, *From Radicalism to Socialism: Foundation of Fabian Socialism 1881–1889* (1975).

S. Maccoby, *English Radicalism, 1886–1914* (1955) deals with left-wing liberals in the British Isles. T. H. Green found a biographer in Melvin Richter, under the title *The Politics of Conscience* (1963). Cf. A. J. M. Milne, *The Social Philosophy of English Idealism* (1962). Further on British socialism: A. B. Ulam, *Philosophical Foundations of British Socialism* (1964); C. Tsuzuki, *H. M. Hyndman and British Socialism* (1961); Stanley Pierson, *Marxism and the Origin of British Socialism* (1973); J. W. Hulse, *Revolutionists in London: A Study of Five Unorthodox*

Socialists (1970), including the great literary converts, William Morris and George Bernard Shaw. Charles A. Barker's excellent study of *Henry George* (1956) should be included in view of this American's extensive influence in Britain. An attractive biography of Beatrice Webb is that by Kitty Muggeridge and Ruth Adam (1967). Peter D'Arcy Jones, *The Christian Socialist Revival in England* (1968) recounts an end-of-the-century revival of a movement begun earlier by Charles Kingsley, F. D. Maurice, and J. M. Ludlow. In *The Responsible Society* (1966), S. T. Glass discusses guild socialism. Martin J. Wiener, *Between Two Worlds: The Political Thought of Graham Wallas* (1972) devotes attention to a British scholar and socialist. There have also been recent studies of G. D. H. Cole by L. P. Carpenter (1973), and R. H. Tawney by Ross Terrill (1973). A useful anthology is Frank Beasley, ed., *The Social and Political Thought of the British Labour Party* (1970).

Some books dealing with the celebrated Russian revolutionary movements: Eugene Lampert, *Studies in Rebellion* (1957), on the generation of Bakunin, Herzen, and Belinsky, and *Sons against Fathers: Studies in Russian Radicalism and Revolution* (1965) on the next generation; Martin Malia, *Alexander Herzen and the Birth of Russian Socialism* (1961); Philip Pomper, *The Russian Revolutionary Intelligentsia* (1970); A. Yarmolinsky (ed.), *Road to Revolution: A Century of Russian Radicalism* (1968). Pomper is author also of a work on *Peter Lavrov* (1973). A brilliant work of intellectual history, Franco Venturi's *Roots of Revolution* (1960) explores the Russian populist mentality, on which see also James H. Billington, *Mikhailovsky and Russian Populism* (1958), Ronald Hingley, *The Nihilists* (1967), and A. Walicki, *The Controversy over Capitalism* (1969). There are other good studies of individual Russian revolutionary leaders, such as Tkachev and Chernyshevsky, by Albert J. Weeks and William F. Woehrlin respectively. Recent additions to this fascinating topic include Abbott Gleason, *Young Russia: The Genesis of Russian Radicalism in the 1860s* (1979), and Adam Ulam, *Ideologies and Illusions: Revolutionary Thought from Herzen to Solzhenitsyn* (1976), also Vera Broido, *Apostles and Terrorists: Women and the Revolutionary Movement in the Russia of Alexander II.* (1977).

Additionally on Christian socialism, A. R. Vidler, *A Century of Social Catholicism 1820–1920* (1964); Josef L. Altholz, *The Liberal Catholic Movement in England 1848–1864* (1960); Lillian P. Wallace, *Leo XIII and the Rise of Socialism* (1966); Matthew H. Elbow, *French Corporative Theory 1789–1948: A Chapter in the History of Ideas* (1953).

To put Marx in the perspective of other nineteenth-century "historicisms," see Herbert Butterfield, *Man on His Past* (1955); Hayden White, *Metahistory: The Historical Imagination in Nineteenth-Century Europe* (1974); Georg Iggers, *The German Conception of History* (1968); on specific historians, Gertrude Himmelfarb, *Lord Acton* (1952); Theodore von Laue, *Ranke: The Formative Years* (1950); Edward K. Kaplan, *Michelet's Poetic Vision* (1977).

Chapter 5

Students of nineteenth-century nationalism include Hans Kohn, *The Idea of Nationalism* (1944), and *Pan-Slavism* (1953); Carlton J. H. Hayes, *The Historical Evolution of Modern Nationalism* (1931) and others including *Nationalism: A Religion* (1960); Elie Kedourie, *Nationalism* (1960); Eugene Kamenka, *Nationalism, the Nature and Evolution of an Idea* (1976); Leon Poliakov, *The Aryan Myth: A History of Racist and Nationalist Ideas in Europe* (1974). M. B. Petrovich, *The Emergence of Russian Pan-Slavism 1856–1870* (1956); Frank Fadner, *Seventy Years of Pan-Slavism in Russia* (1962); and N. Riasonovsky, *Russia and the West in the Teaching of the Slavophiles* (1952) are more detailed studies of Russian nationalist ideologies; see also biographies of the important reactionary nationalist *Pobedonostsvev* by Robert F. Byrnes (1968) and of the pan-Slav *Danilevsky* by Robert E. MacMaster (1967), and Leonard Schapiro, *Rationalism and Nationalism in Russian Nineteenth-Century Thought* (1967). Among the better books on French nationalism is Eugen Weber, *The Nationalist Revival in France 1905-1914* (1959). Weber has also written on the *Action Française* (1962) while Robert Byrnes in *Anti-Semitism in Modern France* (1950) presented the anti-Dreyfusards. Mildred Wertheimer (1924) and, in German, Alfred Kruck (1954) have examined the pan-German League (*Alldeutscher Verband*), leading agent of extreme German nationalism. Salo W. Baron's *Modern Nationalism and Religion* (1947) was a stimulating group of lectures by a notable contemporary scholar. The interesting *Diaries* (1958) of Theodore Herzl throw light on the mind of the founder of modern Jewish nationalism. See also Arthur Hertzberg (ed.), *The Zionist Idea* (1960).

On Nietzsche see Walter Kaufmann, *Nietzsche* (4th ed., 1974) a sympathetic study; F. C. Lea, *The Tragic Philosopher* (1957, reprinted 1973), evocative and penetrating; George A. Morgan, *What Nietzsche Means* (1943, reprinted 1975), one of the first to rescue Nietzsche from misunderstanding in the English-speaking world; Otto Manthey-Zorn, *Dionysus* (1956), a sensitive appreciation; R. J. Hollingdale, *Nietzsche: The Man and His Philosophy* (1965), a serviceable introduction. The older and somewhat hostile treatment by Crane Brinton has been reprinted. Two of the high priests of existentialism have written formidable works on Nietzsche: Karl Jaspers, *Nietzsche: An Introduction to the Understanding of His Philosophical Activity* (English tr. 1965) and Martin Heidegger, *Nietzsche* (1961, 1979). Kaufmann has edited the *Basic Writings* of Nietzsche (1968) and there is another good compilation by Geoffrey Clive, *The Philosophy of Nietzsche* (1965). The definitive edition of Nietzsche's works has only been undertaken in recent years (1967—) in the German publication edited by two Italian scholars, G. Colli and M. Montinari. Christopher Middleton has edited *Selected Letters of Friedrich Nietzsche* (1969). A spate of new interpretations have appeared lately. Arthur Danto, *Nietzsche as Philosopher* (1967) is a critical analysis; *Nietzsche: Collected Critical Essays* was edited by Robert C. Solomon (1973). Volumes of *Nietzsche-Studien* have been appearing annually since 1972. In *The Disinherited Mind: Essays in Modern German Thought and Literature* (revised ed., 1975), Erich Heller explores the Nietzschean spirit, as does Ralph Harper in *The Seventh Solitude* where Kierkegaard and Dostoyevsky are compared to Nietzsche. Another group of recent essays is contained in Malcolm Pasley (ed.), *Nietzsche: Imagery and Thought* (1978). One must leave out a considerable number of other books about Nietzsche in mentioning Joan Stambaugh, *Nietzsche's Thought of Eternal Return* (1973), John T. Wilcox, *Truth and Value in Nietzsche* (1974), and Tracy B. Strong, *Friedrich Nietzsche and the Politics of Transfiguration* (1976). J. P. Stern tried to provide a brief synthesis in the volume on Nietzsche in the Penguin Modern Masters series (1978). The tracing of the German seer's far-ranging influence is the theme of such books as William D. Williams, *Nietzsche and the French* (1952); Patrick Bridgwater, *Nietzsche in Anglosaxony* (1972), also Bridgwater's *Nietzsche and Kafka* (1974); and William J. McGrath, *Dionysian Art and Popular Politics in Austria* (1973) which discovers the influence of both Nietzsche and Wagner in the *fin de siècle* nationalists as well as socialists. Bernice G. Rosenthal's interesting study of the Russian, *Merezhkovsky* (1975), leads to Nietzscheanism in Russia. Christopher Palmer, *Delius* (1977) examines the great musical composer who was an avowed disciple, as was John Davidson (see James B. Townsend's biography, 1961) among many others. Lou Andreas-Salome has found biographers in Rudolph Binion and H. F. Peters.

362   *Suggested Reading*

A good general introduction to Freudianism is Richard Wollheim's volume on *Sigmund Freud* in the Modern Masters series (1971). Some of the background is covered by L. L. Whyte, *The Unconscious before Freud* (1960) and Harry F. Ellenberger, *The Discovery of the Unconscious* (1970); useful also is the article on "Schopenhauer and Freud" by R. K. Gupta in *J. H. I.*, Oct.–Dec., 1975. The classic biography was that of disciple Ernest Jones, *Life and Work of Sigmund Freud* (3 vols., 1953–1955; 1-vol. abridgment, 1956). Freud's writings are available in many editions. Reuben Fine's *A History of Psychoanalysis* (1979) is committed to the defense of Freud; another historical account is Walter A. Stewart, *Psychoanalysis: The First Ten Years, 1888–1898* (1967). Much revealing light may be found in the fascinating *Freud-Jung Letters*, published in 1974. Among the countless reactions to Freud some are gathered together in Benjamin Nelson (ed.), *Freud and the Twentieth Century* (1957); Jonathan Miller (ed.), *Freud* (1972); and John E. Gedo and George H. Pollock (ed.), *Freud: The Fusion of Science and Humanism* (1975). Other important commentaries include J. A. C. Brown, *Freud and the Post-Freudians* (1961); Frederick J. Hoffman, *Freudianism and the Literary Mind* (1957); Herbert Marcuse, *Eros and Civilization* (1966); Paul Ricoeur, *Freud and Philosophy* (1970); Paul Roazen, *Freud's Political and Social Thought* (1968). Criticism of Freud from various angles may be found in S. Fisher and R. P. Greenberg, *The Scientific Credibility of Freud's Theories and Therapies* (1977); Gerald N. Izenberg, *The Existentialist Critique of Freud* (1976); Juliet Mitchell, *Psychoanalysis and Feminism* (1975). T. S. Szasz, *Karl Kraus and the Soul Doctors* (1976) notes the Viennese satirist's hostility to the Freudian school. In *The Hidden Order of Art*, Anton Ehrenzweig (1967) provided a notable application of Freudian theories to art. N. Fodor, *Freud, Jung, and the Occult* (1971) explores another interesting byway.

The Portable Jung is a selection edited by the distinguished Jungian Joseph Campbell, author of *The Masks of God;* Anthony Storr presents the Swiss psychologist in the Modern Masters series, and other introductions are Frieda Fordham, *Introduction to Jung's Psychology* (1956); Joland Jacobi, *The Psychology of C. G. Jung* (1969); Edward C. Whitmont, *The Symbolic Quest: Basic Concepts of Analytical Psychology* (1969). See also Ira Progoff, *Jung's Psychology and Its Social Meaning* (1969); Charles B. Hanna, *The Face of the Deep: The Religious Ideas of Carl Jung* (1967), along with R. Hostie, *Religion and the Psychology of Jung* (1957); J. R. Singer, *Boundaries of the Soul: the Practice of Jung's Psychology* (1972). In *Man and His Symbols* (1964) Jung himself, with the aid of Jacobi, Aniela Jaffé, and others, presented one of the most attractive expositions of his ideas, richly illustrated. Paul J. Stern is the author of a recent intellectual biography of Jung, and among many other recent books touching on him, mention may be made of Miguell Serron, *Hermann Hesse and Carl Jung* (1966). Jacobi with R. F. C. Hull also edited a selection, *C. G. Jung: Psychological Reflections* (1970).

A recent able assessment of Henri *Bergson and His Influence* is by A. E. Pilkington (1976). Older but still serviceable works include Ian W. Alexander, *Bergson* (1957), one of the Bowes and Bowes series of *Studies in Modern Literature and Thought*, a concise introduction; Ben Ami Scharfstein, *The Roots of Bergson's Philosophy* (1943); Thomas Hanna (ed.), *The Bergsonian Heritage* (1962). S. K. Kumar, *Bergson and the Stream of Consciousness Novel* (1963) and P. A. Y. Gunter (ed.), *Bergson and the Evolution of Physics* (1967) trace influences from the philosopher; see also M. Capek, *Bergson and Modern Physics* (1971) and J. J. Gallagher, *Morality in Evolution: The Moral Philosophy of Henri Bergson* (1970). Gerhard Masur, *Prophets of Yesterday* (1961) ranged widely over European literature and philosophy in the age of Freud, Jung, and Bergson. Bergson's own writings such as *Matter and Memory, Time and Free Will, Creative Evolution, The Two Sources of Morality and Religion,* are readily available.

The impact of the new physics can be discerned through the writings of the chief innovators themselves, for example, Max Planck, *The New Science* (1959), Albert Einstein, *The Meaning of Relativity* (5th ed., 1955), and Werner Heisenberg, *Physics and Philosophy* (1959). Successful in making the new concepts comprehensible and significant to the public were James Jeans, *The New Background of Science* (1934), *Physics and Philosophy* (1942), and Arthur Eddington, *Space, Time, and Gravitation* (1920). A more recent scholarly treatment is by the prolific science writer, George Gamow, *Thirty Years That Shook Physics,* a study of the quantum theory (1966). Lincoln Barnett, *The Universe and Dr. Einstein* (1958) is a familiar popularization. The growing interest in the history of recent scientific thought is reflected in L. Pearce Williams (ed.), *Relativity Theory: Its Origin and Impact on Modern Thought* (1965) and the annual series published by the University of Pennsylvania Press, Russell McCormmach (ed.), *Historical Studies in the Physical Sciences,* of which Volume II (1970) centers on relativity and quantum theory. From among many other books on the meaning of the new scientific revolution which extended into the 1920s, see Louis de Broglie, *Physics and Microphysics* (1955); Karl Heim, *The Transformation of the Scientific World View* (1953 in English tr.); C. E. M. Joad, *Philosophical Aspects of Modern Science* (1959); M. Capek, *The Philosophical Impact of Contemporary Physics* (1961). R. Harré (ed.), *Scientific Thought 1900–1960: A Selective Survey* (1969) is more broadly helpful. Arthur Koestler, *The Roots of Coincidence* (1972) has written brilliantly on the startling paradoxes of modern science. Jeremy Bernstein did *Einstein* in the Modern Masters series. Lewis S. Feuer's *Einstein and the Generations of Science* (1974) is an important study in the sociology of the new scientific revolution; Cornelius Lanczos, *The Einstein Decade 1905–1915* (1974), and Gerald E. Tauber (ed.), Albert *Einstein's Theory of General Relativity* (1975) are other recent notable contributions to an understanding of the great physicist. Boris G. Kuznetsov, *Einstein and Dostoyevsky* (1972) suggests some of the dimensions of comparison! There is a massive life by Ronald W. Clark, *Einstein: The Life and Times* (1971).

Books illustrative of religious currents in the nineteenth century include Walter Kaufmann (ed.), *Religion from Tolstoy to Camus* (1961), a convenient anthology; B. M. G. Reardon (ed.), *Religious Thought in the Nineteenth Century* (1966), also an anthology; Owen Chadwick, *The Victorian Church,* Volume II, 1860–1901 (1970); Robert M. Grant, *A Short History of the Interpretation of the Bible* (1963), the Higher Criticism. Reardon has also authored *Liberalism and Tradition: Aspects of Catholic Thought in Nineteenth Century France* (1976). Edward T. Gargan (ed.), *Leo XIII and the Modern World* (1961) presents the pope whose personality wrought a change in the Roman Catholic Church; J. H. Miller, *The Disappearance of God* (1963), the theme of dying faith traced in five nineteenth-century English writers; S. R. Hopper (ed.), *Lift Up Your Eyes: The Religious Writings of Leo Tolstoy* (1960), the leading prophet of the age. In *The Bradlaugh Case* (1965), Walter L. Arnstein examined late Victorian atheism, on which see also some chapters in David Daiches, *Some Late Victorian Attitudes* (1969), and Warren S. Smith, *The London Heretics 1870–1914* (1967). The reprinting of Alfred W. Benn's *History of English Rationalism in the Nineteenth Century* (2 vols., 1906) makes available an older classic. Michele Ranchetti, *The Catholic Modernists* (1970) deals with the reform movement in the Church from 1864 to 1907, as does Lawrence F. Barmann, *Baron von Hügel and the Modernist Crisis in England* (1972). Donald Attwater, *Modern Christian Revolutionaries* (1947) is interesting. Owen Chadwick in *The Secularization of the European Mind in the Nineteenth Century* (1976) brought his learning to bear on large questions, in a work which might be compared with Franklin L. Baumer's older *Religion and the Rise of Scepticism* (1960). See also works previously cited for romanticism, Darwin, Marx, socialism, Victorian era.

The enormous and revolutionary activity in literature and the arts can be approached through such books as Eugen Weber (ed.), *Paths to the Present* (1962), an anthology featuring literary movements, or Roland N. Stromberg (ed.), *Realism, Naturalism, and Symbolism: Modes of Thought and Expression in Europe 1848–1914* (1968). Harry Levin, *The Gates of Horn: A Study of Five French Realists* (1963) is a classic on its subject, including Flaubert, Zola, and Proust. Enid Starkie, biographer of Gustave Flaubert, summed up much in her *From Gautier to Eliot* (1962), concerned with French influence on British literature. Books which set the social scene include C. Grana, *Bohemian versus Bourgeois: French Society and the French Man of Letters in the Nineteenth Century* (1964), and Malcolm Easton, *Artist and Writer in Paris: The Bohemian Idea* (1964); for a slightly later period, Roger Shattuck, *The Banquet Years: The Arts in France 1885–1918* (1958). Valuable for the French scene are the Goncourt brothers *Journal*, edited by Robert Baldick (1962) and André Billy's biography of *The Goncourt Brothers* (1960). Classic accounts of French Symbolism were Arthur Symons, *The Symbolist Movement in Literature* (1919) and Edmund Wilson, *Axel's Castle* (1936); a more recent appraisal is Anna Balakian, *The Symbolist Movement: A Critical Appraisal* (1977), and for the painters Philippe Jullian, *Dreams of Decadence* (1971). Mario Praz, *The Romantic Agony* (1954) looked on the Decadents with unfriendly but penetrating eyes. Holbrook Jackson, *The 1890's* (1913) was a classic account of the Oscar Wilde-*Yellow Book* era in Britain, often reprinted; both Phillipe Jullian and H. Montgomery Hyde have lively accounts of *Oscar Wilde*. Jullian has written also about *D'Annunzio* (1972) and about the Parisian *Prince of Esthetes*, Count Robert Montesquiou. James West is the authority on *Russian Symbolism* (1970); further on the Russian literary movement, George Gibian and H. W. Tjalsma (ed.), *Russian Modernism 1900–1930* (1977); Vladimir Markov, *Russian Futurism* (1969); Carl and Ellendra Proffer, *The Silver Age of Russian Culture* (1971). George Stade (ed.), *Six Modern British Novelists* (1974) includes the great Edwardians, Bennett and Conrad, as does J. I. M. Stewart, *Eight Modern English Writers*, vol. XII of the Oxford History of English Literature (1963), along with Hardy, Shaw, Yeats, Kipling. Samuel Hynes, *The Edwardian Turn of Mind* (1968) stresses the literati and intellectuals, and may be compared with John A. Lester, *Journey through Despair: British Literary Culture 1880–1914* (1968); *Edwardians and Late Victorians*, essays edited by Richard Ellman (1960); S. Nowell-Smith (ed.), *The Edwardian Age 1901–1914* (1964) which includes literature, ideas, the press along with much else; John Alcorn, *The Nature Novel from Hardy to Lawrence* (1977). Treatments of individual writers are far too numerous to begin to mention; but among the giants Zola has been studied outstandingly by F. W. J. Hemmings (1966), Leo Tolstoy by Ernest J. Simmons (2 vols., 1960), Dostoyevsky by Richard Peace (1971), Joseph Frank (1976), and Geoffrey Kabat (1978), as well as the great critic R. P. Blackmur. Dealing generally and philosophically with the Modernist mode are such thought-provoking books as Herbert Read, *The Philosophy of Modern Art* (1952) and *Art and Alienation* (1969); Stephen Spender, *The Struggle of the Modern* (1963); David Daiches, *The Novel in the Modern World* (1939) and *Poetry in the Modern World* (1941); Josef P. Hodin, *Modern Art and the Modern Mind* (1972). On the other than literary arts: John Rewald has written scholarly histories of both *Impressionism* (1961) and *Post-Impressionism* (1956); John Golding, *Cubism: A History and Analysis* (1968), John Willett, *Expressionism* (1970), Marianne W. Martin, *Futurist Art and Theory* (1968) are specimens of valuable monographs on the artistic movements of the 1900s. Remarkable for its sensitive understanding of music's relationship to ideas and culture is Wilfrid Mellers, *Caliban Reborn: Renewal in Twentieth-Century Music* (1967).

The bibliography for the next chapter relates to many themes that were started in the years before 1914. On political and social thought, H. Stuart Hughes, *Consciousness and Society: European Social Thought 1890-1930* (1958) is generally useful. Michael Curtis, *Three against the Third Republic* (1959) ably and interestingly presents the outlook of Sorel, Maurras, and Barrès. Sorel is also the subject of a first-rate book by J. H. Meisel, *The Genesis of Georges Sorel* (1951) and one by I. L. Horowitz, *Radicalism and The Revolt against Reason* (1961). In *Fear of Power* (1967), Preston King compared Sorel with Proudhon and Tocqueville. Richard Vernon, *Commitment and Change: Georges Sorel and the Idea of Revolution* (1978) is a recent addition to the shelf of Sorel studies. Sorel's own writings have been reprinted, not only *Illusions of Progress* and *Reflections on Violence* but a selection, *From Georges Sorel: Essays in Socialism and Philosophy*, edited by John and Charlotte Stanley (1976). On Barrès see Robert Soucy, *Fascism in France: The Case of Maurice Barrès* (1973), and Charles S. Doty, *From Cultural Rebellion to Counter-Revolution: The Politics of Maurice Barrès* (1976). Meisel has also edited Gaetano Mosca's *The Myth of the Ruling Class* (1958). An array of books on the *Action Francaise* and Charles Maurras includes one by Eugen Weber and more recently Paul Mazgaj, *The Action Francaise and Revolutionary Syndicalism* (1979). Another foe of French democracy is examined by Robert A. Nye in *The Origins of Crowd Psychology: Gustave LeBon and the Crisis of Mass Democracy in the Third Republic* (1975). That the Republic had at least a few defenders is indicated in J. A. Scott's *Republican Ideas and the Liberal Tradition in France 1870-1914* (1951). Raymond Aron, *Main Currents of Sociological Thought*, Volume II (1967) covers Durkheim, Pareto, and Weber. Among many students drawn to Max Weber, deserving special note are the biography by Arthur Mitzman, *The Iron Cage* (1970); Reinhard Bendix, *Max Weber, An Intellectual Portrait* (1965), Ilse Dronberger, *The Political Thought of Max Weber* (1971), and Wolfgang Mommsen, *The Age of Bureaucracy* (1974). Other Weber studies are by Julien Freund, Walter Runciman, and Karl Loewenstein. *From Max Weber* (1946), edited by C. Wright Mills and H. H. Garth is a fine selection from the great German sociologist. Vilfredo Pareto's magnum opus has been translated into English as *The Mind and Society,* reprinted in 1963; also available is a selection from Pareto edited by J. Lopreato. Kurt Wolff has edited Emile Durkheim's *Essays in Sociology and Philosophy* (1960) and also Georg Simmel's *Essays in Sociology* (1959). Durkheim is the subject of books by Robert Bierstadt (1966), Robert Nisbet (1965), Dominick LaCapra (1972), Steven Lukes (1972), and Robert N. Bellah, the latter editing a selection from Durkheim's writings (1973). Arthur Mitzman, *Sociology and Estrangement* (1973) examines three German sociologists, Tönnies, Werner Sombart, and Robert Michels. Anthony Giddens, in *Capitalism and Modern Social Theory* (1971) compares Weber and Durkheim with Marx. Philip Abrams deals capably with *The Origins of British Sociology 1834-1914* (1968). Much recent interest in Wilhelm Dilthey is reflected in Rudolf A. Makkreel, *Dilthey, Philosopher of the Human Studies* (1975) and Michael Ermarth, *Wilhelm Dilthey: The Critique of Historical Reason* (1978), as well as in portions of Z. Bauman's interesting *Hermeneutics and Social Science* (1978). Giddens' *Studies in Social and Political Theory* (1977) contains essays on Weber, Marx, and Durkheim. Fritz Ringer, *The Decline of the German Mandarins* (1969) deals in part with sociologists as well as the "socialists of the chair." Classics of political thought from this era, reprinted in popular editions, are Robert Michels, *Political Parties,* and Graham Wallas, *Human Nature in Poli-*

tics. Richard Mandell, *Paris 1900: The Great World's Fair* (1967) is an interesting study in the climate of opinion, as is Carl E. Schorske, *Fin de Siècle Vienna* (1979) and Allan Janik and Stephen Toulmin, *Wittgenstein's Vienna* (1973).

Chapter 6

Many works cited in the previous chapter bear on the mood of the intellectuals at the beginning of the war in 1914. Some additional ones: Walter Laqueur, *Young Germany* (1962) conveys the mood of the youth movement which affected the first days of the war. Peter Stansky (ed.), *The Left and War: The British Labour Party and World War I* (1969) contributes to an understanding of the socialist and workingclass abdication to war, as does Georges Haupt's book translated as *Socialism and the Great War: The Collapse of the Second International* (1972). An article by R. N. Stromberg, "The Intellectuals and the Coming of the War" in *Journal of European Studies,* July, 1973, attempts to analyze the several strains in the war spirit. See also J. D. Ellis, *French Socialists and the Problem of Peace 1904–1914* (1967). Two recent distinguished additions to this literature are Robert Wohl, *The Generation of 1914* (1979) and Paul Fussell, *The Great War and Modern Memory* (1975). Stromberg's forthcoming book is titled *Redemption by War: European Intellectuals in 1914.* Eugen Weber's *The Nationalist Revival in France 1905–1914* (1968) sheds much light on the mood of 1914. Among many more specialized studies, Jon Silkin, *Out of Battle: The Poetry of the First War* (1977) joins a long list of books about the war poets, including Julian Grenfell, Wilfred Owen, Isaac Rosenberg among other soldier poets each of whom has had a recent biographer. An outstanding biography also is D. A. Prater, *European of Yesterday: Stefan Zweig* (1972). Hans Schmitt, *Charles Péguy, the Decline of an Idealist* (1967) views Péguy's turn to nationalism without sympathy. Christopher Hassall, *Rupert Brooke* (1964) is a good biography of the poet who symbolized the pro-war idealism of 1914. A good anthology of war writing is George Panichas (ed.), *Promise of Greatness* (1968); also Guy Chapman (ed.), *Vain Glory* (1968). Bernard Bergonzi, *Heroes' Twilight* (1964) discusses the war literature. I. M. Parsons has edited a volume of war poetry as has Brian Gardner, *Up the Line to Death* (1965). Henry Winkler, *The League of Nations Movement in Great Britain 1914–1919* (1952) dealt with an important wartime body of thought. W. W. Wagar, *H. G. Wells and the World State* (1961) provides an illuminating account of one man of letters heavily involved in this cause.

Lenin and the Bolsheviks: The Intellectual and Political History of the Triumph of Bolshevism in Russia (1965) is by A. B. Ulam. Helmut Gruber (ed.), *International Communism in the Era of Lenin* (1967) is a documentary collection rich in contemporary materials. An anthology of Lenin's writings has been edited by Robert C. Tucker (1975); Robert Conquest, *V. I. Lenin* (1972) is in the Modern Masters series; and among numerous other studies of the great revolutionary, a convenient collections of views is that edited by Leonard Schapiro and Peter Reddaway, *Lenin: The Man, the Theorist, the Leader* (1967). Bertram Wolfe has an essay on "Leninism" in the generally valuable group of essays edited by M. M. Drachkovitch under the title *Marxism in the Modern World.* Vol. II of J. P. Nettl's *Rosa Luxemburg* is useful for the revolutions in the German world. See also, some of the works cited under Marxism in chapter 4, and, below, in the next chapter, the bibliography on communism between the wars.

Much of the bibliography in the previous chapter on literature, social thought, Freudianism, and the new scientific revolution also applies to this chapter, for these were continuing trends in thought. In *Good Tidings: The Belief in Progress from Darwin to Marcuse* (1972), intellectual historian W. Warren Wagar also puts the post-1919 loss of hope in perspective. The neo-orthodox theology of Barth, Bultmann, Berdyaev, Tillich, and others may be approached through numerous editions of their writings, also via collections such as Leonhard Reinisch (ed.), *Theologians of Our Time* (1964), or the analyses in John Macquarrie (ed.), *Contemporary Religious Thinkers* (1968); J. Pelikan (ed.), *Twentieth Century Theology in the Making* (1971). Wilhelm and Marion Pauck, *Paul Tillich: His Life and Thought* (Vol. I, 1976) exemplifies recent scholarly research on this group; more technical is Hans Urs von Balthasar, *The Theology of Karl Barth* (tr. 1971). H. Stuart Hughes, *Oswald Spengler: A Critical Estimate* (rev. ed., 1962) is a commentary on the author of *The Decline of the West*, a most celebrated expression of war and post-war pessimism. Among Aldous Huxley's works, *Brave New World* (1932) has been reprinted along with his later comments, *Brave New World Revisited* (1958). Among other period pieces of the 1920s, J. Ortega y Gasset, *The Revolt of the Masses* (English ed., 1932) is a classic, while Montgomery Belgion, *Our Present Philosophy of Life* was a 1929 commentary; *The Long Weekend* (1941) by Robert Graves and Alan Hodge examined popular culture in Britain between the wars. Beatrice Webb's *Diaries*, Volume II, 1924–1932 (1956) edited by Margaret Cole are among the more interesting sources. Other documents of the times were Joseph Wood Krutch, *The Modern Temper*, and Freud's *Civilization and Its Discontents*, both published in the late '20s. C. E. M. Joad, *Guide to Modern Thought* (1933) found modern physics, psychoanalysis, and Bergsonian vitalism among the doctrines most in need of explaining to the general public; references to these topics in Chapter 5 are therefore still relevant to the 1920s, as also are works on the modernist movement in the arts. The collection edited by C. B. Cox and A. E. Dyson, *The Twentieth-Century Mind* (1972) should be noted: Volume I covers 1900–1918 while Volume II relates to the interwar period. Peter Gay, *Weimar Culture* (1970) and Keith Bullivant (ed.), *Culture and Society in the Weimar Republic* (1978) both encompass a large area within a single country.

Needless to say there is a huge bibliography on the twentieth-century literary revolution. General works, such as Graham Hough, *Image and Experience: Studies in a Literary Revolution* (1960), Walter Allen, *The Modern Novel in Britain and America* (1964) (*Tradition and Dream*), and Germaine Bree and Margaret Guiton, *An Age of Fiction: The French Novel from Gide to Camus* (1958) may be supplemented by studies of specific literary movements, such as Maurice Nadeau, *History of Surrealism* (1965), Herbert S. Gershman, *The Surrealist Revolution in France* (1968), and Wallace Fowlie, *The Age of Surrealism* (1950), and then by the multitudinous works on individual authors. Joseph Frank, *The Widening Gyre: Crisis and Mastery in Modern Literature* (1963) contains essays on Proust, Mann, and Malraux; Joseph G. Brennan's *Three Philosophical Novelists* (1964) are Joyce, Gide, and Mann; George Stade (ed.) added essays on *Six Contemporary British Novelists* (1976), including Graham Greene and Malcolm Lowry, to *Six Modern British Novelists*, previously cited, in which Virginia Woolf and Evelyn Waugh are placed. John Press, *A Map of Modern English Verse* (1969) is an extremely useful compilation of both poetry and criticism. Malcolm Bradbury (ed.), *Modernism, 1890–1930* (1976) may be added to the list of writings on this subject cited in the previous chapter. Among the giants of literary modernism who came into their own after 1919, there are introductions in the Modern Masters series of *Yeats*, by Denis Donoghue, *D. H. Lawrence* by Frank Kermode, *James Joyce* by John Gross, *Franz Kafka* by Erich Heller, *Marcel Proust* by Roger Shattuck, and *T. S. Eliot* by Stephen Spender. On each of these, of course, there is a vast critical literature. One might single out the excellent biographies of *Virginia Woolf* by Quentin Bell (1972), of D. H. Lawrence by Harry T. Moore (*The Priest of Love*, 1974), of Joyce by Richard Ellman (1959); George D. Painter's two-volume biography of *Marcel Proust* (1959, 1965); Hugh Kenner, *The Pound Era* (1972). Kenner also has edited the volume on T. S. Eliot in the useful "Critical Heritage" series, which reprints material showing how writers looked to their contemporaries—volumes also on Lawrence, Joyce, Yeats, and others. Cf. A. Walton Litz (ed.), *Eliot in His Time* (1973); Richard M. Kain and Marvin Magalaner, *Joyce: The Man, the Work, the Reputation* (1965). Roger Kojecky, *T. S. Eliot's Social Criticism* (1972) presents the thought of the poet and essayist whose belated biography we still await. Leon Edel, the biographer of Henry James, has recently written on the Bloomsbury Circle (1979), on which see also Michael Holroyd's biography of Lytton Strachey (1967). The futility of attempting to cite the literature on any of these great writers is indicated in the 10,000 items of a recent Kafka bibliography, equalled or exceeded by Joyce, Lawrence, Yeats. At least ten significant books about Aldous Huxley appeared between 1967 and 1975 (by John Atkins, Peter Bowering, Lawrence Brander, Milton Birnbaum, Peter Firchow, and others.)

Russian writers trying to adjust to an increasingly rigid tyranny are discussed in Robert A. Maguire, *Red Virgin Soil: Soviet Literature in the 1920s* (1968); one of them is given an excellent biography by Edward J. Brown, *Mayakovsky: A Poet in the Revolution* (1973). On the other arts, Peter Blake's *The Master Builders* (1961) conveys the lives and times of the great modern architects; Hans M. Wingler, *The Bauhaus* (1970) is authoritative on the famous German school. Robert C. Williams, *Artists in Revolution: Portraits of the Russian Avant-Garde 1905-1925* (1977) digs beneath the surface. The Modern Master series has a book on *Le Corbusier*, by Stephen Gardiner, and one on *Arnold Schoenberg* by Charles Rosen. In *Léger and the Avant-Garde* (1976), Christopher Green catches the spirit of some of the 1920s artistic style, as did John M. Brinnin in his life of Gertrude Stein, *The Third Rose* (1959), for the Parisian milieu of Picasso and his friends. For the Prague of Kafka, Max Brod's *Streitbares Leben* should be translated.

Among the works dealing with Fascism in general are Ernest Nolte, *Three Faces of Fascism* (1967); Renzo De Felice (the biographer of Mussolini), *Interpretations of Fascism* (1977); *Theories of Fascism*, a special issue of the *Journal of Contemporary History*, ed. George Mosse and Walter Laqueur, 1976 (compare other issues of this journal on fascism, 1966, *International Fascism 1920-1945*, and 1979, *International Fascism: New Thoughts and Approaches*); A. James Gregor, *The Ideology of Fascism* (1969); John Weiss, *The Fascist Tradition* (1967); S. J. Woolf (ed.), *European Fascism* (1968); Hannah Arendt, *The Origins of Totalitarianism* (1966). George L. Mosse, *Toward The Final Solution: A History of European Racism* (1977) is relevant. Among other works detailing the background of German Nazism, Walter Struve, *Elites against Democracy* (1973) contains chapters on a variety of anti-democratic ideologies between 1890 and 1933; cf. Kurt von Klemperer, *Germany's New Conservatism* (1957). Eberhard Jäckel, *Hitler's Weltanschauung* (tr. 1972), and Percy Schramm's introduction to the German edition of *Hitler's Table Talk* are valuable on the roots of the Führer's thought; see also Schramm material edited by Donald Detwiler under the title of *Hitler: The Man and the Military Leader* (1971). Among other works on Hitler especially valuable for ideas is Werner Maser, *Hitler: Legend, Myth, and Reality* (tr. 1974). George L. Mosse's *Nazi Culture* (1966) is a unique record of the Nazi mind. Charles Delzell has edited a collection of documents on *Mediterranean Fascism* (1969). Not translated from the Italian, Renzo de Felice's three-volume biography of Mussolini, of which the first volume, *Mussolini il Rivoluzionaria 1883-1920* appeared in 1964, is the definitive work. Jack Roth's article "The Roots of Italian Fascism: Sorel and Sorelismo" in *Journal of Modern History*, March, 1967, sheds much light on the ideological roots of Mussolini's movement, on which now see also David Roberts, *The Syndicalist Tradition and Italian Fascism* (1979). Adrian Lyttelton, an expert on Italian fascism, has edited *Italian Fascisms from Pareto to Gentile* (1975). H. S. Harris, *The Social Philosophy of Giovanni Gentile* (1960) examined the leading philosopher of Italian fascism. Stanley G. Payne, *Falange* (1962) is an authoritative account of the Spanish variety of fascism.

Robert Benewick, *Political Violence and Public Order* (1969) and W. F. Mandle, *Anti-Semitism and the British Union of Fascists* (1968) are excellent on British fascism. M. D. Biddiss has studied *The Father of Racist Ideology,* the nineteenth-century Frenchman Gobineau (1970). Further on French fascism, William R. Tucker, *The Fascist Ego: A Political Biography of Robert Brasillach* (1975). Peter Dodge, *Beyond Marxism: The Faith and Works of Hendrik de Man* (1966) recounts the career of a Belgian one-time Marxian socialist who, like Jacques Doriot, ended in Hitler's camp. An unusual perspective is that of Robert R. Taylor, *The World in Stone: The Role of Architecture in National Socialist Ideology* (1974).

Chapter 7

Issues of the *Journal of Contemporary History* included *The Left-Wing Intellectuals between the Wars,* edited by Laqueur and Mosse (1966), also *Literature and Politics in the Twentieth Century* (1968), and (Tony Judt, ed.), *Conflict and Compromise: Socialists and Socialism in the Twentieth Century,* a special issue of July, 1978 containing a variety of essays on the 1930's Left. Illustrative of left-wing opinion, the *Left Review* from 1934 to 1938 was reprinted in 1971. George Watson, *Politics and Literature in Modern Britain* (1977) has some incisive essays on the 1930's generation. So does Samuel Hynes, in *The Auden Generation: Literature and Politics in England in the 1930s* (1977). The origins of the Communist parties out of elements of the older Left is the subject of a number of well-researched monographs including Walter Kendall, *The Revolutionary Movement in Britain 1900-1921* (1969); L. J. Macfarlane, *The British Communist Party: Its Origin and Development* (1966); Werner Angress, *The Stillborn Revolution* (1963), on the failure of Communist revolution in Germany 1920-1923; John M. Cammett, *Antonio Gramsci and the Origins of Italian Communism* (1967), dealing with a significant figure of twentieth century Marxist thought; Robert Wohl, *French Communism in the Making 1914-1924* (1966), also Annie Kriegel, *Aux origines du communisme francais* (1964), and Ronald Tiersky, *French Communism 1930-1972* (1974). Further on Gramsci, Martin Clark, *Antonio Gramsci and the Revolution That Failed* (1977).

On the attraction of the intellectuals to Communism, a host of studies is headed by Neal Wood, *Communism and British Intellectuals* (1959) and David Caute, *Communism and the French Intellectuals* (1964), supplemented by such popular books as R. H. S. Crossman (ed.), *The God That Failed* (1950) and Raymond Aron, *The Opium of the Intellectuals* (1962). Caute has added *The Fellow Travellers* (1972). Martin Jay, in *The Dialectical Imagination* (1973) has provided exhaustive treatment of the Frankfurt group of German neo-Marxians which included Herbert Marcuse. George Lichtheim, *George Lukács* (1970) presents one of the more significant East European Marxist theoreticians of the interwar years. Among the more famous memoirs of ex-communists were Arthur Koestler's *Arrow in the Blue* (1952) and *The Invisible Writing* (1954); also George Orwell, in *Collected Essays* (1954) and *Homage to Catalonia* (1952). Such novels as Thomas Mann, *The Magic Mountain* (1930), Ignazio Silone, *Fontamara* (1934) and Koestler's *Darkness at Noon* (1941) provide deeper clues to this ideology-haunted decade than may be found in more formal histories: See also D. E. S

Maxwell, *Poets of the 1930s* (1969); Alex Zwerdling, *Orwell and the Left* (1974). Ronald Clark's biography of J. B. S. Haldane, *JBS* (1969) records the life and works of a British scientist notable for his attachment to Communism. Among other memoirs, Julian Trevelyan, *Indigo Days* (1857); Edward Upward, *In the Thirties* (1970); Kingsley Martin, *Editor* (1968); Simone Weil, *Selected Essays 1934–1943,* edited by R. Rees (1966); Victor Serge, *Memoirs of a Revolutionary 1901–1941* (London, 1965). Julian Symons, *The 1930's* (1975) is an evocative portrait of the mood of the decade. Bernard Zylstra, *From Pluralism to Collectivism: The Development of Laski's Political Thought* (1968) gives attention to a prominent British intellectual of the Left. An older survey still of much value was Volume V of G. D. H. Cole's *History of Socialist Thought, Socialism and Fascism 1931–1939* (1960). John T. Marcus, *French Socialism in the Crisis Years, 1933–1936* (1958) is a well-written account of the struggle with fascism and the emergence of the Popular Front, on which see especially Joel Colton's splendid biography of *Leon Blum: Humanist in Politics* (1966). See also Nathaniel Greene, *Crisis and Decline: The French Socialist Party in the Popular Front Era* (1969) and Daniel Brower, *The New Jacobins: The French Communists and the Popular Front* (1968), along with an article by Donald N. Baker, "The Socialist Party's Left Wing in France, 1921–1939," *Journal of Modern History,* March, 1971. Several books have looked at the Spanish Civil War in its relationship to European writers; among them, Stanley Weintraub, *The Last Great Cause* (1968); J. M. Muste, *Say That We Saw Spain Die* (1966); Frederick R. Benson, *Writers in Arms: The Literary Impact of the Spanish Civil War* (1967).

On the Soviet scene in Stalin's time: Robert C. Tucker, author of *Stalin the Revolutionary* (1974) and *The Soviet Political Mind* (1971) also has edited *Stalinism: Essays in Historical Interpretation* (1977). Joel Carmichael, *Trotsky* (1975) is among the best recent studies of Stalin's defeated foe; among other ill-fated enemies of the tyrant, see Naum Jasny, *Soviet Economists of the Twenties* (1972); Stephen F. Cohen, *Bukharin and the Bolshevist Revolution* (1973). Tucker and Cohen have edited a record of *The Great Purge Trial* (1965). Robert Conquest, author of *The Great Terror: Stalin's Purge of the Thirties* (1971) has also written *The Politics of Ideas in the USSR* (1967). Cf. Vera Dunham, *In Stalin's Time: Middle Class Values in Soviet Fiction* (1976). Biographies and memoirs of the great literary victims of Stalin are the most interesting of materials on the era; see for example Clarence F. Brown, *Osip Mandelstam* (1973), and Nadezhda Mandelstam, *Hope against Hope* (1970); Armanda Haight, *Anna Akhmatova: A Poetic Pilgrimage* (1976). Sylvia Margulies, *The Pilgrimage to Russia, 1925–1937* (1968) records the duping of Western visitors.

G. L. S. Shackle, *The Years of High Theory* (1967) is relevant to the new economic thought of the 1930s, on which theme see also Michael Stewart, *Keynes and After* (1968). Other valuable treatments are Ben B. Seligman, *Main Currents in Modern Economics* (1962); Claudio Napoleoni, *Economic Thought of the Twentieth Century* (1971); Lawrence Klein, *The Keynesian Revolution* (1947). D. P. O'Brien and John R. Presley (ed.), *Pioneers of Modern Economics in Britain* (1980) reviews the neo-classical heritage of economic thought, from Marshall and Jevons to Pigou and Hayek, under attack from the Keynesians in the 1930s.

On philosophical currents of one fashionable sort, Leszek Kolakowski's *Positivist Philosophy* (1972) traces the tradition from Hume down to the twentieth century. Logical Positivism and linguistic analysis can be studied in Viktor Kraft, *The Vienna Circle* (1953); J. O. Urmson, *Philosophical Analysis: Its Development between the Two World Wars* (1956); A. J. Ayer *et al.,* *The Revolution in Philosophy* (1956); Gustav Bergmann, *The Metaphysics of Logical Positivism* (1967). Ayer's *Language, Truth and Logic* (1936) has been reprinted. F. Copleston, *Contemporary*

Philosophy (1956) divides its attention between the analytical and existential schools. I. M. Bochenski, *Contemporary European Philosophy* (1956) is also a sound and lucid guide. A. J. Ayer (ed.), *Logical Positivism* (1959); Margaret MacDonald (ed.), *Philosophy and Analysis* (1966); Barry R. Gross, *Analytic Philosophy: A Historical Introduction* (1970); R. J. Butler (ed.), *Analytical Philosophy* (1963, 1965) are volumes illustrating the trends of professional work; likewise Richard Rorty (ed.), *The Linguistic Turn: Essays in Philosophical Method* (1967). See also J. L. Austin, *Philosophical Papers* (2nd ed., 1970). Anthony Kenny, *Wittgenstein* (1973); David Pears, *Ludwig Wittgenstein*, one of the Modern Master series (1969); David Pole, *The Later Philosophy of Wittgenstein* (1959) are among a large number of works on the most important of the analytical philosophers, whose papers are still being edited for a definitive edition of his complete works, as is the case also with the other philosophical giants of a different school, Edmund Husserl and Martin Heidegger. In *Four Modern Philosophers* (1965), Arne Naess paired Carnap and Wittgenstein against Heidegger and Sartre. Norman Malcolm, *Ludwig Wittgenstein: A Memoir* (1967) is a fascinating look at the great man. Criticisms of the positivistic and linguistic school were noted by Pratima Bowes, *Is Metaphysics Possible?* (1965) and C. W. K. Mundle, *A Critique of Linguistic Philosophy* (1970). Bertrand Russell's fascinating *Autobiography* sheds light on the most colorful of twentieth-century philosophers, who died in 1970 at the age of 98; see also a biography by Ronald W. Clark (1975) and, as an introduction to Russell's philosophy, A. J. Ayer's *Russell* in the Modern Masters series (1972); David Pears, *Russell and the British Tradition in Philosophy* (1967); Pears (ed.), *Bertrand Russell: A Collection of Critical Essays* (1972).

Wolfe Mays and S. C. Brown (ed.), *Linguistic Analysis and Phenomenology* (1972) explores some connections between the two different and often hostile realms of twentieth century philosophy. Edward N. Lee and Maurice Mandelbaum (ed.), *Phenomenology and Existentialism* (1967) relates the two modes of subjectivist philosophizing. Existentialism has given rise to a battery of books. Among the earlier ones, H. J. Blackham, *Six Existentialist Thinkers* (1952) was one of the best, though rather compressed; Walter Kaufmann, *Existentialism from Dostoyevsky to Sartre* (1960); William Barrett, *Irrational Man* (1958), a popular book; David E. Roberts, *Existentialism and Religious Belief* (1963); John Macquarrie, *An Existentialist Theology: A Comparison of Heidegger and Bultmann* (1955); F. H. Heinemann, *Existentialism and the Modern Predicament* (1954); Mary Warnock, *Existentialism* (1970). From Kierkegaard to Sartre, the classics of Existentialism were frequently reprinted. A selection, edited by Nino Langiulli, *The Existentialist Tradition* (1971), brought together fifteen of them. Some of Kierkegaard's writings were selected by Lee H. Hollander (1960), and among the numerous studies of the Dane's thought is Gregor Malantschuk, *Kierkegaard's Thought* (1971), while Walter Lowrie wrote the standard *Life* (1951). Martin Heidegger's *Existence and Being (Sein und Zeit, 1927)*, Gabriel Marcel, *The Philosophy of Existence* (1949) and other writings, and Jean-Paul Sartre, *Being and Nothingness* (tr. 1956) are important existentializing texts; Karl Jaspers, *Philosophy of Existence* has also been reprinted (1971). Rudolf Bultmann, *Existence and Faith* (1960) is a collection of writings by the German scholar and theologian who exerted so great an influence on Protestant religious thought. Alden L. Fisher made available in English *The Essential Writings of Merleau-Ponty* (1969), one of the major French phenomenologists. Writings about the major Existentialists are legion; thus, on Sartre, a mere beginning is Philip Thody, *Jean-Paul Sartre* (1960); Thomas Molnar, *Sartre: Ideologue of Our Time* (1968); Mary Warnock (ed.), *Sartre: A Collection of Critical Essays* (1971); Warnock, *The Philosophy of Sartre* (1965). (For Sartre's further development and role in the 1960's, see next chapter's bibliography.) Robert D. Cummings (ed.), *The Philosophy of Jean-Paul Sartre* (1965) presents key texts. John O'Neill, *Perception, Experience and History: The Social Phenomenology of Maurice Merleau-Ponty* (1970) gives a balanced view of Sartre's colleague. Philip Thody also wrote about Albert Camus, as did John Cruickshank in his *Albert Camus and the Literature of Revolt* (1960), and Germaine Brée, *Camus* (1961). In *European Philosophy Today*, ed. George L. Kline (1965), J. Glenn Gray discussed Martin Heidegger's philosophy. Martin Farber, *The Foundation of Phenomenology* (1968) was a pioneer student of Husserl, on whom see notes in a previous chapter. Leonard H. Ehrlich, *Karl Jaspers: Philosophy and Faith* (1975); William J. Richardson, *Heidegger* (1965); Paul Ilie, *Unamuno: An Existential View of Self and Society* (1967) suggest further dimensions of Existentialism.

Chapter 8

In a 1975 book, *After Everything: European Thought and Culture since 1945,* Roland N. Stromberg attempts, not altogether successfully, to grapple with the richness and fragmentation of recent thought. Few other such surveys exist. The reader is referred to the bibliography in that book. The following tracts for the times could help understand the immediate postwar years: Alfred J. Weber, *Abschied von der Bisherigen Geschichte,* translated as *Farewell to European History* (1946); Georges Bernanos, *La liberté pour quoi faire?* (1953), essays on the European spirit written 1946–1947; José Ortega y Gasset, *The Modern Theme* (tr. 1961); Gabriel Marcel, *Man against Mass Society* (1952); Judith N. Shklar, *After Utopia: the Decline of Political Faith* (1959); Hannah Arendt, *The Human Condition: A Study of the Central Dilemmas Facing Modern Man* (1958); Julian Huxley, *The Human Crisis* (1963); J. H. Plumb (ed.), *Crisis in the Humanities* (1964); R. Guardini, *The End of the Modern World* (1957); Adrienne Koch (ed.), *Philosophy for a Time of Crisis* (1959); Richard M. Weaver, *Visions of Order: The Cultural Crisis of Our Time* (1964); Jacques Ellul, *The Technological Society* (1964); Northrop Frye, *The Modern Century* (1967); Raymond Aron, *Progress and Disillusion* (1968); Daniel Bell, *The End of Ideology* (1960) and *The Coming of Post-Industrial Society* (1973). Christopher Booker, *The Neophiliacs* (1970) stresses the neurasthenic trendiness of current thought.

T. R. Fyvel, *Intellectuals Today* (1968) is a jaundiced view. Lionel Trilling, in *The Liberal Imagination* (1950), *Beyond Culture* (1965), and *Mind in the Modern World* (1972) offered acute commentary on the culture of today. The *New Outline of Modern Knowledge,* edited by Alan Pryce-Jones in 1956, bravely tried to keep up with everything in one volume; a new edition is needed. Attention is called again to the Cox-Dyson *Twentieth-Century Mind,* Volume III covering the English years since 1945. Colin Smith, *Contemporary French Philosophy* (1964) covered a good deal of ground capably. So did Roy Pierce, *Contemporary French Political Thought* (1966).

An attempt to keep abreast of postwar literature might consult books such as Maurice Nadeau, *The French Novel since the War* (1967); Peter Demetz, *Postwar German Literature: A Critical Introduction* (1970); Rubin Rabinovitz, *The Reaction against Experiment in the English Novel 1950–1960* (1967); Malcolm Bradbury (ed.), *The Novel Today* (1977). John Press's study of poetry in the 1950's was titled *Rule and Energy* (1963). Cf. M. L. Rosenthal (ed.), *Chief Modern Poets of Britain and America* (1970); Anthony Thwaite, *Poetry Today, 1960–1973* (1973). On the theater, Frederick Lumley, *New Trends in Twentieth Century Drama* (4th edition, 1972) is a valuable guide which may be supplemented by Martin Esslin's *Theater of the Absurd* (1961), Eric Bentley, *The Theater of Commitment* (1968), and John R. Taylor, *Anger and Afterward* (2nd ed. 1969) Edward Lucie-Smith, *Movements in*

Art since 1945 (1970) struggles manfully with an awkward subject. Cf. Gerald Woods, *Art without Boundaries 1950-1970* (1972). The "New Theology" series edited by Martin E. Marty and Don G. Peerman kept up with recent currents of thought in this lively area.

Mark Poster, *Existential Marxism in Postwar France* (1975) is a work of scholarship which might be compared with Raymond Aron, *Marxism and the Existentialists* (1967). Neil McInnes, *The Western Marxists* (1972) and Maurice Cranston et al., *The New Left* (1971) cast an even larger net to embrace other neo-Marxisms such as Lukacs, Gramsci, and the Frankfurt School. Each of these leftist schools attracted many students as well as disciples. D. G. Cooper and R. D. Laing, *Reason and Violence: A Decade of Sartre's Philosophy* (1975) and James F. Sheridan, *Sartre: The Radical Conversion* (1969) are among handlings of the famous Existentialist's swing toward revolutionary politics. George Lichtheim, veteran Marxist scholar, wrote on "Sartre's Existential Marxism" in his *The Concept of Ideology and Other Essays* (1967); (see also Lichtheim's *From Marx to Hegel*, 1971), as Aron did also in the generally useful M. M. Drachkovitch (ed.), *Marxism in the Modern World* (1965). Dick Howard, *The Unknown Dimension: European Marxism since Lenin* (1972) and Wolfgang Leonhard, *Three Faces of Marxism* (1974), the three being Soviet, Chinese, and East European Humanist, are other works of general coverage in this field. On the Frankfurt School, see again Martin Jay's *Dialectical Imagination;* Albrecht Wellmer, *Critical Theory of Society* (1971); John O'Neill (ed.), *On Critical Theory* (1976); and, among studies of individual authors, Alasdair MacIntyre's *Herbert Marcuse* in Modern Masters series (1970), and Gillian Rose, *The Melancholy Science: An Introduction to the Thought of Theodor W. Adorno* (1978). Lukacs' *History and Class Consciousness* was reprinted in 1971, as also was *Marxism and Philosophy* by Karl Korsch, ed. Fred Halliday (1971). Further on Gramsci, whose influence now was, like Lukacs' and Korsch's, belatedly felt, see Alastair Davidson, *Antonio Gramsci: An Intellectual Biography* (1977), and James Joll's Modern Masters presentation (1977). Gerson S. Sher, *Praxis: Marxist Criticism and Dissent in Socialist Yugoslavia* (1977), and Vladimir Kusin, *Intellectual Origins of the Prague Spring* (1971), as well as Richard T. De-George, *The New Marxism: Soviet and East European Marxism since 1956* (1968) discuss varieties of "humanist" Marxism coming out of the satellites; Erich Fromm (ed.), *Socialist Humanism* (1965) discusses eastern European revisionists, which are examined also in L. Labedz (ed.), *Revisionism: Essays in the History of Marxist Ideas* (1962). Annie Kriegel, *Euro-Communism, A New Kind of Communism?* (1978) adds to the illumination of the western parties which set out on a course of their own in the 1960's; see also Rudolf L. Tokes (ed.), *European Communism in the Age of Detente* (1977). Paul A. Robinson, *The Freudian Left* (1969) and *The Sexual Radicals* (1971), and Richard King, *The Party of Eros* (1972) treat a portion of New Left thought, often seeking to marry Freud and Marx; in the Modern Masters series, Wilhelm Reich is introduced by Charles Rycroft.

The above rather breathless survey can do little more than suggest the prolixity of New Left and neo-Marxist thought, mostly in the stormy sixties. There is also the literature on Soviet Russian dissent and dissidence: Peter Reddaway, *Russia's Underground Intellectuals* (1970); Abraham Rothberg, *The Heirs of Stalin: Dissidence and the Soviet Regime 1953-1970* (1972), and also his *Aleksandr Solzhenitsyn: The Major Novels* (1971); R. L. Tokes (ed.), *Dissent in the USSR* (1975); Robert Conquest, *The Pasternak Affair* (1962); David Joravsky, *The Lysenko Affair* (1970), among others.

Introducing Structuralism, Michael Lane (ed.), *Structuralism: A Reader* (1970); Jean Piaget (ed.), *Structuralism, an Introduction* (1970); Richard and Fernande DeGeorge (ed.), *The Structuralists from Marx to Levi-Strauss* (1972);

Richard Macksey and Eugene Donato (ed.), *The Structuralist Controversy* (1972); E. Nelson and Tanya Hayes (ed.), *Claude Levi-Strauss: The Anthropologist as Hero* (1970); Alex Callinicos, *Althusser's Marxism* (1976). John Lyons writes the Modern Masters volume on Noam Chomsky, while Edmund Leach presents Claude Levi-Strauss.

C. P. Snow's *The Two Cultures and the Scientific Revolution* (1959) began a debate carried on by F. R. Leavis in his (with Michael Yudkin) *Two Cultures? The Significance of C. P. Snow* (1962) and in Snow's *The Two Cultures and a Second Look* (1965). See also Charles Davy, *Towards a Third Culture* (1965); Jacques Barzun, *Science: The Glorious Entertainment* (1964). On another theme of the age, Douglas A. Hughes (ed.), *Perspectives on Pornography* (1970). But the teeming productivity of the contemporary world, embracing dozens of huge academic industries, hundreds of more or less significant creative writers, all kinds of oddities and fads, and an abundance of political polemics defies the bibliographer. If any one periodical comes close to enabling the serious person to keep abreast of the world of ideas, it would be the London *Times Literary Supplement,* with its comprehensive and perceptive coverage of the realm of expression and its occasional special issues devoted entirely to some pertinent special theme.

Locating Additional Books and Articles

The periodical *Isis* prints a critical bibliography of the history of science and its cultural influence every year. *The Philosopher's Index,* issued annually, indexes and also abstracts articles in philosophy, broadly interpreting that term, and is a particularly well-organized guide to the current literature in journals. *Historical Abstracts, Sociological Abstracts,* and other such guides to the current periodical literature in each discipline exist; in English literature, there are the Modern Language Association's *Annual Bibliography,* and the English Association of London's *The Year's Work in English Studies.* A French standard is the annual *Bibliographie de la litterature française du moyen age à nos jours* (Paris). Printed as an adjunct to the *American Historical Review, Recently Published Articles* comes out several times a year covering articles on all kinds of historical subjects. An *Index to Religious Periodical Literature* has been published annually since 1953 at Leiden in the Netherlands. Other guides to current literature include the *International Bibliography of the Social Sciences* and the *International Bibliogrpahy of Political Science* published periodically by UNESCO.

Periodicals such as *Studies in Romanticism* and *Victorian Studies* publish bibliographies for their fields. *Modern Philology* has long published a bibliography in Victorian literature. Volumes 3 and 4 of the *New Cambridge Bibliography of English Literature,* ed. George Watson (1969, 1972) cover the years 1800–1900 and 1900–1950. Boris Ford (ed.), *The Pelican Guide to English Literature* is in seven volumes, of which the last, on the Modern Age, had a third edition in 1975. John Cruickshank (ed.), *French Literature and Its Backgrounds* covers the nineteenth and twentieth centuries in vols. 4, 5, and 6 (1969–1970). Also useful on French literature and culture is Donald G. Charlton (ed.), *Companion to French Studies* (1972). The German equivalent in this Methuen series is Malcolm Pasley (ed.), *Germany: A Companion to German Studies* (1972). The bibliographies published serially by the French Institute of New York, under the titles *French VI, French VII,* and *French XX,* are excellent for French thought and culture.

Josef L. Altholz, *Victorian England 1837–1901: A Bibliographical Handbook* (1970) is one of a series of such guides to the various periods of British history published by Cambridge University Press for the Conference on British Studies. An unusual project is the *Wellesley Index to Victorian Periodicals,* edited by Walter

Houghton (2 vols., 1966, 1972). Another is Paul Raabe's *Index Expressionismus,* translated into English in 1974. The Garland Reference Library publishes numerous volumes of annotated bibliography, such as F Basson et al., *An Annotated Bibliography of French Language and Literature* (1976); William J. Wainwright, *Philosophy of Religion in the Twentieth Century* (1978); Diane L. Hoeveler, *English Prose and Criticism in the Nineteenth Century* (1979). Special bibliographies will be found for every major figure and subject. Helpful in locating the one you want, in addition to the card catalogue of your library (subject index) and the printed volumes of the Library of Congress (subject index) are *The Besterman World Bibliographies* (Theodore Besterman, ed.), in several volumes (1971), and the periodical *Bibliographical Index: A Cumulative Bibliography of Bibliographies.*

In addition to those mentioned, there are other journals the advanced student of ideas should know; among the most relevant are *Journal of the History of Ideas,* the leading periodical for intellectual historians; *Journal of Modern History, Comparative Studies in Society and History, Past and Present, Journal of Social History, History and Theory, Clio* ("an interdisciplinary journal of literature, history, and the philosophy of history"), *Journal of European Studies, Comparative Literature Studies, Journal of the History of Philosophy, French Historical Studies, Journal of Religion.*

Index